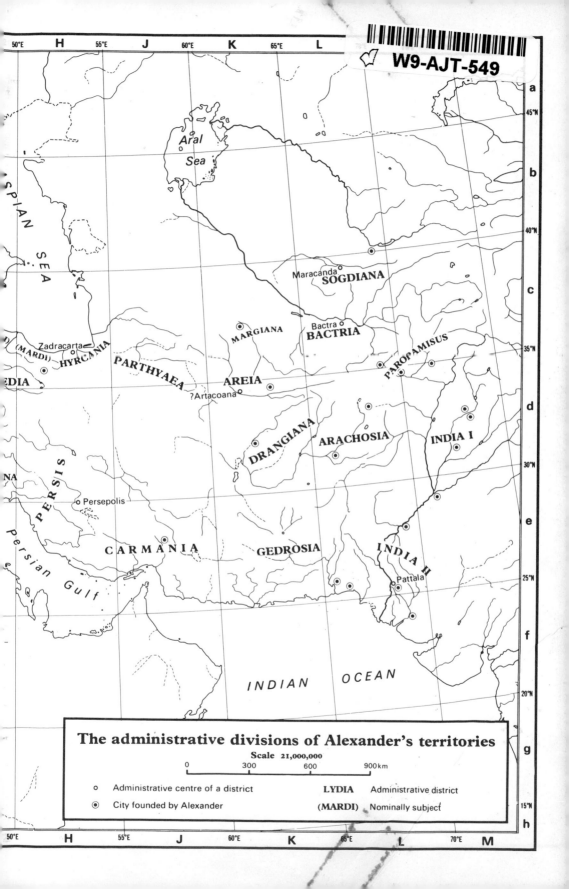

The administrative divisions of Alexander's territories

Scale 21,000,000

0   300   600   900 km

○   Administrative centre of a district

◉   City founded by Alexander

LYDIA   Administrative district

(MARDI)   Nominally subject

W9-AJT-549

ALEXANDER THE GREAT

King, Commander and Statesman

by

N.G.L. Hammond
C.B.E., D.S.O., F.B.A.

NOYES PRESS
PARK RIDGE, NEW JERSEY

Library of Congress Catalog Card Number: 80-18573
ISBN: 0-8155-5058-8
Printed in the United States

Published in the United States of America by
Noyes Press
Noyes Building
Park Ridge, New Jersey 07656

Library of Congress Cataloging in Publication Data

Hammond, Nicholas Geoffrey Lemprière.
 Alexander the Great, king, commander, and statesman.

 Includes bibliographical references and index.
 1. Alexander the Great, 356-323 B.C. 2. Greece--
Kings and rulers--Biography. 3. Generals--Greece--
Biography. I. Title.
DF234.H323   938'.07'0924 [B]   80-18573
ISBN 0-8155-5058-8

PREFACE

Recent studies of Alexander have generally tended towards extreme positions: on the one hand an uncritical acceptance of the evidence, whether good, bad or indifferent, which then yields a colourful but incorrect portrait of Alexander, and on the other hand a sharply critical or even hypercritical undermining of the evidence which loses Alexander altogether in the dust-clouds of demolition. Each has its value, the first for the romantic reader and the second for the debating scholar. The aim of this book is to state most of the evidence and bring the reader into the task of its evaluation; to establish as accurately as possible what Alexander and his Macedonians did do; and to make an assessment of Alexander in his public life as king, commander, and statesman. In order to make an historical appreciation of this kind, it is essential to view the past not from a modern anti-heroic, deflationary, or romantic standpoint but in terms of its own background and outlook. For this a close study of both Macedonia and Greece is essential, and some experience of war and especially of mountain warfare under comparable conditions to those of Alexander's time is desirable; for Alexander was in most things a Macedonian through and through, only in part a Greek by blood and education, and primarily a man of war whose genius is seen most clearly on the field of battle. It is considerations such as these which have determined the proportions and the emphases of this book.

Many fine aids for the scholar and the general reader have been provided in recent years. One may mention Brunt's edition of the first part of Arrian's *Anabasis*, Hamilton's commentary on Plutarch's *Life of Alexander*, Goukowsky's edition of Diodorus XVII, Griffith's *Main Problems* and Badian's bibliography. There has been a great flow of specialised and critical studies on many aspects of the subject, not least from the pen of Badian, and several books on Alexander. These come on top of the fundamental works of earlier decades, notably by Berve, Tarn, Schachermeyr and, in source-criticism, Pearson. The present writer owes a debt of gratitude to these and other scholars for their help both in the portrayal of the Macedonian achievement which he included in his *History of Greece* in 1959 and in this self-standing study of Alexander.

This book has been greatly improved by the keen criticism and the subtle encouragement of G.T. Griffith, whose extensive knowledge and genial friendship have been constantly put at my disposal. Others whose help in personal ways is gratefully acknowledged are M. Andronikos, E. Badian, E.N. Borza, A.B. Bosworth, F.M. Clover, S.I. Dakaris, A.M. Devine, C.F. Edson, J.R. Ellis, E.A. Fredricksmeyer, D. Gillis, C. Habicht, W. Heckel, M.M. Markle, N.T. Nikolitsis, and P.A. Stadter. The British Academy generously made a grant which enabled me to travel extensively in Greece, Thrace, and Turkey, and to visit the battlefields of the Granicus river and Issus; and I have been fortunate enough in the past to have become familiar with the Balkan countries and with the Near East up to Western Iraq and the Libyan desert. The British Academy also appointed me as a Leverhulme Visiting Professor to the University of Ioannina, where part of this book was written, and in autumn 1977 the Institute for Research in the Humanities put its facilities at my disposal when I was teaching in the University of Wisconsin. It has been a special pleasure to work with good friends in the production of this book: Robert Noyes, Martha Gillies, Sarah Jones and Paul Stecher of the Noyes Press, and David Cox of Cox Cartographic Ltd., who have taken infinite trouble on my behalf. And, as always, my greatest debt is to Margaret, my wife, who has put up with my abstraction and helped in compiling the Index.

Clare College, Cambridge   *N.G.L. Hammond*

CONTENTS

LIST OF FIGURES

End Paper. The administrative divisions of Alexander's territories

See also Notes to the Figures for additional comments.

Figures 1-19, 38, 40, 42 and the end paper are by David
A. Cox of Cox Cartographic Ltd., Waterstock, Oxon.

INTRODUCTION

The Macedonian kings, at least from the time of Philip, kept a written record of the king's acts, orders, correspondence, promotions, etc., day by day. These records were known as the *King's Ephemerides* or "Daily Records." They were composed by the king's staff of secretaries, one of them, Eumenes, a Greek from Cardia on Gallipoli, serving first under Philip and becoming chief secretary under Alexander. Since the king was arbiter of all affairs and commander of all forces, his *Ephemerides* were in fact the records of state, and in time of war the reference-book of the king's orders and regulations. It was vital to their purpose that these records were precise and accurate and that they were full and detailed. As documents of state they were confidential, personal to the king and not intended for publication. No doubt it lay with the king to grant access to them. When a king died, his *Journal* (as we may conveniently call it) was presumably closed and deposited at Pella (the capital), or at Aegeae (where the kings were buried). The *Journal* of the new king was then started.

During the eleven years when Alexander was in Asia his *Journal* grew and travelled with him, and it must have been a very large archive (comparable perhaps to twenty volumes) at the time of his death at Babylon in 323 B.C. The king's body and his possessions, including no doubt his *Journal*, were to be taken to Macedonia, but on the way late in 322 B.C. they were diverted to Egypt, where one of his officers, Ptolemy, kept them under his own control. It was the Ptolemy who declared himself king of Egypt in 304 B.C. He wrote a history of Alexander which he published, probably in his old age c. 285–283 B.C. It seems that apart from him writers of histories or memoirs about Alexander after 322 B.C. did not gain access to the *Journal*. However, there were specialist Greek officers on Alexander's staff who had kept their own records of their surveys (i.e., of camp-sites, town-sites, roads, march distances, etc.), their siege-engines, and their engineering works; and some of these records were published.

On the recommendation of Aristotle, late in 335 B.C., Alexander employed Aristotle's nephew, CALLISTHENES, an able and experienced
writer, to accompany him and to prepare a history of the campaign in
Asia which was to be published for the benefit of the Macedonians and
the Greeks. As Callisthenes was in constant touch with Alexander and
with the leading Macedonians and Greeks on his staff, and as he was
probably given access to the *Journal*, he was well placed to describe factual events and indeed had to do so to some extent if his work was to
carry any conviction with contemporary participants. At the same time
he did not publish the battle-orders and the tactics of Alexander's forces,
for instance in the set battles, because Alexander had no intention of re-
vealing these matters in time of war. The interpretation which he put on
those events was no doubt coloured by the wishes of Alexander, in
whom a sense of personal glory and a gift for political propaganda were
highly developed. In 327 B.C. Callisthenes was executed for complicity
in a plot. By then his history had been carried down to 331 B.C. or perhaps to 329 B.C., and it was published perhaps in parts before 327 B.C.
and *in toto* after that. It was certainly first in the field and exerted a wide
influence, but it was generally regarded as too adulatory of Alexander.
The surviving fragments show that he gave a very detailed description
of at least parts of major battles; related Alexander's exploits to a mythical past, especially as that past was portrayed in the Homeric poems;
and indicated that Alexander enjoyed the favour of the gods, indeed was
in some sense "a son of Zeus." We do not know who was appointed to
succeed Callisthenes.

The most influential historian of Alexander had no personal association with the king and was not a participant in the expedition. This was
CLEITARCHUS, a Greek probably of Colophon in Asia Minor, whose
father had written a history of Persia. This Cleitarchus, a young man,
was studying philosophy in Greece when Alexander was in Asia, but he
was already collecting stories in the manner of a modern journalist from
persons who had served with or against Alexander. His first book was
published after the death of Alexander and before 314 B.C. (if we accept
Pliny *NH* 3.57) and the last book around 290 B.C. Besides collecting the
oral tradition, Cleitarchus was able to read other works on Alexander as
they came out. His own history grew into more than twelve books. His
penchant was for fantastic and sensational stories: the Amazon queen
travelling a vast distance and persuading Alexander to beget a child with
her in a thirteen-day affair; Thaïs, an Athenian prostitute, avenging the
Persian sack of Athens by setting fire to the palace at Persepolis; Alexander travelling round with 365 concubines, "one for every day of the
year;" children burned alive in Phoenician sacrifices; and strange devices for catching monkeys.

As a Greek Cleitarchus probably disliked and despised the Macedonians, and as a philosopher he sided with Callisthenes against Alexander. It is possible that he saw in Callisthenes' execution the sign of a degeneration in Alexander, and thereafter attributed to Alexander such atrocities as the massacre of 80,000 Indians in the realm of Sambus. In 308 B.C. or so Cleitarchus moved to Alexandria in Egypt, at the invitation of Ptolemy. There he continued with his history, independently (it seems) of Ptolemy but having an eye to his favour. Thus he included Ptolemy among those who saved Alexander's life at a city of the Malli *honoris causa*; but Ptolemy in his own book which was published later said that he had been elsewhere at the time (see C. 9.5.21).[2] Truth was a minor consideration for Cleitarchus: "a better orator than historian," remarked Cicero, and "brilliantly ingenious but notoriously untrustworthy," said Quintilian, while Curtius thought him careless of the truth and credulous. But being sensational, romantic, readable, and critical of Alexander he appealed very strongly to Greek readers.

In contrast to Cleitarchus there were two writers who had been very close to Alexander. One, MARSYAS of Pella, a Companion of the king, began his history with the first king of Macedon and intended to reach the death of Alexander, but he did not get beyond 331 B.C., his own death sometime after 307 B.C cutting his work short. The important thing is that he judged Alexander as a Macedonian king and described the Macedonian institutions which so few Greeks knew. It was evidently from the work of Marsyas that Curtius drew his account of "mores Macedonici." The other, ARISTOBULUS, a Greek engineer perhaps from Phocis, who clearly enjoyed Alexander's confidence, wrote up his memories in the form of a history of Alexander which was published in parts perhaps between 305 B.C. and 290 B.C., when he was an old man living at Cassandrea in Macedonia. His interests were scientific and geographical rather than military; he had a flair for description and he reported some of Alexander's qualities and in particular the *pothos* or yearning which led Alexander to do unexpected things.

Other Greeks who served with Alexander wrote their own accounts of episodes in which they were particularly involved: NEARCHUS of the voyage from the mouth of the Indus to the Persian Gulf, ONESICRITUS of the marvels of India, CHARES of life at court, and so on. But the most important history by a contemporary was the latest in date, that of PTOLEMY, a Macedonian from Eordaea, published probably c. 285–283 B.C. Like Marsyas, he saw Alexander through Macedonian eyes, knew Macedonian institutions and understood the Macedonian army and its tactics. A close friend of Alexander from youth onwards, a Companion cavalryman, then from 331–330 B.C. a commander (*hegemon*) and finally a King's Own Bodyguard (*somatophylax*), he was better qualified than anyone to write a history of Alexander's military achievements.

Moreover, Ptolemy was able to make use of the *King's Journal*, which he had under his own hand. There he could read the detailed day-by-day record of the twelve years of Alexander's almost constant campaigning, a precise and accurate record such as no man could possibly have recalled by memory alone more than forty years after the events, and also letters and despatches from other theatres which were recorded at the time of receipt. Of course Ptolemy could have used this record for his own purposes. Some have suggested that Ptolemy exaggerated his own achievements, but it should be remembered that he disclaimed the saving of Alexander's life with which Cleitarchus had publicly credited him. To judge from his omissions (precariously inferred from what is not in Arrian's history) whether he was fair to his colleagues is almost impossible, because we do not possess his work but only envisage it dimly through the pages of Arrian's history which was itself very much an abbreviation of Ptolemy's history.

All these and indeed other works of the period 330–280 B.C. were the forerunners of many works written in the Hellenistic period. The dominant influence was that of Cleitarchus. Fictitious versions of previously recorded episodes, fictitious conversations between Alexander and others (e.g., Indian philosophers), fictitious letters, elaborations of technical treatises such as the records of Alexander's marches, fictitious citations allegedly from the *Journal,* and fictitious adventures in distant places—all these sprang up on the fertile soil of Hellenistic imagination and formed some ingredients of the so-called "Alexander Romance." Fragments of papyri have yielded passages from Hellenistic histories, in which there is a total lack of interest in military events.

We owe our information about Alexander mainly to works of the early Roman Empire. Writers in the first century of the Empire, when world-conquest and autocracy were of topical interest, preferred Cleitarchus above all others. Thus DIODORUS, TROGUS, and CURTIUS used him as their main source, while PLUTARCH made citations from him. His sensational, rhetorical style and his picture of Alexander's excesses and degeneration suited the taste and the experience of an age which saw Tiberius, Gaius, Claudius, and Nero degenerate into cruel and licentious tyrants. All four authors made some use of other writers too, but they probably did not draw directly on Ptolemy. A radical change came with the middle of the second century A.D. when ARRIAN, a Greek of Nicomedeia in Asia Minor, published his history of Alexander. Unlike the four authors we have mentioned, he was already a man of military and administrative experience. Promoted by Hadrian to be governor of Cappadocia, he had defeated the Alani who invaded his province in A.D. 135. He had written treatises on two subjects which had been of special interest to Alexander—tactics and hunting.

When he decided to write on Alexander, who had captured his interest as a boy, he had all past histories of Alexander at his disposal. It is most significant that he chose to follow in the main the accounts of Ptolemy and Aristobulus and that he believed them when in agreement to be "completely true." In other words, he judged Ptolemy and Aristobulus to have been truthful in general, and his preference for them implies that he, like Cicero and Quintilian, having read the work of Cleitarchus, regarded Cleitarchus and others as less than truthful. He further remarked on the fact that Ptolemy and Aristobulus had taken part in Alexander's campaigns (whereas Cleitarchus and others had not) and had written after Alexander's death so that they were free from any pressure or any hope of reward which might have led them to depart from what had actually happened (this being an implied contrast with Callisthenes). In addition he gave as a further reason for Ptolemy's truthfulness the point that "it was more shameful for him as a king to lie (i.e., to be seen to lie) than for anyone else." This is as true now as it was then.

"I have also recorded but merely as stories told about Alexander (*legomena*) some matters in the histories of other writers, because I judged them deserving of mention and not utterly untrustworthy." In these words Arrian was referring presumably to the histories of Callisthenes and Cleitarchus and to those who had followed in the Cleitarchan tradition. He felt too that his own history was very different from theirs. "If anyone wonders why after so many had written it occurred to me to write this history, let him express surprise only after reading all their works and then using mine." When we do compare his work with those of the early Empire which have survived, we can see that it differed from them as chalk differs from cheese. For Arrian supplied a consecutive, consistent, objective military account, which was mainly derived from the factual record of the *King's Journal*; he saw Alexander as a Macedonian monarch in pursuit of military glory; and he derived some insights into Alexander's personality from his use of the memoirs of Aristobulus.[3]

Modern historians have varied greatly in their approach to the ancient sources and consequently in their interpretation of Alexander. A generation ago Tarn relied almost exclusively on Arrian and Plutarch, and he regarded Alexander as a military genius and a political visionary, but his Alexander appeared as a unique phenomenon rather than as a Macedonian king who had inherited both Macedonian and Greek traditions. Some writers since then have been attracted by the Cleitarchan tradition and have seen Alexander as a ruthless murderer, an autocratic megalomaniac, and even a bisexual profligate. If Tarn relied too much on the record of the *King's Journal*, these writers have drawn too credulously upon the Cleitarchan tradition. But in each case Alexander has become divorced from his background. Two things were indispensable to Alexander's success: his father's achievement and the Macedonian people.

The first two chapters of this book try to provide the Macedonian background and the setting of Alexander as king of Macedon. The bulk of the book traces in chronological order the problems and the achievements of Alexander in Europe and Asia, reliance being placed particularly on Arrian's account. In the last chapter the aims and the achievements of Alexander in his different capacities are assessed, and some aspects of his complex and fascinating personality are discussed. In the final analysis both record and romance have their place.

I

THE INHERITANCE

(A) MACEDONIA AND MACEDONES[4]

As a geographical term Macedonia comprises both the catchment area of the two great rivers Haliacmon and Axius which flow into the Thermaic Gulf of the Mediterranean Sea, and the adjacent basins on the east which contain lakes (Doiran, Koronia, and Bolbe). The large coastal plain, which has been formed by the alluvial deposits of these and other rivers, is the richest part of Macedonia, and it is fenced off from the interior by a ring of high mountains. The area between the sea and this ring is called Lower Macedonia. The interior beyond the ring is made up of two different terrains, divided more or less by the Axius. The extensive plains of the western terrain stand more than 2,000 feet above sea-level, and the whole terrain is called Upper Macedonia. On the other hand the great areas of flat, fertile land in the eastern terrain are low-lying and less severe in climate. The whole of the interior is separated from its neighbours by a ring of lofty mountains. It is these two rings of mountains which have made Macedonia in the geographical sense easy to defend against large armies, because the entries through the rings are few and generally very narrow. The passes through the outer ring which offer least difficulty are at the head of the Axius valley (via Kačanik and Presevo) and at a junction of the outer and inner rings where the Axius comes closest to the Strumitsa by Valandovo. It was through these passes that the German armies entered Macedonia in April 1941 (Figure 1).

The territory of the people who called themselves "Macedones" and their land "Macedonia" was at first only a tiny part of the geographical unit we have described as Macedonia. Their homeland in southern Macedonia was a small but singularly beautiful district with alpine pastures, tall trees, fertile valleys and abundant water, for which reason it was called Pieria, a Greek word meaning "the rich land." From its alpine pastures one has superb views. Eastwards over the shining waters of the Gulf towards the prongs of Chalcidice; southwards to the towering mass at Mt. Olympus, almost 10,000 feet high, snow-clad from head to foot in

7

mid-winter; northwards to the green gardens of Midas famous for fruit, roses, and wine, and below them the vast plain of alluvial silt, called Emathia, "the sandy land;" westwards to range upon range of mountains which make up the mass of northern Pindus. Alexander climbed and rode and hunted here as a boy. It was above all a place for huntsmen, crofters, and shepherds.

The early Macedones were a pastoral people, their mascot being a goat, and they practised the transhumant form of pastoralism, moving their flocks seasonally from the alpine pastures of summer on high Pieria and Olympus to the lowland pastures of winter by Dium and Ekaterini. They were fortunate in that they had both kinds of pasture within their homeland; they did not need to take their flocks to the remote summer pastures of northern Pindus, as other shepherds did. Because their life was so self-contained, they developed their own dialect of Greek, which was much retarded and so broad that it was almost incomprehensible to other Greek-speakers. In modern times the Vlachs of Olympus and Pieria, with their chief village at Vlakholivadhi, have practised the same kind of pastoral life and developed their own dialect of Vlachic Rumanian. The gods of the early Macedones were Greek, for the Macedones claimed descent from Zeus, enthroned on Mt. Olympus, and they held their autumn festival in honour of Zeus and the Muses at Dium.

While the Macedones were living in Pieria, their king received an oracle from Apollo, god of Delphi. "Go in haste to Bouteïs, rich in flocks, and where you see gleaming-horned, snow-white goats sunk in sleep, sacrifice to the gods and found the city of your state on the level ground of that land." Guided by the oracle, the king founded a city at a place then called Edessa but thenceforward Aegeae, "the haunts of the goat," according to popular etymology. There the king and his successors were to be buried, and as long as that was done, according to another oracle, the kingship would remain in this same family. Alexander, who grew up in the knowledge of the first oracle and perhaps of the second, presided over the burial of his father, Philip, at this very place. Aegeae is at Vergina on the southern edge of the Emathian plain, and the kings lay under some of the three hundred tumuli there—the earlier kings in small graves, the later in fine built tombs.

The Macedonians were not the first, for the kings of the Phryges (or Brygi as they were called by the Macedonians) had been buried there, one of them being the Midas after whom the gardens were named. The royal residence was at some distance above the cemetery on a terrace, where the forested, steep hillside ended. Alexander must have stayed there often in his youth, galloped his horse over the plain, swum and boated on the broad Haliacmon, and explored the river's impressive gorge. One third of the cemetery has been excavated, and in 1976 Pro-

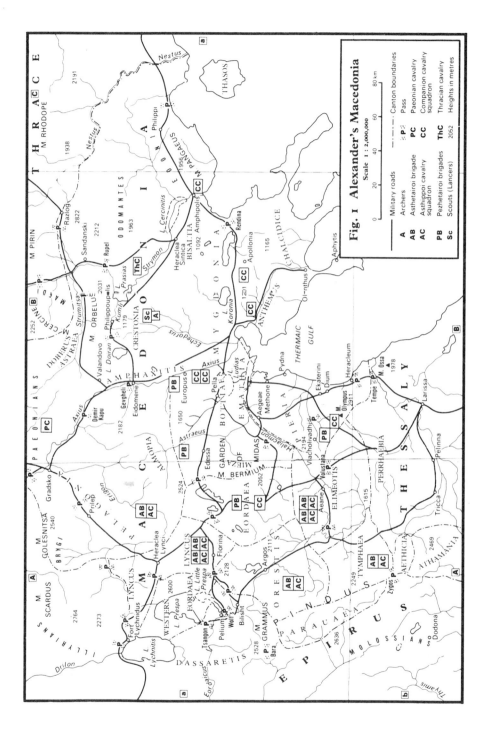

Fig. 1 Alexander's Macedonia

fessor Andronikos found in the largest tumulus of all some head-stones (*stelai*) inscribed with the names of prominent Macedonians of the late fourth and early third centuries. This was clear evidence that friends of the Macedonian kings were buried there as well as the kings. Further, the head-stones had been smashed early in the third century. We are told by Plutarch that some Gallic mercenaries of Pyrrhus at that time broke into the royal tombs at Aegeae, and Professor Andronikos has now found in the broken head-stones the traces of their violence.

From there the Macedones went on to win the gardens of Midas and the Emathian plain almost as far as the Axius. Aegeae became the new capital of the enlarged kingdom, for at that time it lay on the coastal route just where the mountain road from Pieria came down to the plain. As the Macedones advanced, they exterminated or expelled the native peoples and worked the land themselves, becoming settled farmers. At first they kept the divisions into clans or tribes which they had had as highlanders—the leading clan being called the Argeadae—but when they had settled for some time they abandoned the clan-system and organised themselves by places of residence—"cities"—which ringed the plain, a Macedon being defined for instance as a man of Aegeae or of Alorus and no longer as an Argead. Later, when the Macedones conquered east of the Axius, they left most of the native peoples on the land where they were, and planted cities of their own. Very occasionally they destroyed a native town or expelled a leading native tribe, and they annexed one district Anthemus, which was awarded to the crown. But they did not reduce those they conquered to serfdom or slavery. Thus the Macedones remained farmers and shepherds, keeping for themselves the plain and the hills west of the Axius, and east of the Axius coexisting with native tribes, which were of Paeonian and Thracian stocks, who spoke their own languages.

The hinterland west of the Axius, "Upper Macedonia," as it came to be called, was first acquired with the help of Persia c. 480 B.C. The Macedonian kings had been faithful vassals of the Persian Emperor, and when Xerxes was anxious to protect his line of communications through the coastal plain, he gave to Alexander I of Macedon "the rule over the whole region between Mt. Olympus and Mt. Haemus" (J. 7.4.1), the latter being the range which forms the watershed between the Mediterranean Sea and the Danube valley. The native tribes of Upper Macedonia as far as Mt. Golesnitsa near Šar Planina (the ancient Scardus) were Greek-speaking, but their affiliations in race and dialect were not with the Macedones but with the Molossi, who lived on the western side of the Pindus range. Now, however, they were incorporated formally into the Macedonian kingdom; they kept their territorial tribal names Elimeotae, Tymphaei, Orestae, Lyncestae and Pelagones, and they were given the further name "Macedones" (see Figures 1, 5 and 37).

After the departure of the Persians from Europe the incorporation became a dead letter, and some royal houses were fully independent in the years just before Alexander's birth in 356 B.C. Then Philip abolished all independent rule. He gave favoured positions in his service to amenable members of the royal houses, and brought their sons to his court; he recruited highlanders of Upper Macedonia into his army; and he planted "new towns" in Upper Macedonia which he peopled with local men and with lowlanders from one or more of the "cities" of Lower Macedonia. It seems that the Macedonians made a distinction in terminology (as we do) between "new towns" and "cities," the former being *astea* and the latter *poleis*. This distinction is observable in army names, as will be seen later.

The hinterland east of the Axius was a different matter. There Philip had to prove his military superiority in at least two campaigns before the Paeonians submitted to his authority. But once recognised he left the Paeonian king on the throne and allowed him to issue his own coinage, normally a symbol of independence; moreover, he recruited cavalrymen to serve him not as "Macedonians" but as "Paeonians." He used the same methods when he conquered the western Thracians and made the river Nestus the frontier of the Macedonian kingdom (Str. 331); the Thracian king continued to reign and Alexander was served by Thracian troops, who probably came from within the Macedonian kingdom. But Paeonians and Thracians were not recruited into the Macedonian units, as people from Upper Macedonia were; they remained separate, no doubt speaking their own languages.

As a Roman writer put it, Philip "formed one kingdom and one people out of many tribes and races." That is a true assessment. Within the incredibly short space of the twenty years of Alexander's youth Philip did create a united kingdom of disparate original elements. Then Alexander built upon it a vast empire. Thereafter the kingdom remained united until 197 B.C., when the Orestae opted out in favour of Rome. The reasons for the cohesiveness of this Macedonian kingdom were various. One was the fear that everyone had of the neighbouring Illyrians, Paeonians, and Thracians, whose warrior groups were always eager to carry their raids deep into Macedonia. Philip defeated those neighbours decisively in the year of Alexander's birth. Another was satisfaction with the revolution in the economic life of the country which changed the emphasis from transhumant pastoralism to settled agriculture, a revolution such as has occurred in post-war Albania with remarkable effects.

A speech which Alexander addressed to his troops from Upper and Lower Macedonia was reported in the following sense, though not in his *ipsissima verba*. "My father Philip took you over as nomads and paupers, most of you wearing sheepskins, pasturing a few sheep on the mountains, and unsuccessfully fighting in their defence against Illyrians, Triballians, and Thracians, your neighbours; but he gave you cloaks to wear instead of sheepskins, he brought you down from the mountains to the plains, he changed you into worthy opponents of the neighbouring barbarians, . . . he made you inhabitants of cities, and he brought into your lives the orderliness of good laws and customs,"

Another factor was the optimism born of success; for Philip had raised Macedonia to a position of military and political supremacy in southeastern Europe, and had made it the centre of a network of developing trade. The advantages of a united kingdom were obvious to those who had experienced the hazards of disunity. But it all stemmed from Philip. Could his successor maintain it?

Of the natural resources of Macedonia the most important were its Greek-speaking people, physically tough through the open-air life in a country of harsh winters and torrid summers, sturdily independent in the face of constant dangers, hard working and hard fighting. Simple and unsophisticated by comparison with the Athenians of their day, they proved themselves in the field of action to be intelligent, dependable, and loyal. The struggle for independence had taught them the value of discipline, and they had not had the time or the means to engage in soft and luxurious living, as some of their neighbours to the south had done. Their land was rich in timber and minerals, but it needed the genius of a Philip to exploit these resources to the full. Rich too in farm-stock and wild life, which provided more meat in the Macedonians' diet than Greeks were accustomed to, and particularly rich in horses—to which Philip added 20,000 brood-mares from one campaign alone—which were bred for transport and for war.

The shift of emphasis from pastoralism to agriculture was made possible only by controlling flood-water and introducing systematic irrigation, for which an overall authority was essential. Four great rivers—Haliacmon, Ludias, Axius and Echedorus—pour their floods into the coastal plain. In the century before Philip they were so uncontrolled that the Ludias, for instance, flowed at first into the Haliacmon but later changed course and almost flowed into the Axius. The coastline, too, altered very considerably. Philip stabilised the situation. His capital city, Pella (the change from Aegeae occurred late in the fifth century), stood on a low peninsula in Lake Ludias which was fed on one side by the river Ludias and on the other by an artificial channel leading from the Axius; and the outflow of the lake was contained between flood-banks in such a way that it afforded passage for shipping from Pella to the sea throughout the year. An example of land reclamation was seen and reported by Theophrastus, a pupil of Aristotle, near Philippi; there what had been wooded swamp under Thracian ownership became well drained and cultivated under Philip.

Philip's Macedonia was unlike Greece in many ways. The land was in essence continental, not maritime. It had wide vistas, great rivers, and a hard climate in winter, when the ground froze iron-hard and the leaping streams of summer stood silent in icy curtains. Its rapidly developing resources in agriculture, livestock, and minerals made it largely self-sufficient, whereas many of the Greek city-states were dependent on food-stuffs imported by sea. The Greek-speaking people of Lower Macedonia west of the Axius and of Upper Macedonia, who together formed the core of the kingdom and the field army, regarded themselves as "Macedones" and not as Greeks; nor were they regarded by the Greeks of peninsular Greece as anything other than "Macedones" or "barbaroi." For they lacked the essential qualification of Greekness at that time; the emancipated life of the independent city-state and the emancipated mind which had developed Greek culture. The meteoric rise of the Macedonian kingdom to great power seemed to most contemporary Greeks to be comparable with similar phenomena in the past, such as the rise of the Thracian kingdom of Sitalces a century earlier or that of the more recent Illyrian kingdom of Bardylis; and probably, they thought, as liable to sudden eclipse.

It must have seemed to Alexander at the time that his father's energy and will were overcoming all difficulties. For him, as for his contemporaries, the figure of Philip dominated the scene. "Europe," wrote a Greek contemporary, Theopompus, whose pleasure normally was to cut men down to size, "Europe has never produced such a man as Philip, and if Philip continues to observe the same principles in his future policy he will win all Europe." But Alexander knew also the qualities of his countrymen; they too were making Macedonia invincible. It was the combination of Philip the king and the Macedonian people which was raising Macedonia to supremacy. If Alexander could only equal Philip, he knew that the process would continue. When Philip was assassinated, an Athenian statesman, Phocion, may have realised that Alexander would be such a king; for Phocion said that the Macedonian army was the weaker only by one man through the death of Philip.

(B) THE KING AND THE MACEDONES

Constitutional monarchies were defined by Thucydides as "hereditary kingships upon stated prerogatives," and the Macedonian monarchy was a specific example. From the first king of the Temenid house c. 650 B.C. to the last of the line, Alexander's posthumous son who was murdered in 311 B.C., every king was a member of that royal house. It was inconceivable within that time that the Macedonian people would elect anyone else to the throne. This was made clear at Babylon after Alexander's death, when the army, acting as the Macedonian people under arms, elected his half-brother Arrhidaeus, "rejoicing that the strength of authority would remain in the same house and the same family, and that one of the royal stock would assume the hereditary authority, since the people were accustomed to honour and worship the very name, and no one assumed it unless born to be king." In this sense all sons of Philip were born in the purple, and the choice between them lay with the people when Philip was assassinated.

At the demise of a king a leading Macedonian might declare his own preference by putting on his breastplate and moving to the side of his preferred candidate, but it was the Macedonian people, the Macedones under arms, who decided the election, "clashing their spears against their shields as a sign that they would take with satisfaction the blood of any pretender who had no right to the throne." The first duties of the newly elected king were the purification of the people, which was achieved by a ceremonial march of the entire army between the two halves of a disembowelled dog, and the obsequies of the dead king, who was buried with some emblem of his kingship.

Another duty of the king was to maintain the security of the throne by acting as prosecutor in any case of treason before the Assembly of the Macedones, which alone gave and executed the verdict. Such a case arose at once if the previous king had died by assassination. The new king had to ensure the succession by begetting heirs as soon as possible and by training them in the dangerous schools of hunting and war. To this end many Macedonian kings were polygamous. Philip, for instance, "had by his various marriages many other sons [besides Alexander and Arrhidaeus], all legitimate in accordance with the royal custom, but they died, some by chance, others in action." Despite advice to the contrary, Alexander left the begetting of heirs too late for the security of the realm. It was his greatest mistake. Wives were chosen by the king for himself and for his children. As a Greek writer put it, Philip himself married "with an eye to war" (and territorial expansion too); for considerations of state were much involved in royal matches. Thus when the Persians were in Europe the Macedonian king married his daughter to a Persian grandee, and Philip agreed to marry his son Arrhidaeus to the daughter of a Persian satrap.

The chief function of the king in a state which lacked a professional priesthood was religious. He began each day with sacrifice. Alexander, for instance, carried out "the prescribed sacrifices" daily, even during his last illness as long as his strength lasted. The king in person conducted sacred festivals and contests of various kinds. In ceremonial sacrifice he was accompanied by the male members of the royal house, and there were special attendants who interpreted the omens which were revealed then or on other occasions. The king stood on a higher plane than other men in relation to the gods; for he himself was descended from Zeus both as a Temenid and as head of the Macedones. In state justice, which affected relations with the gods and the safety of the realm, the king held the place of the trained judiciary in a modern society. He was sole and final judge in certain cases, some involving the capital sentence. The wise judgements of Philip and the concentration of Alexander in the hearing of cases were proverbial (P. 42.2; cf. 23.3). Further, every subject had the right of appeal to the king against an act of his representative, even against an act of Alexander's "General in Europe," Antipater, in the last year of Alexander's life (P. 74.4-6).

The powers of the king in secular matters were almost absolute. He conducted foreign policy, declaring war and making peace, for instance, at his own discretion. He was sole commander of the Macedonian forces. On campaign he issued orders of all kinds, and he exercised strict discipline, sentencing soldiers to flogging or execution as he thought fit. In battle he led the foremost troops, whether infantry or cavalry, and he himself fought at the point of greatest danger; for this was a warrior kingship as in the epic society which Homer had described. He also led the royal hunt on horseback, in pursuit not of the fox but of lions, aurochs, bears, and boars which were native to the virgin forests of Macedonia. He owned all deposits of gold, silver, copper, and iron, and all forests in his kingdom; he had large hunting reserves and considerable estates; and he raised taxes of various kinds from his subjects. He issued his own coinage, recruited and equipped and paid his own troops, and administered his own property and the state finances. He was himself the government. Because the safety of the realm depended upon him, any step taken to safeguard his life was justified on the principle "salus regis suprema lex esto." Whatever the rights and wrongs of the quarrel between Alexander and Cleitus, once Alexander thought his life was threatened, no Macedonian questioned his right to defend himself by killing Cleitus on the spot.

To assist him the king called upon his male relations in the royal house and upon "Friends" and "Companions" whom he selected himself. For instance, when Perdiccas II made a treaty with Athens, the oath was taken by the king, his relations and then his friends. These assistants acted as officers, envoys, governors, generals, treasurers, estate-managers, and so on, and they were rewarded with gifts in land, money or kind by the king, whose generosity was on an epic scale. If the king wished, he summoned his assistants to give advice on matters of policy or government or war, but it was he who made the decision. The same persons formed the king's court; they attended him in public, fought at his side in war, protected him in the hunt, escorted him on ceremonial parades, and enjoyed his confidence and affection. It was a rare thing for a king to shut himself up in his tent alone, as Alexander was to do on some occasions; for a king's success depended much upon his personal relations with his friends, and he lived most of the time in their company, feasting and drinking in the epic manner.

Another department of court was formed by the royal pages, who were selected by the king from his own relations and from the sons of his Friends and Companions at the age of fourteen. They served as the personal attendants of the king, sitting with him at table, guarding him at night, aiding him in the hunt, handling his horse while he mounted, and fighting near him in war. It was natural that these pages, when they were men, often became the closest friends and companions of the one among them who was elected king, as Hephaestion did of Alexander.

In this man-centered monarchical system the women of the royal house played little part in public life. They were not present at banquets and drinking parties, though courtesans might be, and their role was usually that of the housewife, making the menfolk's clothes, grinding corn, and baking bread. They might become influential in court intrigues and in matters of the succession to the throne, especially when they were queen mothers or queen grandmothers; this happened particularly when the heir was an infant. Even in the personal life of the court the women had less influence on a king and his friends than the men and the boys who shared so many interests in peace and war. It is not surprising that Alexander was as closely attached to Hephaestion as Achilles was to Patroclus; but such an attachment did not exclude love for Roxane and love for Briseis. Attachments between men and boys were more liable to lead to love affairs than attachments between contemporaries, and some conspiracies against the king were attributed to jealousy or chagrin over such affairs.

In writing about the Macedonians we have to be on our guard against using modern terms which imply modern standards of outlook and criticism. Thus it is too easy to label the powers of a Macedonian king as tyrannical, whereas they were in historical fact constitutional; to condemn Philip as profligate for taking a seventh wife in the hope of another heir, unless we recall that the only competent heir, Alexander, had led the cavalry charge at Chaeronea and was expected to lead others in Asia; to select one wife as queen and call the others prostitutes, as Greek writers did; and to speak of divorce between Philip and Olympias, the mother of Alexander, when she withdrew to the Molossian court in Epirus.

Again it is erroneous to call the Friends and Companions of Alexander "Macedonian nobles" or "barons." For the first implies a nobility of birth, a hereditary aristocracy of the English kind, which did not exist at all among the Macedones of Lower Macedonia; and even in Upper Macedonia where such an aristocracy had existed, it was absorbed by Philip into his entourage without any special privileges. Rather there was equality of opportunity to rise in the king's service, and the choice of Friends and Companions was made by the king alone on grounds not of family lineage but of personal quality. When a father and a son, say Parmenio and Philotas, served a king or kings well, we may say that the family of Parmenio was a leading family in Macedonia; but that was by merit. The term "baron" implies a special, mediaeval form of nobility, in which a Great Baron, holding a hereditary domain and recruiting his personal army from his retainers, might challenge the king himself; but in the Macedonia of Philip and Alexander no Friend or Companion had his own troops and there was no possibility of any commoner challenging the king.

The key to the unity of the Macedonian state under Philip and Alexander is to be found in the devotion of the Macedonian people to their king. When Curtius described Alexander's recovery from a serious illness on a campaign, he wrote as follows. "It is not easy to say—quite apart from the reverence which is innate in that people towards their kings—how much they were devoted to this particular king in their admiration, indeed in their ardent affection." At the same time their attitude was not servile or obsequious. On addressing the king in the Assembly a soldier bared his head, but he spoke openly and frankly, whatever his rank. Indeed there was truth in the paradoxical statement that the Macedonians "being accustomed to the rule of a king lived with a greater sense of freedom than any other people."

To this extent the monarchy was a democratic monarchy. The royal house in its attitude to the people had benefited from three centuries of accumulated experience, and its princes inherited a sense of dedication to their subjects and showed an almost instinctive capacity for rule from an early age; so much so that four kings in succession—Alexander II, Perdiccas III, Philip II, and Alexander himself—ruled in their early twenties with assurance, initiative, and authority. The separateness of the royal house from all other Macedonians enhanced its self-awareness and its reputation. Its founder, Perdiccas I, had not been a native of Macedonia but had come from the Greek city of Argos in the Peloponnese as a member of the ruling house there, the Temenidae, which was descended from Heracles, son of Zeus.. The foreign origin of the dynasty, like that of the dynasty in modern Greece, set it apart from any indigenous family and above traditional feuds. It was also valuable in diplomatic contacts with the Greek city-states; for a Macedonian king was a Greek, as well as a Macedonian.

While the Macedonian kingship resembled other warrior kingships in the Balkans, the organisation of the Macedones proper, the conquerors of Lower Macedonia, was peculiar to them. Full citizenship, indicated by the title "Macedon," was held only by men under arms in the service of the king, and their citizenship was further defined by residence in relation to a city, as we have seen. For example, a man is defined in an inscription as "Machatas, son of Sabbataras, a Macedon of Europos," or in a text as "Peucestas, a Macedon of Mieza." When Upper Macedonia was incorporated fully into the realm, each man who attained citizenship there was defined by his canton, so that one might be called "Alexander, a Macedon of Lyncus," and another "Philarchus, a Macedon of Elimeotis." Sometimes a town was added, as in the last case, where he was "a Macedon of Elimeotis from Python." These definitions reflected the system of local government in each area, the city being the civic unit in Lower Macedonia and the canton the civic unit in Upper Macedonia. It is evident that each unit managed its own local affairs, leaving the king and his entourage entirely free to deal with matters of national policy.

We have mentioned the ability of the king to found new towns. The earliest which is known (from excavation only) was founded by Archelaus on land won from Paeonians at Demir Kapu on the north side of the Axius gorge, late in the fifth century. The settlers in these towns were mixed, some drafted from a city of Lower Macedonia and others recruited locally. The town or the territory might be named after a city or a territory of Lower Macedonia; thus the territory above Demir Kapu, having a yellow soil, was named Emathia after the Emathian plain of Lower Macedonia. The most prolific founder of new towns was Philip. He made the men of Upper Macedonia "dwellers in cities," and in general "he transferred at his own discretion peoples and towns, just as shepherds transfer their flocks from winter to summer pastures." Some new towns, we are told, were on the frontiers, so as to face an enemy; others were set in distant places; and others were reinforced with women and children captured in war. When Philip added new territory to his kingdom, he extended existing cantons or named new cantons after them. Thus in the southwest it seems that Lyncus was extended to take in the district by Lake Ochrid, and Elimeotis to include a part at least of Perrhaebia; while the region by Lake Little Prespa was named Eordaea and its river Eordaïcus. In the east there were cantons called Astraea and Doberus; some towns were reinforced, such as Philippi, and new towns, like Philippoupolis, were planted. These developments were of the greatest importance, as the young Alexander was in a position to appreciate. For they served the purposes of frontier defence, internal commerce, cultural fusion, agricultural development, and later military recruitment.

(C) THE BALKAN EMPIRE AND THE GREEK ALLIES[5]

The first considerable land-empire in the history of Europe was created while Alexander was growing to maturity, and in the final stages of its development he was serving his apprenticeship in war and administration. Those experiences shaped the ideas which he was to implement in Asia. The Balkan tribes were as pugnacious as any in Asia, but they failed to combine, partly because they had preyed on one another for centuries. "To be unoccupied is most prestigious, to work the land most shameful; to live by warring and looting is most honourable." This, said Herodotus, was the motto of the Thracians, and it was equally that of the Illyrians and the Danubian tribes. All power was in the hands of tribal kings and aristocrats, fighting as cavalrymen and leading bands of formidable infantrymen, some well-equipped, the majority light-armed, and all bent on slaughter and rapine; sometimes too they reduced their neighbours to serfdom on a huge scale; the Autariatae for instance being credited with 300,000 serfs. Philip hammered these warrior élites into subjection in campaign after campaign and began to impose a new way of life.

Of the Balkan tribes the Illyrians were the most intractable. In 358 B.C. Philip showed the new-found strength of Macedonia by killing 7,000 of the picked forces of the Illyrian Dardanians, who entered battle 10,500 strong. But his chief target thereafter was the enemy cavalry, bearers of authority. When he forced them to capitulate by furious charge and impetuous pursuit, he earned the respect and obedience of their followers. In campaign after campaign he overran Dardanians, Taulantians, Grabaeans, and Ardiaeans, and in 337 B.C. he was attacking Pleurias, king of the Autariatae, in Hercegovina. In these actions Companions and pages fought alongside the king and suffered many casualties; in one pursuit alone in 344–343 B.C., Philip and 150 Companions were wounded and a prince of the royal house was among those killed. Alexander was of an age to fight as a page from 342 B.C.; his prowess in such campaigns earned him the command of the Macedonian cavalry in 338 B.C. When the king of a tribe capitulated, Philip left him in power but required of him "obedience," which normally meant abstaining from wars of his own making but aiding Philip in his wars and perhaps paying some kind of tribute. Philip neither looted nor enslaved; for he had come not to destroy but to impose peace, a peace which could only be maintained by reducing the next marauding tribe. In Illyria he seems not to have planted cities, presumably because Illyrian economy was so predominantly pastoral. There he relied only on his speed of movement and his superiority especially in cavalry to keep control. In the latter part of 337 B.C. Alexander saw this system in operation with his own eyes; for he stayed in Illyria, probably at the court of a vassal-king.

Philip used the same methods of warfare in dealing with the tribes to the northeast and east of Macedonia, and he left some conquered kings in office on similar terms. But he found other kings who joined his side, among them probably the king of the Agrianians at the head of Strymon valley. His aim was to develop the agricultural resources of the fertile plains and valleys of Thrace and expand the field of commerce. To this end he planted a number of cities with a mixture of Macedonian and non-Macedonian settlers, which were intended to serve much the same purposes as his new towns in Upper Macedonia. Some new cities, such as Philippopolis (now Plovdiv), dominated the great plain of inner Thrace, and peasant farmers were helped by peace, irrigation, and sound administration to inaugurate an era of prosperity. The master of the plains had indirect control of the mountain peoples; for they had to bring their flocks down to the plains in winter. The process of pacification within Thrace was not complete at the end of Philip's reign; for Alexander's first campaign, while he was acting as regent in the absence of Philip in 340 b.c., was against some of the Maedi of the middle Strymon valley who had risen in revolt. Driving out those who had broken faith, Alexander founded a new city of mixed population and named it Alexandropolis, both following his father's example and setting a precedent for his actions in Asia.

The policy of pacification in the central Balkans could succeed only if marauding tribes from the north were kept at bay, and that brought Philip into contact with the Danubian tribes, especially the Triballi, Getae, and Scythae. He saw there the importance of the Danube both as a tenable frontier and as a waterway for communication, and he intended to hold it. When a Scythian king crossed the lower Danube, occupied an extensive territory, and tried to make a settlement with Philip, the Macedonian's determination was shown by his demand to sacrifice as of right at the mouth of the Danube and dedicate a statue to Heracles, his ancestor. When this right was denied, Philip summoned Alexander to his side and engaged the very large Scythian forces, famous for their cavalry, in the wide plain of the Dobrudja, in southeast Romania. Philip won a decisive victory and treated the enemy with severity, both to deter other nomadic invaders and because the Scythian king had broken an agreement. He took 20,000 women and children to swell the populations of his new cities; a huge amount of livestock; and sent 20,000 thoroughbred brood-mares to Macedonia. It should be noted that he did not take men to work as slaves, but women and children to increase his free manpower in the future; nor stallions to improve his Macedonian stock, but mares to maintain the great number of horses which he needed. He had been almost too successful; for the Triballi, higher up the Danube on its south bank, demanded a part of his booty as a condition of giving him passage. Philip engaged them in battle. He was severely wounded, the point of the weapon passing through his thigh and killing his horse, and in the alarm and confusion of his troops the Triballi got away with some of the booty. Whether Alexander took command in this crisis, we do not know for certain; but in any case he had his father's injury to avenge.

The foundations of the Balkan Empire were solidly laid. It acted as a shield against the unruly peoples of the middle Danube and north of the Danube, and behind that shield the form of civilization which Macedonia brought flourished for the span of two generations. The commercial development was particularly remarkable; for example, the gold and silver coinage of Philip had an extraordinarily wide circulation throughout the Balkans and in Central Europe, and Macedonian designs and skills were imitated in Thracian gold and in wall-painting. Alexander was able to see some of the fruits of his father's work in the Balkans before he himself was faced with the problems of conquest in Asia.

"A Greek ruling over Macedonians"—so Alexander I spoke of himself in Herodotus' history, and so his successors thought of themselves. To be a Greek was to admire Greek culture and above all to admire Athens as the centre of Greek culture, and the kings invited Greek poets, artists, and scholars to their court and even raised some of them, e.g., Euripides, to the positon of "Companion." The children of the royal house were educated in the Greek manner. Philip hired as tutor for Alexander the best young Greek philosopher of the day, Aristotle, whose father had been employed at court as a doctor. In his relations with the Greeks, as on his coinage, Philip stressed his own worship of the Greek gods and his crusade in the cause of Apollo during the so-called Sacred War of the Greek states; and he evidently impressed his point of view on the young Alexander. But in secular matters his first priorities were the advancement of his kingdom and the security of his Balkan empire, and he was not prepared to let any of the Greek city-states on his coasts serve as a base or a possible base for his enemies. He offered them alliance, which brought considerable economic advantages, but those states which refused or which broke their alliance were forced into subjection.

The warring city-states of the Greek peninsula constituted a separate theatre into which he was drawn by his own ambition as well as by diplomatic and military incidents, and the result in the end was the confrontation at Chaeronea, when he inflicted a decisive defeat on the armies of Athens, Boeotia, Corinth, and some other states. Sparta alone refused to recognise his supremacy. What settlement should he make in this very different world? His thoughts on the matter are likely to have been known to Alexander, who had led the victorious cavalry in the battle of Chaeronea and afterwards headed the military escort which brought to Athens the ashes of her dead—an act of respect which had never occurred in a war between Greek city-states.

Philip's experience with his immediate Greek neighbours, the Thessalians, must have been prominent in his mind. Invited into their internecine disputes, he expelled tyrants and drove back invaders so successfully that the Thessalians elected him President for life of their reconstituted League, commander of their forces in war, and organiser of their finances, which became closely linked to those of Macedonia. He annexed a part of Perrhaebia, from which the hill-people had often raided the Thessalian plain, and he planted Macedonian settlers at Gomphi, renamed Philippi, to check raids by the hill-tribes of Pindus; and these measures proved acceptable to the Thessalians. The result was certainly peace and prosperity in Thessaly, and the Thessalian cavalry served both Philip and Alexander with remarkable loyalty. The views of other Greeks were divided: Demosthenes, the advocate of city-state particularism, condemned the limitation of city-state sovereignty, and Isocrates, who regarded the interminable wars between the city-states as suicidal, congratulated Philip on the justice of his settlement.

In 346 B.C. Philip had publicised his programme for creating "general peace and concord" among the Greek states, and now in the winter of 338–337 B.C. he drew up a detailed programme which embodied these principles. In spring 337 B.C. the delegates of all mainland states except Sparta accepted the proposals and formed themselves into a Greek League, which undertook to apply the rule of law and not war to its internal affairs. The government of what was in essence a Greek federal state was a Council of delegates elected by the member-states, and the Council's majority decisions were binding on the member-states. The formation of this federal state involved the freezing of the status quo and to that extent endorsed the terms of peace which Philip had made with Athens and Boeotia: the former losing some of her imperial possessions, and Thebes being held by a Macedonian garrison. But, as in all such formations of a new community of quondam sovereign states, whether political or economic, the Greek League looked for its justification to the future when there would be "an end to the madness and the imperialism with which the Greeks have treated one another" and a prospect of peace and prosperity within the community.

In procuring this settlement Philip as a Greek had the interests of the Greeks at heart, as he understood them; but as a Macedonian he was concerned to establish peace and cooperation between his kingdom and the Greek League. At the first meeting of the League Council, no doubt at his instigation, an offensive and defensive alliance was formed for all time between the two states, "the Greeks" and "Philip and his descendants," so that this alliance was to be inherited by Alexander. Next the two states declared war on Persia to avenge the sacrilege committed by the Persians under Xerxes in 480 B.C., and the Greek League elected Philip as commander (*hegemon*) of its forces on land and sea and made him chairman of the Council for the duration of the war, with power to appoint a deputy. Troops were mobilised in both states, garrisons of Macedonians were approved at Thebes, Corinth, Chalcis, and Ambracia, and an advance force crossed the Hellespont into Asia to secure a bridgehead for the main body, which was to follow under Philip's command in autumn 336 B.C. Conditions were favourable for a combined operation by the two states. Then Philip was assassinated at Aegeae, at the age of forty-six.

The question for the Greeks at the time and for historians ever afterwards was whether Philip was sincere. Did he intend the Greek states to manage their own affairs within the Greek League? Philip himself did not live long enough to give the final proof or disproof, but Alexander may have been carrying out Philip's intentions in 336–334 B.C. when he referred matters to the Greek League. One general reason for supposing Philip to have been sincere is that he wanted the alliance of the Macedonians and the Greeks to work to their mutual benefit, as he saw it. Another lay in his attitude towards the concept of alliance, an attitude which Alexander inherited.

Sophisticated politicians then, as now, were apt to regard alliances as pawns in a game of deceit, and Athenian politicians in 366–356 B.C., for instance, had been particularly unscrupulous in this regard. But Philip seems to have regarded the religious oaths of an alliance as binding, and he regarded the breaker of those oaths as more culpable than a straightforward enemy. It is to be noted that Philip treated his allies generously, whether Chalcidians, Thessalians, or Athenians, even when they were grudging. But when an ally broke the oaths, he felt free to exact condign punishment: Olynthus was razed to the ground and the bulk of the population sold into slavery, and the Thebans had to pay for the recovery of their dead and the liberation of prisoners of war. Thus Philip's record suggests that the oaths of alliance with the Greek League were seriously undertaken and that he meant to honour them.

For those who took this view of Philip's intentions, the uncertainty was not Philip, but his successor. For the structure inherited by Philip in Macedonia and created by Philip in the Balkans, Thessaly, and Greece depended on the personality of one man in three persons—King, President, and Commander. When the successor proved to be Alexander, Demosthenes pronounced him a Margites, a "Mad-Hatter." That at least he was not; but would he equal "the greatest man that Europe had produced"?

II

THE ARMED FORCES OF THE KING

(A) THE MACEDONES

The relationship between the army and the king in Macedonia was particularly close, in that they were the two parts which made up the Macedonian state: the men under arms being the "Macedones," and the king the head and the superscription of the state. The army chose its commander only when it elected a man to be king, and it was a real choice even if the candidates were restricted to members of the Temenid house by a convention which lasted for more than three centuries. On making the election the soldiers clashed their spears against their shields to indicate their defence of their chosen king, and once elected the king exercised command for the rest of his life without let or hindrance or question, except on the rare occasion when a king was deposed by the army with or without foreign intervention (Amyntas, the father of Philip, for instance, was deposed but subsequently reinstated). Thus Philip and Alexander held the supreme and total command of their armed forces with an absolute constitutional right from the moment each was elected king. Moreover, the king's powers of command were limited only by the condition that charges of treason had to be tried and decided by the army. In all else his orders were to be obeyed. He alone enlisted a man, making him thereby a "Macedon"; he made all appointments and promotions; and he provided pay and bounties, set the conditions of service and granted exemptions, leave, and discharge.

Because so much depended on the choice of his successor, the king brought members of his house into the closest association with the army from the earliest possible age. Thus Philip ensured that as a boy and young man Alexander fought on several campaigns, commanded an army, governed the kingdom as his father's deputy, and led the cavalry at Chaeronea—all before he was twenty. On the few occasions when the army elected a minor to the throne, it chose a regent from the royal house and conferred on him the powers of the king. Thus, according to one tradition, Philip was at first regent for Amyntas, the infant son of the previous king, Perdiccas, Philip's brother; then after a year or two the army deposed Amyntas and elected Philip king. This Amyntas, being both older than Alexander, and of a senior line, was a possible successor to Philip; and it was therefore all the more significant that Philip made Alexander his deputy in 339 B.C.

In the Macedonian army the highest prestige was enjoyed by the cavalry.[6] The king and his entourage were horsemen, hunting on horseback and fighting as cavalrymen, and the king honoured his best cavalrymen with the title "Companion" (*hetairos*). We know that this title was very ancient because there was a worship of Zeus Hetaireios, the god of Companionship, and a festival of Companionship, "Hetairideia," observed both in Macedonia and in Magnesia; and there were athletic and other competitions, including duels between armed men, for which the king and his Companions alone were eligible. To those who, like Alexander, were steeped in the poems of Homer, the ties which bound the king and his Companions were as strong in the religious and the social sense as those which had bound Achilles and his Companions. Already in the period before Alexander II (369–368 B.C.) we know that the king selected from the ranks of his Companions the "Friends" (*philoi*) who were his closest associates and the "Commanders" (*hegemones*) to whom he delegated his own power of command. Entry to the charmed circle of the Companionship depended entirely on the king's favour, and he was concerned to choose men of integrity and ability. But the conditions of horsemanship in war were such that candidature was not open to all men.

Thucydides described the Macedonian cavalry in action against vastly superior numbers of Thracian cavalry and infantry in 429 B.C. as being "brave horsemen and cuirassiers," who "dashed in among the Thracian host wherever they pleased and no one withstood their onset." The men wore the cuirass (a bronze breastplate or coat of mail), their mounts were stronger than the horses of their neighbours, and they fought not as skirmishers but as shock-troops at close quarters. Their horsemanship was superb; for the stirrup being as yet unknown, they had to grip the horse with their thighs and wield a weapon in battle, sometimes with both hands. To acquire this skill it was necessary to start in childhood; already by the age of fourteen the royal pages were so far advanced in horsemanship that they hunted and fought on horseback with the king.

The story which Plutarch tells of Alexander at the age of twelve or so is particularly illuminating. A Greek friend, Demaratus of Corinth, gave to Philip a young thoroughbred horse named Bucephalus ("ox-header"), after the brand-mark of ox-head shape which was used by a famous Thessalian stable. Philip and his entourage came out to inspect the horse's paces, but the horse proved unmanageable and was being taken away when Alexander piped up and said he would handle him. Turning the horse's head towards the sun, so that he would no longer be startled by his own shadow, Alexander calmed him, coaxed him and rode him, to Philip's surprise and delight. Many boys in both Lower and Upper Macedonia must have grown up with horses and mules, but relatively few were trained so early and so expertly in horsemanship of this kind. Those few were often but not always sons of Companions in Lower Macedonia and members of the tribal aristocracies in the cantons of Upper Macedonia.

In the period before Philip the cavalry of Lower Macedonia and Upper Macedonia were separate entities; indeed they sometimes took different sides and even fought against one another. But Philip fused them into one body. His squadrons were named after a centre or centres of recruitment, near which the estates of the Companions were located; for instance, one after Bottiaea, a district in Lower Macedonia, and another after Amphipolis, a city in the coastal basin of the Strymon. One or more squadrons were called the *asthippoi* (a contraction of *astoi hippoi*), "townsmen-cavalry," and were recruited from the towns of Upper Macedonia; some of these served in Alexander's Balkan campaign, being referred to as "the cavalry from Upper Macedonia." Thus there was a territorial basis for the Companion cavalry squadrons. When able Greeks or other non-Macedonians were made Companions by Philip and Alexander, thus becoming "Macedones," they were allocated to the squadron of their place of residence. The total number of the Companion cavalry at the accession of Alexander is uncertain. In Asia Minor Alexander had about 1,800 in eight squadrons of some 225 each. We are told that he left 1,500 cavalry with Antipater in Macedonia; if these included both heavy and light cavalry, as is probable, and the proportion between them was as for the Asiatic campaign, there were about 1,000 Companion cavalry at home, so that the overall total was about 2,800 Companion cavalry in some fourteen squadrons of 200 each.

Thucydides described the Macedonian infantry in 423 B.C. as a mob, inferior to the Illyrians who really were warriors, and liable to panic. It is evident that they were a largely untrained militia, and that Thucydides regarded them with the scorn of the trained soldier. The only exceptions he deigned to mention were the Greeks resident in Lower Macedonia and some trained infantrymen (*hoplitai*) of Lyncus, the latter fighting against the king. Attempts to improve the sorry state of the infantry were made by two kings, Archelaus (c. 413–399 B.C.) who trained and equipped infantrymen on the lines of contemporary Greek armies, and Alexander II (369–368 B.C.), who probably first introduced the title of Infantry Companionship, calling the best infantrymen "Foot-Companions."[7] The latter was an important step; for it placed the best infantrymen on a level with the best cavalrymen, admitted them also to the closest association with the king, and led to a selected number serving as the king's bodyguard. We see these new infantry in action twice, in 359 B.C. as part of an army utterly defeated by the Illyrians with a heavy loss, and in 358 B.C. as the spearhead of victory under Philip's personal leadership against the Illyrians. The transformation was due to the personality and the methods of Philip. "He was not shattered by the great danger of his situation, but he restored confidence to the Macedones by haranguing them in a series of assemblies and encouraging them in eloquent speeches to be courageous; he improved the military formations, equipped his men appropriately with weapons of war, and held frequent exercises under arms and competitions in physical fitness." He was thus beginning to train an army of infantry on professional lines and equip them at his expense.

Names of army units and personnel were used in both a general sense and a restricted one, and their literal meaning is sometimes uncertain. What follows is the author's opinion in a controversial subject. In 359 B.C. (as in most of the preceding decade), the king's authority hardly extended beyond Lower Macedonia. Then Philip drew his "Foot-Companions" (*pezhetairoi*, being a contraction of *pezoi hetairoi*) from Lower Macedonia, and by the end of his reign he had at least six brigades of them. As far as our sources tell us, these brigades of *pezhetairoi* were named after their commanding officer only, e.g., "the brigade of Meleager." Late in the 350s, when Upper Macedonia had been assimilated and new towns were being planted, Philip began to raise and train infantrymen on the same lines from the people of the towns. These were called "Townsmen-Companions" (*asthetairoi*, being a contraction of *astoi hetairoi*). When Alexander went to Asia, he took six brigades, three of *pezhetairoi* and three of *asthetairoi*; and the implication of the equal number is that the total of brigades of each kind was about the same. As a brigade consisted of some 1,500 men and as 12,000 infantry were left behind in Macedonia, the total number of brigades probably was fourteen. The brigades of *asthetairoi* were named, in one source, after both the commanding officer and the canton of Upper Macedonia from which they came; for example, "the brigade of Coenus from Elimeotis" and "the brigade of Polyperchon from Tymphaea."

Within the forces which we have mentioned the king developed certain élites. Seven of the Companion Friends served as personal Bodyguards (*somatophylakes*) to Alexander; and it seems that the assassin of Philip, Pausanias, being both a Bodyguard and a Friend, was one of such a special group during Philip's reign. There was next a special group of *pezhetairoi* who acted as Philip's guard when he was walking on a ceremonial occasion or in action if he was fighting on foot; for example in the battle against the Illyrians in 358 B.C. They were chosen for their courage and physique. Of the Companion cavalry one squadron (*ile*) was the "Royal Squadron" or "King's Own Squadron"; it fought beside the king, and so was sometimes called the Guard (*agema*).

Another group of infantry recruited by Philip was called the Hypaspists ("shield-bearers"). The name was taken from the king's squire who carried his shield into battle (Peucestas did this for Alexander), and it was extended first to the Royal Guard (*agema*) and then to two other brigades. The Hypaspists numbered 3,000, and they all went with Alexander to Asia. They were Companions and Macedones and in a particular sense the King's Own infantry. Their sons were trained for the army, and these sons served in 321 B.C, being named "the descendants of the Hypaspists" or just the "Hypaspists"; for the original corps' name was changed to the "Silver-Shields" (*argyraspides*) just before the invasion of India.

It is probable that the king gave special rewards to the King's Own men: the seven Bodyguards, the royal squadron of Companion cavalry, Philip's guard of *pezhetairoi*, and the royal guard of Hypaspists. These rewards were in land-grants or in cash. In addition, the king paid for the maintenance and training of the royal pages, many of whom were relations of the Companions; he seems to have done the same for the sons of the Hypaspists.

(B) NON-MACEDONES OF THE KINGDOM, BALKAN TROOPS, GREEK ALLIES, AND GREEK MERCENARIES

Some cavalry units which served in Asia with Alexander were not Macedones: Thracians, Scouts (*prodromoi*), and Paeonians—five squadrons in all. That the Scouts, who constituted three of the five squadrons, were recruited from within the kingdom is very probable because they were given no ethnic label in our sources; they came perhaps from the mixed peoples of southeast Macedonia. The Paeonians came presumably from Paeonia which had been incorporated into the kingdom by Philip. If we are right about the Scouts and the Paeonians, it seems likely that the Thracians were also from within the kingdom. The squadrons numbered some 200 men each, and other squadrons of these light-armed cavalry were left behind in Macedonia.

The archers at first had no ethnic label. Although there were Macedones among them, the bulk may have come from east Macedonia and the Balkan empire. Greeks, and especially Thessalians, as well as a few Macedones, developed the siege-train to a high level of efficiency under Philip; and there were probably Greeks as well as Macedonians among the surveyors (*bematistai*), who recorded distances and planned communications. The ancillary services were manned by persons from the kingdom who were not Macedones. Large numbers of grooms and ostlers looked after the cavalry chargers, the remounts, and the horses or oxen which drew the artillery and brought up the supplies. Roads within Macedonia had first been developed by Archelaus (c. 413–399 B.C), who "cut straight roads," i.e., through forested areas; and roads within the Balkan empire were added in the time of Philip. Stones marking distances in stades (units of 185 metres) have been found for the Hellenistic period, and a track with limestone paving, only 1.20 metres wide, on the line of the later Roman road, the Via Egnatia, in central Albania may have been laid first in the time of Philip. Such roads were initially designed for cavalry patrols and pack-horses, and some of them were made later into roads for wheeled vehicles. In 423 B.C the troops of Perdiccas used carts drawn by pairs of oxen, which moved very slowly; so too the Greek army in spring 1941. It is probable that Philip used horses only.

Communication by sea seems to have been developed first by Philip, and for this purpose he created a basin in Lake Ludias by Pella and a banked waterway down to the gulf. Within this safe basin he built a small fleet with the excellent Macedonian ship-timber and made use of the many Greeks in his kingdom for crews. In 340–339 B.C. the Macedonian fleet operated successfully in the Propontis and the Black Sea despite the presence of a hostile Athenian fleet with a centuries-old tradition of seamanship.

To sum up, the forces which came from within the kingdom were of two kinds. The heavy cavalry, called the Companions of the king, and the heavy infantry who fought in the battle-line or phalanx, called the Foot-Companions, the Townsmen-Companions and the Hypaspists—all were Macedones. Together with a few specialists in other arms it was these troops which represented the people under arms who elected the king in an armed assembly. This was apparent most clearly in the assembly and purification of the army which followed after the death of Alexander. Second to them in privilege and not possessing the status of Macedones were the light cavalry, the ancillary services, and the personnel of the fleet. They had no say in the election of the king or the hearing of a case of treason. For example, Callisthenes, a Greek from Olynthus, who served Alexander as the court historian, was not qualified to attend the hearing which resulted in his being put to death. The Macedones in Alexander's expedition to Asia were thus an army within the army and a state within the kingdom.

What proportion of the kingdom was formed by the Macedones in 336 B.C.? Let us take the population figures for A.D. 1928, when the country was at a low ebb after the long Turkish occupation, and let us assume that one person in four was a man of military age. On this basis one man in ten was a Macedon in the areas from which the infantry brigades were recruited, namely Lower Macedonia including Anthemus and Upper Macedonia; or to put it in other words 27,000 out of 270,000 men of military age were Macedones. If we consider the whole kingdom from Lake Lychnitis (Ochrid) to the Nestus, the figure is one man out of eighteen. As the light cavalry and light infantry from within the kingdom who were not Macedones hardly exceeded 2,000 men, the total demand on Macedonian manpower was not heavy. Indeed the loss of men for agriculture may have been made good in Alexander's reign by the effects of a rising birth-rate in Philip's reign.

The Balkan empire was rich in ferocious, if ill-disciplined troops, and there is no reason to suppose that Philip disarmed them. He was able to use some of them against such perpetual enemies as the Scythians and other raiders, and Alexander took to Asia 5,000 infantry who were described as Illyrians, Triballians, and Odrysians, the last being the leading tribe of central Thrace. They were not infantry of the phalanx-line but light-armed skirmishers, useful in mountain warfare and on subsidiary duties. A particularly fine unit of which Alexander made continuous use was supplied by the Agrianes, a tribe at the head of the Strymon valley (near Sofia), whose royal house was on excellent terms with that of Macedonia. Some of the archers who served with Alexander may have been recruited in the empire.

Among the Greek allies the Thessalians provided squadrons of heavy cavalry which rivalled the Macedonians in excellence. Led by a noble house of Heraclid descent, the Aleuadae, they had cooperated with Philip throughout his reign and fought on his side at Chaeronea, taking part in the charge led by Alexander. And for the war against Persia they sent 1,800 horsemen, equal in number and quality to Alexander's own Companion cavalry, who were to play a decisive part. The other Greek allies supplied 600 cavalry, 7,000 infantry, and 160 triremes with a complement of some 32,000 men for the war against Persia. Thus the Greek commitment of almost 40,000 men in all surpassed in number the troops sent from Macedonia and the Balkan empire. The expeditionary force at the start was a well-balanced partnership between the two states, Macedonia and "the Greeks."

A market which was open to all bidders was provided by Greek mercenary soldiers, available in many tens of thousands throughout the Greek world.[8] Philip had made much use of these professional soldiers for training his own Macedonians and for campaigns in the Balkans, and Alexander employed 4,000 Greek mercenaries at the start in Asia. These were mainly infantrymen, probably with different kinds of expertise. It is interesting that he preferred to hire them rather than to take more infantry from his Balkan empire.

(c) EQUIPMENT,[9] MOVEMENT, AND SUPPLY

The Companion cavalryman fought wearing a metal helmet, metal cuirass (sometimes with shoulder-pieces extending to the upper arm), flowing cloak, short tunic, short metal or leather kiltlet covering the abdomen and private parts, and sandal-type shoes. His chief weapon was a lance of cornel-wood, light and tough, with counterbalancing butt and tip of metal, which he wielded with one arm. In a massed charge the lance gained its momentum from man and horse alike and was broken or dropped on impact, lest the rider was himself unseated. The Macedonians were the first to use the lance successfully. Next he fought with a rather long, slightly curving sword, of which the blade was designed for slashing. He did not normally carry a shield in battle; but a groom might be at hand to provide one at need. Thus equipped the cavalrymen rode in a close wedge-shaped formation, apex to the enemy, so that they could readily incline to right or left and charge into any gap (a formation used on occasion by Epaminondas of Thebes, but regularly first by Philip; Xen. *HG*. 7.5.24 and Arr. *Tact*. 18.4). It required much training, for every man had to keep his eyes on the one leader, "as happens in the flight of cranes" (Ascl. 7.3; cf. Arr. *Tact*. 16.8 and 25.7). Their function was to shatter the enemy cavalry by the shock of their onset, and they proved under Philip superior to the fine horsemen of Illyria, Thrace, and Scythia. They could not charge an infantry-line; but as soon as an infantry-line lost its cohesion, they could push their way in, using the lance and the horse's weight, and they were deadly in attacking the open flank or the rear of an infantry force, and in pursuing a broken enemy, as Philip showed in his victory over the Illyrians in 358 B.C. The mounts were usually geldings, controlled by a spiked bit and spurs. They were bred from sturdy stock and expertly trained, but were often killed or wounded in battle, and maimed in long pursuits, since they were not shod. The relatively light armour of these cavalrymen, as compared with that of some Persian cavalrymen or the medieval knight, was in part due to the fact that Macedonian horses were less heavily built and smaller, perhaps around fourteen hands.

Light-armed cavalrymen, drawn probably from the eastern part of the Macedonian kingdom, served in Philip's time, as they appear early in Alexander's activities. Of these the Paeonians and the Thracians were armed with missiles as well as side-arms; and the Paeonians at least had no breastplate but used a shield (*Itin. Alex*. 25). The Scouts or Lancers (*sarissophoroi*) carried a long *sarissa*, similar to that of the Companion infantryman which we shall shortly describe. As Alexander was sometimes portrayed wielding such a *sarissa*, it is possible that the Companion cavalrymen were trained to fight on occasion with the *sarissa*.

For centuries the Thessalian nobles had bred the finest horses and been the best cavalrymen in Greece. Equipped in the Greek manner, they carried two short spears, hurling one as a javelin and using the other as spear or javelin to suit the occasion and they were armed with a curving sword for slashing. They wore protective armour like the Companion cavalrymen, but sometimes had bronze guards on the forehead, chest, and flanks of their chargers. Thessalians were said to have invented the diamond formation.

The Companion infantrymen, both *pezhetairoi* and *asthetairoi*, were equipped with a metal helmet, metal greaves, a metal circular shield some two feet wide which was suspended from neck or shoulder, a long pike (*sarissa*) of light cornel-wood to be wielded with both hands, and a dagger as a second weapon. Pikes varied in length, probably from 15 to 18 feet; they were held in the middle by a metal band; and the foot-long blade at the tip was counterbalanced by a spiked butt of metal. During much of Philip's reign only the officers seem to have worn a metal cuirass, but in his later years, as prosperity developed, the wearing of it or of a metal frontlet (a "semi-cuirass") probably became general. This was so under Alexander. This equipment was designed primarily for fighting in the long close-packed line, known as the phalanx, against an enemy line of a similar kind. Normally each man in the front rank occupied a metre of space.

Behind him there were at least seven men. His front was protected not only by the blade of his own 15-foot pike but also by the blades of three or four pikes from behind him, these being progressively longer. When they faced an enemy of a different kind, other formations were adopted, such as a wedge or column. On the march into action the infantrymen were quick to change their pace and direction, and they had to maintain their dressing on different kinds of terrain. Strict discipline and precise drill were essential, and the best training of all was provided by experience in battle. For this reason Alexander chose not young but seasoned infantry-men for the brigades which went to Asia.

The Hypaspists were equally infantry of the line in that they formed part of the phalanx in every set battle. Then they too used the pike, which was the characteristic weapon of the Macedonian phalanx, and had the same equipment as the Companion infantrymen except that the cuirass was worn only by their officers. To be without a cuirass made for greater mobility on forced marches and night operations. Thus the Hypaspists were used sometimes with light-armed units for special tasks. They saw more action and had a greater reputation for toughness and endurance than any other soldiers.

That the men of the phalanx, *when in that formation*, fought with the pike is clear from the battles at Chaeronea and Pelium, where the king was leading his best infantrymen (whether called *pezhetairoi* or *hypaspistai* at the time) and also from the battle at Gaugamela, for the serried points were mentioned in the descriptions. It was this weapon which gave the Macedonians the advantage over Balkan infantry and Greek hoplites; and it did so also in the set battles in Asia against both cavalry and infantry. Ideally they fought on flat ground, but also on difficult ground, for instance on the steep banks of the Granicus and Pinarus rivers. That they were able to fight with other weapons under other conditions is obvious; for instance when mounted in the final stage of the pursuit of Darius, or in leading an assault on a breached wall at Tyre, or in mountain warfare. The shaft of the *sarissa* seems to have been made of two pieces joined together; these were probably dismantled on the march, and one length alone was of a normal spear's length and may on occasion have been used as such.

The Agrianians, who were frequently associated with the Hypaspists, were armed in their native style and were probably recruited from the personal "shield-bearers" of the Agrianian king. Their equipment was based on that of the *peltast* who carried a small shield, long spear and long sword, and wore light body-armour. The other Balkan troops were armed each in their own style, but the details of their equipment are not known.

The infantry known as *hoplites* were the Greek equivalent of the Companion infantry. They were more heavily armed, having helmet, breastplate and greaves, a large bronze shield with two grips which was attached to the left arm at elbow and hand, a spear, six to eight feet long, and a sword. They too were trained to fight in a close-packed phalanx, eight men deep, but one which was less flexible and needed flatter terrain. Because their weapons and their methods did not marry with those of the Companion infantrymen, they were not used as troops of the line in Alexander's major battles.

The remarkable feature of the European army which Alexander inherited from his father and led into Asia was its composite nature and the specialised expertise of each part. Alexander had at his disposal almost every known variety of cavalry and infantry, heavy or light, regular or irregular, as well as experts in siegecraft, artillery, roadmaking, bridge-building, surveying and so on. Each unit was the best of its kind, properly equipped and highly trained. The fleet too, though relatively small, was supplied by the leading naval states in Greece, Athens among them, and the reputation of Greek triremes and Greek seamen was still the highest in the Mediterranean.

"Philip used to train 'the Macedones' for dangerous service by taking them on frequent route marches of some 37 miles, fully armed with helmet, shield, greaves, pike and, as well as their arms, rations and all the gear they needed for daily life." This type of training, familiar today in commando or parachute courses, was of general application, and it produced the physical fitness and capacity for endurance which were found in the best guerrilla troops of the Balkan resistance movements of World War II. On such marches over rough country there was no question of keeping step in a column of fours or waiting for a soup kitchen. The troops spread out and each man made his best speed; each man too was his own mule, carrying a load which might include a month's stock of flour, and he prepared his own food in his metal dixie (the Macedonian name being *kotthybos*).

Whereas a Greek hoplite had a slave boy to carry his shield and gear, Philip allowed only one bearer (carrying grinders and ropes) to ten soldiers on the march. Troopers and horses were trained on similar lines so that they were capable of maintaining long pursuits over rough country. Philip allowed only one groom to a cavalryman.

The movement of goods and especially of heavy materials for the building of siege-towers and bridges was best undertaken by a fleet, whenever possible, as in Philip's campaign of 340–339 B.C. and in the early phase of Alexander's expedition to Asia. On land, when advanced troops had repelled an enemy, the baggage-train followed at its own slow pace, wheeled carriers and wagons being drawn by horses or by requisitioned oxen, and men also putting their shoulders to the task. But sometimes, as in Alexander's Balkan campaign, the baggage-train had to keep up with a fast-moving army; and this was achieved by careful planning, frequent relays of draught-animals, and knowledge of the country.

Communications and supply were related matters. We have already mentioned road-making in Macedonia and the Balkans, and Alexander put his Thracian troops to the task of making a road in mountainous Lycia, for example. Even where there were Persian roads or newly-made roads surfaced with rubble or flagstones, haulage was slow; and messages carried by riders or cross-country runners took months even in summer to pass from Macedonia to India. Philip and Alexander had to find local solutions as far as possible to the problems of supply. The army often split and moved in separate groups, so that they could live mainly on foodstuffs officially requisitioned or privately purchased from the villagers; and where local supplies were short, the army had to make double speed to get into a better feeding-ground for men and horses, as between Susa and Persepolis. Hardships were relieved by feasting and drinking at times of rest and relaxation. Even so, long-term plans had to be made and executed when shipwrights and their equipment were brought from Phoenicia to the Indus valley, or an army was marched across the Hindu Kush. That these problems of communication and supply, which Wavell regarded as the supreme test of generalship,[10] were solved by Alexander is one of the clearest signs of his genius.

III

ALEXANDER IN EUROPE

Alexander's mother, Olympias, was a member of the Molossian royal house in Epirus, which believed itself and was generally believed by other Greeks to be descended from Achilles, son of the goddess Thetis Olympias' mother was of the royal house of the Chaones in Epirus, traditionally founded by Helenus, son of Priam of Troy. So her claims to be of heroic descent were as strong as Philip's. The situations of the two families were similar. They were Greeks ruling over "barbarian" subjects, Molossians and Macedones alike being outside the circle of city-state life, although Greek-speaking. Both peoples suffered terribly from the same enemy, the Illyrians, and it was probably Philip's victory over them in 358 B.C. which led Arybbas, the Molossian king, to give his niece in marriage to Philip. They are portrayed in Figures 29 and 30. Their first child, Alexander, was born in the summer of 356 B.C.

Intermarriage between royal houses was as common then in the Balkans as in Victorian Europe, and it sometimes affected the line of succession. In Molossia, Arybbas had taken the throne after the death of his elder brother, King Neoptolemus, who had left three children. Of these Arybbas married the elder daughter himself, gave the younger daughter to Philip, and kept the third child, another Alexander, at his court; but since Arybbas had a son older than this Alexander, it seemed likely that his son would succeed, until Philip intervened, took young Alexander away, brought him up as one of the royal pages, and then in 342 B.C. put him on the Molossian throne, expelling Arybbas and his sons, who fled to Athens where the people voted to restore him by force. Philip soon strengthened the relationship by giving his own daughter by Olympias, called Cleopatra, to Alexander in another case of uncle-niece marriage. Thus the two Alexanders, who had grown up together in their teens and were very close friends, became brothers-in-law.

The love-life of royalty attracts the sensationalist writer of every period. That of Philip and his seven or eight wives is no exception, and some of the stories about them deserve as much credit as a modern strip-cartoon. For example, Philip, it was said, on his way to join Olympias in bed put one eye to a chink in the bedroom door and saw Olympias having intercourse with a snake. This turned him off for some weeks. Meanwhile Olympias found she had conceived a child who proved to be Alexander. Philip consulted the oracle at Delphi about what he had seen, and the god replied that Philip would lose that sacrilegious eye, for the snake was none other than Zeus Ammon. Satisfied by this explanation, Philip resumed marital relations with Olympias and got at least one more child by her. Olympias, of course, could not keep a secret; she told Alexander how she had conceived him, but asked him not to make it public, lest Hera, the divine wife of Zeus, become jealous. Sure enough, Philip lost that eye during the siege of Methone.

Royal pages too, provided good homosexual material for the sensationalists; Philip, they held, made most of them his victims, not sparing even Olympias' young brother, the Molossian Alexander, according to the lubricious Justin.

Rows in the royal family and drunken orgies were good starting points for gossip. In 337 B.C. Philip married Cleopatra, the ward of Attalus, a leading Companion. As has already been discussed, it was important to beget more heirs, and now that five of his wives, including Olympias, were past child-bearing age it was sensible of Philip to marry a younger woman. The story of the gossip-writers was this: Philip, although too old for marriage (at forty-five!) fell in love and married a young girl, Cleopatra, and at the wedding banquet her uncle Attalus drank too much and asked the company to pray for a legitimate heir to the throne by his niece. Thereat Alexander, with a shout "Am I then a bastard?", hurled a wine-cup at Attalus; Attalus threw a tankard at Alexander; Philip drew his sword against his son but was so drunk that he tripped and fell flat on his face. Alexander had the last word. Standing over the drunken king he cried, "Ready to cross from Europe into Asia, you cannot even get from one chair to the next." Splendid comedy, indeed! But not to be taken as accurate reporting. No Macedonian would have thought of suggesting that the king's deputy in office and the king's commander of the cavalry at Chaeronea was not in fact his son. After this disgraceful scene, the story ran on, Alexander and his jealous mother, Olympias, went off to the Molossian court, and Alexander went on alone and stayed in Illyria. It took a Greek gentleman, Demaratus of Corinth, to bring Philip to his senses and end the quarrel between father and son. One ancient author (Justin) and some modern writers go further and claim that Philip 'divorced' Olympias and banished Alexander; if so, he certainly would not have sent them, or let them go into exile in the two areas where they would have been best able to foment trouble.

Another story was concerned with secret negotiations between

Philip and Pixodarus, satrap of Caria in Asia Minor, which were prompted by Philip's expected advance deep into Persian territory in 336 B.C. Pixodarus offered his daughter and Philip proposed his retarded son, Arrhidaeus, to make a match. The story ran that Olympias got wind of this, worked Alexander into a fit of jealousy and suggested that Philip was making the half-wit his heir. Persuaded of all this, Alexander sent a secret messenger to Pixodarus to say that Arrhidaeus was not only subnormal but a bastard as well; so Alexander himself was the man Pixodarus should be seeking. Philip in turn got wind of this secret message, took Philotas as a witness and confronting Alexander in his room ridiculed him for wanting to marry the daughter of a mere Carian. Such claims of knowing what goes on in secret negotiations and in private conversations between mother and son, and father and son, were common enough with the Hellenistic writers, as with some journalists today. But they provide no basis for historical reconstruction. The story in its unabbreviated form was probably totally imaginary, and Alexander's part in it seems to bear the mark of malicious fiction.

To gain currency these stories had to based on some fact or facts. For example, Olympias as a worshipper of Dionysus was a snake-handler; Philip lost an eye; Pixodarus did negotiate with Philip; and the marriage of Philip and Cleopatra did cause a rift in Philip's relations with Olympias and Alexander. The last needs some investigation, because it was connected by some with the assassination of Philip. Arrian, our least sensational source, wrote as follows in a short digression. "Because there was suspicion between Alexander and Philip, since Philip had married Eurydice (Cleopatra) and dishonoured Alexander's mother Olympias, Harpalus was banished because he was loyal to . . . [a lacuna, the name probably being Alexander], and on the same ground Ptolemy, Nearchus, Erigyius and Laomedon." Since this Ptolemy wrote a life of Alexander, which Arrian used as one of his two main sources, we may be confident this passage came from Ptolemy himself and the banishment was correctly associated with the marriage (and not with the later affair of Pixodarus to which Plutarch attached it). Presumably these friends of Alexander had associated themselves with some protest or demonstration against Philip which brought about their banishment by the assembly of the Macedones, if it was on the grounds of treason, or by the king, if on military grounds. Thereafter Philip and Alexander were reconciled, perhaps with the help of Demaratus of Corinth.

The murder of Philip in June 336 B.C. was a sensational affair. The story ran as follows. The assassin, Pausanias, had once been Philip's favourite but had been displaced in Philip's affections by a young page, whom Pausanias—considerably older and very distinguished—proceeded to insult. The page complained bitterly to another lover, Attalus, and then lost his life while protecting Philip in battle in 337 B.C. Attalus took revenge on Pausanias in 336 B.C.: he invited him to dinner, got him drunk, and handed him on to the grooms, who assaulted him sexually. Pausanias then asked Philip to punish Attalus and his men for the outrage. Philip promoted Pausanias to high rank by making him one of his seven Bodyguards (*somatophylakes*), but he did not punish the offenders in any way. So Pausanias decided to take revenge on Philip. That this was Pausanias' motive was stated by Aristotle, a reliable contemporary, and may be accepted as true. The fact that Pausanias had a personal motive did not exclude the possibility that he was one of several conspirators, the others having different motives. And the circumstances of the murder led people to believe that others had been involved.

The opportunity for the murder occurred on the day after the state wedding between Alexander the Molossian king and Cleopatra, Alexander's sister, which we have already mentioned. This day was to begin with a festival of the arts, and the theatre at Aegeae was packed at dawn with leading Macedonians, delegates of the empire, and ambassadors of the Greek allies. The procession approached—first the statues of the gods, then Philip walking between Alexander the bridegroom and Alexander his chosen heir, with the special guardsmen round them, and then Philip's Bodyguards and Friends. When they reached the entry (*eisodos*), the two Alexanders and the Friends went ahead to take their places by the throne. Then the special guardsmen stood away, and the Bodyguards dropped back, so that the king, wearing a white cloak, entered alone into the *orchestra*. At that moment Pausanias leapt upon him, killed him outright, and sprinted off to some horses which were waiting near the gateway. Hotly pursued by three of the Bodyguards, Pausanias tripped, fell, and was killed by the weapons of his pursuers as he was getting up.

The first need was to elect a new king, and the first man to declare for Alexander was Alexander the Lyncestian, who put on his breastplate and stood beside Alexander, in accordance with the traditional procedure (A. 1.25.2; C. 7.1.6). The assembly of the Macedones, being those under arms at Aegeae and nearby, then elected Alexander, clashing their spears against their shields. The next step was for the new king to prosecute and the assembly to judge those accused of treasonous conduct in connection with the late king's death. Those who had held the horses for the assassin may have escaped or had nothing to disclose, as they do not appear in the accounts; but the fact that the horses were there showed that the murder had been premeditated. Our first suspects, if we had been in Alexander's position, would have been those who had let the king be by himself, unprotected—the group of Friends, the Bodyguards who had failed in their duty, and the special guardsmen who had stood aside. Further, as the assassination was obviously planned for this ceremony but an opportunity to strike might not have arisen until later, one should consider also those who were to have been seated near the king's throne in the front row of the theatre. In fact we have a fragmentary papyrus which, as tentatively restored by the present writer, described the verdict of a trial and also the third step, the burial of the dead king. It reads thus: "And they acquitted those with him in the theatre and the special guards and those round the throne, but he [i.e., Alexander] delivered the diviner to the Macedones to punish. And they crucified him. And the body of Philip he handed over to the attendants to bury. . . ." No doubt the defence put forward by the first two groups of defendants was that they had acted on the orders of Philip. The diviner had evidently taken the omens that day and declared them favourable; that might have been enough for the assembly, or there may have been other evidence against him.

Acquittal did not end suspicion. The Bodyguards must have seemed the most likely accomplices, especially those who killed Pausanias and thereby prevented enquiry. The names of three of these were recorded in our sources—Leonnatus and Perdiccas, who were both of the royal family, and Attalus, whose niece Philip had married. When enquiry was made into the background of the assassin, the connection between Attalus and Pausanias must have appeared suspicious; was the story of Pausanias being maltreated by the servants of Attalus merely a cover for their collaboration in a plot? Attalus was by now back in Asia, in command of a Macedonian army, with which he was very popular, and in contact with Greeks who might join in a revolt. Alexander sent one of his Friends with some troops on a secret mission: to bring Attalus back alive or, if he could not manage that, to kill him. In fact the Friend killed him, and there is a report in our sources that Attalus had been in treasonable correspondence with Demosthenes, who was then leading the opposition to Alexander at Athens. If Attalus had been brought back alive, he would presumably have been prosecuted by Alexander and judged by the assembly of the Macedones. We are in no position to declare Attalus either guilty or innocent.

The killing of Attalus led to the killing of his ward, Cleopatra, and the child she had just born Philip (whether a boy or a girl is uncertain). On whose orders? The sensational sources made Olympias do the killings and Alexander regret them, but their veracity is very dubious. It is possible that the assembly of the Macedones made the decision in accordance with the tradition that "those related to a traitor in blood" were executed (C. 6.11.20; 8.6.28).

Three sons of Aëropus were accused of complicity in the murder of Philip: Alexander Lyncestes who had been first to hail Alexander as king, and Heromenes and Arrhabaeus. It is probable that these three men were members of the royal house, being descended from Perdiccas II through Aëropus II (see stemma facing p. 176 in Mac. II)[10a]. There were those in Macedonia who thought that a son of Aëropus had a better right to be king than Alexander; for we learn from Plutarch that on Philip's death the discontented "looked towards Amyntas and the sons of Aëropus." They were no doubt tried—Alexander Lyncestes was later judged a traitor who was to have been placed by Persia on the throne of Macedonia (see p. 184); the other two were found guilty and executed.

Even so Alexander doubted whether he had got to the bottom of the plot. It was suggested that he asked the god at Siwah whether all the conspirators had been punished. In any event, Alexander should have learnt one lesson, that a king cannot trust any close friend, not even a Bodyguard especially chosen to protect his person. From then on Alexander was forewarned. It is a sign of his awareness that he demoted Leonnatus and Perdiccas for their failure to protect their king. He chose other men to be his Bodyguards, and only some years later restored these two to this trusted rank. The Macedones too had learnt the lesson that the safety of the realm, in the person of the king, was precarious. If Philip could be killed on such an occasion, and killed at that by a high-ranking officer, the life of his only capable heir, Alexander, must be protected by all practical means.

When mystery surrounds the assassination of a head of state, whether king or president, the wildest theories may be advanced, and each theorist is sure he knows the answer. Such a one was Justin. "Olympias," he wrote, "was believed to have set Pausanias to the task." And a sentence or two later the belief is presented as fact. "Olympias had the horses ready for him . . . and that night she put a gold wreath on the head of the crucified corpse, and later had a tumulus made for him on the spot and arranged for sacrifices in his honour." Justin's view collapses under these absurdities. In any case it requires us to suppose that Olympias deliberately chose to have her husband murdered at the celebration in honour of the wedding of her only daughter to her brother, and that in the presence of her son. Justin and Plutarch are both hesitant in mentioning the wildest theory of all, that Alexander was a party to her plot and himself promoted the murder of his own father (parricide being a heinous offence by the moral and religious standards of the Greeks), Alexander now choosing as the occasion the wedding of his own sister to his close friend in the presence of delegates from the Greco-Macedonian world, and thereafter prosecuting persons he knew to be innocent with brilliant, cold-blooded hypocrisy. This would be hard to believe of any Machiavellian prince, and it certainly is incompatible with the personality of Alexander as his contemporaries, Ptolemy and Aristobulus, portrayed him.[11]

Let us bear in mind the impact of the years 340–336 B.C. on a young man of deep sensitivities and strong emotions: the thrill of command as king's deputy against the Maedi, the campaign to the Danube, the elixir of leading the cavalry charge at Chaeronea, the escorting of the ashes of the dead to Athens, the rift with his father, the sympathy with his mother, the banishment of his close friends, the reconciliation with his father, experience in Illyria, the walk beside his father to the theatre at Aegeae, the sight of his father standing alone, triumphant, then struck dead. The last was a searing experience, an indelible memory.

The tributes paid to Philip in his death have become known to us through the excavation of the Great Tumulus at Aegeae (Vergina) by Professor M. Andronikos.[12] The first unplundered tomb to be found there was certainly that of a Macedonian king of our period and almost certainly that of Philip. For the three miniature heads, shown in Figures 29, 30, 31 are portraits of Philip, Olympias and the young Alexander. The king buried there, close to the shrine, was to be the recipient of worship after death; one of his wives, a victim probably of suttee, was buried in the adjoining chamber; and the offerings placed with them were costly and magnificent. The rites were derived from a long tradition, of which we find mention in the *Iliad* and the *Odyssey*; and in the fourth century they were not Greek but barbaric and specifically Balkan in character. We learn from literary sources that the corpse of the assassin was crucified, exposed and then burnt above the tomb, his sons were executed there and those convicted of complicity were killed at the tumulus over the tomb. The cremated horse-trappings which were found within the top of the tomb's small tumulus were perhaps those of the horses which had awaited the assassin. These examples of human and animal sacrifice and other details remind us that the Macedonian kings, Alexander included, were closer in their religious ideas and funerary practices to the Getae, the Scyths, and the Celts than to the Greeks in the fourth century B.C.

Alexander had been elected to the throne in preference to Amyntas, son of Perdiccas III, an elder brother of Philip. This Amyntas, representing an older line and himself older than Alexander, had been king (*IG* VII 3055) albeit as a minor in 359 B.C., had married Philip's daughter Cynna and had probably led the envoys to Thebes in 339 B.C.; and after Philip's death, when Macedonia was "festering with discontent, it was looking to Amyntas and the sons of Aëropus" (Plut. *Mor.* 327 C). The trial immediately after the assassination did not involve the name of Amyntas but led to the execution of two sons of Aëropus. It was only later, before summer 335 B.C., that Amyntas was condemned to death for conspiring against Alexander. Mentions of that plot in our sources are casual, not descriptive (C. 6.9.17, 6.10.24; J. 12.6.14; A. in *FGrH* 156 F.9,22; Plut. loc. cit.), but that is no ground for dismissing them as false.

It seems probable, then, that Amyntas was arraigned for treason and executed. One of his friends, another Amyntas, son of Antiochus, who had been honoured with him at Oropus in Boeotia (Tod 164), fled at this time and took service with Darius; and the surviving son of Aëropus,

Alexander the Lyncestian, was later in treasonable correspondence with this Amyntas. Whatever the rights and wrongs of the case—and we are in no position to weigh them—the death of Amyntas freed Alexander from his fear of an immediate rival. The only close relative was his half-brother, the defective Arrhidaeus, and he was destined to accompany the king on the campaign in Asia. There were descendants in other branches of the Temenid house, Leonnatus and Perdiccas and Alexander Lyncestes among them, but rightly or wrongly Alexander felt confident of their loyalty.

His father avenged and his throne secure, Alexander must have felt free to proceed with his own personal ambition. It was contained in his favourite line of his favourite book, the *Iliad*: to be "both a good king and a mighty warrior" (Plut. *Mor.* 331 b, quoting *Iliad* 3.179). Simple in word, but rich in possibilities.

(B) THE ASSERTION OF AUTHORITY
(see Figure 2)

Because the structure and the direction of Macedonian power depended solely on the king, there was a time of paralysis after the murder of Philip. During it Alexander had to make his mark and impress his will. When the funeral was over and the embassies were about to leave, Alexander reminded the Greeks among them that they had taken oaths of alliance with "Philip and his descendants," so that his intention to hold them to the alliance was clear. But his first aim was to consolidate his position in Macedonia. There he was fortunate in commanding the loyalty of Philip's closest Friends, Antipater and Parmenio, both men of Lower Macedonia in their sixties, widely experienced in war, diplomacy, and administration; but, what was more important, he was already known and trusted by the rank and file of the army, because he had been able to gain experience and show his abilities before he was twenty years of age to a degree which would have been impossible for anyone but a chosen prince. As in so many things, he acted as Philip had done: he kept the men under arms, trained them rigorously, enforced strict discipline, and made some changes in the higher command. When autumn came, he left Antipater in charge in Macedonia and Parmenio in Asia Minor and set off southwards to win the personal positions which his father had held—President of the Thessalian League and Commander of the Greek League forces against Persia. Would this young man of just twenty commend himself as worthy of such positions of trust? Or was he a mere "Mad Hatter," as Demosthenes had described him?

The narrow Vale of Tempe, almost impregnable against a frontal at-

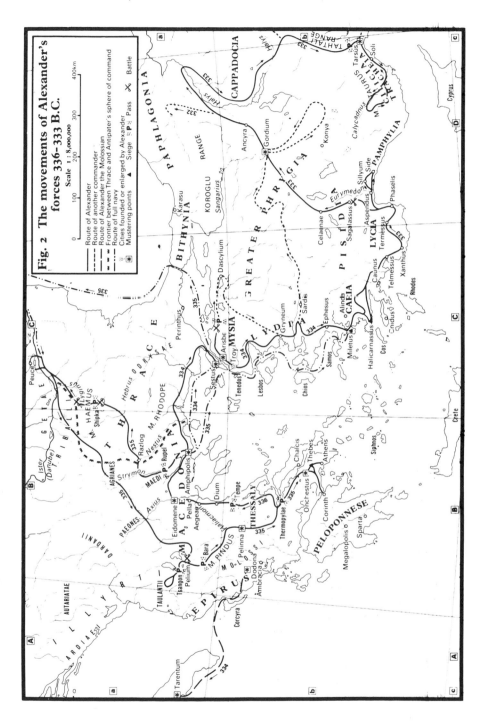

Fig. 2 The movements of Alexander's forces 336–333 B.C.

tack, was held by a force of Thessalians. Like guerrilla bands in 1943, Alexander cut his way not down but across the Vale, his men swimming the river or using boats. He was at the head of a small, mobile force, and he and his men, skilled in mountaineering, cut steps known as "Alexander's ladder" up the cliff face of Mt. Ossa and turned the position of the Thessalians.

Arriving in Larissa, where the ruling clan, the Aleuadae, were related and loyal to the Macedonian kings, Alexander stressed his personal affinities with the Thessalians as a descendant of Heracles on his father's side and of Achilles on his mother's side and emphasised his good will towards them.

At a meeting of the Thessalian League Alexander was elected President, he was entrusted with the organisation of its revenues, and he was promised its support in Greek League affairs. He could now rely on the finest cavalry force in Greece and a strong voice in the Council of the Greek League. His next aim was the Amphictyonic Council, in which the Thessalians and their neighbours whom Alexander now dominated had a majority vote. Alexander convened a special meeting. The Council gave him its full support. A rapid march brought him to Thebes, where the people had voted to expel the Macedonian garrison. The opposition to him was overawed. Ambassadors of Athens hastened to avert the anger of Alexander, who believed—probably correctly—that Demosthenes had intrigued with Persia and conspired with Attalus against Macedonia and Greece. Their apologies were accepted. The Athenians bestowed even greater honours on Alexander than they had conferred on his father.

The way was now clear for a majority vote in his favour at a meeting of the Council of the Greek League which he convened. The delegates of all tribes and city-states of Greece proper, except Sparta which remained proudly defiant, reaffirmed the principles of the Greek League, and in response to a tactful speech by Alexander appointed him commander (*hegemon*) of their forces for the war against Persia. Alexander returned home with all objectives gained; but, like his father, he left Macedonian garrisons in position at Corinth, Thebes, Chalcis, and Ambracia, in the last of which he approved a change of constitution from oligarchy to democracy. He had shown remarkable adroitness in advancing stage by stage and in not making an issue of the opposition at the Vale of Tempe, of the Thebans voting to expel the garrison, of Demosthenes' activities and Sparta's defiance. He had pressed on to his main objective, the Council of the Greek League.

Once elected hegemon, he was on a different footing with the Greeks, since every state on the mainland, except Sparta, had bound itself by the following oath.

"I swear by Zeus, Earth, Sun, Poseidon, Athena, and Ares, by all gods and goddesses, I shall abide by the peace and I shall not break the agreement with Alexander the Macedonian. . . . If anyone acts in any way contrary to the treaty and its articles, I shall go to the help of the injured party as they may enjoin and I shall fight against the transgressor of the common peace in whatever way seems good to the general Council and may be enjoined by the hegemon."

The background to the agreement between Alexander and the Greeks was in everybody's mind: the battle of Chaeronea, fought little more than two years before.[13] Although Philip had offered negotiation more than once, the states of the central part of the peninsula, led by Boeotia and Athens, had been determined to force a decision by arms; for they had been confident that their superior numbers of citizen infantrymen, stiffened by professional mercenaries, would defeat the Macedonians. They had been mistaken. Philip had outmanoeuvred the Greek generals and routed the Greek heavy-armed infantry, 30,000 of them, by his coordinated use of infantry and cavalry in a set battle. He was following the example of Pelopidas and Epaminondas, the brilliant generals of Thebes in the 360s B.C., but the troops which he led and Alexander inherited were to prove themselves superior to any Greek forces. To us who enjoy hindsight the victory was decisive; for the brilliant withdrawal by the Macedonian pikemen under Philip's personal command on the right wing and the dashing charge of the Macedonian cavalry under Alexander on the left wing demonstrated the superior skill and quality of the Macedonian army and established its predominance over Greek arms for the future. But the Greeks did not necessarily see the situation thus at the time. Sparta had not participated; Thebes had fought with distinction; and the inferior discipline of the Athenians could be blamed for the defeat. Alexander too must have realised that the verdict of Chaeronea was not accepted as final by the Greek states or by the Greek heavy-armed infantry in the world.

(c) THE BALKAN CAMPAIGN[14]
(see Figure 2)

"As soon as it was spring [in 335 B.C.] Alexander set off for Thrace against the Triballi and the Illyrians who, he had learnt, intended to revolt. . . . Setting out from Amphipolis, he invaded that part of Thrace which is occupied by the independent Thracians, keeping on his left Philippoupolis[15] and Mt. Orbelus, and having crossed the river Nestus he came to Mt. Haemus on the tenth day."

Such is the concise narrative with which Arrian started his account. In fact some months passed before Alexander reached the Illyrians, and we may assume that his aim was to assert his authority throughout the Balkan Empire. His route from Amphipolis was probably through the Rupel pass of the Strymon river to Sandanski on the side of Mt. Pirin; thus he left to the west of him Philippopolis in the Kumli valley and the range of Plaskovitsa-Belasitsa (ancient Mt. Orbelus). The high mountains of Pirin and Rila, exceptionally steep and exuberantly forested, were the home of Dionysus-worship and formed centres of the "independent" republican Thracians (as in Herodotus 7.111). Traversing Mt. Pirin he descended to Razlog, crossed the Mesta (ancient Nestus) and entered the central plain of Thrace near Tatar Pazardzhik. If there was any fighting before Tatar Pazardzhik, it was in difficult country. In the central plain his cavalry enforced the peace, and there another, larger Philippoupolis (now Plovdiv) was the seat of administration.

To the north lay Mt. Haemus, forming the watershed between the Aegean Sea and the Danube valley. Rather than circumvent it Alexander chose to cross the range by a high pass (probably Shipka rather than Kajan), and he found that the top of the pass was blocked by a force of local tribesmen and some of the "independent" Thracians, who had made what appeared to be a defensive laager of wagons. Alexander guessed that their intention was to launch the wagons against his infantrymen as they advanced up the steep, narrow part of the defile. Accordingly he issued orders to the men to open ranks, where space allowed, and crouching or even lying, to form a "testudo" or roof of shields over their heads, where they had no room for manoeuvre. This done, when the wagons were let loose, they passed through or over Alexander's men without killing anyone. The infantry then charged uphill with shouts of *alalai*, corresponding to the modern Greek battle-cry *aera*. Alexander had intended to make this charge part of a concerted attack, the archers giving enfilading fire from his right and he himself attacking from the left at the head of the Royal Guard of Hypaspists, the other Hypaspists and the Agrianians. But the archers' fire and the frontal charge broke all opposition before Alexander could come into action. The enemy lost 1,500 men. All women, children, and gear were captured and sent to the coast to be shipped to Macedonia. Alexander had no intention of being caught encumbered by booty, as Philip had been in 339 B.C.

Coming down from the watershed, Alexander reached the headwaters of the Lyginus river (probably the Rositsa). He was now three days' march from the Danube. The Triballi and the Thracians north of the mountain had dispersed and some had fled to a large island in the Danube, called Peuce ("Pine Island"), where the Triballian king, Syrmus, concentrated the women and children.

When Alexander was marching down the Lyginus valley, he learnt that the bulk of the Triballi had doubled back and were now behind him. Returning at once, Alexander caught them pitching camp in a narrow glen near the river, where they formed their order of battle in a confined space. Alexander had to tempt them into the open, which he did by sending the archers and the slingers forward first. Stung by their fire, the Triballi came out, whereupon Alexander ordered the heavy cavalry of Upper Macedonia to charge from the right and the squadrons of heavy cavalry from Bottiaea and Amphipolis to ride in from the left. While they pinned them from both flanks, Alexander himself led the phalanx to the attack, protected by a screen of light cavalry armed with throwing-spears. At first the Triballi held their own. But when Alexander and the phalanx in deep formation charged and the cavalrymen drove their horses among them and wielded their swords, the enemy broke, leaving 3,000 dead. The thickness of the woods and the fall of night made pursuit impossible. Alexander lost eleven cavalrymen and some forty infantrymen according to Ptolemy.

Three days later Alexander reached the Danube and descended to its delta, where he met a small fleet of warships which he had sent ahead through the Bosporus into the Black Sea. After failing to force a landing on Peuce, because he had too few ships and the current was strong, he decided to cross to the other bank and cut off the Triballian king. At the same time he felt a yearning (*pothos*) to go beyond the great river. The fact that the Getae held the far bank with a force estimated at 4,000 cavalry and 10,000 infantry did not deter him. He ordered his men to fill their leather tent-covers with straw, so that they could be used as floats for rafts (as in Xenophon, *Anabasis* I. 5); he collected a large number of the local dugout tree-trunk boats (*monoxyla*, used still in southern Albania); and himself embarked on one of the ships. In the course of one night in June he brought 1,500 cavalry and 4,000 infantry across the river and, concentrated them in a field of high-standing corn, where their presence was undetected.

When dawn broke, they set off upstream, Alexander ordering the infantry to hold their pikes obliquely and so smooth down the standing corn; the cavalry was to follow. On reaching uncultivated land, Alexander led his cavalry forward to his right wing and ordered the phalanx to adopt a square formation (usual in facing superior numbers of cavalry, as in 358 B.C.), but the enemy fled at the unexpected sight of the bristling close-set phalanx and at the violent charge of the wedge-shaped formations of cavalry. Alexander pursued, taking due precautions against an ambush (cavalry in front and infantry hugging a river-bank), until he reached their ill-fortified town, from which they fled again, far into the steppe country, taking as many of their women and children on their horses' cruppers as they could.

Alexander plundered and razed the town, entrusted the booty to two of his brigadiers, sacrificed on the river bank to Zeus the Saviour, Heracles, and the river-god, Ister, for their safe crossing, and returned without the loss of a single man to his main body on the south bank. There embassies came to him from the independent Thracians and the Triballian king (no doubt making submission), and also from the Celts near the head of the Adriatic, with whom he exchanged oaths of friendship and alliance. These tall, proud warriors said that they were afraid not of Alexander but of the sky falling upon them (this arising because their oaths were provisional upon the sky not falling, the earth not opening and the sea not rising). "What boasters Celts are!", Alexander is said to have remarked.

The narrative which you have read comes entirely from Arrian, who himself was drawing on the accounts of Ptolemy and Aristobulus. In other parts of his history Arrian made occasional use of subsidiary sources, but not here. Ptolemy was the source of the two detailed references to this campaign in other writers (Str. 301–2 and Polyaenus 4.3.11), and the lack of an account in Diodorus, Justin and Plutarch is best explained by the hypothesis that the writers they followed (such as Cleitarchus and Callisthenes) had not covered this campaign. Thus we have here an unadulterated use by Arrian of Ptolemy and Aristobulus, and primarily of Ptolemy who was particularly concerned with military actions.

What then was the character of Ptolemy's account? It was much fuller than what we have in Arrian. It contained the army's movements day by day, the orders issued by the king, the actions of the king, and the actions of the king's subordinates. It was concerned as much with the king as with the actual events. Thus at the Haemus Pass the king intended to lead in person an attack from the left; this intention is recorded although the attack was not actually delivered (A. 1.1.11–12). How was the king's intention known to Ptolemy? Presumably either from a record of the king's orders at the time or from a conversation with Alexander later. Ptolemy evidently gave a very full and detailed account of movements day by day and of officers involved in actions. Arrian selected only some items, such as a place or two on the line of march, an occasional officer's name, and now and then the number of troops engaged. Yet the consistent character of Arrian's narrative with its detail, clarity, and vividness in these chapters is likely to mirror the character of Ptolemy's account.

To decide what Arrian took from Aristobulus is harder: probably the yearning (*pothos*)[16] of Alexander to go beyond the Danube, the description of Danubian fishermen's ways (1.3.6), and the mention of the "parasang" as a unit of distance in defining the position of the Getae's city. The details which are indicative of the eye-witness may have come from either Ptolemy or Aristobulus. With these points in mind let us go on to the second part of the Balkan campaign and notice for ourselves some indications of Arrian's sources and Arrian's methods.

Although it is not apparent from Arrian's abbreviated account, Alexander spent four months in the eastern Balkans before he turned westwards and entered the territory of the Agrianians (they lived south of Sofia round Mt. Vitosha, the ancient Scombrus). There he learnt that Cleitus, son of Bardylis II, who ruled in what is now Kosovo over the Dardanians, and Glaucias, king of the Taulantians (near Tirana in Albania) were in revolt, and that another Illyrian tribe, the Autariatae, planned to intercept him on the march. His intelligence proved to be correct. The king of the Agrianians, who commanded his own corps d'élite, known to Arrian as "the hypaspists," undertook to raise more troops and divert the Autariatae by invading their territory (in Hercegovina). This he did successfully. The Autariatae were an independent tribe whom Philip had defeated but not reduced. Meanwhile Alexander marched to intercept the forces of the two rebel kings before they could invade western Macedonia.[17] As their forces were likely to be greater than any he had met so far in the campaign, he evidently took the entire force which he had at hand, namely 3,000 Hypaspists, six or seven brigades of phalanx troops (9,000 to 10,500 men), at least 600 Companion cavalry, a force of light-armed cavalry, Agrianians, archers, slingers, siege-train, and baggage-train; perhaps in all 25,000 men and 5,000 horses. Marching at speed, probably via Kjustendil, Kratovo, Štip, Gradsko, and Prilep, into the headwaters of the Erigon (Cerna Reka), he swung south and then west to reach the Eordaïcus river, where he encamped close to Pelium, a fortified city in Illyris which Cleitus had already occupied (see Fig. 2). Next day he moved up to the city, whereupon the troops of Cleitus on the surrounding hills sacrificed three boys, three girls, and three black rams and came down to engage the Macedonians. They were routed so thoroughly that they abandoned their original positions and left their sacrificial victims lying there.

During the march Alexander had not waited to get news of the enemy's whereabouts, but his exceptional speed of movement paid him well. He blocked the easier routes into Macedonia, first above Florina and then at Bilisht, and now he stood between the Dardanians and Bilisht. Moreover, he caught one enemy army—larger evidently than his own—before a second army came up, and he blunted the edge of its courage by inflicting a rapid defeat. Then he moved up to Pelium and prepared to invest it. During a visit to Albania in 1972 I was able to identify Pelium with the fortified site at Goricë (see Fig. 21). Until some time after 1805 the overflow of Lake Little Prespa formed a river which issued from Wolf's Pass (it was later impeded by a rock fall) and joined the Devoll by Goricë. This river was the Eordaïcus (see Fig. 3).

Next day the second army came up, the Taulantians under Glaucias, and Alexander found himself very heavily outnumberd. Investment of the city was out of the question, and any move was hazardous. The most pressing problem was supply for both men and horses, as he had already stripped the country behind him and was near the end of his transported stocks. Back in his base camp, he sent out all his transport, protected by a screen of heavy cavalry under Philotas; it was to move with all speed through the Tsangon Pass some eight kilometres away and enter the great plain of Koritsa, rich in grain (harvested by now, late July or early August) and in swampy pasture for horses. Glaucias was unable to block the Tsangon Pass in time; but he occupied the hills around that part of the plain, hoping to catch Philotas on his return and wipe out his men and horses when night fell. But Alexander gave him no such chance. Taking advantage of the enemy's divided forces—some in Pelium, some on the surrounding hills and those with Glaucias around the Tsangon Pass—Alexander led a powerful, fast-moving group consisting of heavy cavalry, Hypaspists, archers, and Agrianians (perhaps 5,000 men in all), dislodged Glaucias from the hills by the Tsangon Pass, and cleared the way for Philotas to return with his loaded carts and well-pastured horses. Meanwhile the rest of his army kept the enemy in and round Pelium in check. But in terms of supply it was a brief respite. Alexander had to move or starve, and yet movement too seemed dangerous. Arrian, no doubt citing the opinion of a participant, whether Ptolemy or Aristobulus, wrote as follows: "Cleitus and Glaucias seemed still to have caught Alexander on difficult ground; for they held the commanding heights with large numbers of cavalry, large numbers of javelin-men and slingers, and no small force of heavy-armed infantry as well, while the garrison of Pelium was likely to fall upon the Macedonians as they made off." Retreat over flat ground would be difficult enough, but retreat over hilly, rocky terrain would be fatal when the enemy were so superior in light-armed cavalry and infantry. Yet any line of retreat from Pelium would sooner or later bring the army onto great areas of such country.

Alexander did the unexpected (see Figure 3). He decided not to retreat but to advance straight through the enemy, thus splitting them again into three groups. This meant forcing his way through a defile between cliffs, today called Wolf's Pass (Gryke e Ujkut in Albanian; see Fig. 22), which lay over two kilometres from his camp. Arrian described the defile through the eyes of a participant: "It appeared narrow and wooded —narrow because it was confined on one side by a river (Eordaïcus) and on the other there was a very high mountain (Mt. Trajan) and cliffs on the mountain side (especially by Kalaja e Shpelles), so that there would not have been passage for the army even at four abreast." The choice of this route for some 25,000 men would have seemed foolhardy if the enemy had known his intention. But they knew nothing, and deception was Alexander's best card.

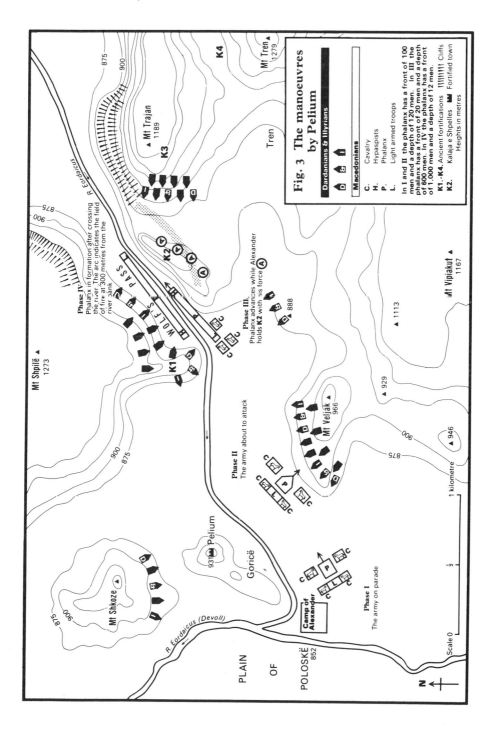

Fig. 3 The manoeuvres by Pelium

Dardanians & Illyrians

Macedonians

C. Cavalry
H. Hypaspists
P. Phalanx
L. Light armed troops

In I and II the phalanx has a front of 100 men and a depth of 120 men. In III the phalanx has a front of 20 men and a depth of 600 men. In IV the phalanx has a front of 1,000 men and a depth of 12 men.

K1.–K4. Ancient fortifications |||||||| Cliffs
K2. Kalaja e Shpelles ▰ Fortified town
Heights in metres

On this occasion Alexander drew up the army with the infantry-phalanx 120 men deep in each file and a squadron of 200
cavalry on each flank, ordering them to keep silence, so that
they could pick up the words of command smartly. The first
order he issued was to the infantry to raise their pikes upright,
then to bring them to the ready at the word of command, and
to swing their serried points in close formation now to the right
and now to the left. He also moved the phalanx smartly forward and then kept changing direction, now to one flank, now
to the other. In this way he went through many manoeuvres
and changes of formation within a short time.

The Dardanians and the Taulantians had a grandstand view of this
splendid parade-ground performance from their positions on the walls
of Pelium and the surrounding hills (see Fig. 21). No one knew what
the Macedonians were up to, but it could be seen that the siege-train
was on parade and the baggage-train was not. Perhaps it was drill and
then an assault on the city walls. But no, for "Alexander formed the
phalanx on his left into a wedge (see Fig. 4) and led it forward against
the enemy, who had for long been amazed by the sight of such smart
and orderly drill; and now that those around Alexander were bearing
down on them they did not wait but abandoned the first hills." Mean
while from behind him the Taulantians rushed down to attack his rear
but the phalanx about-turned in order, raised the battle cry and clashed
their pikes against their shields (the usual preliminary to a pike-charge)
The enemy turned tail and fled towards Pelium. Alexander had now
cleared both flanks of his intended but unrevealed line of advance.

Alexander saw some of the enemy—not many—in possession
of a hill beside which his passage lay (Kalaja e Shpelles), and so
he ordered the Bodyguards and his personal cavalry Companions to mount their chargers and take their shields on horseback and charge towards the hill; and if the enemy did not
withdraw from the position on their arrival, to attack with half
their number on horseback and with the other half dismounted
and fighting on foot among the cavalrymen. When the enemy
saw the onset of Alexander they abandoned the hill and withdrew to the mountains on either side. Then Alexander occupied the hill, summoning the Agrianians and the archers up to
2,000 strong to join the Companions. And he ordered the Hypaspists to cross the river, and after them the brigades of the
Macedonians (the phalanx), and immediately on crossing to extend to their left, so that the phalanx should appear thick-set as
soon as they got over. He himself, being in an advanced covering position, was watching the movement of the enemy from
his place on the hill. On seeing the force crossing, the enemy

came down the mountains to oppose them, intending to set upon the troops with Alexander as they withdrew last.

For now that his army and siege-train were safely across, Alexander's men were the rear-guard. How could they get away?

> When the enemy were already close, Alexander and those with him delivered a sudden attack, and the phalanx raised the battle cry as being about to charge through the river. With everyone heading towards them the enemy gave way and fled. At this moment Alexander led forward the Agrianians and the archers at the double towards the river. He himself got over first; on seeing the enemy pressing upon those who were last he mounted his engines on the bank and ordered all the missiles to be fired at extreme range, and he ordered the archers to go into the river and fire from midstream, them too. The troops of Glaucias did not venture to come within range. The Macedonians meanwhile crossed the river in safety. Not a single man was killed in the course of their withdrawal.

The brilliance of the operation needs no underlining. With an accurate memory of the ground from his earlier mission in Illyris, precise planning of each move up to his seizure of the key position and the crossing of the river, and brilliant improvisation thereafter, he enacted his preconceived plan exactly as he had envisaged it. Now he held the almost impregnable position within Wolf's Pass which his enemy had failed to occupy, and he could move his troops back into the basin of Lake Little Prespa, where there was excellent pasture and the lines of supply were open (see Fig. 22). At each point he took the initiative, he issued the orders, he led each decisive movement; it was Alexander's personal triumph, given a superbly disciplined army. His opponents seemed amateurs in comparison. But we should not forget that the Dardanians alone, without the Taulantians to support them, had killed 4,000 Macedonians in battle some twenty-five years before.

The Dardanians and the Taulantians thought indeed that Alexander had withdrawn in fear of their superior numbers. For he had not only abandoned his camp and baggage-train, but he had also left Wolf's Pass and withdrawn further into the plain round the lake. But he had left some men to watch from the cliffs, and he learnt from them that the enemy were encamped in an unduly long line without the guardposts, palisades, and ditches which were customary with the Macedonians. Before dawn on the fourth day after his withdrawal

> while it was still night Alexander crossed the river unobserved, taking with him the Hypaspists, the Agrianians, the archers and the brigades of Perdiccas and Coenus. He had also ordered the rest of the army to follow, but when he saw an opportun-

ity for attack he did not wait for all his troops to concentrate but
sent the archers and the Agrianians forward. Their attack was
unexpected; they struck the enemy line at one end, where their
own attack, being at its strongest in a deep formation, was
likely to hit the enemy at his weakest point.

Once the right of their line was broken with heavy loss of men killed
and captured, the enemy fled in a panic except for Cleitus who led a
force into Pelium.

"The pursuit by Alexander's Own Cavalry was carried up to the
mountains of the Taulantians, and all who did escape threw away their
weapons to save themselves." The pursuit by cavalry for some days
over a distance of some ninety-five kilometres made the victory as decisive as that of Philip in 358 B.C. Other business drew Alexander south
at once, reunited now with his baggage-train. But Glaucias submitted
and was left on his throne; Cleitus burnt Pelium, withdrew to join Glaucias and later made his peace with Alexander, on what terms we do not
know.

The Balkan campaign was completed. Without employing Philip's
best generals, Antipater and Parmenio, Alexander had shown his ability
to cope with a wide variety of situations and he had won the confidence
of the army. Posting himself at the spearhead of action repeatedly he
had set the highest example of personal courage at the cost of a wound
during the final pursuit. His men had suffered a surprisingly small number of casualties by carrying out his orders to the letter, and they knew
that they had as their commander a second Philip. He was now a seasoned general in several departments of war and had no need of advice
from others. The fact that he was twenty-one years of age was no handi-
cap in a king; if it served to delude some Greek politicians into thinking
of him as a youthful amateur, or if it was exploited by romantic and sensationalist writers in praise of Parmenio or depreciation of Alexander,
no Macedonian was deceived. Alexander might consult his Council of
Friends, but he, like his predecessors on the throne, decided for himself,
and led the way in implementing his decision.

The nature of the campaign gives us some insight into the structure
of the Balkan empire. Within the extended kingdom of Macedonia and
in the great plains and lowlands of Thrace Alexander inherited a stable
situation which was full of economic promise. We know from an inscription that he gave orders for some land-reclamation works in the vicinity
of Philippi; and in general, pacification was followed by commercial development. His purpose in Thrace was to subdue the warring mountain
tribes who had so often raided the plains in the past, and it was for this
reason that he had chosen to drive through the mountains of Rila and
Pirin and then Haemus. His invincible power once demonstrated, he received their submission and let them be. In the Danube valley he had to

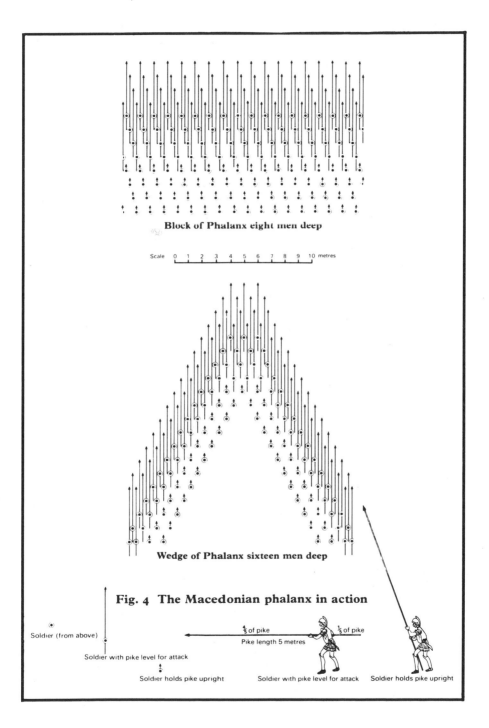

Block of Phalanx eight men deep

Scale 0 1 2 3 4 5 6 7 8 9 10 metres

Wedge of Phalanx sixteen men deep

Fig. 4 The Macedonian phalanx in action

Soldier (from above)

Soldier with pike level for attack

Soldier holds pike upright

⅘ of pike

Pike length 5 metres

⅕ of pike

Soldier with pike level for attack

Soldier holds pike upright

defeat the Triballi who had wounded Philip and taken his booty, and he had to strengthen his position along what was proving to be an unstable frontier. He achieved his purpose partly by battle and partly by out-manoeuvring the leaders of the local tribes who took refuge on Peuce.

As Arrian put it, without specifying the terms they received, "ambassadors came to Alexander from all the independent tribes in the Danube valley and from Syrmus, the Triballian king." Syrmus gave gifts to Alexander and offered his friendship. The south bank was now secure; and the demonstration of Macedonian power across the river made the Getae fly "as far away as possible from the river into the desert (i.e., the steppes)."

The situation in Illyria was quite different. The Dardanians occupied the fertile plains of southern Yugoslavia. They had always been a military power and had threatened the very existence of the Macedonian state in the first half of the century. The Taulantians too held extensive plains in the central part of what is now Albania, and they were second to none in the hit-and-run warfare of tribes accustomed to live by rapine, "rapto vivere assueti," Curtius described them (C. 3.10.9). Alexander had known in early spring that they were planning a national uprising, and he must have realized that, if all the Balkan tribes did likewise, "there would be no withstanding them." He chose first to confirm the loyalty of the Thracians in the plains, secure his northeastern frontier and then deal with the major threat.

The campaign at Pelium was not a frontier incident but a decisive conflict between the northwestern tribes and the Macedonians. It was rendered decisive above all by the long pursuit, directed primarily against the enemy cavalrymen who were the tribal leaders. When they were destroyed or disgraced by defeat, resistance collapsed. Thenceforth Alexander recruited Illyrian troops to his service, and the client kings kept the peace at home. By this whirlwind campaign (from April to September) Alexander "reduced all the neighbouring barbarians to his rule" (D. 17.8.1).

The word "barbarians" in this quotation from a writer of Greek outlook has an overlay of contempt. Alexander thought otherwise of the Balkan peoples. For instance, he honoured the king of the Agrianians as a close friend and equal, bestowed on him "the greatest gifts" and would have given to him his own half-sister, the princess Cynna, in marriage, if he had not died of an illness. What Alexander sought to create in the Balkans was a strong power, created indeed by military supremacy but held together by goodwill or respect and by mutual interest. That his aim was capable of fulfilment was shown by this same king volunteering to attack the Autariatae, in order that Alexander should re-establish that power in the west. For such a power was a shield against the unrelenting pressure of the tribes of northern Europe, protecting not only the Balkan peoples but also the Greek city-states. It held firm for some fifty years.

Finally let us return to the matter of Arrian's sources which we have already mentioned for the first part of the Balkan campaign. In the second part the same prominence is given to each day's movements, the orders issued by the king and the king's actions. Arrian has abbreviated his source at the beginning and the end, causing some obscurity, but in general it seems that his account is of the same dimensions as that of Ptolemy and contains the same material. What is remarkable is its precision, its vividness, and its topographical detail. It is so thorough that on two occasions orders of Alexander were cited for situations which did not eventuate (A. 1.6.5 "if the enemy stand their ground, do so and so," and 1.6.10). Also the details of the units engaged in the actions are precise.

It has sometimes been suggested that Ptolemy recalled all these details by power of memory alone. To do so he would have had to know them, all of them, including Alexander's orders and even his unfulfilled orders at the time when he was serving as a combatant in the Companion cavalry; and not only in the Balkan campaigns, but in campaigns which extended almost continuously over some twelve years and were packed with episodes. Further, the distance of time between the Balkan campaign and his writing was probably some fifty years. To recall at such an interval the day-to-day movements, orders, dispositions, unit-commanders, strengths of special groups, losses (as in the Lyginus glen), depth of the files (as on the parade near Pelium) and hundreds of similar details over the twelve years of campaigning seems to me utterly impossible; indeed to judge from personal experience in trying to recall the relatively few episodes of a five-years war some thirty years ago most of these things are just what one did not know at the time and certainly not the kind of things one remembers.

There is to me no doubt whatever that Ptolemy was drawing on the *King's Journal* for the bulk of this narrative and reinforcing it with his own memory of what he personally had seen. In other words the great bulk of what we read about the Balkan campaign came not from the inevitably patchy memory of a man of eighty or so but from the accurate record kept in detail at the time and not written for publication. It was no doubt checked by Alexander himself.

(D) THE REVOLT OF THEBES AND THE ARRANGEMENTS IN GREECE
(see Figure 2)

What drew Alexander south was the report that Thebes was in open revolt. Fearing for the safety of his garrison there and anxious to forestall help from other insurgents, Alexander chose the quickest route which would at the same time enable his approach to be unheralded until the last moment[18] (Figs. 5, 37). Following a southern tributary of the Eordaï-cus, he marched "alongside" (i.e., west of) the western Eordaea, crossed the Grammus ridge by the Bara Pass and at heights of 5,000 feet at times traversed the slopes of Grammus and Pindus which bordered Parauaea on the west and Tymphaea on the east (here in the summer season of transhumant herdsmen there were unlimited supplies of pasture, milk, cheese, and meat, and an abundance of horses and mules). He then descended to the south of Grevena, skirted southern-most Elimeotis and on the seventh day entered Pelinna, a city loyal to the Macedonian cause, in western Thessaly.

Alexander had come through 120 miles of thinly populated, high country ahead of any possible report. We may assume that there was a day of rest before the army set off again at speed. His aim was to seize "the Gates" of Thermopylae before the insurgents could do so. Taking the western side of the Thessalian plain, far from normal traffic, he crossed the hills into the upper Spercheus valley and swooped down on the Gates of Thermopylae. They were unoccupied. Continuing at speed, he entered Boeotia on the sixth day from Pelinna—again a matter of some 120 miles—and reached Onchestus at the moment when a report of an army having passed through the Gates was delivered to the insur-gents at Thebes. This march, made without a siege-train and with only pack-horses for equipment and supplies, was one of the most remark-able which Alexander's army achieved. The nature of the terrain can be seen in the satellite photograph in Fig. 37.

The Greeks were taken totally by surprise. On the other hand Alex-ander had arrived just in time to anticipate a coalition of forces. Demos-thenes, who was in correspondence with the Persian commanders in Asia Minor, had persuaded the Athenians to support the Thebans; they had already sent a supply of weapons but had not yet despatched an army. Contingents from the Peloponnese—from Arcadia, Argos and Elis, according to Diodorus—were on the way to join Thebes; they were already at the Isthmus of Corinth when they heard of Alexander's ar-rival. The Thebans had already risen in revolt. They had killed two un-suspecting Macedonian officers and were besieging the Macedonian garrison, which was protected by the massive walls of the citadel but was cut off by a Theban ring of deep trenches and strong stockades. While the other insurgents froze in their tracks, the enemies of Thebes in Central Greece sent troops to help Alexander: in particular Phocis, Plataea, Orchomenus and other Boeotian cities. Had he gone from Pelium to Macedonia, collected reinforcements and marched south at a normal speed, he would have had to fight a second battle of Chaeronea. As it was, he isolated Thebes and proceeded to besiege it. The month was now October of the year 335 b.c.

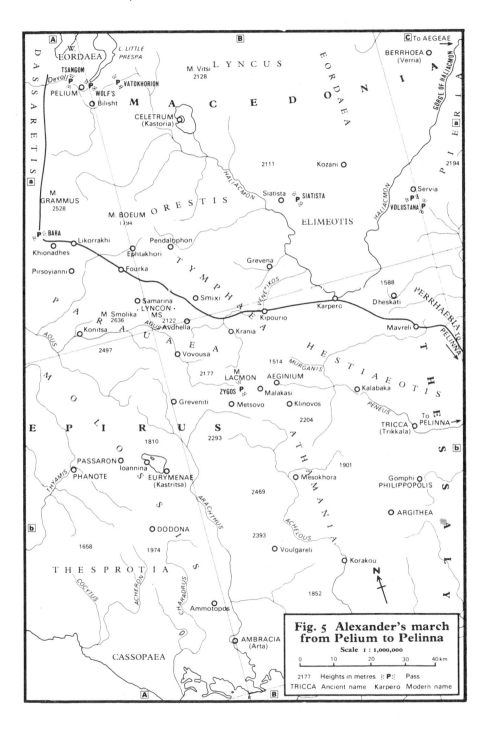

Fig. 5 **Alexander's march from Pelinna to Pelinna**

Scale 1 : 1,000,000

0   10   20   30   40 km

2177   Heights in metres   P Pass
TRICCA   Ancient name   Karpero   Modern name

There are two versions of the siege of Thebes, one common to Diodorus[19] and other writers which is based on Cleitarchus, and the other in Arrian which is based on Ptolemy and Aristobulus. Let us take the former: Diodorus has Alexander "return into Macedonia," take the entire strength of Macedonia, "30,000 infantry and more than 3,000 cavalry"—the very army on which he relied to defeat Persia—and arrive outside Thebes, where the leaders and the people were unanimous in fighting it out despite the willingness of Alexander to come to terms and make concessions. Finding himself despised and taunted by the Thebans, Alexander lost his temper. He decided in advance to destroy Thebes utterly, and in a rage he mounted his siege-engines for the attack. While everyone else in Greece despaired of their chances, the Thebans showed the greatest courage, upset though they were by a string of horrible omens, and prepared to fight outside the city, while their cavalry manned the stockades and the liberated slaves, refugees and resident aliens manned the walls. Thereupon Alexander divided his army into three parts: one to attack the stockades, one to attack the Thebans outside, and one to sit as a reserve. The second of these engaged the Thebans who were many times outnumbered (D. 17.11.2 and P. 11.10). As they met,

> the troops on both sides shouted the battle cry with one voice and hurled their missiles at the enemy. These being soon expended and all engaging in sword play, a great contest ensued. The Macedonian might was hard to resist because of the number and weight of the phalanx, but the Thebans being of stronger physique and fitter through constant training and having the advantage of great spiritual exaltation faced every danger.

Finding his force failing, Alexander brought up his reserves. This action (like the bringing in of reserves in a game of football) caused the Thebans to say the enemy were now admitting their inferiority; and they excelled themselves, fighting on with unsurpassable élan. At this moment Alexander spotted a small gate which had been deserted by its guards and through it fed Perdiccas with an adequate force into the city. Aware of this, the Thebans tried to withdraw into the city, but the cavalry galloped all over the infantry and dashing into narrow streets and ditches crashed, fell, and were killed on their own weapons. To top it all, the garrison of Macedonians sortied from the citadel and caused havoc among the confused Thebans.

That this account is worthless is obvious. The Homeric echoes include the decision to fight in front of the walls, the discharge of missiles, and the duels with swords. In fact neither Theban hoplites nor Macedonian phalangites used missiles; they fought with spear and pike re-

spectively. The arming of slaves, etc., is reminiscent of the Athenian decision to defend their city after the Battle of Chaeronea. The second
wave of assault troops is reminiscent of the Persian assault on the
Greeks at Thermopylae. In fact the Thebans would have been insane to
put their entire infantry force outside the city in the open and leave the
defence of the walls to scratch troops without proper training. The battle
as composed by Cleitarchus is a fantasy, expressed in an epically rhetorical style and shot through with Greek pride in themselves and Greek
hatred of the Macedonians and their bad-tempered, vicious king.

In Arrian's account the instigators of revolt in Thebes brought back
some men who had been exiled by Philip, and combining together they
killed the two Macedonian officers. They then persuaded the people to
revolt, partly by telling them that Alexander was dead. When Alexander
arrived, he gave the Thebans a time within which to reconsider their attitude; but they used the respite to sally forth with cavalry and light-
armed troops and killed some Macedonians. Still Alexander did not re-
taliate. Next day he moved his camp to the point closest to the citadel
within which the garrison was now in considerable danger. At this point
the Thebans held a double stockade; and they faced the brigade of
Perdiccas which had an advanced position.

According to Ptolemy (evidently Aristobulus did not mention it),
Perdiccas started the attack without waiting for the signal from Alexander; for he went ahead of his men, broke through the first stockade
and led a charge against the advanced troops of the Thebans.[20] The
nearest brigade, that of Amyntas, followed the brigade of Perdiccas. To
prevent them from being cut off Alexander brought the rest of the army
up. He ordered the archers and the Agrianians to go forward at the
double into the space between the two stockades, but he still kept the
Royal Brigade (*agema*) and the two other brigades of the Hypaspists outside. In attempting to force the second stockade Perdiccas fell seriously
wounded, but the troops continued to drive the Thebans back along a
sunken road as far as a precinct of Heracles, where the Thebans counter-
attacked and drove their enemy past the stockade, killing some seventy
archers, including their commander, Eurybotas, a Cretan.

As the Thebans pursued hotly in disordered formation, Alexander
was waiting for them (it was the tactic he had employed in the Lyginus
glen). He launched his line in formation at the charge, drove the
Thebans through the field defences and through the gates of the city
walls in such panic that they failed to shut the gates behind them. The
walls there not being manned because of the posting of so many advanced
troops, the Macedonians streamed in through the gates. Within the
walls most advanced to the city centre, but some, joining hands with the
garrison, occupied the higher ground. As the attacks were pressed
home, Alexander appearing now here and now there, the Theban

cavalry broke out and fled away over the plain. "In the heat of the action it was not so much the Macedonians as the Phocians, Plataeans and other Boeotians who killed the Thebans when they ceased to defend themselves in any organised way."

This account is of a piece with those of the Balkan campaign: day by day movement, disposition of troops, some topographical detail, orders, one action without an order, Alexander's acts, units, unit-commanders, and notable Macedonian losses. It has as good reason as its predecessors to be regarded as factually correct on the Macedonian side. The Thebans were experts in the use of field defences, as they had shown against the Spartans, and they thought that Thebes was impregnable, as it was by the standards of Greek warfare. Not so for the Macedonians. On the third day in Boeotia, the army being concentrated at one place and poised for attack, Perdiccas acted on his own initiative—a point noted presumably in the *King's Journal* and so known to Ptolemy; but it was Alexander who broke into the city and conducted the fierce street-fighting in which so many were killed, women and children included. That the Greeks on Alexander's side went on killing is only too likely; for they were repaying past massacres by the Thebans.

What was to be done with the captured city? The record of Thebes vis-à-vis Macedonia was one of breaking treaties, and Alexander had as good cause to punish Thebes as Philip had to punish Olynthus in 348 B.C., by selling the population into slavery and razing the site. But it was not Alexander's intention to act as a Macedonian king. In trying for a peaceful settlement he had asked Thebes to rejoin "the Common Peace" within the charter of the Greek League, and he had represented himself in the role of hegemon acting against a defaulter from the League and an ally of Persia, the common enemy of the League and Macedonia. So now he referred the decision to a special meeting of the Council of the Greek League, which he attended in a personal but influential capacity as hegemon.

Greek states had often been ruthless with a defeated enemy. Athens had killed all adult males and enslaved the remainder at Sestus, for instance, and Thebes had done the same at Orchomenus within living memory. A similar fate for the people of Thebes, said to have numbered over 30,000, was proposed by some Councillors, but the majority decision was to sell the people as slaves, outlaw from the League's territory any Theban who had escaped, and raze the city to the ground, leaving only the temples. The only acts of mercy were attributed to the intervention of Alexander: priests and priestesses, personal friends of Philip and Alexander, official representatives of Macedon, those who had opposed the decision to rebel, and the descendants and the house of Pindar were exempted, and the widow of a Theban general who had been raped by a Macedonian officer and had killed him in revenge was given her freedom together with her children.[21]

The capture in a few hours and the elimination of the strongest military state in Greece had an immediate effect on the other Greek dissidents. The Arcadians condemned to death their anti-Macedonian leaders, the Eleans recalled their pro-Macedonian exiles, the Aetolians asked forgiveness for rising in support of Thebes, and the Athenians congratulated Alexander on his safe return from Illyria and on his quelling of the Theban revolt. He took no steps except to demand the surrender of some anti-Macedonian leaders at Athens, Demosthenes being one of them, on the ground that they had been as guilty as the Theban leaders in promoting the revolt; but when Athens appealed he contented himself with the exile of Charidemus, a mercenary general who had fought repeatedly against Macedonia. A regular meeting of the Council of the Greek League was held late in October[22] at which arrangements for the spring offensive against Persia were finalised, and the Greek League undertook to provide 2,400 cavalry, 7,000 infantry and 160 warships with crews and marines totalling some 32,000 men.

Returning to Macedonia, Alexander celebrated one of the great national festivals which were a feature of Macedonian life. In the narrow plain of Dium below Mt. Olympus the king conducted the traditional sacrifice of thanksgiving to Zeus of Olympus, the national god of the Macedonians. He then celebrated the Olympian festival at Aegeae;[23] and it was there too that he instituted the nine-day dramatic competition in honour of the Pierian Muses in the theatre. The festivals were attended by the Macedones, and the king distributed largesse to them in the form of animals for sacrifice.

During the festivals day after day the king entertained his personal guests—Friends, Commanders, and ambassadors sent by the Greek states—in a great marquee known as a "hundred-coucher" (each guest reclining on a couch). The lay-out of the marquee was perhaps similar to that of the later "palace" at Aegeae, where a central courtyard was flanked by eleven-couch dining-rooms, six in all but in pairs of descending grandeur to fit the degrees of dignity accorded to the guests.[24] Alexander arranged that the materials for constructing a similar marquee should be taken to Asia, where it was to serve as the Royal Headquarters. At Aegeae the splendid pomp and ceremony of the national festival served to lay the ghostly memory of the death of Philip in that very theatre.

Alexander's activities since Philip's assassination afford a good example of his strategic planning. He had at the outset four areas to consider: Macedonia, the Balkans, Greece, and Persia, with which he was already at war. First he secured his home base thoroughly; then Thessaly as an important adjunct to his military power; then his position as hegemon in Greece in late 336 B.C. By being conciliatory and accommodating he then created a period of delay during which anti-Macedonian leaders like Demosthenes did negotiate with Persia but the people of the various states refused to commit themselves. It was during that period of delay that Alexander held his military front in northwest Asia Minor and secured the essential background to that front and to any advance beyond it, namely full control of the Balkans. The final act, precipitated by the revolt of Thebes, was to secure the Greek area and as far as possible to enlist Greek aid. Throughout this series of operations the greatest danger was an effective collaboration between dissidents in Greece and the Persians, who could have supported revolt in Greece by sending not only subsidies but also a superior fleet and a sea-borne expedition. As it happened, Persia was distracted by internal troubles at the time. But the danger remained until Alexander was able to cut the lines of communications between Greece and Persia.

In terms of strategic planning the destruction of Thebes was effective. The Greek states toed the line, sending their contingents to Asia and remaining quiescent long enough for Alexander to cut Greece's communications with Persia. But in a wider context the destruction of Thebes was a disaster. If Alexander was to make the entente between Macedonia and Greece into a form of positive cooperation, as Philip seems to have planned, it was necessary for Alexander to forgive and forget and forgive again.

As the average city-state was a democracy, its foreign policy depended on two things, the convictions of the citizen body and the state of play between party-leaders. An outside power could affect that foreign policy by appealing to the interest of the citizen body for whom peace and prosperity were important considerations, and by supporting those party-leaders who were sympathetic. Philip and Alexander succeeded well enough on these lines with Athens. But the fundamental conviction and the overriding consideration of the citizen body was its right to liberty; indeed the very worth of the city-state as a cultural and political form stemmed from its sense of liberty. Philip respected that sense in Athens, when he sent Antipater and Alexander with the ashes of the Athenian dead after the battle of Chaeronea, and Alexander respected it when he remitted the demand for the surrender of the anti-Macedonian leaders. But the destruction of Thebes was the negation of liberty. It revealed the mailed fist of Macedon.

SOURCES

(A) D. 16.91-96; 17.2 and 5.1-2;J. 9.5-7;J. 11.2 and 5.1; *POxy* 1798 = *FGrH* I48 F1; *Itin. Alex.* 5; A. I.25.2; C. 7.1.6; P.9-10

(B) A. I.1.1-3; D. I7.2-4;J. 11.2.1-5; Polyaenus 4.3.23

(C) A. 1.1.4-6.11; P. 11.5-6; D. 17.8.1

(D) A. I.7-10; D. I7.8.2-I5.6; P. 11.6-I4;J. 11.3-4; Tod I83

IV

THE CONQUEST OF ASIA MINOR

(see Figures 2 and 6 as well as 7 and 8)

The Macedonian empire and the Persian empire were immediate neighbours with an open frontier, formed by the waters of the Black Sea, the Sea of Marmara and the Aegean. Traffic across these waters was normally lively, particularly between Greece and Persia, which employed a very large number of Greek mercenaries, and there was thus no difficulty in obtaining information about military and other resources. Philip, for instance, had given refuge to a distinguished satrap, Artabazus, and to a Greek mercenary commander, Memnon of Rhodes, who had fought for and against Persia; and he had been on close terms with Hermias, an independent ruler on the Asiatic coast south of Troy. Later Artabazus and Memnon returned to the Persian court, and Hermias was captured and tortured by the Persian king, Artaxerxes Ochus. Both kings sought allies in Greece. Artaxerxes won Thebes, Argos, and later Athens; and when hostilities between Persia and Macedonia started in 340 B.C., it was Athenian sea power, Persian money and Persian mercenaries which prevented Philip from capturing Perinthus and Byzantium on the European side of the Bosporus. Thus Persia won the first round of the struggle.

As soon as Philip defeated the Greek allies of Persia at Chaeronea and brought the Greek League into existence, he planned to establish a bridgehead on the Asiatic side of the Hellespont and thus to make it difficult for any Persian fleet to dominate the Hellespont and the Bosporus. In spring 336 B.C. an army of several thousand Macedonians and Greek mercenaries was ferried over to Abydus and proceeded to carry out its orders "to liberate the Greek states" on Asiatic soil from Persian rule. The commanding officers, Parmenio, Amyntas, and Attalus, acting fast before the satraps had organised their forces, brought about the overthrow of many pro-Persian dictators and established democracies in their place on the offshore islands and on the coast as far south as Ephesus. Altars were dedicated to Zeus Philippius at Eresus on the island of Lesbos and a statue of Philip was placed in the temple of Artemis at Ephesus (or Diana of the Ephesians, as she was called later). Philip's success in this phase was due in part to the distractions of Persia; for the death of Artaxerxes Ochus in 338 B.C. was followed by two years of dynastic confusion, and it was shortly before the death of Philip in 336 B.C. that a member of another branch of the Achaemenid royal house, by name Codomannus, was crowned as Darius III.

In 335 B.C. when Alexander was campaigning in the Balkans, Persian agents visited Greece and played some part in promoting the revolt of Thebes. Concurrently, an offensive against the Macedonians in Asia was conducted by Memnon, the former guest of Philip. He defeated Parmenio at Magnesia on the Maeander, captured Ephesus and garrisoned its citadel with a force of Greek mercenaries. Then he switched his attack to the north. He failed at the head of 5,000 Greek mercenaries to capture Cyzicus, an important base on the shore of the Propontis; but with his superior numbers he drove one Macedonian force back to Rhoeteum. If Memnon had had the cooperation of a Phoenician fleet in 335 B.C., he might well have forced the Macedonians to leave Asia. As it was, Darius made a fatal error in leaving the initiative at sea to Alexander.

Alexander had to assess the needs of defence in Europe against those of his offensive in Asia; for he realised that Persia might use her navy to intervene in Greece and open a second front. He left with Antipater, his general in Europe, eight brigades of phalanx-infantry to a strength of 12,000 men and 1,500 cavalry, of whom perhaps 1,000 were Companion cavalry mainly of Upper Macedonia. Antipater was probably authorised to call up the local militia[25] in Macedonia, raise troops from the Balkan dependencies and seek help from Macedonia's allies in Greece in the event of need. In the early spring of 334 B.C. Alexander mustered the expeditionary force of Macedonian and Balkan troops in Amphaxitis and marched by the Kumli valley to the mouth of the Strymon. There he was awaited by the Greek forces and the Graeco-Macedonian fleet, which had taken on board the expedition's siege-train and supplies. The joint forces proceeded to Sestus and crossed the Dardanelles unopposed. The army and its baggage-train covered some 350 miles from Amphaxitis to Sestus in twenty days, which meant that a daily march was almost 20 miles, if we allow some days of rest (A. 1.11.5; *Itin. Alex.* 8, from Amphipolis).

The army which was reviewed on landing in Asia numbered some 32,000 infantry and 5,100 cavalry.[26] These totals broke down into the following contingents: 12,000 Macedonian phalanx-infantry, 1,000 archers and Agrianians, 7,000 Balkan infantry (Odrysians, Triballians and Illyrians), 7,000 Greek allied infantry and 5,000 Greek mercenary infantry; and 1,800 Companion cavalry, 900 light cavalry from within Macedonia

(Paeonians, Thracians and Lancers or Scouts), 1,800 Thessalian cavalry, and 600 Greek allied cavalry. It is probable that there were a further 8,000 infantry, mainly Greek mercenaries, up and down the west coast, but these were not called back from their task of holding land already gained. There were also a siege-train, a baggage-train with only one month's supplies, engineers, surveyors, camp-planners, secretariat, court-officials, medical services, grooms for the cavalry, and muleteers for the baggage and supply services. The fleet of 182 warships, of which 160 were provided by the Greek allies, had a complement of some 36,000 men. There were in addition supply vessels, which could bring equipment and stores to the Asiatic coast; these were the more necessary because Alexander ordered his troops to abstain from foraging and pillaging. Thus the whole expeditionary force, on land and sea, of which more than half was Greek, was in the region of 90,000 men—the same total, more or less, as that of the force sent by Darius I to attempt the conquest of Greece in 490 B.C. Alexander's financial resources were strained to the utmost.

The crossing from Europe to Asia was associated in Alexander's mind with the Trojan War, in which his ancestors had been involved on both sides of the conflict. On the European shore he sacrificed at the grave of Protesilaus and prayed for a happier landing than Protesilaus, whom a Trojan had killed "as he leapt from his ship, far the first of the Achaeans" (*Iliad* 2.702). Alexander then led a flotilla of sixty warships to the Troad, sacrificing in mid-channel to the deities of the sea—Poseidon (so hostile to the Greeks in the Trojan war), Amphitrite, and the Nereids. He was the first to spring ashore on Trojan soil, hurling his spear into the ground as a preemptive claim that the land of Asia was his, "won by the spear" and "granted by the gods" (Figure 6).

Then passing through the ancient walls of Troy, he dedicated his armour to Athena, goddess of Troy, and took from her shrine a sacred shield, dating (it was believed) from the Trojan War, and made sacrifice at the Altar of Zeus to avert the anger of Priam, whom his ancestor, Achilles' son, Neoptolemus, had killed. Leaving Troy he visited Achilles' tomb in the plain and placed a wreath on it, while his friend Hephaestion placed one on the tomb of Achilles' friend, Patroclus. On his order altars were erected on either shore where he had gone aboard and landed, and he sacrificed to Zeus Apobaterios (protector of disembarkation), Athena, and Heracles, his ancestor. Alexander was living fully in the world of his gods and his ancestors, as they had been portrayed by his favourite poet, Homer, whose *Iliad* was his constant companion, and as they still lived in his imagination and belief.

Alexander was actuated also by practical considerations. His claim, "from the gods I accept Asia, won by the spear" (D. 17.17.2), was to be repeated by him time and again. It is important to understand it fully.

"Asia" was a gift from heaven to him. He did not claim for himself the Persian throne and the Persian empire, though some scholars have interpreted "Asia" so; for that would have been the quickest way towards alienating the support of those who were suffering under Persian rule within the Persian empire. No, he would be king of Asia—the whole continent of Asia, as we shall see—in his own personal right, and he would give just and beneficent treatment with heaven's favour to those who were willing to accept his leadership; for he came both as a liberator and a leader. That was to be his propaganda for the future. At the moment he went from the Troad to Arisbe, where the army was already in camp. For Parmenio had conducted the crossing of the expeditionary forces by ship from Sestus to Abydus and had sent each detachment forward to Arisbe.

In 497 B.C. Darius I had sent three army groups and the Phoenician fleet to deal with a much less serious threat than Alexander presented. Now, though it was the third year of Persian operations in northwest Asia, Darius III merely sent reinforcements to cavalry and left the local satraps to form their own strategy with the advice of Memnon. If they should try to stop Alexander from advancing southwards by holding one of the mountain ranges which run from the interior westwards to the Aegean coast, they would have hostile Greek cities in their rear and the Greek fleet could turn their position by landing troops behind them. They decided therefore to occupy a position inland and to draw Alexander eastwards. So they concentrated their forces at Zelea (see Figure 6).

Memnon's advice was to avoid a pitched battle, because "the Macedonian infantry was far superior." His assessment was based no doubt on the victories of that arm over the Greek mercenaries of Onomarchus in 352 B.C. and over the citizen hoplites of Thebes and Athens in 338 B.C.; past experience had not indicated what a decisive role Alexander's cavalry was to play in Asia. The satraps and Memnon must have known that Alexander had in Asia a total of some 40,000 infantry and 5,000 cavalry; what they could not know was that he would advance with less than half that number of infantry. The next part of Memnon's advice was to withdraw eastwards, burning all crops, fodder, stores and even towns, so that Alexander would have to abandon the pursuit for lack of supplies; and then (presumably) to harass his withdrawal and threaten his communications with Europe. But the satraps, six Persian nobles who distrusted Memnon as a Greek (Alexander had increased their distrust by leaving Memnon's estate near Abydus unharmed), decided to defend their satrapies and offer battle, under conditions chosen by themselves, on the right bank of the river Granicus.[27]

Alexander was aware that the enemy were concentrating a superior number of cavalry and a large army of Greek mercenary infantry in the district of Zelea. He set off with his best troops only, no doubt because

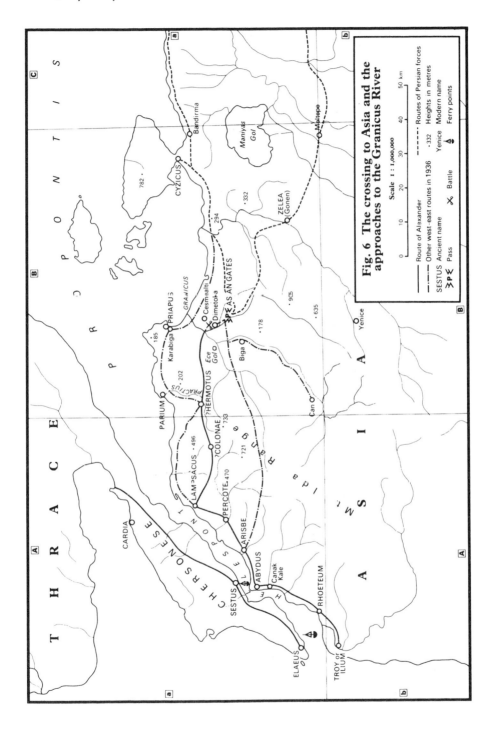

Fig. 6 The crossing to Asia and the approaches to the Granicus River

he would be more mobile and he was not confident of the loyalty of the Greek allied infantry and the Greek mercenary infantry in an engagement with Persia's Greek infantry; nor did he take the Balkan infantry, apart from the highly trained Agrianians. On the third day after the completion of the landing, when he knew the enemy were not far off, he began to cross the wide plain west of the Granicus river in a formation which was suitable for defence, if he was attacked by superior cavalry forces.

The Lancers and 500 light-armed troops reconnoitred ahead; then came the phalangites, 12,000 strong, marching with a front of 750 men and a depth of 16 men, but with an interval between the eighth and the ninth man, so that it was a "double phalanx" (the rear phalanx could face about to meet an attack from the rear); the cavalry rode on each flank of the phalanx; and the baggage-train brought up the rear (A. I.13.1; see Figure 7). Alexander was "not far from the river when scouts galloped back" to tell him of the enemy position on the far bank of the river. It was already after noon on a late May or early June day. Should he withdraw to higher ground, encamp where he was in the open plain, or go at once into the attack?

The Persians had so positioned themselves as to close the "Asian Gates" (P. I6.1). These gates are a gap through which the Granicus river (Kocabaş Çay) flows from the hills into the plain, and it was through this gap that the main west-east roads ran until recent times. This gap is called "the Dimetoka gap" after a village of that name (probably the ancient Didymoteichus). As the Persian line was on the bank and not straddling the river, it should be placed alongside and downstream from Dimetoka. The Persian cavalry were in front; they held both the right bank and the level area behind the bank. The Greek mercenaries who were the strength of the Persian infantry were arrayed in a long line on a ridge above the level area. Such a ridge is formed by the first rise of foothills between Dimetoka and Çesmealti (see Figure 7), and its length, being of some three kilometres, is appropriate to the numbers in the battle.

When I visited the site on June 15 and 16, 1976, this ridge was almost treeless, still grassy, and fairly uniform in height; there are some re-entrants like small bays, but the slopes are not steep or precipitous. Fig. 23 shows the ridge. Features today which correspond to those described by the ancient writers are the wide, level plain of Adrasteia, the steep clay banks of the Granicus, and the deep pockets in its clay bed. The plain consists of stoneless alluvial clay, deposited over the millennia by the river of Biga and the Granicus.

The differences are that there was a stronger flow and more water in antiquity before the days of deforestation and irrigation by motor-pumps; that there were no trees and shrubs on the banks whereas now there are very many; and that the course of the Granicus was uncon-

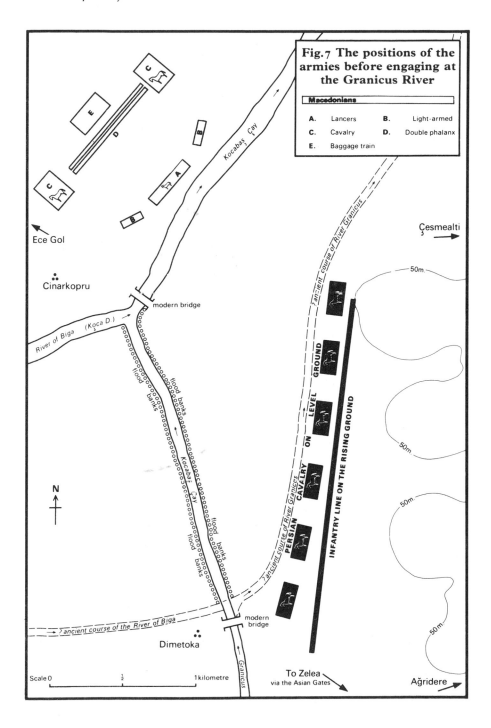

Fig.7 The positions of the armies before engaging at the Granicus River

Macedonians

A. Lancers   B. Light-armed
C. Cavalry   D. Double phalanx
E. Baggage train

trolled in antiquity, whereas today it is stabilised by artificial flood-
banks which enable the trees and shrubs to establish themselves (see
Fig. 24). Left to itself, the Granicus in flood bears to the right, and the
ancient description of the Persian position indicates that the river flowed
then close to the ridge of foothills, as shown on Figure 7. Since no mention was made of a second river, it seems that the river of Biga then joined
the Granicus by Dimetoka. If so, their combined waters in late May or
early June were considerable. Even then, we should imagine the river
not filling the thirty-to-forty-metres wide bed but meandering within it
(as it does today in June) with varying depth (see Fig. 24).

Having set the geographical scene, let us consider the earliest version
of the battle which has come down to us, that of Diodorus, drawn, it
seems, from an original account by Cleitarchus. Diodorus first provides
suitable omens which foreshadow victory for Alexander in a great cavalry battle, and he attributes the satraps' rejection of Memnon's advice
to withdraw to the satraps' high spirit (*megalopsychia*). Then Diodorus
has the armies encamp on opposite banks of the river Granicus. Only its
waters separated the more than 10,000 cavalry and 100,000 infantry of
the Persians from the army of Alexander. "At dawn Alexander in bold
mood took his army across the river, and he was the first to draw up his
army for the contest" (D. I7.I9.3). The Persians put the mass of their cavalry in front, facing all Alexander's line, and arrayed their infantry behind. There were two rounds to the contest. First, cavalry versus cavalry
during which Alexander's personal gallantry is demonstrated ("chance"
matching him against the enemy leaders); second, infantry versus infantry (D. I7.2I.5). The Thessalian cavalry fought best. There is no mention
of any Greek infantry on either side. Persian losses were 10,000 killed,
including 2,000 cavalry; and 20,000 taken prisoner.

Like the account of the battle at Thebes, this is a romantic fantasy.
The impossible is achieved: the crossing of a river defended by 110,000
men is completed without a blow by forces much inferior in number. No
explanation is offered. Cleitarchus has waved his fairy wand. A gentle-
manly battle ensues, since Alexander refrains from using the outstand-
ing quality of Macedonian generalship, the coordinated use of infantry
and cavalry; instead, cavalry fight cavalry, infantry fight infantry, and
never the twain shall meet. Let us waste no more time on this version.

Arrian's version, apart from the opening speeches, is not romantic
but factual, like his reports on the Balkan campaign and the Theban action. It gives the Macedonian order of battle; the units and their commanders, usually with patronymic; Alexander's orders, movements and
actions; topographical details; and figures of some losses. The account is
a careful record, derived from Ptolemy, who had the *King's Journal* to
draw on, as we have argued before. In its general point that the battle
was fought in the afternoon, and also in some particulars, Arrian's ac-

count is supported by the independent evidence of Plutarch, writing before Arrian and drawing probably on Aristobulus.

Arrian's introduction to the battle is cast in the traditional form of two opposing speeches, not to be regarded as authentic but deployed simply to put the pros and cons in a dramatic form. Parmenio proposes that Alexander should camp on the river bank and cross next day, and points out the dangers which Alexander will run by immediate action, i.e., by making a frontal assault. It will not be possible, Parmenio claims, to take the army through the river in an extended line; consequently it will emerge on the far side in disorder, and any break-through group, pushing ahead of the others, will come out onto the level ground in column and be ridden down by the enemy cavalry. Alexander, of course, replies that his decision is for an immediate assault. Thanks to Parmenio's speech we know the difficulties he will encounter and we shall be interested to see how he overcomes them.

Alexander's order of battle is then given (A. I.I4.1-3). It is shown on Figure 8. Alexander put Parmenio in command of the left half, and he took command himself of the right half. We infer from the units named by Arrian that the total force was probably 5,100 cavalry and 13,000 infantry, equally divided between Parmenio and Alexander. They were in an extended line some two-and-a-half kilometres in length, the cavalry on either wing being some ten troopers deep, and the phalanx forming the centre and being eight men deep. They saw across the riverbed 20,000 Persian cavalry in an extended line of the same length at a depth of some sixteen troopers; the cavalrymen were arrayed on the lip of the bank and also on the level ground behind the lip (A. I.14.4 and I.15.4). They could also see on the ridge behind the level ground an infantry force forming a line of equal length; this force consisted mainly of 20,000 Greek mercenary hoplites in a phalanx eight men deep. We may note that Alexander had not given the Persians any time within which to alter their dispositions. He had deployed from his marching order into his extended line without delay, and he thereby offset his enemy's much superior numbers by pitting his one extended line against their two extended lines, of which only one could engage at the outset. The Persians saw Alexander, conspicuous in a white-plumed helmet, and his entourage, and they massed the pick of their cavalry on the bank and the level ground opposite him.

Alexander acted first, in such a way as to deceive the enemy. While he ordered a special assault force to make a frontal attack on the opposite bank, he himself led all the forces of the right wing into the riverbed with the men shouting the war-cry and the trumpets blaring. The Persians of the opposing wing stood firm, expecting an immediate attack. But the troops to the right of Alexander's entourage turned right and thinned out, moving progressively upstream, so as to extend their line to the right and indeed outflank the Persian left (Polyaenus 4.3.16). Where the troops met a strong current in the river, they moved obliquely against the current and maintained their line (thus overcoming one of the dangers mentioned by Parmenio). During this movement sideways the Persians held their fire, as the Macedonians were not yet at close quarters.

Meanwhile the special assault force had gone into action. It consisted from left to right of the Royal Brigade of Hypaspists, the Lancers and the Paeonian cavalry, and ahead of them the Companion Cavalry Squadron of the day, commanded by Socrates. This squadron in particular suffered heavy casualties, as it emerged first from the river and tried to force its way up the bank, some five metres high and varying in steepness. The Persian cavalrymen had advantages: a supply of javelins to hurl from above, heavier and partly armoured horses to repel any Macedonians by sheer weight on the slope, and the ability to strike downwards at close quarters. Some cavalrymen, led by Memnon, rode down to the water's edge first and engaged with spear and scimitar. The effect of the assault force operating in depth was to pin down and weaken the pick of the Persian cavalry.

At the critical moment when the survivors of Socrates' squadron were falling back, Alexander swung the forces of the right wing into frontal attack in line. He himself at the head of his entourage and the Royal Squadron of Companion cavalry attacked on the right of the Paeonian cavalry and forced their way up the bank. Their exceptional strength, their experience and the long reach of their lances in close combat began to tell. Alexander and his entourage were the first to break through and onto the level ground, but in disorder. This was the moment for the Persian commanders and their picked men, who were ready in formation on the level ground. They charged with Mithridates at the apex of a wedge-shaped formation. Alexander rode out at Mithridates, and unseated him with his lance. But the following mass was upon him. Rhoesaces sheared off part of his helmet with a scimitar. He speared Rhoesaces through the cuirass with his lance. As he was doing so, Spithridates from behind raised his scimitar on high to give Alexander the coup de grâce. At that moment Cleitus the Bodyguard cut off the sword arm of Spithridates.

During this desperate action more and more Macedonian cavalry on the right were forcing their way in line onto the level ground. They were helped by the archers and the Agrianians, who had outflanked the Persian line and were now attacking the enemy horses with deadly effect. But it was Alexander and those near him who first routed their immediate opponents, namely the enemy commanders and their picked horsemen. Yet the first general collapse was that of the Persian centre. There the Macedonian infantry-phalanx had gone into action, pushing the

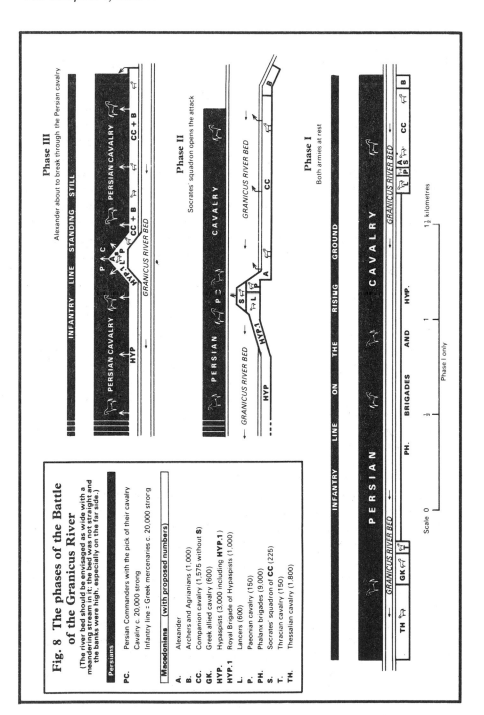

Fig. 8 The phases of the Battle of the Granicus River

(The river bed should be envisaged as wide with a meandering stream in it; the bed was not straight and the banks were high, especially on the far side.)

Persians

PC.   Persian Commanders with the pick of their cavalry

Cavalry c. 20,000 strong

Infantry line = Greek mercenaries c. 20,000 strong

Macedonians   (with proposed numbers)

A.   Alexander
B.   Archers and Agrianians (1,000)
CC.   Companion cavalry (1,575 without **S**)
GK.   Greek allied cavalry (600)
HYP.   Hypaspists (3,000 including **HYP.1**)
HYP.1   Royal Brigade of Hypaspists (1,000)
L.   Lancers (600)
P.   Paeonian cavalry (150)
PH.   Phalanx brigades (9,000)
S.   Socrates' squadron of **CC** (225)
T.   Thracian cavalry (150)
TH.   Thessalian cavalry (1,800)

Phase III

Alexander about to break through the Persian cavalry

INFANTRY   LINE   STANDING   STILL

PERSIAN CAVALRY

PERSIAN CAVALRY

GRANICUS RIVER BED

Phase II

Socrates' squadron opens the attack

PERSIAN   CAVALRY

GRANICUS RIVER BED

Phase I

Both armies at rest

PERSIAN   CAVALRY

GRANICUS RIVER BED

INFANTRY   LINE   ON   THE   RISING   GROUND

PH.   BRIGADES   AND   HYP.

Scale 0   ½   1   1½ kilometres

Phase I only

Persian cavalry back with their long pikes and keeping close formation all along their line. Soon both wings broke also into flight. Pursuit was short; for Alexander turned his forces towards the enemy infantry.

The Greek mercenaries, amazed at the suddenness of the action, stood still, there where they had been posted on the ridge of higher ground. Alexander led his infantry line in a frontal attack and ordered his cavalry to take the enemy in flanks and rear. The mercenaries fought to the death, apart from 2,000 who gave up and were taken alive. Plutarch adds that as Alexander was leading this attack his horse was killed under him by a sword-thrust. The Macedonian losses according to Arrian were 25 men of the advanced squadron of Companion cavalry, 60 or more other cavalry, and up to 30 infantry. Aristobulus, cited by Plutarch, gave 34 men of whom 9 were infantry; when he wrote his account of this battle, he evidently did not have access to the *King's Journal*.

Alexander had won what might well have been his last battle. He owed his life only to the metal of his helmet and the quickness of Cleitus. But he had demonstrated the superior quality of his cavalry over that of Persia in close combat, and he had destroyed an even more formidable enemy, Persia's first army of Greek mercenaries. The Macedonian phalanx, too, had defeated Persian cavalry in close combat under adverse conditions and had confirmed the victory of the Macedonian pike over the Greek hoplite's spear. But more significant still was the ability of Alexander to coordinate heavy infantry, heavy cavalry, light cavalry and light infantry in a single attack. It was this above all that defeated an enemy which had failed totally to coordinate its excellent cavalry and its professional infantry, and therefore exposed first one and then the other to total defeat.

Alexander paid special tributes to his dead: they were buried with their weapons and equipment, and Lysippus, the most famous sculptor of the day, created bronze statues of the twenty-five members of the heroic squadron of Socrates who had fallen in the first assault, which were set up at Dium. Alexander also honoured the enemy dead by giving formal burial to the Persian commanders and to the Greek mercenaries. The parents and children of the Macedonian dead were granted exemption from land-tax, property-tax and personal services; and Alexander made a tour of the wounded, inspecting their injuries and hearing their stories.

The services of his Greek allies[28] were commemorated by the dedication of 300 sets of Persian armour to Athena of the Acropolis at Athens with the inscription: "Alexander, son of Philip, and the Greeks, the Lacedaemonians excepted, gave these from the barbarians in Asia." And as traitors to the Greek cause, the Greek prisoners-of-war were sent in chains to work in Macedonia, a sentence which compared favourably with the crucifixion of Greek mercenaries in Carthaginian service by Dionysius of Syracuse. On his way south Alexander made dedications to Athena at Troy and declared the city free and exempt from paying tribute (Str. 593).

(B) THE LIBERATION OF THE GREEK CITIES AND THE WINNING OF THEIR NEIGHBOURS
(see Figure 2)

The actions of Alexander in the months after the battle give us an insight into his mind. As Macedonian king he showed his love for his men and their dependents and with typical consideration he gave leave to recently married officers and men to spend the winter in Macedonia. As commander in the field he was quick to reward and commemorate deeds of valour by his Companions and his soldiers. On the other hand there was no relaxation of discipline, no bounty, and no indulgences; pillaging was still forbidden, the camps were in the countryside and the men were not billeted in the towns. Spoils were mainly armour and weapons, not captives to be kept or sold as slaves, and the spoils from the enemy headquarters, which fell to Alexander by Macedonian custom, were mostly sent to Olympias.

As hegemon of the Greek League he gave credit to the Greeks as well as to the Macedonians; rightly so, since almost half the victorious cavalry were Greek and it was the Greek fleet and the Greek allied troops which provided the indispensable base of operations.[28] The wording of the dedication at Athens, once desecrated by the Persians, represented the crusade as a joint operation of the Macedonian state (for which "Alexander, son of Philip," was the normal term in diplomacy) and of the Greek League.

As possessor of Asia, Alexander levied taxes on his subjects, Greek and non-Greek. Greek cities were normally required to pay "contributions" towards the expenses of the liberating forces (A. I.26.3; Tod 185,15), whereas non-Greek communities paid "tribute." A defaulting Greek state was sometimes made to pay "tribute" to Alexander or "the Macedonians" (A. 1.27.4; the terms were politically significant, as in the Delphic inscription of 325 B.C. in *Mélanges G. Daux* 22 and 24). There is no record of any Greek city in Asia seeking or being granted membership of the Greek League. Within any Greek city "liberation" involved a change of government. Previous "liberators," Athens and Sparta, had each supported or imposed its own type of government, and they had punished any revolt or secession by harsh indemnities and loss of rights. Alexander was fortunate in having no ideology. While Philip had favoured oligarchy on the Greek mainland, Alexander now favoured democracy in Asia.

Both Philip and Alexander tried to arrest the endemic disease of Greek politics, *stasis*, the violent party-strife which was as common then as in the modern world. Thus at Ephesus, when the incoming Greek democrats tore suppliants from the altars and stoned them to death, Alexander banned all "interrogation" and any further victimisation of those who had been in power. Whereas Athens, for instance, as an imperial power, had sometimes punished opposition or secession by the Greek form of genocide called *andrapodismos* (execution of adult males and sale of the remainder as slaves), and Parmenio had punished Gryneum in Asia in this way, Alexander pardoned Ephesus and even in the heat of the siege tried to save the citizens of Halicarnassus. By these humane methods Alexander won the support of the Greek cities in Asia more effectively than either Athens or Sparta had done in the fourth century.

The Greeks regarded non-Greeks, whom they called "barbarians," as subjects for imperialistic exploitation, and even Greek intellectuals—men such as Isocrates and Aristotle,—expected Alexander to enslave the barbarians in the service of their Macedonian and Greek masters. But Alexander did nothing of the kind. He honoured Greek and Persian dead alike, even as Philip had honoured the Athenian dead after Chaeronea; and he paid special honour to the Persian commanders who had come so close to killing him, for he respected heroism in action. This was characteristic of him throughout his life; after his victory at the Hydaspes river "he ordered the burial of the dead, his own and the bravest of the enemy" (*Epit. Metz* 62, *post ut solitus erat mortuos sepeliri iussit suos atque hostium fortissimos; Itin. Alex.* 15). Except for the Greek mercenaries he let the defeated go free. He did not demand indemnities or impose conscription, and when hillsmen came down to surrender he sent them back to cultivate their own properties in peace. He expressly "liberated" one Asian people, the Lydians, who were allowed to practise their own ancestral customs and administer their own affairs. They were, of course, not exempted from the taxes and services which were due to Alexander as king.

Since Alexander did not make the Asians subject to Greek masters or to Macedonian masters (as they were, for instance, in the territory of a Greek city-state in Asia), he had to devise an economic method of control in relation to his very limited Macedonian manpower. He found the model in Philip's organisation of the Balkan empire. The first essential was to win the respect and cooperation of the native peoples by lenient and generous treatment. For instance, Alexander gave a position of honour in his own entourage to the first Persian commander who joined him, Mithrenes, and himself accepted adoption by a Carian princess, Ada, who made him her son. He took over the Persian system of administration to which the native peoples were accustomed, and he improved it by dividing civil, military and financial powers which had in the past been concentrated in the hands of one Persian satrap or governor in each satrapy or province. For example, in Caria he made Ada civil satrap, a Macedonian officer military commander, and a third person (unknown) financial administrator, each being independently responsible to himself. Thus at the outset he took a step which Rome failed to take until the principate of Augustus. Moreover, by such delegation of powers he kept his own hands free from the burdens of direct government. Where troops were needed for garrison duty and for lines of communication, he used Greek allies or Greek mercenaries, so that his Macedonian field army was kept intact.

The methods which Alexander adopted in the months after his victory must have seemed very novel to those who were familiar with the imperialism of Sparta, Athens, and Thebes. That Alexander sought military and political power was obvious, but the profits of power were not given to the Macedonians and the Greeks in any tangible form. The Macedonian people did not draw imperial revenues, such as had made Athens prosperous, and the Greek League received neither lands nor slaves but only such spoils as the hegemon chose to send.

This was made possible by the fact of the Macedonian kingship and the personality of the king. He could and did formulate all policy himself, and he was able to enact his policy so long as he commanded the loyalty of the Macedonians and the cooperation (or at least the neutrality) of the Greek League. What he had in view was the overthrow of Persia. At his first landing he had claimed Asia for himself "won by the spear and granted by the gods," and during the first winter in Asia he told some Athenian envoys that he would release the Athenians captured at the Granicus river "at the end of the Persian War." To anyone else this reply might have served as an excuse for procrastination; but to a king as confident and as far-sighted as Alexander it was a statement of fact.

The strategic problem for Alexander was much as it had been for the Spartan king Agesilaus in the 390s B.C. Each had the military strength to conquer the west coast of Asia Minor, each had the supremacy at sea for the moment, and each was faced with the same dangers: that a Persian army descending from the Anatolian plateau along one of several valleys could cut the coastal strip in two, and that a Persian fleet, if fully manned, could sweep the Aegean and raise revolt on the Greek mainland. Agesilaus failed to find a solution. Alexander first consolidated his base in northwest Asia Minor by extending his control inland to Dascylium and Sardis. Next he moved rapidly against two Persian bases—Ephesus, from which the Persian garrison of Greek mercenaries fled, and Miletus, where the garrison held firm in the inner city; meanwhile other detachments confirmed his authority along the coast to the north of Miletus. He brought his fleet of 160 ships to Lade, an island off Miletus, and he put troops on the island to secure it as a naval base.

Three days later the Persian fleet, of which he must have had some information in advance, came to anchor off Cape Mycale: 400 ships, with crews and marines totalling some 80,000 men. At this point Arrian makes Parmenio advise what Alexander chooses not to do: fight a naval battle. Instead, Alexander set his siege-engines to work, delivered an assault on the defences of the inner city, and brought his fleet under oar into the harbour of Miletus, where they blocked the entry against the Persians. The Milesians and the Greek mercenaries in the inner city saw no hope of relief and tried, unsuccessfully, to escape. Alexander offered a pardon which the Milesians accepted. When 300 Greek mercenaries were prepared to fight to the death he respected their courage and gave them employment in his own service. The fall of the greatest Greek city in Asia before the eyes of the Persian fleet was an object-lesson to the Greek states from Miletus to the Bosporus. They stayed loyal to Alexander and the Greek League.

At this point Alexander disbanded the bulk of his fleet. Since it was not capable of challenging the enemy fleet at sea, it was now an expensive liability in terms of money, supplies, and shore-based troops and had little or no strategic value. In some respects it had served its purpose admirably by transporting and supplying the expeditionary force at the outset and by assisting in the capture of the seaboard as far as Miletus. By now Alexander had solved the problems of supply, for the granaries and the depots of the Persian satrapies were at his disposal, and tribute and contributions were coming to hand.

But his financial commitments were very great. He had to pay large numbers of mercenaries, Thracian as well as Greek, who were better able than an inactive fleet to protect the Greek cities on the coast from Persian intervention. With their aid he was able to deny Persia the use of the harbours and even the coast, as he had demonstrated at Miletus, where his harassing tactics forced the Persians to leave Cape Mycale. We are told by Arrian the cautionary tale of an omen, an eagle perching on shore astern of the Greek fleet, to which Alexander gave the proper interpretation: "he would master the Persian fleet from the land," by capturing the bases which were constantly needed by warships under oar.

His next objective, therefore, was the Persian base at Halicarnassus. Marching his army through Caria, he received the support of Ada and the Carians en route, and his siege-train and supplies were brought by the residue of his fleet by sea to the coast just north of Halicarnassus. This part of the original fleet had been chosen for its dependability in facing a much larger Persian fleet, and it included twenty Athenian triremes. Its services now and later were of great importance to Alexander.

Strong by nature, Halicarnassus was fortified with massive walls six feet thick, faced with masonry and solid with stone rubble, high masonry towers, battlements and sally ports, and it was surrounded by a ditch fifteen feet deep and twice as wide. A strong garrison of Greek mercenaries and Persian troops had been reinforced by sailors and marines from the Persian fleet which held the harbour and brought in supplies, and the defence was well equipped with bolts and arrows as ammunition for their catapults.

After preliminary moves Alexander filled part of the ditch, protecting his men under wheeled sheds, such as Philip had had at Methone, and then brought up his battering rams. A resolute sally at night was rebuffed; there were losses on both sides, many Macedonians being wounded as they were not wearing their protective armour. Eventually two towers and the intervening curtain were felled by the rams. But the defenders built a crescent-shaped brick wall and then a 150-foot tower, armed with catapults, behind the debris. When some Macedonians, the worse for drink, attacked this wall, a general engagement developed in which the defence had the advantage; for Alexander requested a truce to recover his dead. Two Athenian officers urged refusal, but Memnon, as commander-in-chief, granted it in accordance with normal practice

Although the defenders used cross-fire to good effect and delivered another partly successful sally, it became apparent that Alexander's siege-engines would break a way into the city. A dawn sortie of the defenders in three coordinated groups was then carried out with great skill and came near to success. But the king himself was in the thick of the fighting, his catapults and stone-throwers raked the enemy with their fire, and at the end of the day a company of Macedonian veterans drove the Greeks and Persians back in disorder and might have broken into the city if Alexander had not sounded the retreat in order to spare the citizen population. Shaken by their heavy losses, the garrison-commanders decided to withdraw into the two citadels by the harbour, but first that night they fired the houses near the walls.

Alexander broke into the city, killed all incendiaries and forbade any reprisals against the citizens. Next day he razed the buildings near the citadels and left a force to contain the enemy there. He had not achieved his purpose entirely, since the harbour was still in Persian hands. But he had limited the purposes to which it might now be put; for the citizens of Miletus preferred his methods to those of the Persians.

Arrian and Diodorus gave accounts of the siege, the former from the Macedonian viewpoint of his sources, and the latter from the defenders' viewpoint as supplied to his source, whether Cleitarchus or another. Each belittled their opponents' achievements; but neither denied the courage and tenacity shown by both sides. The techniques of defence and attack were highly developed after two centuries of Persian, Phoenician, and Greek siegecraft. At Halicarnassus these included massive walls nearly 150 feet high, a tower of that height to overlook walls or towers almost as high, and a crescent-shaped wall to permit of enfilading fire against the attackers. Hitherto the odds had been in favour of defence, as Philip had found at Perinthus and Byzantium in 340 B.C.; but now Alexander used not only more powerful bolt-shooting catapults, in which twisted horse-hair, anchored in a wooden frame reinforced with metal plates, provided the propulsive power (these being known as "torsion-catapults"; see Figure 9), but also for the first time stone-throwing engines, which fired from inside his siege-towers. The king's patronage and money seem to have inspired the Macedonian engineers to develop new devices.[29]

The loss of Halicarnassus town was serious for the Persians. They had hoped to use it, as the British used Tobruk, for the landing, launching, and supplying of a Persian army which could attack Alexander's lines of supply and communication. Now the harbour was of little more use than the many harbours on the Aegean islands, and the defence of the citadels was costly in terms of good mercenary troops. As the sailing season was coming to a close, Alexander was free to turn inland and embark on a large-scale strategic plan, of which the *raison d'être* is to be found in the geography of Asia Minor.

(C) THE SUBJUGATION OF THE ANATOLIAN PLATEAU
(see Figure 2)

The remarkable feature of Asia Minor is the huge area of upland plateaus, fertile for growing cereals, rich in pasture and probably then, as now, devoid of trees, which lies between the great ranges of Köroğlu in the north and Toros (Taurus) in the south. This area, known as the Anatolian plateau, was ideally suited to supply Alexander's army and to provide fodder for his horses, and it was excellent cavalry country, such as he had known in Macedonia and in Central Thrace. It was, in addition, the area through which the main routes of the Persian system of made-up roads ran on their way from the Hellespont and Ionia towards the East.

The main entries into the Anatolian plateau from the west are at Eskişehir, Afyoi, and Dinar. The first and probably the second of these were to be the objectives of Parmenio, who was sent in late 334 B.C. with the bulk of the cavalry, the allied troops, and the baggage-train to reduce the tribes of the interior and gain control of Greater Phrygia, feeding his forces meanwhile off the territory of the enemy. Presumably because the operations of Parmenio were not recorded in the *King's Journal*, we are told nothing of them by Arrian but they were of vital importance; for they denied to the enemy and secured to Alexander the western part of the road-system. By the spring of 333 B.C. Parmenio was in possession of the northern part of the plateau. On the other hand,

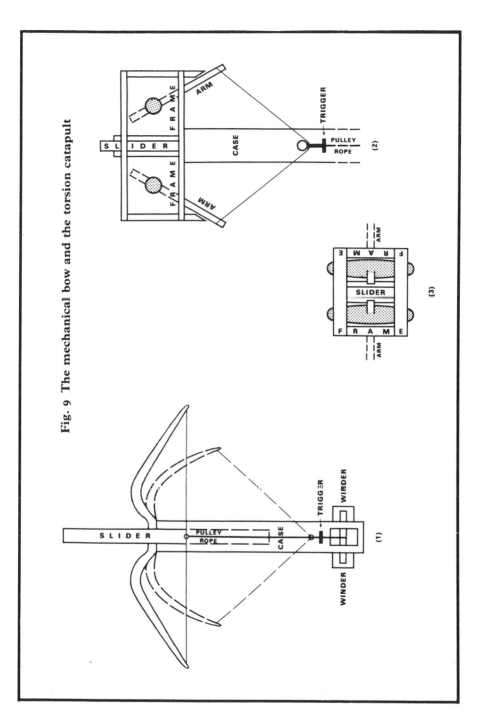

Fig. 9 The mechanical bow and the torsion catapult

Alexander concerned himself that winter with the southern part of the plateau and with the south coast, which is remarkably dangerous for sailing vessels except where there are large coastal plains at Antalya and Mersin. Entry into the plateau from the south coast is best made from these same coastal plains. Thus Antalya and Mersin were what the Persians most needed if they wished to use their navy on the south coast for the landing or the supporting of armies which could invade the plateau or simply block Alexander's progress southwards and eastwards. As it turned out, the Persians did not act, and Alexander achieved his objectives in three stages. First, he reached Antalya and swung north to enter the plateau and meet Parmenio at Gordium (west of Ankara). Then he overran the eastern part of the plateau, finally coming down southwards into the coastal plain of Mersin. If Darius had taken the field earlier, Alexander might not have had the chance to complete the final stage.

Having given this overall view of the campaign, let us take it in detail. After the fall of Halicarnassus Alexander reduced a Carian city, Myndus, which had opposed him during the siege of Halicarnassus, and probably other centres of resistance, and appointed his adopted mother, Ada, satrap of Caria. Next, with an army mainly of Macedonian and Balkan infantry he marched through the broken and mountainous countryside of the Lycians, a warlike people, who were later to resist Rome for many generations. Opposition was bitter; when the defenders of one stronghold, Marmara, realised that they could no longer hold it against the determined assaults of the Macedonians, they burnt their houses and escaped into the mountains. By midwinter all resistance was overcome. The largest cities came to terms without fighting—Telmessus (Fethiye), and Xanthus, Pinara, and Patara, a trio in the valley of the Koca Cayi; for their citizens were partly Hellenised, many speaking Greek as well as Lycian, and they knew that Alexander would defend them against the marauding mountaineers. Some thirty small towns followed suit. It is significant that Alexander by-passed Cnidus, a Greek city, and Caunus (Dalyan), partly Hellenised, which were held as ports of call by the Persians. His aim was to control the native people and the interior.

After appointing Nearchus, a Cretan, as satrap of Lycia, he struck northwards in order to open up the entry towards Phrygia—with what success we do not know. Later he came back to the coast at Phaselis (Tekirova), a Greek city, which had offered its friendship and sent him a golden crown. He helped the Phaselites to destroy the stronghold of some Pisidian raiders. Other people on this (the eastern) coast of Lycia joined him willingly. Marching on towards Antalya, he sent the main force by a mountainous route inland, where his Thracian road-builders cut steps, presumably for pack-animals, in the rock. He and the rest marched along the shore to a point where a passage was impossible against a south wind. As he approached, the south wind, which had been blowing, veered, and a north wind sprang up, enabling the men to pass along this dangerous coast waist-deep in water. The change of wind was attributed by Callisthenes, the court-historian, and by others to divine favour, but Alexander mentioned it in his letters without any such suggestion. By conducting mountain warfare in the depth of winter—a rare undertaking in Greek or Persian history—Alexander won a remarkable success; for he demanded and obtained, both in the town and the countryside, formal submission to himself and to his delegated officials. In what capacity? As king of Macedon or as king of Asia? Perhaps he did not give the answer. It was enough that they submitted to Alexander.

Entering Pamphylia in the vicinity of Antalya, Alexander received the submission of the Greek cities—Perge, Aspendus and Side—but was resisted at Sillyum (Asar Köyü), strongly held by Greek mercenaries and Pamphylians. He let Sillyum be, put a garrison in Side and turned back to threaten Aspendus, which had reneged on its agreement. Overawed by his presence, the citizens of Aspendus accepted the terms which he offered: surrender of hostages; payment of the tribute in the form of horses which had hitherto been paid to the king of Persia, of 100 talents as a fine, and of an annual tribute "to the Macedones"; to be subject to the satrap appointed by Alexander; and to accept his adjudication in a current frontier dispute. These terms, which Arrian reported either via Ptolemy from the *King's Journal* or from a source familiar with an actual treaty, show that a Greek city in Asia was usually not subject to Alexander's satrap and did not pay money "to the Macedones." Under an earlier agreement, which Arrian reported, the payment of horses and of 50 talents by Aspendus had been expressly "for the army as pay," presumably as a contribution to the war of the Greek League and Macedonia against Persia. Now the treasonable conduct of Aspendus lost it the status of a Greek city. No doubt it was garrisoned by Alexander; for it was important to deny to Persia the use of the Eurymedon River, which had been the mustering point for a Persian army and fleet in 467 b.c.[30]

The next phase was the advance through Pisidia into the Phrygian part of the Anatolian plateau. Whereas the modern road from Antalya runs northwards along limestone coombes and slopes which are uninhabited, Alexander marched from one Pisidian city to another: first through a narrow pass to Termessus (northwest of Antalya), whose resistance he did not try to break; then, after making alliance with an enemy of Termessus, Selge (Sirk), founded by Lacedaemonians, he attacked Sagalassus (Ağlasun) near the source of the Eurymedon River. The Sagalassians occupied a position on a rocky ridge, unsuitable for cavalry, and Alexander led the Royal Brigade of Hypaspists to the assault. On this occasion he had the Hypaspists, the three brigades of *pezhetairoi*, the archers, the Agrianians, and the Thracian light-armed infantry. The natives being without protective armour suffered heavy losses, and Alexander at the head of the Hypaspists pressed so hotly on their heels that he broke his way into the city. The archers lost their commander and twenty men in the action.

Warned by the example of Sagalassus, a number of Pisidian fortresses surrendered. Dividing his forces, Alexander took some others by assault. Then he advanced past Lake Ascania (Burdur) and four days later reached Celaenae (Dinar), a key point in the communications between Phrygia and the Aegean coast and between Phrygia and Pamphylia. The fortified city was held on the orders of the Persian satrap of Phrygia by a garrison of 100 Greek mercenaries and 1,000 Carians. These troops agreed to surrender on a specified date, if no relief force reached them. After resting his army for ten days Alexander left a force of 1,500 men to keep a watch on the garrison and pressed on, unopposed, through excellent cavalry country to Gordium (near Polati, west of Ankara). There he was joined by Parmenio's part of the army and by substantial reinforcements from Europe, which had accompanied the Macedonians returning from their compassionate leave at home. By now it was probably late in April 333 B.C.

At Gordium Alexander was on the northern side of the watershed; for the Sangarius river (Sakarya Nehri), which flows past the city, enters the Black Sea at Karasu. Proceeding to Ancyra (Ankara), Alexander received the submission of the Paphlagonians who lived towards the Black Sea; and then later he invaded Cappadocia, where he won territory on both sides of the river Halys (Kizilirmak), which drains the eastern side of the Anatolian plateau. These operations, of which no details are known, may have lasted into July.

Some fifteen months had passed since Alexander first set foot on Asiatic soil. His amazing progress was due above all to the boldness of his winter campaign, such a campaign as had never been executed by a Greek army. Agesilaus, the Spartan king, had conducted summer campaigns deep into the hinterland of Asia Minor in the 390s B.C., but his failure to capture bases and establish a system of supply had resulted in his achievements being nothing more than tip-and-run raids.[31] On the other hand Alexander and Parmenio laid the foundations of a firm system of control in a single winter. Before a year had passed, he had dispossessed Darius of most of Asia Minor, including the great Anatolian plateau, and he had added to his domain a country as rich and as large as Philip's Balkan empire. It was of course not fully conquered; for there were still scattered Persian garrisons and some defiant tribes. But the bulk of the Greek cities in Asia were liberated, the majority of the native peoples pacified, and the military power of Macedonia demonstrated.

The satraps whom he appointed would be able to consolidate their control—among them two natives, Ada in Caria and Sabictas in Cappadocia (in the eastern part of the plateau by Kayseri).

Alexander's lines of communication ran now from supply points on the Bosporus and on the Aegean coast via Eskişehir and Dinar into the plain of Konya and thence towards the Cilician Gates. Greater Phrygia held the key position on this route, and Alexander entrusted it to one of his ablest officers, Antigonus Monophthalmus (the One-Eyed).

(D) THE SECOND PLOT; THE KING OF ASIA; AND THE WAR AT SEA

In the winter of 334–333 B.C. Parmenio caught a Persian agent, Sisines, and was informed by him of a plan to kill Alexander. He sent Sisines to Alexander, then at Phaselis. When Alexander heard what Sisines had to say, he laid the matter before his Council of Friends.

Sisines' story was this. When Amyntas, a prominent Macedonian, had deserted to Darius, he had brought a letter in which Alexander the Lyncestian had made proposals to Darius. Sisines had been sent by Darius to urge this Alexander to kill the king, and to offer as a reward a thousand gold talents, marriage into the Persian royal house, and the throne of Macedonia. We can understand Darius' choice if the Lyncestian was a member of the royal house and a respectable candidate for the throne. Suspicion was increased by the fact that the two brothers of Alexander the Lyncestian had been executed for complicity in the murder of Philip in 336 B.C., and that he himself had been tried on the same charge and had owed his acquittal largely to the intercession of Alexander. Since then he had been promoted to high positions by the king and was now commander of the largest group of cavalry, the 1,800 Thessalians, with whom he was very popular.

The Council of Friends had no doubts. They urged the king to get rid of the Lyncestian at once. Speed and secrecy were necessary in case the news of Sisines' arrest alerted the Lyncestian and he staged a mutiny. The brother of the brigade-commander Craterus set off in native dress with local guides and delivered a verbal message to Parmenio, who carried out the arrest and sent the prisoner to the king. The evidence which convinced the Council of Friends would certainly have led the Macedonian Assembly to execute the Lyncestian, if the king had prosecuted him. But the king did not; he simply kept him under guard. Some scholars have supposed that he did not wish to alienate Antipater, whose daughter the Lyncestian had married; but it is unlikely that Antipater would have questioned the verdict of the Macedonian Assembly. Rather, the king had a strong affection for the Lyncestian and was reluctant to accept the evidence or to act upon it, as in 336 B.C. At the same time the incident must have shaken his confidence in the dependability of even his highest commanders and in his own ability to select loyal officers.

The account which we have given came through Arrian from one of the Friends, presumably Ptolemy or Aristobulus. It is preferable to that of Diodorus (17.32.1–2), in which the warning is given not by Parmenio but by Olympias, the transference being due probably to Cleitarchus. Arrian's account shows the faith which the Friends and Alexander himself put in the interpretation of the omens. Sometime before the Sisines affair a swallow had landed on the head of the king once when he was drowsy, and it had not flown away until he became fully awake. The king's most trusted seer, Aristander of Telmessus, claimed that this portended a plot by one of the Friends which would be revealed. But who among the Friends? Sisines' story seemed to provide the answer. "Alexander himself put the two together" says Arrian, drawing probably on Aristobulus, who was a personal confidant of the king.

An incident at Gordium in April, 333 B.C., shows more strikingly what signs and omens meant to Alexander. The temple of Zeus at Gordium housed the wagon of the Phrygian Gordius, who had left Macedonia and won the kingship of Asia,[32] and the local belief was that the first person to untie the knot of the binding on the yoke of this wagon would become king of Asia. On coming to Gordium Alexander felt a "yearning" (*pothos*) to see the wagon and the knot, and he tried but failed to undo the knot. Unwilling to accept defeat, he seized the yoke-pin which went through the knot, drew it out and thus detached the yoke from the pole. The assurance that he had untied the knot was given that night by thunder and lightning, both being manifestations of Zeus.

So next morning Alexander sacrificed to the gods who had shown him how to untie the knot and had sent the signs of thunder and lightning. From then on Alexander believed that he would be by divine favour King of Asia; and no doubt many Macedonians and many Asians shared his belief. This account of what happened at Gordium came evidently from Aristobulus and was confirmed in part by Ptolemy (A. 2.3.7 and P. I8.3, citing Aristobulus). A different account, that he cut the knot with his sword, is less credible (C. 3.1.14–19; J. 11.7.16).

Alexander's successes in the hinterland of Asia Minor did not diminish his anxieties about the situation at sea. In fact Darius decided to mount an offensive by sea and appointed Memnon in the winter of 334–333 B.C. as supreme commander of all naval forces and of the coastal areas in the Mediterranean. Memnon's preparations were so efficient that he set sail in late March from the Phoenician ports with 300 warships and some 60,000 men, which included a strong force of Greek mercenary soldiers. Entering the Aegean without opposition and estab-

lishing bases on the islands, he captured Chios by treachery and all of
Lesbos except Mytilene by the end of April. News of his advance
reached Alexander at Gordium. It was evident that Memnon's next
move might be to the Hellespont, where he could cut Alexander's lines
of communication, or to the Greek mainland where Sparta and other
states might join the Persian side. In either event Alexander would have
to turn back to Europe, as Agesilaus had had to do in 394 B.C. under
similar circumstances. Alexander took immediate steps to defend the
Hellespont by putting two Macedonian officers in charge of all forces
there and ordering them to take the offensive at sea, and by instructing
the Greek League Council to send a fleet to hold the Hellespont. He sent
500 talents to meet the cost of the offensive. Antipater and his officers in
Greece were given 600 talents in order to raise naval forces and hold the
western Aegean. Alexander was indeed in an awkward situation. Because he had kept his financial reserves under his own hand, his officers
in the Hellespont and in Europe could not act effectively until these
large amounts of coinage were transported to them.

Although Alexander was unaware of it, Memnon 'sat down to
blockade Mytilene, unwisely, since the slackening of his rapid offensive
gave the Macedonians time to organise resistance at sea. Then Memnon
fell ill and died, probably in June, and there was an interval of inactivity
until his successor, a Persian, Pharnabazus, was appointed in July.
During that interval Darius arranged for the Greek mercenaries with the
fleet to be brought back to serve with himself; probably in the belief that
the naval offensive could not win success in what was left of the sailing
season, he had decided to assume the offensive on land. Thus part of
Pharnabazus' fleet had to bring the mercenaries to Tripolis in Syria
(A. 2.13.2), and the effectiveness of the Persian naval offensive was considerably reduced.

The news of Memnon's death reached Alexander in July. By then he
was campaigning farther east in Cappadocia; for he intended, if he had
to turn back to the Hellespont, that any forces he left should be able to
defend Asia Minor against Darius. His army and ancillary services, well
over 50,000 men and great numbers of horses, were amply supplied
from the Anatolian plateau, and now in Cappadocia he controlled the
approaches from the east through the Taurus range and the Tahtali
range, which were narrow and difficult. Moreover, he had sealed most
of the coast against seaborne landings of any significant size, and he
controlled the Hellespont. His position in the Konya plain was a central
one in relation to the enemy; he could move west if he needed to reinforce the coastal cities or the Hellespont, and he could extend his conquest eastwards, if opportunity should offer. The news of Memnon's
death was followed by the report that Darius had withdrawn the Greek
mercenaries from the fleet. In view of this Alexander's inherent desire to

continue his anabasis towards the east was strengthened (P. 18.5). Early in August he translated his desire into action.

SOURCES

(A) D. 16.91.-2; I7.2.4-6 and 5-7; I7.16-21; A. 1.11-16; P. 15-16; J. 11.5-6

(B) D. I7.21.7-27.6; A. I.17-23.5; P. I7.1-2

(C) and (D) D. 17.27.6-29; 32.1-2; A. I.23.6-29; 2.1.1-2.2.2; 2.3.1-2.4.2; P. I7.3-I8.5; C. 3.1; J. 11.7

V

THE CONQUEST OF THE
EASTERN MEDITERRANEAN COAST

(A) THE OCCUPATION OF CILICIA

Cilicia, the territory round the Gulf of Issus, presents grave problems for any army of invasion. It is flanked by two roughly parallel ranges, Taurus and Amanus, each pierced by two passes: Taurus by one leading into the valley of the Calycadnus (Göksu Nehir) and by another, "the Cilician Gates," which leads to Tarsus; and Amanus by a northern pass (Hasanbeyli), to which there are viable but more difficult alternatives, and by a coastal pass in the south, known as "the Pillar of Jonah." In consequence the communications of any army invading from west to east are exposed to danger as it passes through Cilicia; for a hostile force can descend from the interior into the plain, or a hostile fleet can land troops on the coast to cut the lines of communication or of retreat and occupy one or more of the narrow passes. Alexander was certainly aware of these strategic problems; for having read Xenophon's *Anabasis* he knew how Cyrus had passed that way, and he was in touch with the Greeks of the locality (see Figures 10, 38 and 39).

The Persian road which Alexander decided to follow passed through the "Cilician Gates," a spectacular cliff-bound pass of considerable length, which admitted only four men abreast at its narrowest point. Properly defended, it would have been impregnable. Alexander encamped a long way short of the pass and took his Hypaspists, archers and Agrianians on a forced march that night, hoping to surprise the enemy at the pass at dawn. Although the element of surprise failed, the enemy force fled when it was seen that Alexander in person was leading the attack. Such was the terror his name inspired! Twenty-four hours afterwards the whole army began flowing through the "Cilician Gates." Alexander sped on again with a body of cavalry and light-armed infantry, covering over ninety-five kilometres (57 miles) in a day (J. 11.8.2),[33] and occupied Tarsus before the Persian satrap could carry out his intended plundering of the city.

There Alexander fell dangerously ill. The cause has been disputed (P. 19.2). According to Arrian, Aristobulus thought the cause was fatigue, understandably, since Alexander had been leading every attack and had spared himself nothing in physical effort. Others said that he was hot and sweaty when he plunged on a midsummer day into the icy waters of the river Cydnus and was seized with a cramp. Whatever the cause, all the doctors despaired of his life except an Acarnanian doctor called Philip, a friend of Alexander since boyhood. As Philip was preparing a special potion, a despatch was delivered to Alexander. It contained a warning from Parmenio that Philip had been bribed by Darius. As Alexander took and drank the potion, he gave Philip the despatch to read, thus "demonstrating to Philip his trust in him as his friend, and demonstrating to the company of friends not only a confidence in them which rose above suspicion but also his own steadfastness in the face of death."

Such is Arrian's account, derived through Ptolemy or Aristobulus or both from the company of Friends who were present. Other accounts, less credible, specified the bribe as 1,000 talents and a royal princess in marriage; made Alexander keep the despatch for a day or two "under his pillow," informing no one and (more incredibly) making no enquiry of Parmenio; and made him gaze at Philip to see if Philip showed signs of guilt. Plutarch and Curtius may have got this more dramatic version from Cleitarchus.

Throughout August and most of September, while Alexander lay ill at Tarsus, Pharnabazus, the Persian admiral, was conducting operations in three sectors. He captured Mytilene and then Tenedos, from which he threatened the entry to the Hellespont; he stationed ten ships at Siphnos on the way to the Peloponnese and sent subsidies to his sympathisers in mainland Greece, in particular Sparta; and his sea-borne forces, landing at Halicarnassus and other points, established a bridgehead on the Carian coast. Alexander's communications by sea were cut completely. If Pharnabazus were to adopt a strategy of concentration rather than dispersal, he might cut Alexander's overland communications either by entering the Hellespont and capturing bases there, or by driving inland from the Carian coast. With such threats to his rear Alexander was wise to keep his army at Tarsus. Then, in early October, the news reached him that Darius had mustered a great army at Babylon and was evidently intending to engage the Macedonian army in battle. Should Alexander await him at Tarsus, where his own front would be protected by the Pyramus river[34] and he had access to the Anatolian plateau for supplies or withdrawal? If he did so, Darius would reach the Gulf of Issus and receive the support of a Persian fleet, which could not only supply his army but also land troops behind Alexander's lines. Alexander decided to have the best of both policies. He kept his main army at Tarsus and sent Parmenio ahead to occupy the coast of the Gulf (see Figure 10).

Parmenio's force, consisting mainly of the Thessalian cavalry and Greek allied and mercenary infantry, and numbering some 14,000 men, swept the forces of the Persian satraps aside and won over two Greek cities, Magarsus and Mallus. Operating from there he captured and garrisoned the narrow pass of Kara Kapu (by Akpinar) and occupied Castabalum on the Persian Royal Road at the head of the Gulf. He was now at the junction of the two routes which crossed the high Amanus range: the northern one through the "Amanian Gates" (the Hasanbeyli Pass) into the upper valley of the Karasu, and the southern route involving two passes—the "Pillar of Jonah" near the coast over an outlier of the range, and the Belen pass over the actual range. Parmenio took the latter route, established his main base at Issus (near Dörtyol) and occupied the Jonah Pass. He cleared the westward flank of Mt. Amanus of Persian troops. The advanced posts of the Persian satraps were now at the Hasanbeyli Pass and at Myriandrus, south of the Jonah pass. Alexander's small fleet could now use the Gulf, and Parmenio's troops could close its harbours to Persian warships, some of which lay at Tripolis on the Lebanese coast.

When Alexander recovered his health completely in mid-October, he moved from Tarsus not eastwards to join Parmenio but west to invade Cilicia Tracheia ("Rough Cilicia"), so named from the precipitous slopes of the Taurus range on the seaward side. In a week of mountain warfare, conducted at top speed by three brigades of Macedonian infantry, the archers and the Agrianians, he forced the hill tribes to submit. His aim was probably to secure the rear of the position at Tarsus against any seaborne landings and to open another route to the Anatolian plateau up the valley of the Göksu Nehir (Calycadnus), because the main route had a serious disadvantage for movement and supply, the bottleneck at the Cilician Gates. At Soli, on his way back, he learnt that the Persian force in Caria had been decisively defeated by his commanders in Asia Minor. This changed the whole situation on land. Moreover, at sea the approach of winter weather would confine the Persian fleets to their Aegean bases and their home ports. In his jubilation Alexander held a national festival and a parade of his army at Soli. It was now early November.

It was obviously desirable to concentrate his scattered forces for a decisive battle. Abandoning the Tarsus position, he bridged the Pyramus, moved his baggage-train across the river, and made sacrifices at Magarsus to the war-goddess Athena and at Mallus to Amphilochus, a hero who hailed from Alexander's ancestral home, Argos. While he was at Mallus, a report reached him, no doubt from Parmenio, that Darius was encamped at Sochi in Syria, two days' march beyond the Jonah Pass. He hastened on to Castabalum, where he met Parmenio, and advanced to Issus, where he left those who were sick together with his siege-train and main supply dumps; for he intended to seek out the enemy.

At Issus Alexander consulted his staff.[35] The question was whether to await Darius on the borders of Cilicia or to advance into Syria. The staff favoured advance. But by which route? The coastal route and then the Belen Pass seemed better, because supplies could be carried by sea to Myriandrus (near Iskenderun) and forage and granaries would be available in the plain of Myriandrus and the basin of Antioch for his more than 30,000 men and 10,000 horses. Marching from Issus he reached Myriandrus in two days, as Cyrus had done in 401 B.C., and drove the Persian troops back towards the Belen Pass. That night there was a severe storm with much wind and rain, and next day Alexander rested his men and horses at Myriandrus.

Meanwhile, unknown to Alexander, Darius had decided to advance from Sochi into Cilicia. He chose the northern route, because he knew that Parmenio held the Jonah Pass. In preparation for the advance he had sent his baggage-train and treasure to Damascus; for he drew his supplies mainly from the south and probably intended to follow up the defeat of Alexander by a move in that direction. At the time of his decision Darius believed that Alexander's forces were spread out from Cilicia Tracheia or Tarsus to the Jonah Pass and that his own army, descending from the Hasanbeyli Pass and some lesser passes to Castabalum, would cut the enemy forces in two. In fact Darius reached Castabalum without opposition, captured Issus and mutilated or killed the sick. There he learnt to his surprise and delight that Alexander was not at Tarsus but had left Issus two days before en route for Myriandrus. He was sitting on Alexander's tail with a larger army, and he knew that Alexander would have to turn back and fight his way through or starve. So he advanced next day to the best defensive position, the line of the river Pinarus, and encamped there. On that day Alexander was resting his army at Myriandrus[36] (see Figures 38 and 39).

(B) THE BATTLE OF ISSUS
(see Figures 10 and 11)

The news that Darius was not in front of him but behind him reached Alexander at Myriandrus during the ensuing night or early next day. He was at first incredulous. He sent some of his Companions in a thirty-oared boat to ascertain the truth. They not only found where Darius was but they rowed right into the mouth of the Pinarus and noted the disposition of his forces. Their action was the more courageous, because the Persians must have commandeered and manned any shipping along the

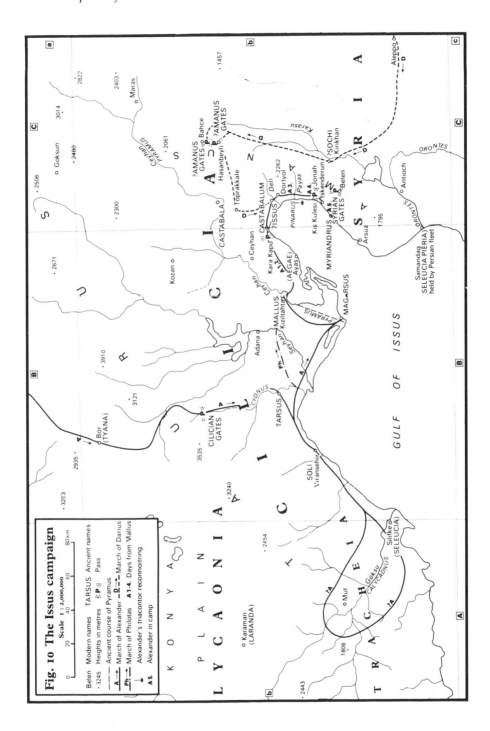

Fig. 10 The Issus campaign

coast. When they reported back, Alexander consulted his staff. He then ordered his men to take their afternoon meal and started back as night was falling. The army reached the Jonah Pass at midnight; detachment after detachment marched through the narrows and slept among the crags. Both Alexander and Darius knew that a decisive battle was about to be fought on or near the Pinarus river.

It is this battle which scholars have named the Battle of Issus. It was not fought there, but there has been considerable argument as to which of the rivers north of the Jonah Pass was the Pinarus. One important source of information is Callisthenes, the court historian, who stood high in the confidence of the king. He was probably present at the battle and could have obtained information on the spot. As Tarn observes, Callisthenes must have read his account to Alexander; and he must have had comments from him and other participants. Matters of fact then are as certain to be correct as anything can be, and it is these matters of fact which enable us to establish the scene of the battle beyond any reasonable doubt.

We owe our knowledge of Callisthenes to Polybius, who read and criticised his predecessor's work and so transmitted to us some of Callisthenes' statements. One is that when Alexander, having already passed "the narrows" (i.e., Jonah's Pass) going south, learnt of the presence of Darius in Cilicia (i.e., at the Pinarus river), they were 100 stades (18.5 kilometres) apart (Polybius 12.19.4). Alexander heard this news at Myriandrus. Since the distance from Iskenderun to the Payas river is 20 kilometres by the modern motor-road, the Pinarus river should be identified with the Payas. Most scholars prefer to identify it with the Deli Cayi, 10 kilometres farther north. Its distance from Iskenderun, 30 kilometres, is incompatible with the distance given by Callisthenes.[37]

Callisthenes says that when Alexander led his army forward in deployed formation (12.20.1)—that is "on first coming into the wide ground" (12.19.6)—he was about 40 stades distant from the enemy. As one descends from the Jonah Pass, one first encounters wider ground by Erikli, which is some 7 to 8 kilometres from Payas. This corresponds to "about 40 stades." On the other hand, no one could postpone the *first* entry into wider ground until that distance from the Deli Cayi, because the plain is already 4 kilometres wide near Payas. Further, Callisthenes reported that the distance from the coast to the mountainside at the place of battle was "not more than 14 stades" (2.6 km) (Polybius 12.17.4). The distance at the Payas river today is some 4 km, but we have to bear in mind that the coast may have advanced since 333 B.C. Callisthenes' measurement, then, may be compatible with the Pinarus being the Payas. On the other hand, the corresponding distance at the Deli Cayi is 6.7 km. It is difficult to believe that the coast of the plain, flatter than the shelving Payas plain, could have advanced four kilometres since 333 B.C. On all these grounds we may dismiss the Deli Cay as a claimant.

Another measure of distance has come down in the accounts of Diodorus (17.33.1) and Curtius (3.8.23), which were independent of one another; but it is practically certain that they both obtained the measure ultimately from Callisthenes. It is that 30 stades (5.5 km) separated the armies at the moment when the scouts sent forward by Alexander reported back to him.

The scouts were certainly mounted on fast horses; they had to get close to the enemy in the early light, return with their report at full speed and inform Alexander before he had marched very far. If Darius held the Deli Cayi and we apply the interval of 30 stades, it follows that Alexander would have marched some 17 kilometres before the scouts reached him; but if Darius held the Payas, only some two to three kilometres. This means in the former case that his well-mounted scouts covered only some 24 kilometres, while his army was marching on foot some 17 kilometres; and in the latter case that they rode some 9 or 10 kilometres to the army's 2 or 3 kilometres. Once again the Payas has to be preferred over the Deli Cayi, because a well-mounted man should move three or four times faster than a marching army, when relatively short distances are involved.

If we ask how Callisthenes came to know these distances, the answer is from Alexanders' surveyors, the *bematistae*. Alexander had been a student of war from boyhood and as a commander he had to assess distances in relation to battle-formations with an accurate eye. If then, the distance between coast and mountainside at the Payas river, as given by Callisthenes, is not the same as it is today, the logical deduction is not that Alexander or Callisthenes got it wrong,[38] but that the terrain has changed since 333 B.C.

Callisthenes described the river Pinarus as follows (Polybius 12.17.5): (a) In its upper part after emerging from the mountain "the sides of its bed were torn away." (b) Where the river ran through level areas as far as the sea, its bed was marked by "precipitous ridges, hard to climb"; and Callisthenes described this feature as "the eyebrow of the river, precipitous and thorny," i.e., an overhang with briars at the foot of the bank (12.22.4). We may infer by comparing (a) and (b) that in the upper part the banks were neither precipitous nor hard to climb in general and that the bed was wide rather than confined. Callisthenes made other remarks to which we shall come later.

I visited the scene of the campaign first in January 1941. Then I studied the terrain of the Payas river on June 18th, 1976. The Amanus range, running roughly parallel to the coast, is scarred by very deep rifts in the limestone face which looks towards the Gulf of Issus. These rifts are usually at right angles to the line of the range, and from them issue rivers which flow into the Gulf. In times of heavy rain they are roaring torrents, but in November 333 B.C. the water was evidently low enough for a man to wade across. The course of the Payas between the mountainside and the sea is divisible into three parts.

(1) The first part runs from the rift to a little below the first bridge. Here the riverbed is 30 to 40 metres wide with shelving sides, but at one place on the north side the water had undercut the gravel bank and torn away a short piece, leaving a steep side. The bed is mostly of sand and gravel but has a generous sprinkling of large and medium-sized boulders. This is shown in Fig. 25. This part is similar to section (a) of Callisthenes' description. Men or horses could pick their way across it, but a cavalry charge would be impossible.

(2) Between the first bridge and the second bridge the river is no longer sweeping down a gently sloping hillside, but it is confined within a channel of varying width, which has been cut through a level and deep stratum of conglomerate rock. Fig. 26 shows the river, just below the first bridge, entering the confined channel between its conglomerate sides. Most of the north bank, and particularly the upper half of the stretch, has precipitous cliffs from 3 to 7 metres in height; at some places a cliff is overhanging and at others a chunk of cliff had fallen into the bed. But on this north side there are some ways down between precipitous sections, one of which is gradual and wide enough for carts to go up and down. The south bank has some precipitous places in the upper half of this stretch, but access to the river is easier and at more places than on the north side. In the lower half down to the second bridge the precipitous places on the north side are fewer than they are higher up, and the south bank is mostly shelving. The worst features of this stretch correspond to those of Callisthenes' description (b). There is a good deal of rubble in the bed of the river, but not of a size to impede progress.

(3) Below the second bridge (shown in Fig. 27), the river issues into an open bed of gravel and sand and proceeds gently down towards the sea. It is crossed by a road bridge and a railway bridge, and a lot of gravel and sand has been taken from the bed and its sides for road building. This last part could be crossed readily by a squadron of cavalry in formation.

The ground north of the right bank is uneven in the first part; unusually level in the second part; and gently sloping seawards in the third part. The ground to the south of the left bank is different. Between the mountainside and almost the second bridge there is a gentle ridge or swell, which is parallel to and contains the riverbed; to the south of this ridge the ground falls and forms a low, flattish area, which is invisible to anyone standing on the right bank and is from that point of view "dead ground." In Fig. 28 we are looking south from the top of the ridge by the first bridge; one can see the dropping "dead ground" and the sickle of high ground beyond. From just above the second bridge to the coast there is no such ridge; the ground south of the river is generally flat.

Returning now to the point where the river emerges from the rift and looking south, one has to one's left a steeply falling hillside, which curves towards the southwest and ends in a diminishing promontory of high ground. It forms the background of Figs. 25 and 28. This curving run of high ground embraces the top end of the ridge and overlooks the "dead ground" south of the ridge. Fig. 28 shows the view from the right bank, looking south; one can see the ridge and beyond it the promontory of high ground, which has the shape of a sickle, the handle lying near the riverbed and the point being formed by the promontory. Callisthenes' description of the upper and middle of my three parts, and Arrian's description of the third part (towards the sea) as being more suitable for cavalry manoeuvres (2.8.10), show that changes in the upper and middle parts since antiquity have been few. Once the river had cut its first channel in the belt of conglomerate rock aeons ago, it was bound to stay within it. All that has happened there since 333 B.C. is that the channel has been deepened by the scour of torrential floods and widened by the occasional collapse of a piece of overhanging cliff.

On the other hand Callisthenes said that the river ran *obliquely* or *diagonally* across the space between the mountains and the sea, and this means that the river below the second bridge ran farther northwards than it does today. This fits the fact that the coast was different in 333 B.C. For when Alexander sent men by boat to see where Darius was, they found him more easily since he was encamped along the Pinarus river (the Payas), and the coast there took the form of *a bay* (A. 2.7.2). What is meant presumably is that by rowing their thirty-oared boat into the bay the men could see the course of the river.

The coast at this point is now convex, not concave, and the reason is undoubtedly that more than two millennia of river-deposits have pushed the coast forward into its present form. Indeed, Admiralty Chart No. 2632 shows that the process is continuing; for the water inshore by the outlet of the Payas is shallower than elsewhere. Further evidence comes from *The Mediterranean Pilot* 5 (1961) 190 on the subject of Payas: "The ancient port is now partly inland and filled with sand and stones; the moles are still visible." This ancient port was of the Roman period, when the place was called not Payas but Baiae. In the time of Alexander the coast was no doubt farther inland still. Indeed Callisthenes' report of the distance from mountainside to coast shows that the coastline in 333 B.C. was 1.4 kilometre inland of the present coast and formed a bay, as indicated in Fig. 11. There are many parallels. The river Baphyras in Pieria, for instance, had deposited so much silt that the distance from Dium to the sea has increased from 1 kilometre to 3 kilometres between 169 B.C. and the present day.[39]

We may take some points in Arrian's account which become clearer now that we have described the terrain. When Darius held the north bank of the river, looking south, he placed 20,000 men "on the mountain to his left" and some of these later found themselves in the rear of Alexander's right wing (2.8.7). They were evidently stationed on what I have called the sickle of higher ground and enclosed the eastern part of the "dead ground," where Alexander's right wing became deployed. For Arrian says (2.8.7) that "the mountain where they were drawn up had recesses in places to some depth and was somewhat like a bay on a sea-coast; and then it advanced at a curve, so that men placed on the slopes were behind the right wing of Alexander" (see Figure 11).

In the middle part of the river's course, where Darius placed himself for battle, the attacking Macedonian infantrymen "found in many places precipitous banks and were unable to keep formation or maintain the line of the phalanx" (A. 2.10.5). On the other hand, Darius could not see the dead ground, and this is why he was unaware of the last changes which Alexander made in his order of battle (A. 2.9.1; cf. C. 3.11.3). Lastly, near the coast the Persian cavalry operated freely, and the Thessalian squadrons practised their wheeling tactics in formation (A. 2.11.2 and Curtius 3.11.13–14); for the ground here was free and unencumbered.

Darius was in camp at the Pinarus river for more than thirty-six hours before Alexander's army appeared. His choice of the Pinarus position was therefore deliberate. It may seem to us that he could have put his superior numbers to better effect by positioning himself on either of the rivers father north, the Uzerli Cayi or the Deli Cayi, because the distances there between coast and mountainside were almost twice as much as at the Payas river, and his cavalry forces in particular would have had more space to manoeuvre. But the banks of these rivers lacked the runs of precipitous places which we have seen at the Payas river. We must conclude then that Darius preferred to man these precipitous places even at the cost of being unable to put his superior numbers to the best effect. How did he intend to use these places? Evidently as means of defence for the infantry which he placed on the north bank; which is clear from the fact that he had stockades built on such accessible places as occurred between the precipitous ones. The plan then was to hold the centre by the defensive action of Darius' best infantry, fighting against the only force which could attack them frontally, the Macedonian phalanx. Curtius was then correct in saying that Darius believed the chief strength of the Macedonian army to be its phalanx (3.10.11, *phalangem Macedonici exercitus robur*). The very erection of the stockades meant that Darius did not intend his best infantry to take the offensive. Callisthenes made a similar point (Polybius I2.I7.6).

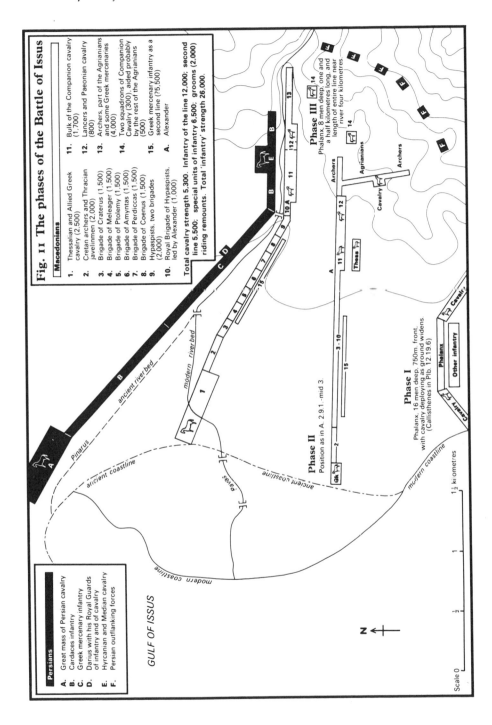

Fig. 11 The phases of the Battle of Issus

Macedonians

1. Thessalian and Allied Greek cavalry (2,500)
2. Cretan archers and Thracian javelinmen (2,000)
3. Brigade of Craterus (1,500)
4. Brigade of Meleager (1,500)
5. Brigade of Ptolemy (1,500)
6. Brigade of Amyntas (1,500)
7. Brigade of Perdiccas (1,500)
8. Brigade of Coenus (1,500)
9. Hypaspists, two brigades (2,000)
10. Royal Brigade of Hypaspists, led by Alexander (1,000)
11. Bulk of the Companion cavalry (1,700)
12. Lancers and Paeonian cavalry (800)
13. Archers, part of the Agrianians and some Greek mercenaries (4,000)
14. Two squadrons of Companion Cavalry (300), aided probably by the rest of the Agrianians (500)
15. Greek mercenary infantry as a second line (75,500)
A. Alexander

Total cavalry strength 5,300. Infantry of the line 12,000: second line 5,500; special units of infantry 6,500; grooms (2,000) riding remounts. Total 'infantry' strength 26,000.

Persians

A. Great mass of Persian cavalry
B. Cardaces infantry
C. Greek mercenary infantry
D. Darius with his Royal Guards of infantry and of cavalry
E. Hyrcanian and Median cavalry
F. Persian outflanking forces

GULF OF ISSUS

Phase I
Phalanx, 16 men deep, 750m. front, with cavalry deploying as ground widens. (Callisthenes in Plb. 12.19.6)

Phase II
Position as in A. 2.9.1.–mid 3.

Phase III
Phalanx, 8 men deep, one and a half kilometres long, and length of entire line near river four kilometres.

Scale 0   ½   1   1½ kilometres

The best infantry, being heavy-armed, were the Greek mercenaries (30,000 according to Callisthenes); next came their Persian imitators, the Cardaces (60,000 according to Arrian). When the whole force was encamped, before the Macedonian army appeared, Darius had his cavalry on the right near the sea, then the Greek mercenaries along the river, and then the Cardaces (Callisthenes in Polybius I2.I7.7; also A. 2.8.6). When the enemy first began to approach, Darius sent across the river towards them a cavalry force of 30,000 and a light-armed infantry force to the number of 20,000. One effect of this was to screen Darius' rearrangement of the infantry, which is mentioned by Callisthenes but not by Arrian. Darius summoned the Greek mercenaries to the centre where he stationed himself (Polybius 12.18.9); presumably he moved part of the Cardaces to the position vacated by the Greeks, i.e., to the right wing of the infantry line, next to the cavalry. Thus he put himself and his finest infantry in the most defensible place. There was also with him the 3,000-man Royal Cavalry Guard. The revised positions, as indicated by Callisthenes (Polybius I2.I8.9), are shown in Figure 11.

In advance of his left wing Darius placed troops on the foothills which curved round in the shape of a sickle. They were in position before the Macedonian army reached the point of the sickle. When the enemy came closer, Darius recalled his cavalry by signal and stationed the majority on the right of the phalanx and a part only on its left. But even of this part he withdrew most and reallocated them to his right wing, the reason being that they were cramped for suitable space on the left wing (A. 2.8.I0–II). We learn from Curtius (3.9.5) that the cavalry who stayed there were Hyrcanians, Medes, and a heterogeneous squadron. They fitted between two groups of Cardaces (A. 2.8.6).[40]

The Persian order of battle, in its final form, is shown on Figure 11, apart from archers, slingers, and other skirmishers (C. 3.9.1–5). Darius clearly intended to deliver an attack with the cavalry massed on his right by the sea, and at the same time to deliver a left hook with the forces on the sickle-shaped high ground taking the enemy in the flank and partly in the rear. Meanwhile his phalanx had to hold firm and keep the Macedonian phalanx at bay. Success against both wings or even one wing would enable the successful troops to take the Macedonians in the rear.

Let us turn now to Alexander. On the day before the battle he learned from the Companions who rowed into the bay of Payas that the order of the encamped troops from coast to mountainside was cavalry, Greek mercenaries, and "peltasts," who were Cardaces or others. Just before dawn, when he was mustering his army near Jonah's Pass, he sent horsemen off to reconnoitre. The column of march formed at dawn. It was led by the phalangites, 12,000 strong. When the strip between the sea and the mountainside became a kilometre or so, the column deployed into a front of 375 men and a depth of 32 men. When the strip widened to two kilometres, the front changed to 750 men and the depth to 16 men (Callisthenes in Polybius 12.19.6). At about the time of the change-over, the horsemen returned to report what they had seen at dawn, namely that the Persian army was standing to arms in the order of encampment as reported on the previous day, and that some troops were moving on the higher ground of the mountainside south of the Pinarus river. As the march continued, Alexander riding ahead saw the 30,000 Persian cavalry and the 20,000 light-armed coming towards him. But they were soon recalled by Darius and withdrew north of the river.

When the Macedonian phalanx, sixteen men deep, passed the tip of the sickle-shaped high ground, it began to enter the flat area of the dead ground and its extension to the coast. Here the front of the phalanx was extended to 1,500 men and the depth reduced to eight men, the normal depth for engaging an army of hoplites; and he was able also to deploy his cavalry. Alexander himself rode immediately on the right of the phalanx. He had under his command there the Companion cavalry, the Thessalians, the Lancers and the Paeonians. He posted the Greek cavalry and the allied cavalry on the left of the phalanx and put them under the command of Parmenio. A force of Cretan archers and Thracian infantry was brought forward to form a link between Parmenio's cavalry and the left of the phalanx. The remainder of the infantry marched as a second phalanx behind the Macedonian brigades (A. 2.9.3).

From this point, perhaps two kilometres from the river Payas, Alexander made his army advance very slowly, with frequent halts. There were two reasons for this. He wanted to see the final dispositions of Darius before his own men left the dead ground, in which they were out of sight of Darius and his staff. He also had time to deal with the threat to his right flank and—as he advanced—to his right rear, for he deployed a force of Agrianians, archers, and cavalrymen at a right angle to the line of his advance and ordered them to attack the enemy on the sickle-shaped higher ground (A. 2.9.2 and 4). This they did successfully.

When the right hand half of the line was about to reach the ridge where they would see and be seen by the enemy on the Payas river, Alexander made his last dispositions. He knew now the final dispositions of Darius, because he or his aides riding to the top of the ridge could watch the enemy movements. He moved the Thessalian cavalry from the right wing to the left wing, but he made them ride *behind* the phalanx, i.e., in the dead ground, so that Darius and his staff did not see the change of disposition. In the second place he filled the gap created through the withdrawal of the Thessalian cavalry by bringing forward the archers, some of the Agrianians, and some Greek mercenaries (the last from the second phalanx) and making them into an extension of the line on the right wing. He also detached two squadrons of Companion cavalry and sent them to a position on the right which they were to reach unobserved by moving *behind* other troops (A. 2.9.3–4). He did this, says Arrian, because his right wing up to that point was not strong and was in danger of being much outflanked by the longer Persian line. He posted 300 cavalrymen, evidently those of the two squadrons of Companion cavalry, to his right rear to deal with any threat from the enemy on the sickle-shaped piece of high ground.

The front men of the Macedonian army came slowly over the top of the ridge and across the level ground near the coast in the final order of battle, which is shown in Fig. 11. They were in perfect line, cavalrymen and infantrymen,[41] as on a parade ground. They halted at the order of Alexander. He rode along the front of the line, some four kilometres in length. While he harangued the troops, the enemy made no attempt to attack. When his 31,000 or so men roared their approval, he returned to his position on the right of the phalanx, and the slow advance was resumed "step by step" (A. 2.I0.3). As the line came within range of the Persian archers on the far bank of the river, some eighty metres away, the Royal Infantry Guard, led by Alexander on foot, charged "at the double" into and through the river to hurl themselves upon a battalion of Cardaces, the Hyrcanian and Median cavalry being on the Cardaces' left (Alexander crossed the river at a place between Figs. 25 and 26).

We must pause to emphasise the point that the charge was on foot and not on horseback. The expression "dromo" which I have translated "at the double" is generally used of an infantry charge, though not exclusively. More decisive is the nature of the ground. Cavalry at the charge would have broken the horses' legs in the boulder-strewn riverbed described above. But Alexander, his entourage, and the Royal Brigade of Hypaspists (A. 2.8.3) could pick their way at the run through the riverbed and emerge in line on the far side. It was, indeed, an axiom of ancient warfare that cavalry never delivered a frontal charge on an infantry line. Scholars have assumed this to be an exception, because the Cardaces were Persians, albeit trained as hoplites (A. 2.8.6); but there is no need to postulate such an invidious exception.

As in the case of the other battles, the attention of the narrator and so of the reader is focussed upon the doings of Alexander and any unit he is leading. We hear less of what happened in other parts of the battlefield. Of course, once the two lines were locked in conflict, no one had an overall knowledge of what was happening, far less any overall control. Alexander had anticipated this by decentralising the command in advance: he had given to Parmenio command of the entire left half of the line with orders not to lose contact with the coast (i.e., not to be outflanked), and within that command he had given command of the left half of the phalanx to Craterus, himself commander of the leftmost brigade of phalangites (A. 2.8.4).[42] Alexander retained command of the

entire right half of the line, both infantry and cavalry. He led the Royal
Infantry Guard in the initial charge, and later, as we shall see, a group of
Companion cavalry. As he was himself to be a combatant, he must have
given his orders to unit commanders in the right half of the line before
he had led the charge. We may assume that what ensued in this part of
the line came about through the execution of these orders.

Alexander and his Royal Infantry Guard succeeded brilliantly. They
punched a hole through the line of Cardaces, and as they did so the Hypaspists, Coenus' battalion, and Perdiccas' battalion were coming into
action against the Cardaces (up to almost the middle of the Persian line),
and on Alexander's right the Companion Cavalry crossed the wide river
bed in their own time and attacked the Hyrcanian and Median cavalry.
Further to the right, lancers, Paeonians, Agrianian infantry, and archers
swept into action, outflanking and overwhelming their opponents.
After some fighting[43] the whole of the Persian left wing gave way and
fled. The task of Alexander's right wing was now to swing left and
attack the Persian centre on the flank and in the rear; and he himself,
now mounted, went first with his own Companions and the leading
squadron of cavalry, forcing his way through the disrupted battalions of
Cardaces towards Darius and his Royal Cavalry Guard, conspicuous
among the sea of infantrymen (see Figure 33).

Meanwhile the left half of the Macedonian line was in considerable
difficulty. Whereas Alexander had taken the initiative on his right, the
cavalry of the Persian right had crossed the river and attacked the Greek
and Thessalian cavalry under Parmenio. Although the Persian cavalry
far outnumbered their opponents in this part of the field, the actual front
was so narrow that it is doubtful whether there was much disparity at
first between the numbers effectively engaged. Squadrons of heavy Persian cavalry, in which man and horse were both protected by corselets
of metal discs, overbore one Thessalian squadron by the weight of its
charge; but other Thessalian squadrons, being quicker in movement,
and using the wider space behind their infantry for regrouping, outmanoeuvred and slaughtered the Persians.

As the limitless Persian reserves came through the gap, the cavalry
battle became very fierce. The connecting link of infantry seems to have
held its own, but the four battalions of the left half of the Macedonian
phalanx had to deal not only with some beetling cliffs on both sides of
the river and some stockades on the far side but also with the opposing
Greek mercenaries, whose fighting quality was high (their superior
numbers was not a factor, since the limited space made the numbers
equal in the first eight files). It was not possible for the Macedonians to
maintain the phalanx line either in getting down into the riverbed or in
forcing their way up the accessible parts of the opposite bank and
through the stockades. Whenever a group of Macedonians established a

bridgehead on the north bank, the Greeks charged them and tried to hurl them back into the river.

Both sides fought with a bitterness in which racial animosity played its part. One battalion commander, Ptolemy son of Seleucus, and 120 phalangites lost their lives in this struggle. There was also some dislocation on the right half of the phalanx line, where a sudden shift to the right had been made necessary by the impetuous charge of Alexander (A. 2.10.4–7).

While the fate of the left half of the line was hanging in the balance, Alexander was drawing near to the Persian Royal Guard. Alexander and his Companions evidently passed behind the Greek mercenaries in order to make a drive on Darius, and it was the victorious infantry Guardsmen, the Hypaspists, and the phalangites of Coenus and Perdiccas who were coming in on the flank and in the rear and mowing down the Greek mercenaries. In this way the phalangites of the left part of the line received relief, and the Greek mercenaries were in danger of being surrounded (A. 2.11.3 fin.). However, Alexander and the Companion Cavalry had pressed on towards the extreme left wing, where the Persian cavalry were at last being driven back. Aware now of the complete defeat which Darius had suffered and of Darius' own flight, the swarms of Persian cavalrymen set off at the gallop for any routes of escape through the Amanus range.

The pursuit, led by Alexander, the Companions, and the Thessalians, lasted as long as there was light. The distance covered, 200 stades (37 km) (D. 17.37.2), is that from the Payas river to Toprakkale, beyond which the enemy turned east into the hills. Alexander did not submit his tired horses to pursuit in the hills as darkness was falling. This is another indication that the Payas is to be identified with the Pinarus; for if the Deli Cayi is proposed, he had to carry the pursuit into the hills for some ten kilometres. The pursuit was directed not against the Greek mercenaries (who escaped in large organised units) but against the Persian Empire's élite, the cavalrymen of the central and eastern satrapies, and Darius himself. The losses in men and mounts on the Persian side were very great, some narrow defiles being filled with their corpses; but Darius rode through the night and collected survivors next day, including 4,000 Greek mercenaries, before crossing the Euphrates to safety. Alexander lost 150 cavalrymen and 302 infantrymen; he was one of the 4,500 wounded. The proportion of killed to wounded is a testimony to the effectiveness of protective armour.

To criticise Darius is not difficult. The position which he chose for the inevitable battle had grave defects. It was too narrow for the full deployment even of his best troops, let alone the mob of light-armed who became engaged only in the horrors of the flight. For example, if the 30,000

Greek mercenaries had been used in the same depth as the 12,000 Macedonian phalangites, they would have had a front of 3.75 kilometres, whereas in fact they were concentrated beside the king with a front of probably less than half a kilometre. The great numbers of fine Persian cavalry had the same experience on the Persian right wing. There were more squadrons than could be used there, whereas the Persian left wing failed partly through a shortage of good Persian cavalry.

Darius' personal example, in choosing a safe place behind his centre instead of leading the left wing, may have been the sort of factor which caused the light-armed infantry on the higher ground to show so little spirit. Arrian makes criticisms on such lines. "Some freak of chance led Darius to the very place where he did not derive any great advantage from his cavalry or from his great number of men, missiles and arrows" (2.6.6). "God put it into the mind of Darius to bring his own forces, from wider ground into a narrow space, where the great numbers of the Persians were useless but the distance was just right for the deployment of the Macedonians" (2.7.3).

In the preliminary phase Darius seems to have made changes of disposition rather through indecision or miscalculation than for tactical reasons. It was the view of Callisthenes that Darius meant at first to fight on his left wing where he would face Alexander if Alexander followed the usual practice of Greek commanders, but that later he decided otherwise and moved to the centre where he held a backward position (Polybius I2.22.2; C. 3.9.4). If he thought he and his staff could direct the course of the battle better from there, once action started, he was mistaken. Again, his motive for moving the Greek mercenaries from the right wing, where they had the best chance of breaking and outflanking the left wing of the Macedonian phalanx, seemed tactically unwise. Perhaps the transfer of them to the centre gave him a greater sense of security. The moving of cavalry units from one wing to another seems to have been due to changes of mind or miscalculation, and the final result was to weaken the left wing which had to face the superb Companion Cavalry.

Alexander might well have been disconcerted when he realised that his sick and wounded had been captured, his lines of supply cut, and his return barred by an army of superior numbers in a strong defensive position. However, when he called a meeting of his commanders, he said they had grounds for confidence. Then he ordered his army to take their main meal—the last they were to have for some twenty-four hours. When night fell, he led the army back to Jonah's Pass. There, after a few hours of sleep, they began a slow confident march down towards the enemy. The deployment in three stages from a marching column to a moving line of battle was a superb piece of drill, executed by more than 30,000 men, and was itself a demonstration of the cohesion and integration of the various arms and races in Alexander's army. Thus the men realised their interdependence and their interdependability on the eve of action.

Whereas Darius failed to use so many of his men, Alexander used his men with a precise economy. The threat to his right wing and right rear was contained finally by 300 cavalrymen. The phalanx, about one and a half kilometres in length, was of the standard depth, eight men, although the enemy infantry was in much greater depth. The right number of Companion Cavalry to break through the opposing Persian cavalry was so assessed that two squadrons could be detached to ensure the outflanking of the Persian left wing. The distribution of his 5,000 or so cavalry between the two wings when they faced some 30,000 Persian cavalry was so capably calculated that he ensured success on his right and held the enemy on his left. It is not possible to fault his final order of battle, either in theory or in practice, and that is a very remarkable thing when we realise that Alexander developed it stage by stage during a slow but continuous march, in such a way that it fitted the final dispositions of the enemy. He made the last moves, and he made them so that they were not seen by Darius and his staff.

The decentralisation of command was another thing which distinguished Alexander from Darius. The authority entrusted in advance to Parmenio enabled him to hold together the hard-pressed left wing, and that entrusted to Craterus enabled him to coordinate the four battalions which were under severe pressure, whereas the Persian left wing seems to have disintegrated rapidly. But this was only possible because Alexander's planning mind gave him a clear idea of the way in which the whole action would develop. "It turned out as Alexander supposed" (Arrian 2.10.4).

"Alexander carried out the duties of a soldier no less than those of a commander" (C. 3.11.7). Even in the more remote relationships of modern warfare the known courage in action of a Field Marshal—Birdwood, Montgomery, Harding for instance—is an inspiration to officers and men, a challenge to emulation. Alexander had the fearlessness of the born fighter. In the deadly struggle of the Macedonian infantry against the Greek mercenaries on the precipitous banks "it was the conspicuous success of Alexander in action which made the Macedonians determined not to fall behind him and not to dim the glorious record of the phalanx, famed as invincible up to that day" (A. 2.10.6).

Both as a commander and as a fighter, whether on foot or on horse, Alexander knew his officers and men with a personal intimacy which it is impossible to conceive as ever existing between the Great King of Persia and his subjects. "When the two armies were already close to one another, then Alexander rode all the same along the line, calling upon his men to be courageous and naming with the appropriate honours those of the commanders, squadron-leaders, captains, and mercenaries who were widely known for their reputation or for some act of prowess. And on all sides the shout came to him: 'do not delay but charge upon the enemy'" (A. 2.10.2). When he led the charge of the Royal Guard, he knew that every man in the army would play his part in the ensuing action.

For our account we have drawn almost exclusively on the data of Callisthenes, as preserved by Polybius, and on the narrative of Arrian, whose chief source in military matters, Ptolemy, derived his information about the Macedonian battle-order and the orders and acts of Alexander from the *King's Journal*, at least in our opinion. A very different version is given by Diodorus (17.33–34), who made Alexander arrange his cavalry all along the front of his army and place his infantry-phalanx behind in reserve (33.1); he then provided a cavalry battle, which resulted in the flight of Darius, and thereafter an infantry battle which was of short duration (34.9). The pattern is familiar from Diodorus' account of the battle of the Granicus, already discussed. Here too Cleitarchus, who is the most probable source, has waved his fairy wand and made the Pinarus river disappear from the battlefield. Here too we find the epic manner and the Homeric form of fighting: missiles fly so thick that their impetus is impaired and every hand-to-hand blow finds a mark in so dense a mass of contestants; but there is still room for the champions to show their prowess—Oxathres for instance facing Alexander. Darius' transfer from one chariot to another chariot in the press of battle is a ludicrous fantasy. The version is as worthless to the historian as that of the Granicus battle.

Curtius has provided a confused version which seems to arise from the conflation of two accounts. Thus Darius crosses the Pinarus river and advances southwards (3.8.16), but that river is still between Darius and Alexander when they march towards one another later on in the account (3.8.28). Curtius' description of the order of march during Alexander's descent from the pass (3.9.7-12) was taken no doubt from Callisthenes. Next comes a cavalry battle, as in Diodorus, but with more details, some of which have a different timing in Arrian's account (3.11.1-3); an epic description of fighting so crowded that weapons could not be poised, and of missiles so numerous that they got in each other's way; combat sword to sword, buckler to buckler, foot to foot, as with pairs of opposing champions; finally Oxathres in combat with Alexander, a pile of corpses in front of Darius, and the same Persian nobles killed (as in D. 17.34.4-5). These and other points such as the high praise of the Thessalian cavalry indicate that Curtius and Diodorus had a common source, probably Cleitarchus. That Greek writers felt free to alter the record or just invent for sensational effect should not surprise us, when we note that Chares, a courtier of Alexander, portrayed a personal combat between Darius and Alexander. Others had no interest in military matters; Plutarch felt it enough to mention Alexander's outflanking of the enemy's right. (*OxyP* I798.44 and the *Fragmentum Sabbaiticum* 3 were even more perfunctory.)

All the accounts we have mentioned were written at a later date, when the myth of Alexander's invincibility was already established. They conceal the fact that only a freak of chance prevented Darius from cutting Alexander's forces in two, and that only the folly of Darius gave Alexander the opportunity to fight under favourable conditions and recover from being outmanoeuvred. The victory was commemorated later by the foundation of Alexandria ad Issum, named in relation to the Gulf of Issus rather than to the town of Issus; for the new city was placed where Iskenderun (previously Alexandretta) now is.

As usual, Alexander visited the wounded and held a ceremonial funeral of the fallen, which was attended by the army on parade in battle-order. In his address he praised individual actions, seen or reported, and he announced generous bounties to the families of the dead. Notable Persians too were interred with all due honour. He gave thanks to the gods, erecting altars on the bank of the Pinarus to Zeus, Heracles, and Athena, to whom he had prayed at Magarsus. The victory was celebrated by magnificent gold coins with the head of Athena on the face, and, on the reverse, a winged Victory; one emblem on the reverse, a *stylis*, referred to the daring Companions who had "singed Darius' beard" by rowing into the mouth of the Pinarus and observing his dispositions.[44]

On this occasion he did not send spoils to Greece, as he had done after his victory at the Granicus river. Perhaps the Council of the Greek League had failed to reinforce the fleet at the Hellespont, as he had ordered, and he may have been disconcerted by the response of many Greek states to the advances of Pharnabazus. Some Greek envoys who were captured in Persian company were treated individually: Thebans released as having sought Persian help justifiably after the sacking of their city, an Athenian Iphicrates kept but honoured as son of the Iphicrates who had served Macedonia well, and a Spartan kept under guard but released later. By now he had completed the liberation of the Greek cities in western Asia, and Greek susceptibilities were less in his mind as he faced the future.

(C) THE OCCUPATION OF THE SOUTHWESTERN SATRAPIES
(see Figure 12)

The victory at Issus opened up alternative courses: to pursue Darius into the Persian homeland before another army could be recruited, or to "master the Persian fleet from the land," a policy enunciated first at Miletus. Pursuit must have been tempting; for Alexander could have advanced rapidly into Babylonia without encountering any serious opposition. But he judged it essential first to conquer the seaboard of the Eastern Mediterranean, so that the Persian fleet would collapse cut off from its bases. At the time of the battle Pharnabazus with the main fleet of 100 ships had been at Siphnos conferring with Agis, king of Sparta, who planned to go to war with Macedon and requested ships, men and money. Other squadrons lay at Cos and Halicarnassus, and a Persian garrison held Chios, the main base. The news of Darius' defeat drew Pharnabazus back to Chios, and Agis got no more than ten ships and thirty talents, with which he tried to win support in Crete (see Fig. 2).

Men looked towards the east, as Alexander marched through north Syria, while Parmenio captured Darius' treasure and the wives of many Persian commanders at Damascus. Alexander then came down from Homs via Krak des Chevaliers to the first Phoenician cities—Aradus (Arvad), Marathus and others—in the realm of Gerostratus, who was serving with the Persian fleet. They all submitted. Byblus (Gebal) and Sidon (Saida) followed suit. Envoys from Sidon's rival, Tyre, offered to obey Alexander's orders. He asked to enter the city and sacrifice to Heracles (with whom the Tyrian god Melkart was identified); consent would mean that they accepted him as their overlord. The envoys reported his request. The people of Tyre refused, believing their fortified island to be impregnable and the issue of the war to be undecided. Alexander explained to his officers (though not in the *obiter dicta* of A. 2.17) why it was necessary to undertake the Herculean task of capturing Tyre. In fact it cost him some seven months. But it was time well spent. His strategic concept was correct: to consolidate a base of operations which included Greece and the Aegean as well as the Eastern Mediterranean seaboard, before he embarked on a major campaign against Persia.

That Alexander did in fact regard his march south as merely a preliminary to the invasion of the Persian homeland was made apparent during his negotiations with Darius. At Issus the tent of Darius was the personal spoil of Alexander, and in it the womenfolk and children of Darius were found to be weeping for his supposed death. Alexander sent Leonnatus, a member of his own royal house, to tell them Darius was alive and Alexander would treat them as royal personages. "So Ptolemy and Aristobulus," writes Arrian. He then retails the following story for which he does not vouch (it is found also in Diodorus, Curtius, and Plutarch). On the following day, when Alexander and Hephaestion, dressed alike, entered the tent, the Queen Mother did obeisance to Hephaestion as the taller and was much embarrassed when an attendant told her she was mistaken. "No mistake has been made," said Alexander, "for Hephaestion too is an Alexander."

The story, probably untrue, was certainly in character. Then and thereafter Alexander treated the royal family with compassion and respect. Thus the ladies were in his charge, when envoys came to Marathus from Darius, asking for their restoration and offering friendship and alliance in return. Alexander's letter in reply listed the wrongdoings of Persia and Darius, including an accusation of complicity in the murder of Philip; Alexander claimed that the gods had given him territory in Asia, and he represented the Persian survivors of the battles as his willing subjects.

> You must come to me since I am Lord of all Asia. . . . and in future send to me as the king of Asia and tell me of your needs, addressing me not as an equal but as master of all your possessions. Otherwise, I shall deal with you as a miscreant. If you dispute the kingship, stay and fight and do not run away, since I shall go wherever you are.[45]

Alexander made a total demand: all Asia. There is no suggestion that Persia is to pay tribute to "the Macedones" (as Aspendus had to do), or to be subject to Macedonians and Greeks, or that Alexander intends to dethrone Darius and enthrone himself as king of Persia. The matter in dispute is the kingship of Asia, a position which kings of Persia had claimed as their perogative; if, then, Darius makes that claim, he must stand and fight. Otherwise he can come to Alexander, recover his family and be treated with generosity.

A different version, derived by Curtius from some other source, is much inferior to that of Arrian which I have given above. The original letter was certainly recorded in the *King's Journal*. If I am correct in supposing that Arrian got his version (genuine in substance, not verbatim) through Ptolemy from that *Journal*, then the personal aims of Alexander in the winter of 333–332 B.C. are plain.

Descriptions of the siege of Tyre, themselves clearly abbreviations of longer versions, have survived in Arrian and in Diodorus and Curtius, the last two sharing points in common, such as a marine monster, omens, and crucifixion of 2,000 Tyrians after the fall of the city, which seem to be improbable. In any case the course and the nature of the siege and the defence are reasonably certain.

The Tyrians were an exceptionally able and brave people, excelling in naval warfare, fortification and artillery, and their city, half a mile offshore on an island-fortress, was thought to be impregnable. The circuit-wall round the coast was of masonry set in gypsum—not dry masonry in the Greek manner—and it stood 150 feet high (like the tower at Halicarnassus) where it faced the mainland. The population was of the order of 50,000, more than enough to man the circuit-wall which was nearly

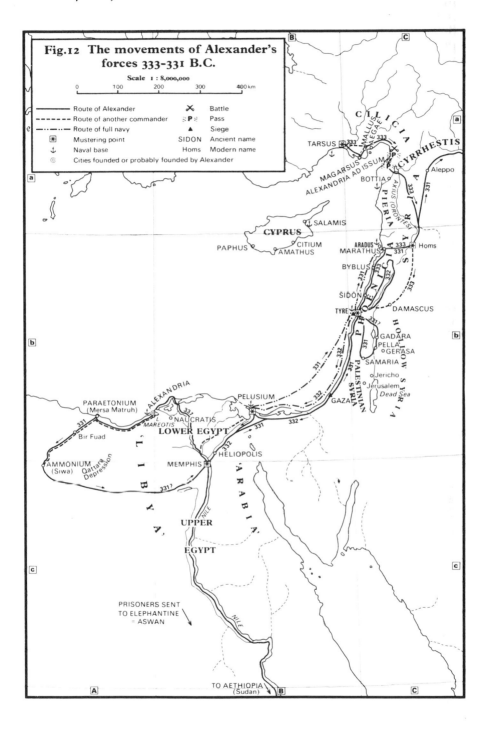

Fig.12 The movements of Alexander's forces 333-331 B.C.

Scale 1 : 8,000,000

0   100   200   300   400 km

——————— Route of Alexander
--------- Route of another commander
-·-·-·-·- Route of full navy
⊞ Mustering point
↓ Naval base
◎ Cities founded or probably founded by Alexander

✕ Battle
P Pass
▲ Siege
SIDON Ancient name
Homs Modern name

three miles long, and the city was well stocked with supplies and materials of war. Although a squadron from Tyre was away with the Persian fleet in the Aegean, the Tyrians still had eighty triremes; and they expected help from Carthage, a colony of Tyre. Moreover, the Persian fleet was supreme in the Aegean. All the odds seemed to be in favour of Tyre.

Alexander began in January 332 B.C. to build a 200-foot wide mole from the mainland towards the island (the basis of the present isthmus), employing soldiers and natives alike. When the mole approached the island and the water deepened to some eighteen feet, the Tyrians went into action with catapults from the wall and missiles from their ships. Work on the mole stopped until two 150-foot towers were built with Lebanese timber, protected on one side with raw hides against incendiary arrows. These were hauled to the top of the mole-end, so that catapultists from the top could sweep the parapet of the wall and from lower stories attack the ships with their missiles. With great ingenuity and daring some Tyrians towed a large fire-ship to the mole-end and others landed from small boats elsewhere on the mole to add fuel to the flames. All the siege material was destroyed, and the Tyrians captured some Macedonians whom they disabled in the water. Alexander started to build a wider mole, beginning from the mainland end.

The second phase of the siege began pursuant to Alexander's policy of "defeating the Persian fleet on land"; for the Phoenician squadrons of the Persian fleet, Tyrians apart, came over to join him, the Cyprian squadrons followed suit, and other ships (following the mainland coast which his forces held) arrived from Lycia, Rhodes, Soli, and Mallus. One even got to him from Macedonia, and soon afterwards 4,000 mercenaries arrived by sea from the Peloponnese. Now he had more than 200 ships. The Tyrians refused battle at sea, and they blocked their two harbours, which Alexander then blockaded, placing his fleet by the nearby mole. Thereafter he pushed his wider mole to within spear's throw of the wall, but at the same time he probed other parts of the wall by bringing his ships as close as possible.

He used horse-transporters, triremes, and triangular platforms, made by tying two quadriremes, bows together and joining their sterns with long beams. Anchoring the vessels was one problem, for the Tyrians cut the ropes, either using armoured boats or diving underwater, until the Macedonians replaced the ropes with chains. Another difficulty was caused by great rocks dropped by the Tyrians to snag the approaches; these were raised by loops of rope suspended from yard-arms and dumped elsewhere. The closer they got to the wall, the more the Macedonians suffered from deluges of red-hot sand and volleys of missiles.

As the pressure was now mounting, the Tyrians made a surprise sortie at midday against the Cyprian ships which lay at anchor, mostly unmanned. They succeeded there, but before they could get back they were defeated by Alexander who manned ships rapidly, sailed round the island and caught them unawares. They had no longer any hope of escape or of relief from Carthage and Persia. Yet the defenders invented new ways of resistance, building wooden towers on top of their 150-foot wall, mounting spin-wheels to intercept artillery fire, hanging padded bolsters to weaken the effect of stones hurled by the stone-throwers against the wall, and cutting the ropes of the rams with sickles on long poles. The Macedonians suffered month after month from enemy missiles and from wind and weather which undid much of their work, but in the end they devised not only a form of decked-over platform on which a powerful ram could be wielded by a large number of men but also a way of anchoring it firmly against the wall. Once this method was in use, they cracked a length of wall on the south side of the island.

On a July day with a calm sea Alexander delivered attacks all round the island, but the concentrations were against the two harbours and the cracked wall, where he and his men brought up the ram-carrying ships, opened a large breach, rowed in with gangway-dropping ships and forced a way onto the battered wall. The assault-troops were Hypaspists led by Admetus, who reached the wall first and was killed, and one of the *asthetairoi* brigades, that of Coenus from Elimeotis. Alexander and his personal companions were on the heels of Admetus and established a bridgehead, from which they moved into the city.

Meanwhile at one of the harbours the Cyprians took possession and advanced into the city from that side. The Tyrians concentrated their forces and street fighting ensued. "The Macedonians went to all lengths in their rage, embittered by the length of the siege and by the Tyrians having killed Macedonian prisoners in the sight of the army, hurling them from the 150-foot wall into the sea."

These words are from Arrian. He gave the Tyrian losses at the end as 8,000 killed, and the Macedonian throughout the siege as about 400; but the wounded and maimed Macedonians were probably over a thousand. Suppliants at the altar of Heracles were spared, many escaped to the Phoenician towns, especially Sidon, and the rest of the people, around 30,000, were sold as slaves. Alexander made a lavish sacrifice to Heracles in accordance with his original request. Honours were paid to Heracles and to the Macedonian dead by the military and naval forces in a ceremonial review and in athletic contests.

The siege had tested to the full the tenacity and the fighting spirit of both sides but especially that of the Macedonians.[46] When Alexander had the Tyrian fleet under blockade, he might have been tempted to abandon the siege, as he had just lost his towers and his siege equipment, but he knew that local superiority at sea was not enough; for the rest of the Persian fleet was wintering in the Aegean and might sail to the relief of Tyre. The final assault was brilliantly planned. Against a defending force of more than 10,000 Alexander could bring only two ships at a time to the main point of attack, and these delivered only the first wave of the Royal Brigade of Hypaspists (1,000 in all) and of the phalanx-brigade (1,500) which was named first in the orders of the day. Even when driven off this part of the defences, the Tyrians far outnumbered the Macedonians and had a good chance of defeating them before reinforcements could be brought up by sea.

Like Thebes, Tyre had bitter enemies in the neighbouring city-states, and it was the Cyprians and to a lesser extent the other Phoenicians who made victory possible, not only at sea but in the final assault. Whether the Tyrians tried to surrender is very doubtful; for the Phoenicians were fanatical fighters, as the Sidonians had shown in 345 B.C., when 40,000, it was said, burnt themselves and their houses as the city was falling to the Persians. Whether Alexander could have stopped the street fighting is no less doubtful. In any event he fulfilled his inexorable purpose, to eliminate Tyre as a naval base.

When he advanced southwards with fleet and army together, he met resistance at Gaza, Phoenicia's southernmost city, which commanded the entry to the route through the desert to Egypt. The engineers who had made victory possible at Tyre advised Alexander that this populous and garrisoned city was impregnable, but he was only the more determined to capture it for reasons of strategy and prestige. As Gaza occupied a plateau 250 feet high and had strong walls, he decided to build a great mound of earth to the same height all round it. When it was nearing completion and had the appropriate height on the south side where the wall appeared less strong, siege-engines and towers were wheeled up, but with great difficulty and some loss of life, since they sank in the sandy soil. On the day planned for the assault an omen caused Alexander to consult his preferred seer, Aristander, whose interpretation was: "O king, you will capture the city, but this day you yourself must be on your guard." Accordingly Alexander stayed out of range when the assault began; but when the garrison sortied under covering fire and began to drive the Macedonians off the mound, he went into action with the Hypaspists and restored the situation but was wounded by a catapult bolt, which passed through shield and cuirass into his shoulder, causing much loss of blood. Although the wound was cured only with difficulty, Alexander took heart from the omen, thinking he would capture the city.

During his illness the siege-engines used at Tyre were brought by sea, and the mound was augmented so as to be uniformly 250 high and 400 yards wide all round the city. This vast earthwork, like the mole at Tyre, was constructed by the whole army working with Chinese concentration and requisitioning transport and draught-animals in the vicinity. Once the towers were positioned on the mound, the fire of the catapults drove the defenders off the parapet and covered the parties of men who undermined the wall by tunneling and those who swung the battering-rams. The defenders built wooden towers on top of their wall in response and warded off three assaults. In November 332 B.C., the second month of the siege, a fourth assault, delivered on all sides by the 12,000 infantry of the phalanx, proved successful, the first man up the ladder and onto the wall being Neoptolemus, a member of the Molossian royal family. The Persian garrison and the Gazaeans fought to the last man.[47] The number of dead was probably comparable to that at Tyre, and the women and children were likewise sold into slavery. Alexander re-peopled the site with local tribesmen, placing a garrison in it for the time being.

The successes at Halicarnassus, Tyre, and Gaza gave Alexander con-fidence to attempt the apparently impossible later. Much depended on the inventiveness of his engineers, Diades and Charias, pupils of Philip's chief engineer Polyidus, a Thessalian, and upon the craftsman-ship of carpenters and shipwrights—Macedonian, Greek and Phoeni-cian—who constructed higher towers, stronger rams and larger floating platforms than ever before. Torsion and non-torsion catapults, long lad-ders raised by block and tackle, manoeuvrable gangways, mantlets, and stone-throwers were improved and in some cases invented. The other thing on which Alexander depended was the readiness of officers and men to lead the assault on the top of a swaying ladder or dropping gang-way. This was forthcoming until late in his campaigning.

During the sailing season of 332 B.C. Macedonian admirals regained control of the Aegean area, where the Persian policy of imposing tyrants and enlisting pirates had proved most unpopular (see Figure 2). The peoples of Tenedos, Chios, and Cos rose with Macedonian help and ex-pelled the Persians, while Macedonian forces drove the Persians out of Lesbos. Pharnabazus was captured at Chios, but he escaped later. Rhodes, controlling the entry to the southeastern Aegean, placed itself under the orders of Alexander.[48] The only island even partly in Persian hands was Crete, where Agis, king of Sparta, was operating with a group of Greek mercenaries who had escaped from the battlefield of Issus. In November 332 B.C. the sea lanes were open and Alexander sent ten triremes from Gaza to Macedonia to fetch reinforcements. These successes at sea did more than the victories in Asia to alter the ambiva-lent attitude of the Greek states of the mainland. It was probably then at an autumn meeting and not at the earlier Isthmian festival that the Coun-cil of the Greek League voted to crown Alexander with a golden crown for his victory at Issus and his services as hegemon in the cause of Greek liberty. Better late than never.

In the course of the year many operations, of which we know little since the king was not personally involved, were undertaken to consolidate and extend the areas under Macedonian control. In Asia Minor, Antigonus Monophthalmus, satrap of Greater Phrygia, beat off some Persian attacks and invaded Paphlagonia (north of Ankara), Lycaonia (north of Karaman in the Konya region), and Cappadocia, inland of Cilicia. While Alexander was taking control of the fertile and then populous Syrian plain, Parmenio was sent ahead with the Thessalian cavalry to capture Damascus, which became a Macedonian base. While Alexander was on the Phoenician coast, Parmenio was operating with the bulk of the cavalry forces in the interior, removing all signs of Persian rule and requiring submission to Alexander.

During a pause in the siege of Tyre, Alexander conducted a ten-day campaign with some cavalry, the Hypaspists, the Agrianians, and the archers in the valley of Ba'albek between the Lebanon and the Anti-Lebanon ranges. During this campaign a story about Alexander is told by Chares, a court official. When the troops were attacking the mountaineers of the Anti-Lebanon range, Alexander went out alone at night, killed two enemy soldiers at their camp fire and returned with a burning brand, so that his companions could light a fire themselves. The story is certainly untrue, since the Bodyguards and the pages were always with the king, but it is of a piece with other such stories that appeal to the common man.[49]

The consolidation of Alexander's control over new territories was marked by the appointment of satraps: Socrates of Cilicia, Philotas of Phoenicia (with Tyre as its centre), Arimmas of Syria (probably Aleppo to Homs), and Andromachus of "Hollow Syria," i.e., low-lying Syria, which probably comprised the Ba'albek valley, Damascus, and the Jordan rift to the Dead Sea. This last area became known to the Macedonians; for the balsam woods of Jericho were mentioned (Pliny *NH* I2.25.117). By incorporating these, the western parts of the Fertile Crescent, Alexander brought his domains up to the desert which separated Syria from Mesopotamia. The region southwest and west of the Jordan rift was known as "Palestinian Syria," extending from the hill-country round Nablus, then called Samaria, to as far as Gaza. When Alexander was besieging Tyre, he demanded allegiance and supplies from the High Priest of the Jews at Jerusalem, and no doubt he obtained them without difficulty.[50]

The march from Gaza to Egypt, across nearly 140 miles of the Sinai desert, was carried out with the most careful planning. The fleet, sailing along the coast for most of the way, carried the heavy gear, supplies, and water (of which the horses needed a great quantity); and the men, the wagons, and the draught-animals overcame hard conditions even in late November. The fleet then went ahead to occupy Pelusium, the first

Egyptian fortress, situated by the eastern mouth of the Nile (near Port Said). The army reached Pelusium unopposed on the seventh day, having averaged over twenty miles a day. The Egyptians issued in crowds to welcome Alexander as their liberator from Persian rule, so recently reimposed in 343 B.C., a rule which had been marked by the plundering of temples and undisciplined behaviour of mercenary troops. Indeed Amyntas, the Macedonian deserter who had brought a corps of Greek mercenaries to Egypt after the battle of Issus, had just been killed in a native uprising. No opposition was offered to Alexander as he marched to Heliopolis (near Cairo) and joined his fleet on the Nile. Crossing the river, he advanced to Memphis, where the Persian satrap formally surrendered Egypt to him. The richest country on the Mediterranean coast had come into his possession without the loss of a Macedonian or an Egyptian life. In the ensuing winter envoys from Cyrene brought gifts and concluded with Alexander a treaty of friendship and alliance. The whole of the eastern Mediterranean seaboard was finally in his hands.

The incompetence of Darius had been a factor in Alexander's success. We have already mentioned Darius' slowness at the outset, his folly in relying on his fleet to distract Alexander and then in weakening it by withdrawing the Greek mercenaries, and his failure to bring Alexander to battle until November 333 B.C., at Issus. Equally bad was the totally inadequate supply of money for stepping up the naval operations (while Alexander had sent 1,100 talents to his officers in the Aegean for naval purposes, Pharnabazus gave Agis only thirty talents), and the failure to reinforce the Persian garrisons in the satrapies of the southeastern Mediterranean, from which in fact Darius took troops away. By the end of 333 B.C. it was obvious that what Darius had done was too little and too late. Even then a determined offensive in 332 B.C., designed to cut the narrow waist of Alexander's position by the Gulf of Issus, would have put Darius in touch with his fleet, drawn Alexander away from Tyre and threatened his communications. Again Darius procrastinated. When his offer to pay an indemnity and cede all of the empire west of the Euphrates was refused, it was too late, at least in his opinion, to mount an offensive that year, and the mustering of an army was put off into 331 B.C.

On the other hand, Alexander's successes were neither slow nor ephemeral, and his combination of quickness and thoroughness won him the control of wide territories and huge resources. It is probable that he founded, now or in 331 B.C., a number of Macedonian cities at strategic points: Aegae on the west side of the Gulf of Issus, Alexandria ad Issum on the east side; probably a settlement Bottia near the later city Antioch on the Orontes, then renamed the Axius; Arethusa (Er Rastan) between Hama and Homs; Gadara east of Lake Tiberias; Pella (Khirbet

Fahil) near Beisan; and Gerasa (Jarash) farther east in Jordania. That Alexander founded Alexandria, Pella, and Gerasa is attested, and he had a considerable number of wounded and maimed Macedonian soldiers whom he chose to settle together with native people in these new towns. It was probably they who gave names from Macedonia to their new country, such as Pieria (the region north of Latakia), Cyrrhestis (the region of Antioch extending to the Euphrates), and other town-names such as Heraclea, Cynthus, and Beroea.[51] Moreover, his methods in contrast to those of Persia were calculated to win the native peoples to his side.

In the narrative of Arrian (2.25), the arrival of envoys from Darius was placed before the fall of Tyre, which was in July 332 B.C., and the offer was 10,000 talents for the persons of the Queen Mother, the Queen and the children, the cession of all territory west of the Euphrates, the hand of Darius' daughter, and the conclusion of a treaty of friendship and alliance. Alexander refused.

Arrian evidently did not find any details of Alexander's refusal in Ptolemy and Aristobulus, and in the case of Ptolemy the reason was presumably that the *King's Journal* merely noted that the envoys departed without achieving anything. This is not surprising as Darius' offer was simply a raise of his earlier offer, received at Marathus, and Alexander's reasons for refusing this one were as before (i.e., as stated in the letter cited by Arrian at 2.14).

However, "as a tale told by others in their accounts" (A. Preface), Arrian went on to report (2.25.2) that in a conference of the Companions Parmenio said to Alexander, "If I were Alexander, I should be content to end the war on these terms and avoid further danger," and that Alexander replied, "Were I Parmenio, I should do so, but being Alexander I shall reply to Darius as follows."

Then comes a report of the alleged reply, brief but with some points common to the letter cited by Arrian. In particular, there is the suggestion, that, if Darius will come to Alexander, he will receive generous treatment. This is spelt out more fully in an account of the negotiations in Diodorus (17.54), who tells the same story of Alexander and Parmenio and reports that if Darius will accept Alexander's order he may be "king over other rulers," thanks to the generosity of Alexander. In other words Darius will remain, it is hinted, king of the Medes and Persians and rule over them in the traditional feudal manner.

While we shall consider this last point later, the accounts in Diodorus and in Curtius (4.11) are inflated with rhetoric and less likely to be accurate than that of Arrian. Both writers shift the exchanges to shortly before the battle of Gaugamela in 331 B.C., a more dramatic moment indeed but a most unlikely one, since Darius had made immense preparations for a pitched battle and his commanders would have demanded it. The actual occasion was certainly the summer of 332 B.C. When his offer was refused, Darius began to muster a great army for a decisive campaign. The reasons for Alexander's refusal were as they had been at Marathus, and they were fortified by his confidence that Tyre would soon be captured. The conversation between Parmenio and Alexander lies probably in the realm of fiction; for the older generation of Macedonian officers might well have settled for a viable frontier with Persia, but the decision lay not with the officers, old or young, but with the king.

SOURCES

(A) and (B) A.2.4.2-12.1; P. 18-6-20; C. 3.2-11; D. 17.30-37.2; Callisthenes in Polyb. 12.17-22; Polyaenus 4.3.16; J. 11.8-9.10

(C) A. 2.12.2-27.7; P. 21, 24-25, 29.7-9; C. 3.12-13; 4.1.1-33; 4. 2-6; 4.11; D. I7.37.3-47.6; 48.2-7; 54; J. 11.9.11-11.I0.14; I2.1-4; Josephus *AJ* 11.320,325

VI

THE WIDENING HORIZON

Alexander left Gaza as King of Macedon, Hegemon of the Greek League, President-for-life of the Thessalian League and adopted son of the Carian queen, Ada, and he took on an additional *persona* in Egypt. On arriving at Memphis, the religious and secular centre of the country, he sacrificed "to the other gods and especially to Apis"; and in making these sacrifices to the gods of Egypt he was deliberately contrasting himself with two Persian kings who had slaughtered the Apis, the sacred bull of their day, and he was behaving publicly as the King of Egypt in accordance with Egyptian custom.

That he was indeed accepted as "Pharaoh" by the priests and the people of Egypt has been made certain by the survival of some hieroglyphic inscriptions which mention the following cult-titles of Alexander: "Horus, the strong prince," "King of Upper Egypt and King of Lower Egypt, beloved of Ammon and selected of Ra," and "Son of Ra," to which "Alexandros" was added. What distinguished him from preceding Pharaohs was a new title attached to his Horus-name: "He who hath laid hands on the lands of the foreigners." Thus Alexander was regarded by Egyptians as the incarnation of their greatest god. He returned the compliment by worshipping the Egyptian gods at Memphis who included Ra, Isis, Apis, and in particular the deified form of the dead bull, Osor-hapi, or in the Greek form, Sarapis, in whose precinct Imhotep, the god of healing, was regarded by Greeks as Asclepius.

What did this mean to Alexander? On grounds of political expediency, no doubt, he chose to become the legitimate king of the Egyptians, a unique people with age-old and distinctive traditions, and this entailed the concept of being a god on earth in their eyes. There is no indication that Alexander ever regarded himself outside Egypt as a god incarnate. On the other hand, it was well within the orbit of Macedonian and Greek ideas to be a son of a god and yet human, since many heroes were sons of gods in that sense, for example Heracles, the ancestor of Alexander in the royal family. Again to see Greek gods in foreign deities was a commonplace among Macedonians and Greeks alike. Macedonians gave Greek names to Paeonian and Thracian deities, and Herodotus had long ago identified Isis with Demeter. "Zeus Ammon," a fusion of a Greek and a Libyan god, was recognised and worshipped not only at the oracle of Siwah but also at Dodona in Epirus and at Aphytis in Chalcidice, shrines with which no doubt Alexander himself was familiar. There was, then, a sense in which to be called "Alexandros, son of Ra" came very close to being called "son of Zeus" in a society which was not nationalistically exclusive in its religious ideas but readily syncretistic.

On the same occasion at Memphis, Alexander held a festival of athletics and arts, which was entirely Macedonian and Greek in character. This part of the celebration had been planned in advance; for leading athletes and artists had been brought over from Greece. Later Alexander sailed down the Nile, accompanied by the Royal Squadron of Companion Cavalry and the Hypaspists, archers and Agrianians. His fleet which had sailed up from Pelusium to meet him at Memphis took him and his troops down the western outflow of the Delta to Canobus. There he sailed round Lake Mareotis and saw that the rising ground (then some four metres higher above the sea than today) was suitable for a Macedonian city, such as Pella by the outflow of the Axius. The openness and the very slight elevation of the site were much as at Dium and Pella, and he planned to fortify this site with walls, just as Philip had fortified Edessa and other cities in Macedonia.

Seized with a yearning (*pothos*) to found a new Alexandria, "he in person laid down markers for the plan of the city, where the city-centre was to be built within it, how many temples and to which gods, some being Greek but Isis being Egyptian, and where the circuit-wall was to be made. And thereupon he made sacrifice, and the sacrifice proved favourable" (A. 3.1.5). Something of Alexander's zest and vigour are conveyed by Arrian, drawing on Aristobulus. The date was probably 20 January, 331 B.C.

In marking out the line of the walls, Alexander used the meal which the soldiers carried as hard rations in their kits; Arrian said that this was *faute de mieux;* but we learn from Curtius (4.8.6), drawing evidently on Marsyas of Pella, that it was a Macedonian custom to mark the bounds of a new city with pearl-barley. A further addition by Curtius is likely to be also from Marsyas, that when flocks of birds flew down and pecked the barley, the seers prophesied the coming of many citizens and prosperity for the city. Arrian refers probably to the same incident in remarking that Aristander and other seers said the city would prosper and especially from the fruits of the earth. As Demeter was the giver of those fruits and Demeter was identified with Isis, we can see why Isis in particular among Egyptian gods and goddesses was to be honoured at the new Alexandria. In fact the worship of the counterpart of Isis, Demeter, is attested early in the city's history.

That the lay-out was on the grid-system with most streets facing the sea, which washed three sides of the site, and that the area within the walls was very large is made probable by the fact that Alexander was planting not a small Greek city of the acropolis or colonial type but a large Macedonian city, comparable to Dium, Alorus, Pella, or Macedonian Amphipolis. A large territory was no doubt assigned to it, and a large native population was drafted into it from nearby villages and towns; here too the analogy is with new cities founded in Upper Macedonia or in the Balkans under the Macedonian monarchy and not with the Greek city. The names of the chief local divisions, "demes," were taken from the gods and heroes and the members of the Macedonian royal family. The names were probably chosen by the founder himself.

The status of the city was like that of a Macedonian city in that it was subject to the edicts of the king but otherwise self-governing; and on leaving Egypt Alexander did not place a garrison in it. The top grade of citizens was defined legally by membership of the deme, just as a "Macedon" in the home country was defined by membership of a town (e.g., "Marsyas Macedon Pellaios"). The second grade of citizen was simply "Alexandreus," in the same way that a "Marsyas Pellaios" in the home country belonged to a second grade of citizen who was not a Macedon. As Alexander was launching a full-scale city, the two grades of citizen were evidently original to the foundation.

Any Macedonian, Greek, or Balkan soldier who had served his time or who wished to settle was included in the top grade, and it was the members of this grade who carried arms and conducted the control and defence of the city; for it was a time of war. To judge from the names, citizens of both grades came from Macedonian and Greek areas, especially the latter and especially from the Aegean islands. The constitution was that of a Greek democracy in accordance with Alexander's predilection, and the citizens had as usual their Assembly, Council, and Boards of Magistrates; for the citizens were predominantly of Greek origin.

Although some Egyptians or other foreigners may have adopted Greek ways and names and entered the citizen grades, the native Egyptians drafted into the city were unprivileged in terms of citizenship. They and resident or visiting foreigners practised their own religions and ways, and native Egyptian law was administered by Egyptian judges. A slave class was present, as in contemporary Greek cities and in much of the Near East. All inhabitants, both free and slave, were subject to the city's laws, which were based on those of a number of Greek cities, but the rights of citizenship were restricted to that small proportion of the total population which was registered with membership of a deme.[52]

Alexandria was ideally situated for maritime commerce, having two sheltered harbours and being connected or connectable by canal with the Nile which in flood was difficult to enter from the sea (similarly Pella was connected by canal with the Axius); and there was much to export, primarily grain, the gift of Demeter-Isis, other food stuffs, minerals, papyrus, drugs, spices, perfumes, etc. No place was better able to attract traders and settlers from the Mediterranean and particularly from the Greek world, and to create international exchange within Egypt and with the Mediterranean peoples. The worship of both Greek and Egyptian gods was symbolical of its cosmopolitan future, which was destined to last until 1961.

The circuit of the walls as planned by Alexander was eighty stades (fifteen kilometres) according to Curtius (4.8.2). This is probably correct, when we allow for the level of the sea there being some four metres lower and apply the ancient comparison of the outline of the city to that of a Macedonian cloak (*chlamys*). From the outset the city covered all the area between the sea and the lake which existed then. Its military importance was considerable, since it was to become a bastion comparable to Pelusium and its harbours were to enable the Macedonian fleet to guard the western entries to the Delta. As in Macedonia, the upper grade of citizens was to provide a reservoir for military recruitment, a feature which Polybius was to find so repugnant later (34.I4); this was certainly a major consideration in Alexander's planning. It is a remarkable instance of Alexander's confidence in the future and his foresight in many aspects of human affairs that he founded Alexandria where, when, and as he did.

On leaving Alexandria Alexander followed the coast to Paraetonium (Mersa Matruh) and struck inland to visit the oracle of Ammon at Siwah, famous for centuries throughout Greece and the East.[53] Many accounts survive, and we shall take them in the chronological order mentioned at the beginning of this book (see Figure 12).

Plutarch has preserved the summary of a report of the visit which Alexander wrote in a letter to his mother, Olympias, namely that he had received certain secret responses from the oracle which he would himself tell her and only her on his return. This is so different from the accounts which were generally put about, that it is much more likely to have been derived from a genuine letter at the time than from a letter forged later.

Callisthenes attributed the visit to Alexander's "love of glory," the glory being to emulate Perseus and Heracles who had gone there (similar to his emulation of history at Troy). Lost in a dust-storm of several days, Alexander and his force were saved from thirst by rainstorms and guided by two crows. On their arrival at the shrine in the oasis of Siwah the others were directed by the priest to change their clothes, but the king was sent without changing into the inner sanctum. Then the others were directed to stay outside the sanctum, but the king was to be inside to hear the oracle-givings, which were expressed not by words but generally by nods and signs, the priest acting the part of Zeus. Alexander was expressly told by "the fellow" (Plutarch's word for the priest) that he was the son of Zeus. Such in outline was the "official" version in the sense that Callisthenes must have shown it to Alexander and received his approval before it was published. It gives an insight into Alexander's "love of glory"—in terms not of posterity but of emulating the heroes of the past—and it shows that no account was published of the "oracle-givings" at all. This is, of course, not a variance with the summary of the letter which said the responses were not to be divulged even by him to his mother until his return.

No named fragment of Cleitarchus has a mention of the visit. Aristobulus is the source of the following: Alexander had a yearning (*pothos*) to visit the oracle; his route was along the coast through a desert which was not waterless as far as Paraetonium, a matter of some two hundred miles (i.e., from Alexandria, a correct reckoning); on the next stretch two crows flew ahead, guiding Alexander; the return was made by the same route.

On the other hand, Ptolemy said that two snakes, uttering cries, led the way there and back, and that the return was on a direct route towards Memphis (by Saqqara)—which is a practicable route.

Arrian's account seems to contain an amalgam of Aristobulus and Ptolemy, with a note of the disagreement between them. Points additional to those in Callisthenes are that, as the myths made Perseus and Heracles sons of Zeus, Alexander "was to some extent trying to trace his own birth to Ammon"; and that he heard from the god "what was, so he said, to his liking." This does not state but merely suggests indirectly that Alexander was told that he was the son of Ammon.

The stated reasons for Alexander making the visit seem to be impeccable. The implied reason that he wanted to trace his birth to Ammon is only speculation by Aristobulus-Ptolemy. The fact that the priest called Alexander "son of Zeus" in whatever language and form, whether as Zeus, or Zeus Ammon, or Ammon, or Ra, and that he directed him into the inner sanctum, shows that the priest welcomed Alexander as the reigning king of Egypt. Alexander let Callisthenes make this point. Those who knew Egyptian ways—and Alexander was one of them—attached no importance to the details of the priest's welcome, but less informed Macedonian and Greek soldiers might think otherwise. What "secret responses" did the god give? Only the priest and Alexander knew; and neither revealed them, except inasmuch as Alexander said he had heard what was to his liking—the sort of remark he might have made to Aristobulus or any questioner.

Inevitably many writers, ancient and modern, have added their speculations on what questions Alexander asked and what answers he got: was Philip his father? Had all conspirators against Philip been apprehended? Was Alexander invincible? Would he conquer the whole world? Was he the Son of God? All these questions and the most flattering answers to them have been supplied, for instance, in the accounts of Diodorus(17.49.2–51.4), Curtius (4.7.5–30), and Plutarch (*Alexander* 26.6–27.5), which have a great deal in common. These speculations are, of course, worthless except for the light they throw on the speculators. Cleitarchus, for example, was certainly an early speculator; and if, as is generally believed, he is responsible for much that appeared in Diodorus, Curtius, and Plutarch, he provided the most sensational claims for Alexander to be acclaimed already as invincible, world-conqueror, Son of God, and destined after death to be a god. Cleitarchus was in fact totally irresponsible in his assertions.

The important thing, historically, is that Alexander did not allow any claims to be made for him in Callisthenes' "official" record, except the (to him) unimportant greeting by the priest. Neither Aristobulus nor Ptolemy made any speculations; their sense of history was too scrupulous for them to do so, but being human they dropped the hint which Arrian picked up, that Alexander "was to some extent trying to trace his own birth to Ammon." Arrian too refrained from speculating. The differences between Aristobulus and Ptolemy are of interest. That the episode of the two crows was the correct version is clear from Callisthenes alone. Such crows are common at Siwah; faith in signs from birds was as primaeval as Prometheus; and it was a fair guess that crows in flight would be bound for the oasis. But two talking serpents! That must have been added by Ptolemy as king of Egypt for local consumption, because a talking serpent, "Neheb-Kau," served as the gods' intermediary whenever they wished to give information to a pharaoh. Thus Ptolemy was not above altering the record to suit his local interest.

The route from Mersa Matruh to Siwah, that normally taken by pilgrims, was not particularly difficult for Alexander's lightly equipped party with their guides and camels (C. 4.7.6–12); but unexpected rains and crows leading the way when a sandstorm had obliterated the track were interpreted as signs of divine favour. In fact they made good time, covering some 160 miles across the desert in eight days (D. 17.49.3–6). No doubt most of them returned by the same route, but Alexander in his usual adventurous spirit may have taken others on the direct route to Memphis. If Ptolemy was one of them, we can see why he made a point of correcting what had become the accepted view.

One thing we do know for certain is that the visit to Siwah made a very deep impression on Alexander. He referred repeatedly to Zeus Ammon or to Ammon, and he was punctilious in carrying out sacrifices and rites enjoined, as he believed, by the god; and not least at times of emotional stress. It was the observation of this by others and especially by his soldiers, and not any knowledge of what the priest said to Alexander, that fed the popular belief that Alexander believed himself to be literally and physically the son of the god Ammon.

The Roman poet Lucan (I0.272–5) mentioned the sending by Alexander of an exploratory mission, which penetrated far up the Nile into "Aethiopia" (as the Sudan was then called) but was halted "by the blazing zone of parched sky." Callisthenes, while serving with Alexander, was said to have been in Aethiopia and to have discovered that it was the enormous rainfall there which caused the Nile to flood (F 12a); and the best explanation of his going there is that he was a member of this exploratory mission. As a nephew of Aristotle, who like so many philosophers had wondered why the Nile should flood in summer, he was an obvious choice; and it was no doubt his report which led Aristotle to make the pronouncement "This is no longer a problem" (Fr. 246, Rose). Indeed Alexander himself had the yearning (*cupido*) to visit Aethiopia and the palace of Tithonus, the prisoner of the Sun, at the confines of the inhabited world.

Early in the winter the prisoners of war from the Greek islands were brought to Memphis by Hegelochus, the Macedonian admiral. Some of them were sent to the scene of their crimes, in particular the pro-Persian tyrants; this was a practice which Alexander was to follow in his Asian domains. In this case they were judged by their fellow citizens and put to death with torture in the Greek manner (C. 4.8.11). The oligarchs who had betrayed Chios to the Persians were not sent back to Chios, where they would certainly have met the same fate. They were kept instead under guard at Elephantine near Aswan in Upper Egypt (A. 3.2.7). It is probable that when the sailing season opened in the early summer they were to be sent to Greece and tried as traitors to the Greek cause by the Council of the Greek League; for Chios had been admitted to membership of the Greek League (Tod 192). Rewards were given to those who had helped in the war at sea. Compensation for their expenditure and a gift of additional territory were granted to the people of Mytilene, and special honours were accorded to the kings of the states in Cyprus.

At the end of the winter many embassies from the Greek states came to Alexander at Memphis. Particularly welcome were some envoys from Miletus who reported that Apollo of Didyma, an oracular shrine silent since the Persian occupation, had now spoken and declared Alexander to be "born of Zeus" and forecast his future. Then too came a prophecy by the Sibyl of Erythrae on the mainland opposite Chios: she affirmed his "exalted birth." Both declarations were published later by Callisthenes (F. 14) in his official history, evidently with the approval of Alexander. As sceptics, we may suppose that news travelled fast from Siwah to the coast of Asia Minor and back to Memphis; or that coincidence was at work. But Alexander was a believer; he may have been confirmed in his belief that he was in some sense a son of Zeus.

In political matters he was conciliatory towards the Greeks. He returned to Soli the hostages and a part of the fine which he had exacted for their support of Persia, and he settled in the interest of Chios and Rhodes the disputes which they had had with Alexander's garrison troops. Envoys from the states of the Greek mainland, including Athens, were granted most of their requests. His generosity was prudent at a time when he expected trouble from Sparta.

With the approach of spring Alexander held a festival at Memphis in the Macedonian tradition, with the entire army on parade in full armour and with competitions in athletics and the arts. There he made sacrifice to Zeus the King. It was this aspect of Zeus which had been portrayed on the victory coins after the battle of Issus, and it was appropriate to invoke his aid for the coming campaign.

The arrangements which Alexander made before leaving Egypt were remarkable for their use of different nationalities and their decentralisation of authority. He appointed two Egyptians as civil governors to administer their traditional system in Upper Egypt and Lower Egypt; a Greek born in Egypt at Naucratis, Cleomenes, as civil governor of the southeastern district "Arabia" along the Gulf of Suez, and another Greek as civil governor of the western frontier district, called "Libya;" two Macedonian generals in command of 4,000 troops in Egypt; and an admiral to command a fleet of thirty triremes which defended the approaches to the Nile. Each of these seven men was responsible directly to Alexander. In addition he appointed two Macedonian officers to command garrisons at Pelusium and Memphis—again responsible directly to him—and he set up a special system to control the Greek mercenaries: an Aetolian Greek commanded them, a Macedonian administered all their affairs—including payments—and a Macedonian and a Rhodian acted as inspectors of mercenary troops. Alexander made these additional appointments in the hope of preventing any coup d'état; for he knew that Greek mercenary troops had often supported a military adventurer, and that such an adventurer could hold Egypt against attack, if he was in possession also of Pelusium and the navy.

The detailed military arrangements operated no doubt only in peacetime; and in the event of a counter-attack by Persia the Macedonian generals must have been empowered to exercise command of all officers and forces in Egypt. The taxes were raised as in the past by native "nomarchs" or regional officers, apparently at the same rate. All taxes were to be sent on to Cleomenes, who held a central treasury on behalf of Alexander.

During the winter one of Alexander's closest friends, a younger son of Parmenio called Hector, was drowned in an accident on the Nile. Alexander showed the deepest grief for him and honoured his memory with a magnificent funeral, a tribute also to the young man's father, his close friend and adviser. The Nile and the canals to the east were bridged in preparation for the departure, and in early spring 331 B.C. Alexander led his army over them and marched to Tyre, where his fleet joined him. The gathering of his forces was celebrated by a magnificent sacrifice to Heracles at Tyre and by athletic and artistic competitions, in which plays selected and subsidised by the kings of Cyprus were judged.

Alexander hoped that his friend Thessalus, an actor, would be in the winning play; when the verdict went elsewhere, Alexander expressed his approval of the judges but said he would gladly have given a part of his kingdom to see Thessalus victorious. The winning actor had broken an engagement at the Athenian Dionysiac festival in order to act at Tyre, and when the Athenian people fined him the actor asked Alexander to intervene. Alexander refused to do so, but paid the fine. At the time the Athenian ship-of-state with a special mission on board lay in the harbour. Alexander granted all the Athenian requests, including the liberation of the Athenians captured in the Persian ranks at the Granicus river. The care with which he handled Athens was to bring its own reward later.

In the early months of summer 331 B.C. Alexander was active in Phoenicia and Syria. We know of only one campaign, conducted against a Jewish stronghold at Samaria (Beit Umrin, north of Nablus). The people of Samaria had captured Andromachus, the satrap of "Hollow Syria," and had burnt him alive, and Alexander went in person to suppress the revolt and punish the atrocity. The Samarians surrendered those responsible, who were executed on the spot, and Alexander then expelled the population and founded a Macedonian settlement.

Leonnatus, now a bodyguard of Alexander, was charged with some responsibility for the settlements at Samaria and at Gerasa, where honours were paid to him. It must have been clear to Alexander that, if he succeeded in overthrowing Darius, a very important centre in his communications would be Syria; so he took all possible steps to strengthen the Macedonian control of that vital area. He did not yet advance eastwards across the Euphrates for a number of reasons. It would suit Alexander better if Darius came east of the Euphrates, so that Alexander's supply lines were short and Darius' long—an important consideration, as the campaigns of Rommel and Montgomery made clear to us; and Alexander had no intention of lengthening his own lines, unless he had no alternative. Meanwhile he would keep an eye on the situation in Greece, where Agis of Sparta was known to be disaffected and in receipt of Persian money.

He was also in closer touch with Antipater in Macedonia. He sent an order, perhaps in June, requiring Antipater to send very large forces from Macedonia, Thrace, and the Peloponnese to join the army in Asia.

These reinforcements set out in July or perhaps later still, at which time the situation in Greece was quiet, and Alexander may have hoped they would join him before there was a decisive encounter with Darius.

Another consideration was that of supply for an army of 47,000 soldiers and their ancillary services, and for a great number of horses, probably not far short of 20,000 (the baggage-train alone of Darius at Damascus had had 7,000 horses; C. 3.13.16). There were excellent areas for summer pasture in the Orontes valley and inland of Antioch, and the satrap of that area, "Syria," had been made responsible for bringing in the necessary stocks. He failed in his duty. He was dismissed from his post and replaced by another Macedonian, Asclepiodorus. It was essential to allow time for the grain-harvest of 331 B.C. to be harvested on the Syrian plateau and for the winnowed grain to be collected and transported to points near the Euphrates. Thus it was not until late July that Alexander decided that he was ready to march to the east. It was by then clear that Darius had no intention of coming west.

(B) THE MOVEMENTS OF ALEXANDER AND DARIUS IN MESOPOTAMIA
(see Figure 13)

With the decisive battle of Gaugamela in prospect our sources of information become fuller. They may be divided into two groups: Diodorus-Curtius-Plutarch, which have a number of significant points in common but go back to more than one account; and Arrian, drawing on Ptolemy and Aristobulus in the main. Diodorus and Plutarch took only a few episodes from a long account or accounts, and Curtius took more episodes and elaborated them himself. Arrian too abbreviated his sources' accounts but systematically, so as to give a consecutive account himself.

In the first group the Persian side is portrayed in a grandiose but rather simple-minded manner. Darius had a million men, trained them carefully and equipped some with larger weapons than hitherto. Yet he feared they would fall into confusion as they spoke so many languages (as if Persians had not commanded multilingual armies for two centuries); many had no weapons at all; and horses were brought in great numbers to be broken and ridden by infantrymen who were converting themselves into cavalrymen (as if cavalrymen were made in a day or two). Darius then considered one strategy after another: withdrawal into the remote eastern provinces, a scorched-earth policy to starve the enemy army and keep it out of reach, and holding the bank of the swift-flowing Tigris as a barrier of defence.

The commander of the advanced force, Mazaeus, behaved in an inexplicable manner. Although there seems to be some confusion between the Euphrates and the Tigris in Curtius' account, yet the orders of Darius were given to the effect that Mazaeus had to hold the Tigris with 6,000 cavalry. Nevertheless, Mazaeus let the entire Macedonian army ford the Tigris and reform for battle (as at the Granicus river in Diodorus' account of that battle). Only then did he send cavalry into the attack, not 6,000 as we had been led to expect, but a mere 1,000. In this, we are told, Mazaeus was careless; for he had thought the river to be impassable. Such was Alexander's "perpetua fortuna"! The burning countryside is graphically described, but only *east* of the Tigris; and there is nothing to explain why the Macedonians did not starve, as Darius had hoped.

According to Arrian, Mazaeus had orders from Darius to defend the Euphrates with an army of 3,000 cavalry, 2,000 Greek mercenaries, and some other infantry (number lost in the transmission of the text, but probably 1,000). Alexander's advance force at Thapsacus built the greater part of two bridges across the 750-metres wide river (Xen. *Anab.* 1.4.11), before Alexander arrived; that is they either drove wooden piles into the river bottom (as was done in the Strymon) or built stone piers on the river-bed but had stopped short of Mazaeus' troops on the opposite bank. When the main army approached, Mazaeus withdrew. The last piles or piers, we may assume, were then made by the engineers, long beams were laid on them, and the army crossed over the two bridges. The troops remained at rest for some days, during which Alexander may have misled Mazaeus about his future route; no doubt baggage and supplies were also being brought up during these days.

Then Alexander set off, not on the royal road from Thapsacus (probably Jerablus) down the valley (see Xen. *Anab.* 1.4.11), but up the valley "because it was easier there to obtain pasture for the horses and supplies for the army and because it was less hot, keeping the Euphrates and the mountains of Armenia on his left and proceeding through "the country called Mesopotamia" (so also *Itin. Alex.* 22). As the Armenian mountains" are those from which the Euphrates flows (A. 7.21.2), and as the most southerly of them cannot be put south of Saryekshan (2561 m), he went north to Karacali Dag into the northern part of "Mesopotamian Syria." Meanwhile Mazaeus had misread the intentions of Alexander, and he lost touch completely with the Macedonians, as they did with him.

After an unstated interval of time Alexander captured some of the Persian scouts who had been sent far and wide to look for him, and he learnt from them that Darius was encamped on the Tigris and planned to stop any attempt by Alexander to cross the Tigris. Alexander then "went in haste towards the Tigris" (A. 3.7.5), reached it at an undefended place and with difficulty forded its fast-flowing waters. He then rested the army for some days, and an eclipse of the moon occurred (which astronomers date to the night of September 20–21, 331 b.c.). Alexander sacrificed to Moon, Sun, and Earth as the deities involved, and the eclipse

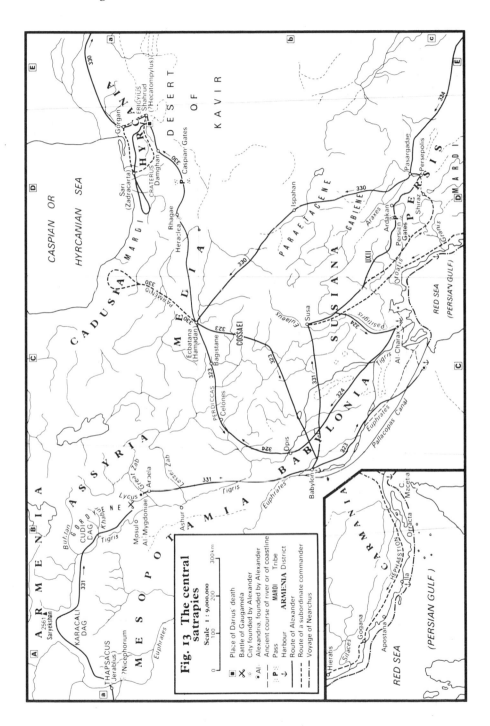

Fig. 13 The central satrapies

was said to signify victory for Alexander that month. This interpretation, provided by Aristander the seer, comforted the Macedonians,
who, like the Athenians in 413 B.C. at Syracuse, had been terrified by the
eclipse.

Advancing from their crossing place, the Macedonians passed
through the narrows between the river and "the Gordyenian mountains" (presumably Cudi Dag, 2089 m), and on the fourth day made first
contact with the enemy by capturing some of a select cavalry force, 1,000
strong. From them Alexander learnt that Darius and his large army were
not far off. He now halted his army for four days of rest. Then, having
fortified his camp and left there his baggage and unfit soldiers, he led
forward his fighting troops, encumbered with nothing but their arms,
and next day (September 30th) he saw the enemy camp, some three or
four miles away. His own fortified camp was about the same distance
behind him. He now made a new camp. On the following day, October
1st, 331 B.C., battle was joined.

The choice between Diodorus-Curtius-Plutarch and Arrian is too obvious to need discussion. But even if we add some points about the Persian movements from Diodorus-Curtius-Plutarch, we are still left with
this problem: as Alexander reached Thapsacus during the lunar month
of Hecatombaeon (c. 10 July to 8 August) and as he started his rapid
march to the Tigris c. 14 September, what was he doing in the intervening weeks? If Arrian had not curtailed his sources' account, we should
have been informed. As it is, we can be sure that Alexander did not
allow his army to be idle.[54]

We may be confident in the conjecture that he was busy subjugating
a large area of northern Mesopotamia, so that he could safeguard his
supplies and communications with the west, acquire a satisfactory base
of operations, and ensure himself against any attack from the north; for
he must have learnt his lesson from having been outmanoeuvred just
before the battle of Issus. At the same time he might receive his reinforcements from Europe and he might draw Darius out of the plain into
the hills, as he had done by delaying at Tarsus in 333 B.C.

While Alexander campaigned out of sight and out of touch, what did
Darius do? At first he waited at Babylon, expecting Alexander to come
south and seek him out. Then he advanced north but kept in the plain
"between the Euphrates and the Tigris" (C. 4.9.6). In what was to some
extent a war of nerves, it was Darius who first decided to retire behind
the Tigris, perhaps at Ashur (Ash Sharqat), and to use the Tigris as a defensive line. He supplied his army by river as well as by road, and he
sent some of his best cavalry to hold places where Alexander might try
to bridge the river. An inkling of his strategy is given by Arrian (3.7.4)
and Diodorus (17.55.1).

As the armies had lost contact with one another, Darius sent scouts in various directions. Some were caught by Alexander c. 13 September. Learning where Darius had been earlier in September and ascertaining or guessing his plans, Alexander moved with speed from his camp (its name is corrupted in C. 4.9.14), made a forced march of four days and reached the Tigris at a point much farther north than any of Darius' cavalry squadrons. Fording the river with difficulty (probably above the Khābūr-Tigris confluence), he rested the army until the baggage-train arrived. Heavy gear and wagons were presumably left on the far bank; necessary baggage was manhandled over the fast river, and it was carried from then on by pack-animals (*skeuophora*, A. 3.9.1). He was about to move, when the eclipse of the night 20-21 September delayed him. Setting off on the 22nd, he took the only possible route which runs between the river and the Gordyenian mountains (Cudi Dag, 2089 m) through a well-supplied region, as Xenophon had noted (*Anabasis* 3.5.1-14). On the 25th he made his contact with the 1,000 select Persian cavalry (A. 3.7.7; *Itin. Alex.* 22).

Meanwhile Darius moved northwards himself; for he realised from scouts who returned c. 14 September, that Alexander was considerably farther north than he had supposed, and that Alexander's plan was to turn the Tigris position in the north. He marched from Ashur some seventy miles to Arbela, where he established his base of supply and centre of communications; for from it there were made-up roads leading to Babylon, to the east and to the north. He then advanced his army to the river Lycus (Greater Zab), where he built a bridge or bridges and spent five days getting his army across. Finally, he marched another ten miles to the river Boumelus (Khazir), beyond which he encamped and prepared the ground for a confrontation with Alexander.

He was in position on 25 September when Alexander captured some of the 1,000 Persian cavalry and learnt from them where Darius was. Alexander camped at once and rested his army, while his baggage was coming up. Then he made a base camp, fortified to protect his sick and the bulk of the baggage. On the night of September 29th he set out with his fighting-troops and some pack-animals carrying, for instance, barley for his warhorses, and early next day he sighted the enemy army in the plain below.

While Alexander had been adding to his conquests and making ready for the next advance, Darius may be blamed for inactivity. But he had little option. His large, unwieldy army had little chance of catching and defeating Alexander in the hills of Northern Mesopotamia, and his best hope was to bring Alexander to battle against his own superior numbers on the ground of his own choice. This Darius had now succeeded in doing; and to that extent he had won the game of move and counter-move. Two of our sources, Diodorus (17.55.2) and Curtius (4.9.7 and 12; 4.8.23-24; 4.10.14; and 4.12.1-5), aimed their criticisms at

Mazaeus, certainly with exaggeration and probably unfairly, because Darius trusted him throughout and gave him high command in the battle. Their attitude may have been due to their use of a pro-Persian account which branded Mazaeus as a deserter (since he submitted later to Alexander), and which sought to diminish Alexander's achievement by implying that Alexander would have been defeated but for his "perpetua fortuna."

We have referred already to the way in which Diodorus and Curtius shifted Darius' offer of friendship and alliance to a time shortly before the battle of Gaugamela, a timing which was more dramatic but less credible. Another event too, the death of Darius' wife, the beautiful Stateira, was put shortly before the battle by Diodorus and Curtius. Indeed Curtius had it lead to a sensational outburst by Darius, who, being amazed that Alexander had not raped her, cried out: "If it is all up with me, let so merciful a victor be king" (4.10.34). A detail in Curtius' account, that Alexander saw Stateira only once, namely on the day she was captured, provides a link with the probably untrue story of Alexander and Hephaestion visiting the captives. Nor is it credible that he had never seen her since that day.

Much the same story appears in Plutarch (*Alexander* 30), but he placed it before Alexander's march to the Euphrates. One incident in Curtius' account and in Plutarch's account, the escape of the eunuch attendant on Stateira, was mentioned by Arrian (4.20) as happening soon after the battle of Issus, and he gave the same sort of exclamation to Darius; but Arrian gave it all as a "story" (*logos*), not taken from Ptolemy and Aristobulus and not vouched for as true. Certainly we can dismiss Plutarch's detail that Stateira died in childbirth, since with Plutarch's timing that would have needed an eighteen-months pregnancy. When Arrian chose to include this story, he must have known several versions of it and preferred to give the date of her death as soon after the battle of Issus. It is best to follow his judgement in the matter.

On sighting the army of Darius at Gaugamela, Alexander summoned his commanders. The great majority urged immediate attack, but Parmenio urged and Alexander accepted the need for reconnaissance. The army camped on the spot. When the ground had been inspected by him he told the commanders to exhort their men appropriately and to order them in particular during the advance next morning to maintain silence, keep position, and pass orders promptly (as at Pelium). One story which Arrian mentions without vouching for it, made Parmenio recommend a night attack and Alexander reply "I do not steal victory" (the story recurs in P. 31.7 and C. 4.13.4).

Another story, which Arrian does not trouble to cite, made the Macedonians panic twice and Alexander dither and sacrifice with Aristander until dawn, when he fell into so deep a sleep that, when it was time to arm, he could not be roused until Parmenio went in and shook him. But Arrian reports as a fact that Darius kept his forces standing in battle-order, men and horses alike, throughout the night. The Macedonians no doubt slept in their camp and were fresh when they stood to arms at dawn.

(C) THE BATTLE OF GAUGAMELA
(see Figure 14)

Diodorus describes the battle very much as he described the battle of Granicus and that of Issus. According to him, the Persians in all three battles had their cavalry in a line in front and their infantry in a line behind; and in this battle Alexander did the same. Except that the scythed chariots came within range of the Macedonian infantry, the fighting was all between cavalry units. The Thessalians were again better than any other cavalry; indeed when Parmenio had failed to obtain help from Alexander, the Thessalians got Parmenio out of disaster. The Macedonians suffered two major defeats, and they won only because of a misunderstanding, when Alexander's javelin, missing Darius, happened to knock his driver to the ground and the bystanders thought it was Darius who had fallen. So they ran away, exposing the flank of Darius, who also ran away.

All in all, it is a childish and worthless account. It is decked out with trumpets, shouts, cracking whips, whinnying horses, and falling men; throngs of missiles, clouds of dust, and ghastly forms of death dealt by the scythed chariots—men cut to the vitals, shield-gripping arms amputated, and decapitated heads wearing the expression of the moment as they rolled. We owe this account to Cleitarchus' vivid imagination, perhaps with some inept touches added by Diodorus. Some details of the battle-order, especially of the Macedonian infantry who figure not at all in hand-to-hand fighting, may be salvaged and used when we come to a more acceptable account.

It is evident that Curtius has conflated two or more accounts to make up his own account, and one of them was that used by Diodorus, since we find in Curtius (4.15.28–4.16.6) the same picture of the driver's fall, the din, the clouds of dust, Parmenio's appeal for aid, the Thessalians rallying to the attack, and their success. The earlier part of the battle is drawn from somewhere else; for the chariots had more success and then were repulsed by other methods than in Diodorus' account, Alexander and his cavalrymen were nearly surrounded and saved only by the "Agrianian cavalry" (otherwise unknown) coming to his rescue, and there was much more fighting around the Macedonian baggage than in Diodorus' account. A peculiar feature of this part of the battle is that

Alexander is represented as receiving a silly question from Parmenio ("What about the baggage, Sir.", 4.15. 6), as being himself concerned about what was happening in the baggage-camp (4.15.13), and as becoming a rallying-point for fugitive Macedonians whom he inspired to go back into action (4.15.19). These details were provided by some writer who failed to realise that the king was always in the thick of the fight, not a detached general overlooking the scene. Only the beginning and the end of the battle emerge fairly clear from the confused welter of incidents; so too it must have been at the time for individual participants in the battle.

Plutarch gives only a few episodes. His story about the baggage is as in Curtius (4.15.6–8); he, like Curtius (4.15.26–7), has Aristander the seer, clad in a white robe, pointing to an eagle over Alexander's head and encouraging the troops; and again like Curtius (4.16.3) Plutarch represents Alexander as furious at Parmenio's folly. Plutarch is alone in giving a full description of what Alexander was wearing (32.5–6), and his extraordinarily graphic description of the scene when Alexander was attacking and Darius' chariot-horses were rearing in panic (33.3–5) was inspired probably by an actual painting or mosaic of that moment in the battle. Plutarch cites Callisthenes, the court historian, for two of the points which he makes (33.1 and 33.6), to which we shall refer later.

Arrian's account is of a different order altogether, being based upon Darius' written battle-order, which, according to Aristobulus, was captured after the battle, and upon the Macedonian battle-order as recorded in the *King's Journal* (in my opinion), which came to him through the writings of Aristobulus and Ptolemy, if we accept his own account of the sources which he used. There is from the outset a full understanding of the overall plan of Alexander, which is brought out by the report of his orders issued in advance and subsequently executed. Detailed description of the action itself is limited in general to the part played by Alexander and by the units under his command. This is explicable if the main source was the *King's Journal* in which his acts and orders were recorded. Barely enough is said to explain what happened elsewhere on the battlefield.

Although Diodorus and Plutarch wrote before Arrian did, they made no use of Aristobulus and Ptolemy (as known to us through Arrian), because detailed battle-orders were not to their taste. Curtius, being an omnivorous reader, may have drawn some points or names from them, but in the main he preferred more sensational writers and more rhetorical matter (as at 4.14.1–7 and 9–26). The original sources also were of two kinds. Callisthenes and Cleitarchus wrote for a popular audience to which epic encounters, miracles, and paradoxes were the spices of battle, and their accounts were in circulation first. The memoirs of Aristobulus and the dull, factual account of Ptolemy were written primarily for those interested in recollected and recorded facts and even in dry military history. To us the account of Arrian appears to be much more dependable.

Darius was in command of a large and formidable army. He had recruited the finest cavalry of all his satrapies, extending eastwards to Uzbekistan, Afghanistan, and the borders of Pakistan, and he had been reinforced by the Sacae, an allied Scythian tribe to the east of the empire, who excelled in mounted archery. Each unit was a racial entity, and the units formed groups by territory, each group under a satrap who held his command from Darius. Thus Mazaeus commanded such of the cavalry from "Hollow Syria" as had escaped Alexander's attentions and also the cavalry of "Mesopotamian Syria." There is no doubt that all the cavalry units supported Darius to the full, and it is a special sign of loyalty that some units came from Cappadocia and Armenia by devious routes. The total number of cavalry, according to Arrian (3.8.6), "was said" to be 40,000 (Diodorus gave 200,000!). Arrian's expression means that Ptolemy and Aristobulus, and consequently in our opinion the *King's Journal*, did not give over-all figures for enemy strengths, and that Arrian adopted from other writers a conservative figure, which even so may be inflated. Darius had rearmed some cavalry units with lances instead of javelins and with long swords of Greek type instead of scimitars in view of his experience at Issus, but most of the units were armed in their own traditional manner. In some Persian and Scythian units both man and horse were protected by iron plates linked together into one piece (C. 4.9.3), effective in a scrimmage but putting a brake on any manoeuvre.

The best of the infantry were the loyal and highly paid Greek mercenaries, and the Persian Royal Guard of distinguished record. It seems that the Cardaces—Persians trained and equipped as hoplites to serve with the Greek mercenaries in phalanx-formation—had been disbanded since their ignominious defeat at Issus. In general the infantry served in their traditional equipment and had no standard formation in battle; many of them simply supported their own cavalry units (A. 3.11.3). While Arrian reported the figure of a million infantry as "said," Curtius (4.12.13) gave 200,000, which provides a reasonable proportion of infantry to cavalry; but again the number may be inflated.

Darius produced a special type of scythed chariot as his new weapon. Drawn, some by two horses abreast and some by four horses abreast and driven by one charioteer, the chariots carried razor-sharp blades set upon the shuttering of the axles and on sides and the front end of the yoke-pole. The intention was that these chariots, launched at full speed, would break up the formations of the enemy cavalry and infantry alike and that the Persian cavalry, each unit in formation (usually a rectangular column), should charge into any gap or attack disordered units of the enemy. But as a chariot needs a flat race-track, Darius prepared three fairways at specified distances apart. He also sowed some areas with caltrops, spikes set to cripple horses.

Thus Darius tied himself down to using a fixed piece of terrain, thereby sacrificing the initiative to Alexander and inhibiting his own movement. Although it cannot be pinpointed, this terrain was part ploughland and part pasture, as it is today (see pictures in Fuller 168), and it lay in an extensive plain most suitable for cavalry. Darius hoped to use his huge numbers of cavalry in such a way as to prevent Alexander from taking his army off the fixed piece of terrain in either direction.

A written order of battle of the Persian forces was captured after the battle (A. 3.11.3). The capture was reported by Aristobulus, as Arrian says, but it is not clear whether Arrian took the battle-order (which he reproduces) from Aristobulus' memoirs or from the history of Ptolemy who was himself using Alexander's papers. In any case there is no reason to doubt that it did represent the disposition of Darius' troops on the day before the battle. It was as follows (Figure 14).

The whole army was drawn up in a straight, continuous line of varying depth. The centre, where Darius placed himself in his chariot, had the greatest depth. There in the very front fifteen Indian elephants and fifty chariots were supported by Indian cavalry, whose horses had been trained to fight alongside elephants. Behind them came "deported Carians" (deported long ago from their homeland to inner Asia), Mardian archers and the two Royal Guards—first, the cavalry guard of 1,000 nobles, known as the "Kinsmen Cavalry," and behind them the infantry guard of 1,000 Persians, called the "Apple-bearers" because there was a golden apple instead of a spike on their spear-butts. On either side of the Apple-bearers were the Greek mercenary infantrymen, probably 6,000 in number. Behind these forces in the centre there was a reserve line of infantry in a formation more than eight men deep.

Each wing was formed by a mass of cavalry. In front on the left, enumerated from the left, Scythians and Bactrians and 100 chariots; behind them Bactrians, Dahae, and Arachotians. In front on the right, enumerated from the right, Armenians and Cappadocians and 50 chariots; behind them Syrians and Medes. Between the rear parts of the cavalry wings and the centre there were on the left mixed contingents of cavalry and infantry (Persians, Susians, and Cadusians), and on the right some mixed contingents but a higher proportion of cavalry (Parthyaeans, Sacae, Topeirians, Hyrcanians, Albanians and Sacesinae).

This order of battle and the preparing of the ground show that Darius hoped to break the enemy line into disorder by the attack of his chariots and elephants and to envelope the whole enemy force with his massed cavalry wings. He put twice as many chariots, more infantry, and his best cavalry (Persians, Scythians, and Bactrians)—apart from

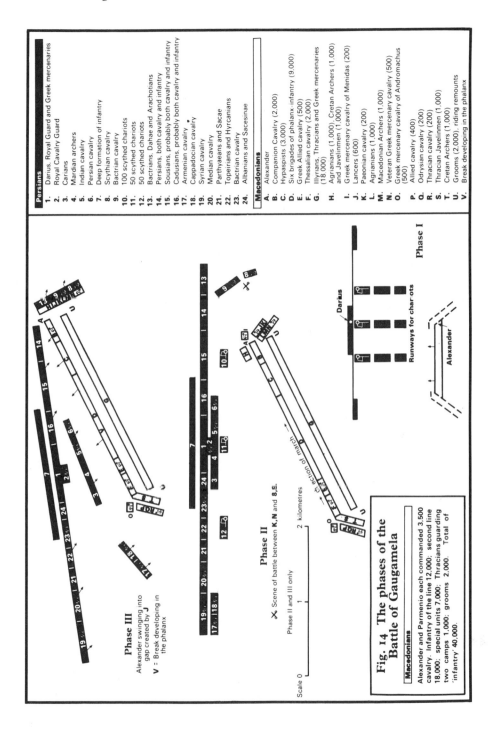

Persians

1. Darius, Royal Guard and Greek mercenaries
2. Royal Cavalry Guard
3. Carians
4. Mardian archers
5. Indian cavalry
6. Persian cavalry
7. Deep formation of infantry
8. Scythian cavalry
9. Bactrian cavalry
10. 100 scythed chariots
11. 50 scythed chariots
12. 50 scythed chariots
13. Bactrians, Dahae and Arachotians
14. Persians, both cavalry and infantry
15. Sousians, probably both cavalry and infantry
16. Cadusians, probably both cavalry and infantry
17. Armenian cavalry
18. Cappadocian cavalry
19. Syrian cavalry
20. Median cavalry
21. Parthyaeans and Sacae
22. Topeirians and Hyrcanians
23. Bactrian cavalry
24. Albanians and Sacesinae

Macedonians

A. Alexander
B. Companion Cavalry (2,000)
C. Hypaspists (3,000)
D. Six brigades of phalanx-infantry (9,000)
E. Greek Allied cavalry (500)
F. Thessalian cavalry (2,000)
G. Illyrians, Thracians and Greek mercenaries (18,000)
H. Agrianians (1,000), Cretan Archers (1,000) and Javelinmen (1,000)
I. Greek mercenary cavalry of Menidas (200)
J. Lancers (600)
K. Paeonian cavalry (200)
L. Agrianians (1,000)
M. Macedonian Archers (1,000)
N. Veteran Greek mercenary cavalry (500)
O. Greek mercenary cavalry of Andromachus (500)
P. Allied cavalry (400)
R. Odrysian cavalry (200)
S. Thracian cavalry (200)
T. Thracian Javelinmen (1,000)
U. Cretan Archers (1,000)
U. Grooms (2,000), riding remounts
V. Break developing in the phalanx

Phase III

Alexander swinging into gap created by **J**

V = Break developing in the phalanx

Phase II

✗ Scene of battle between **K, N** and **8**

Direction of march

Scale 0   1   2 kilometres

Phase II and III only

Darius

Runways for chariots

Alexander

Phase I

Fig. 14 The phases of the Battle of Gaugamela

Macedonians

Alexander and Parmenio each commanded 3,500 cavalry. Infantry of the line 12,000; second line 18,000; special units 7,000; Thracians guarding two camps 1,000; grooms 2,000. Total of 'infantry' 40,000.

the Kinsmen Cavalry—on the left side of the line, in case Alexander himself concentrated his best cavalry on his right, as he had done at Issus.

Darius put his Greek infantry where he hoped they would oppose the Macedonian phalanx (A. 3.11.7). The plan was of course to be subject to change when Darius knew Alexander's dispositions, again as at Issus, and we know indeed of one change: the elephants were not among the forces seen at close range by the Macedonians (A. 3.13.I) but were captured in the camp (3.I5.4); and "at the time in the battle" some Bactrian cavalry were "drawn up with Darius" (A. 3.16.1). But whatever changes Darius might make later, the trap was intelligently set. Everything depended on Alexander walking into it.

Aware of Darius' dispositions (which his scouts may have checked at dawn), Alexander left such baggage as he had at his overnight camp under the guard of some Thracian infantry, and paraded his men in battle order on the forward slopes of the hills some hours after dawn, thus extending the time during which the enemy stood under arms. He marched them as on a parade-ground for some three miles across the plain, keeping on the left-hand half of the prepared ground in order to make Darius think he was entering the trap. It was during this march that Darius is likely to have moved his best Persian cavalry and some Bactrian cavalry from his left to a place by the front of his right centre. On coming close enough to distinguish Darius and enemy units in the centre, Alexander suddenly changed direction, moving his whole force "rather in the direction of the right" (A. 3.12.1). By then, if not from the start, his line was in the oblique formation invented by Epaminondas, his right advanced and his left retarded, as shown in Figure 14.

The dispositions of Alexander's army and his orders are given by Arrian. Of the continuous line the units from right to left were the Royal Squadron and seven other squadrons of Companion Cavalry, the Royal Brigade and two other brigades of Hypaspists, six brigades of phalanx-infantry (the commanders from right to left being Coenus, Perdiccas, Meleager, Polyperchon, Simmias, and Craterus), some Greek allied cavalry and the Thessalian cavalry.

Subordinate commanders for sections of the line were, from right to left: Philotas, son of Parmenio, in charge of the Companion Cavalry; Nicanor, son of Parmenio, in charge of the Hypaspists; and Craterus in charge of the left-hand part of the infantry line. Parmenio was in full command of the left half of the whole line. Alexander, leading the Royal Squadron himself, held the command of the right half of the line.

Attached to either end of the line were flank-guards, obliquely placed in relation to the main line. On the right, attached literally to the Royal Squadron, came half of the Agrianians, then the "Macedonian archers" (the first appearance of this unit), and last the "old-timer

Greek mercenary infantrymen" (probably light-armed from Philip's reign); and in front of the Agrianians and archers, the Lancers and the Paeonian cavalry. To the front of the whole flank-guard an advanced place was taken by those Greek mercenary cavalry who were commanded by Menidas. And to the front of the Companion Cavalry an advanced place was taken (from right to left) by half of the Agrianians, half of the Cretan archers, and the "Javelin-men of Balacrus," the last being placed opposite to the scythed chariots (A. 3.12.4, probably the central group of chariots, in view of 3.13.I). The flank-guard on the left was attached to the Pharsalian squadron of the Thessalian cavalry. Its troops were, from right to left, the Thracian javelin-men and the other half of the Cretan archers (C. 4.13.3I and D. I7.57.4), and in front of them probably the rest of the Greek allied cavalry, the Odrysian cavalry and, as they figure nowhere else, the squadron of Thracian cavalry. To the front of this flank-guard was a squadron of Greek mercenary cavalry under Andromachus.

Finally, behind the infantry section of the front line Alexander placed a second line of infantry at an interval, so that the formation was a "double phalanx," such as he had employed on the approach to the Granicus river; this second line was composed probably of Illyrians, Greek mercenaries, and Thracians (C. 4.13.3I). The commanders of the second line received orders from Alexander to face about if they should see Persian troops encircling them; and the commanders of the infantry sections of the flank-guards were to be prepared either to fall back and close the gap between the two infantry lines or to swing forward and so extend the length of the front line. In the former case a box-like formation of infantry would be created, "looking in every direction if they were surrounded" (cf. Frontinus, *Strat.* 2.3.I9). One further order was given in advance: Menidas, in front of the right-hand flank guard, was to incline to the right and charge any enemy cavalry which might try to encircle the right wing. The other orders were general ones, circulated through subordinate commanders: that each man should keep his position, maintain strict silence during the advance and make a concerted shout only at the appropriate moment; and that each subordinate commander should be quick to accept, pass on, and execute each order; and that one and every man should do his duty. The army of 7,000 cavalry and 40,000 infantry was much smaller than that of the Persians and took up much less space (A. 3.12.5; *Itin. Alex.* 23 also gives 7,000 cavalry).

When the entire Macedonian army changed direction at Alexander's probably prearranged order and inclined to the right, Darius responded by extending his line sideways to his left. However, being cumbrous in its deep formation, it moved much less rapidly, except in the front, where the Scythian cavalry swung forward to ride facing the flank-guard. Meanwhile, Alexander marched still further to the right and his leading troops were clear now of the Persians' left-hand fairway for chariots. Anxious to keep Alexander within chariot range, Darius ordered the advanced cavalry of his left wing to encircle Alexander's right wing and stop his rightwards movement. Alexander countered by putting into effect the prearranged order: Menidas charged the first encircling troops. The Scythians and Bactrians counter-charged, driving Menidas back; but Alexander countered by ordering into the attack the Paeonians and the "old-timer" Greek mercenary cavalry, thereby incidentally extending his line to the right, as he had foreseen in such a contingency (A. 3.12.2). At first, their attack made the enemy cavalry fall back. But fresh Persian squadrons, including the rest of the Bactrians on Darius' left wing, joined in and restored the fight. The Persian troops in general, being superior in number, and the Scythians in particular, horse and man being equipped with defensive armour, caused heavy casualties; but the Macedonians fought back, kept formation squadron by squadron, and charging in formation broke up the enemy lines. Meanwhile Alexander kept on towards his right, bringing more of his line clear of the prepared ground.

Before it was too late Darius launched his three groups of chariots. The 100 chariots on his left, charging towards Alexander, were in part intercepted by the Agrianians and the Javelin-men of Balacrus, who hurled their weapons into the horses, knocked the drivers off, and surrounded and killed the horses; other chariots caused no harm because the Macedonians opened ranks, as Alexander had ordered in advance (as at the Shipka pass), and the horses were overpowered by Companion Cavalry grooms in the rear and by some Hypaspists of the Royal Brigade, who had reached that fairway. Arrian says nothing of the other two groups of chariots, except that the opening of the ranks was particularly effective. It was, of course, a piece of drill previously arranged and practised. The second group must have hit the middle of the six infantry brigades; there the pikemen opened ranks and drove their pikes into the passing horses (C. 4.15.14–15). The noise of shouting and banging, which Alexander had ordered in advance, served to scare the horses and turn them back onto their own ranks; this was effective on the Macedonian left, which was almost clear of the fairway (D. 17.58.2–3).

Together with the launching of the 200 chariots Darius had ordered a general advance. His line swept forward, cavalry ahead and vastly outflanking the retarded Macedonian left, but hardly outflanking the Macedonian right, because the Bactrian, Scythian, and related cavalry had already been expended in the preliminary cavalry battle. As more cavalry, now Persian in nationality, tried to encircle his right wing, Alexander ordered the Lancers under Aretes—the last cavalry reserve of the right flank-guard—to charge them at the point of hinge with their main line. While this was happening, Alexander was still continuing the advance to his right front. But when the Lancers under Aretes broke through and created a gap in the main line, Alexander turned his line some ninety degrees to his left front and charged at full speed into the gap, the Companion Cavalry and the Royal Brigade of Hypaspists forming a deep, wedge-like spearhead and every man shouting the war-cry *alalai alalai*. The redirected line arrested and then pierced the leftwards-shifting line of Darius. It then drove forwards "in the direction of Darius himself," Alexander and his cavalrymen on the right shoving back the Persian cavalrymen and aiming their lances at their enemies' faces, and the brigades of Hypaspists presenting a solid hedge of bristling pike-points (A. 3.I4.3). Beyond them brigade after brigade of phalanx-infantry engaged at close quarters, driving the cavalry back relentlessly, as they had done at the Granicus river.

Darius, high in his chariot, saw the left and now the left-centre crumbling before his eyes, and he realised that Alexander and his entourage were fighting their way through to kill or capture him. He turned his chariot and fled, his imperial banner conspicuous above him. Out on the Macedonian right the charge of Aretes and his Lancers to the right (A. 3.14.I) had succeeded, and "here the Persian flight was complete" (A. 3.I4.3–4). As the cavalry of the left centre began to follow Darius in flight, Alexander and his entourage were pressing hard on them and the Hypaspists were encountering the tougher opposition of the Greek mercenary line.

Here we must turn to the other half of the Macedonian line. Since Alexander's advance to his right front inevitably drew the left of his line towards the centre of the battlefield which Darius had prepared, the obvious course for the Persians should have been to encircle and attack the Macedonian left wing at once and so halt the whole operation. But Darius, retaining the over-all command in his own hands, delayed unwisely in order to make a general attack with the chariots and the cavalry, and by that time Alexander was already within striking distance. When the massed forces of the Persian cavalry under Mazaeus' command did encircle the Macedonian left wing, they brought to a halt the whole of that wing, up to and including the brigade of Simmias, so that a widening gap arose between that brigade and the brigade to its right which was still advancing, and also between the corresponding parts of the second line.

Into this gap some Indian and Persian cavalry of Darius' right centre made a charge. Breaking through entirely, they did not wheel to attack the flank of Simmias' brigade and the second line, but they rushed on to Alexander's overnight camp, in order to liberate some prisoners and seize loot (A. 3.12.5 and 3.14.5–6 refers to the camp as "the baggage-animals").[55] The small force of Thracian guards was overwhelmed, but the commanders of the second line of the phalanx, carrying out their prearranged orders, turned their troops about and killed most of the enemy, relatively few escaping in headlong flight. It is probable that these troops came from the right-hand part of the Macedonian second line.

Meanwhile the left-hand of the Macedonian line was at first attacked on the front and on the left wing and was exposed at the rear and on the right. Promptly, in accordance with the prearranged orders, the infantry of the flank-guard fell back, the second line made an about-turn, and Simmias' brigade closed the right flank, so that the enemy were now faced on all sides. While Parmenio was under the maximum pressure, he sent a messenger or messengers at the gallop across the open gap and behind the victorious Macedonian line to reach Alexander who was just on the brink of pursuit. The message was that the left was held up; it was in difficulties and help was needed. Alexander, who was already behind the Persians' original line, "still abstained from pursuit." Instead he wheeled his Companion Cavalry round to the left and set off at speed (A. 3.15.1). Forcing their way at a charge across a stream of withdrawing cavalry—Parthyaeans, Indians, and others of the enemy right centre—the Macedonians clashed head-on with some unbroken formations, deep and solid, of excellent cavalry and in particular of "the finest and most numerous Persians" (including perhaps some of the 1,000 Kinsmen). In this situation it was a matter of push and stab at close quarters, as it had been at Tegyra when Thebes' best hoplites and Spartan hoplites had clashed head on. Many of the enemy broke through, killing sixty Companions on their way. However, the rest of Alexander's force drove on and came within range of Parmenio, only to find the enemy there also in flight because the Thessalian cavalry had delivered a brilliantly successful counter-attack.

Alexander and his Companion Cavalry now led the pursuit, with the Thessalian cavalry a close second. By nightfall, when they reached the Lycus river (the Greater Zab, some twelve miles away), Alexander stopped to water the horses and rest them and the men until midnight. Meanwhile Parmenio was sent to execute the coveted task, the capture of the Persian camp. From midnight until far into the next day the Macedonians pressed the pursuit up to Arbela, the Persian base, seventy-five miles from the battlefield. Five hundred of the Companion Cavalry horses (twenty-five percent) died in action or foundered in this pursuit (Allenby's 5th Cavalry Division lost only twenty-one percent of its horses on a long pursuit). But Darius got away and rode east towards Media, accompanied by the select Bactrian cavalry, the Kinsmen and a few of the "Apple-bearers" who took to horse. Two thousand of the Greek mercenaries made their way out and rejoined Darius later. Otherwise the greatest army Darius had ever mustered was shattered. The losses on the Macedonian side were given by Arrian as about a hundred men killed and more than a thousand horses; by Curtius as under three hundred men killed; and by Diodorus as five hundred killed and a very great many wounded, including Hephaestion, Perdiccas, Coenus, Menidas, and other commanders. [56]

In assessing the generalship of Alexander at Gaugamela, one has to recall that as he intended to be a combatant himself he had to commit himself to a number of prearranged orders, made possible only by his prevision of each step and of contingent situations. Of these orders we know those designed to nullify the effect of the charging chariots, to use the flank-guards in one or the other of two ways (either as forward-moving units to extend the line or as backward-moving units to form flaps between the two lines of the double phalanx), to convert the second line of the double-phalanx into a rear-guard action, and to check by immediate charge the very first move of the enemy to encircle the right wing. Every such order was implemented in the action with total success, the right flank-guard, for example, moving forward and the left flank-guard moving backward. Next, Alexander had to calculate in advance the precise moment at which to change direction from straight ahead to right incline; to anticipate the length of time the units on his right could hold off the Persian cavalry; to ensure that before the end of that time the head of his line, advancing at the pace of a walking horse, would be within striking distance of the enemy; and to anticipate the position which he and his Royal Squadron would then hold in relation to Darius.

As soon as he was engaged in the cavalry charge, Alexander knew that his control of the overall situation was gone. But he had given orders to Aretes and to the commanders both of the battered units and of the fresh infantry units of the right flank-guard which ensured the defeat of the enemy out on the right. He would normally have left Parmenio to fight his own battle on the left, and he would himself have plunged into the pursuit. If he had done so, his victory would have been more complete and the losses of the Companion Cavalry would have been much smaller. But given the message from Parmenio, Alexander made an honourable, if unwise, decision. With the possible exception of his reaction to Parmenio's message Alexander's generalship was faultless on the first and second days of October 331 B.C., which saw the collapse of the two-centuries-old Persian Empire. It is to be noted that Alexander singled out Parmenio now, as after the victory of Issus, for the signal honour of capturing the enemy camp. There is no indication whatever that he had any grudge against Parmenio. [57] Indeed the victory was due in large part to the complete understanding and trust between Alexander and his commanding officers, which resulted from their being constantly in one another's company in and out of action.

Given the disposition which Darius had made of his much more numerous cavalry and very large infantry forces, he failed through losing the initiative, delaying the attack by his right wing, tying his tactics to an ineffective new weapon, and not committing his one thousand Kinsmen to an all-out attack on Alexander in person. His flight at Issus had been to fight another day. At Gaugamela he fled too soon, and his flight ended any hope of fighting again. Perhaps his greatest fault in war was never fully to delegate command, even to such capable officers as Mazaeus and Bessus. He alone matched his brains and his courage with Alexander's, and he was inferior in both. The defeats at Issus and Gaugamela cost his subjects dearly. When we recall that Philip killed 7,000 out of an army of some 10,000 Illyrians, we should estimate Persian losses in tens of thousands.

For Issus we have only propaganda figures of Persian losses which are absurd; but for Gaugamela the figure of 40,000 "so far as the victors could determine" (C. 4.16.26) is not impossible, since the plain was extensive, the Persian infantry was poorly equipped and the cavalry pursued to Arbela. Prisoners were not mentioned as a feature at Issus, but they outnumbered the dead at Gaugamela according to Arrian, drawing on Ptolemy. They were probably sold or held to ransom not by individual captors but by Alexander; for Philip had so dealt with Theban prisoners at Chaeronea, and Alexander so at Issus. It is not surprising that Mazaeus, satrap of Babylonia, decided not to expose the people to further suffering in the cause of Darius, or that Bessus, satrap of Bactria, should doubt the competence of Darius to lead the national resistance.

As hegemon of the Greek League, Alexander reported to the Greek states the overthrow of the apogee of tyrants and the establishment of freedom for all Greeks, to live under their own laws; he promised to rebuild for the Plataeans the city which they had sacrificed in 479 B.C. in the war for freedom against Persia; and he sent a part of the spoils to Croton, which, alone of Greek cities in Italy, had shared in the victory at Salamis. In his letter to Darius after the battle of Issus, Alexander had said, "If you dispute the kingship of Asia with me, stand and fight." Now that dispute was settled. At a ceremony at Arbela which included magnificent sacrifices to the gods, Alexander was officially proclaimed "King of Asia" (P. 34.1). The very words with which he described himself after his victory appear on the oxheads which he dedicated to Athena of Lindus in Rhodes: "King Alexander, having mastered Darius in battle and having become Lord of Asia, made sacrifice to Athena of Lindus in accordance with an oracle" (*FGrH* 532 F I, 38). This is one of the few places where Alexander's actual words have been preserved.

SOURCES

(A) A. 3.1-5; P. 26.3-27.11; D. 17.49-52; C. 4.7-8; 4.11; J. 11.11-12; Str. 792, 814; Lucan 10.272-5.

(B) A. 3.6-7; P. 29.1-6; 30-32.7; D. 17.53, 55, 56; C. 4.9-12.5; J. 11.12.5.

(C) A. 3.8.1-16.2; P. 32.8-34.4; D. 17.57-61; C. 4.12.5-16; 5.1.1-10; Polyaenus 4.3.6, 17 and 18; J. 11.13.1-14.7; *FGrH* 532 F I.38.

VII

FROM MESOPOTAMIA TO AFGHANISTAN

(A) THE KINGDOM OF ASIA

What did it mean to be proclaimed "King of Asia"? When had such a kingship been mentioned or implied before the time of this proclamation? On his first landing in the Troad Alexander "accepted Asia from the gods, land won by the spear," that was, as his personal possession (D. 17.17.2). He believed at Gordium that he was to be "ruler of Asia," the gods themselves having shown him how to undo the knot and having confirmed his future by thunder and lightning (A. 2.3.6 and 8). He maintained that if victory should be granted at Issus the only task remaining was the taking possession of "all Asia" (A. 2.7.6; cf. C. 3.10.4). He challenged Darius to recognise his claim ("I hold the land because the gods gave it to me") and address him as "King of Asia" (A. 2.14.7). He defined the issue at Gaugamela as being "the rule of all Asia" (A. 3.9.6; cf. P. 16.1 "at the gates of Asia . . . for rule ⟨of Asia⟩ "). On riding into battle at Gaugamela Alexander was reported by Callisthenes, his official historian, to have shifted his lance to his left hand, raised his right hand in appeal to the gods and prayed: "If in truth I am descended from Zeus, guard and strengthen the Greeks" (P. 33.1). Thus Alexander encouraged the view that the gods themselves gave him victory at Gaugamela. It was they who had first given him Asia and it was they who now ratified his claim to be "King of Asia."[58]

As King of Asia, Alexander claimed from the start to be liberating his people—the Asians—from the tyrannical rule of Persia. In that capacity he honoured the dead of both sides at the Granicus river, retained no Asian prisoner there, sent the hillmen back to their farms, respected the religion and customs of Lydia and Egypt, and himself made sacrifice to Phoenician Heracles, Egyptian Apis, and Babylonian Ba'al. This was not at all what Greek intellectuals such as Isocrates and Aristotle had hoped he would do: "Compel the barbarians to be the serfs of the Greeks" had been their advice (Isoc. *epist.* 3.5). Nor was he acting as Philip had acted in the Balkans, subjecting hostile peoples to the rule of the king of Macedon, or even as Philip had acted in Greece when he became in person *archon* of the Thessalians and *hegemon* of the Greeks. The kingship of Asia was a god-given, spear-won prerogative, vested in Alexander alone. The Greeks and the Macedonians were helping him to take possession of the kingdom, but they were not, and were not to be, either its rulers or its exploiters. Such a concept as Alexander's was almost inconceivable to a Greek mind; for the peoples of all Greek states from Athens to Thebes, whether following a Pericles or an Epaminondas, had insisted on ruling and exploiting to the full those whom they had conquered by force of arms. Alexander's idea was intelligible, but not on that account acceptable, to some Macedonians; for they understood from their own experience of the Macedonian kingship that the king alone decided the uses to which he put the Macedones, and that the king regarded spear-won land as his own.

After his victory at Gaugamela Alexander knew that he faced a major decision. To suppose that the Greeks would continue to support and enforce his claim was chimerical; he did not delude himself into the belief that they would proceed beyond the liberation of their fellow-Greeks and the exaction of vengeance on the Achaemenid house of Persia which had sacked the temples of Greece. The question was whether the Macedonians would follow their king and enable him to take possession of a new kingdom, that of all Asia. The fact that they did proclaim him on that day at Arbela "King of all Asia" committed them, in his view and theirs, to this task (P. 34.1). He even told Athena of Lindus in his proleptic way that he was "Lord of Asia" (*FGrH* 532 F I, 38). He himself seems to have had no doubts. A man of twenty-five, confident in five years of kingship and victory, assured of divine aid and of Macedonian support, he did not hesitate in the face of his task, a small fraction of which was to daunt the Roman Trajan when he too approached the shore of the Persian Gulf.

The question we may ask is this: was Alexander justified in pressing on towards the east? Indeed should we apply to him the judgement that has been passed on Trajan, that already he "had advanced too fast and too far"? Strategically, of course, it was clear to any Macedonian that possession of the alluvial plains was not enough; for as in the Balkans, so in Mesopotamia it was essential to conquer and hold "the upper provinces," as the Macedonians were soon to call them, if the kingship of Asia was to be secured. What was in question was whether the resources of Alexander were already stretched beyond the reasonable limit. If they were, the wise course was to withdraw to the line of the Upper Euphrates by Thapsacus. If they were not, a further advance was justified; but Alexander must have known already that such an advance had to be carried into areas which were very distant from Babylon, let alone from Pella. We must therefore turn back and consider whether Alexander's resources were overstrained by the end of 331 B.C.

˙ (B) DEMANDS ON MEN AND MONEY IN EUROPE AND ASIA

During Alexander's campaigns in Asia most of the reinforcements from Europe of whatever nationality were mustered by Antipater in Macedonia and sent on from there or collected there by officers sent home for that purpose (A. I. 29.4, Macedonians, Thessalians and Eleans; 3.5.I, Greek mercenaries and Thracians). Thus when we are informed by Polybius, who was summarising some statement in Callisthenes, that "5,000 infantry and 800 cavalry came from Macedonia as another rein- forcement for Alexander when he was about to invade Cilicia," this tells us nothing about the nationality of the troops (Polyb. I2.I9.2 = Callis- thenes F 35). Further, even when the word "Macedonian" is used, it is frequently in contrast to "Persian" or "Greek," and it does not then have the specific sense of Macedonian citizen. Thus when we are told by Arrian that Alexander received at Gordium 3,000 Macedonian infantry, 300 Macedonian cavalry and 150 Elean cavalry (A. I.29.4), we should not conclude that these Macedonians were all those élite citizens, the "Macedones" proper, who were qualified to serve in the Hypaspists, the phalanx-brigades and the Companion Cavalry.

Nor should we take the two accounts of reinforcements, that of Polybius and that of Arrian, and regard them as variants of one act of re- inforcement. For they differed both in numbers and in time. Arrian's re- inforcements reached Gordium about April 333 B.C., and Polybius' rein- forcements reached Alexander when he was about to invade Cilicia, i.e., in July/August 333 B.C. It was a contingent of the latter which was de- scribed at the battle of Issus in November 333 B.C. as "Agrianians recently arrived" (C. 3.9.I0). Thus returning to Callisthenes (F 35), we see that Agrianians were among the 5,000 infantry "from Macedonia," and that the word "another" implied that Callisthenes had mentioned an earlier but not remote army of reinforcement (namely, that at Gordium).[59]

What were Alexander's needs? On the basis of the numbers which we have given for his three great battles in Asia, Alexander maintained the Hypaspists and the phalanx-brigades at the same strength and in- creased the number of Companion Cavalry only slightly, by some 200. As his losses in dead at the Granicus were in tens, at Issus 150 cavalry and 302 infantry all told, and at Tyre about 400 all told, replacements for the dead in these special units were not high in number; on the other hand large numbers were wounded, and some proportion of these must have been unfit for further service in these units. It seems probable that Alexander could have maintained the strength of these units by taking only each year's output of new soldiers in Macedonia (say 1,000 a year for the phalanx and 100 a year for Companion Cavalry).

Thus Alexander did not need to draw at all from the army of Mace- donian citizens which he had left with Antipater; that he did not do so is what we should expect of a capable commander in years when the Persian fleet was active and Agis was fomenting revolt in Greece. In this connection it is important to note that these special units were constantly on operations in the field and formed the spearhead of the attack in all three battles; it was this continuous action and specialised use which gave them their remarkable esprit de corps, and even the sick and wounded among them were taken on campaign in the hope of rejoining their units (so at Issus). They were not diverted or frittered away for garrisoning, blockading, and guarding lines of communication; these duties were carried out by Greek allied troops, Greek mercenaries, light-armed Balkan troops, and allied or mercenary cavalry (e.g., A. I.I7.7–8; I.23,6; 2.I.4; 2.I3.7). Indeed even within the first line troops Alexander tended to keep the three special units under his own hand, for instance, in autumn 333 B.C. when he sent Parmenio ahead not with any Macedonian troops but with the Thessalian cavalry, the Thracian javelin-men, the Greek allied infantry and the Greek mercenaries (A. 2.5.I).

For garrisoning and similar duties he had at the outset 7,000 Greek allied infantry, 7,000 Balkan infantry, and probably 13,000 Greek mercenaries, and he drew on all of them in these years. Demands were particularly heavy in the years between the Granicus and Issus, when Alexander had to put garrisons in the islands, in places on the Asiatic coast, and especially in the Hellespontine area. Moreover, he knew that for the confrontation with Darius he would need to implement his army with a large force of additional infantry. In fact at Issus as compared with the Granicus we may estimate that he had the following additional troops: 200 more Companion Cavalry, 200 more Thessalian cavalry, 1,500 more archers and Agrianians, 1,000 Thracian Javelin-men, 1,000 "Macedonian" (as opposed to "Cretan") archers, and 7,500 Greek mercenary infantry. It seems likely, then, that the bulk of the troops who came out as reinforcements were Balkan rather than Macedonian, and Greek mercenary rather than Greek allied. Moreover, he also recruited Greek mercenaries in Asia, e.g., at Miletus and Chios.

When we compare his forces at Issus and at Gaugamela, as we have estimated them, we find the following increases: 400 Greek allied cavalry, 1,200 Greek mercenary cavalry, 200 Odrysian cavalry, 500 Agrianians, and 10,500 Balkan and Greek mercenary infantry. Part of these must have come from Europe; but he also recruited troops who had been in enemy service at Issus (A. 2.I4.7). Altogether we know of 7,500 Greek mercenaries, obtained from Antipater and direct from the Peloponnese and from Chios, and of 500 Thracian cavalry sent by Antipater; but there is little doubt that we should allow for a large number of additional Balkan troops (perhaps 5,000) who are not mentioned in our sources. During this period he had some additional commitments: mercenary garrisons at Memphis and Pelusium (A. 3.5.3; numbered at 4,000 by C.

4.8.4), a fleet of 30 triremes defending Egypt, and considerable naval operations in the Aegean (A. 3.6.3). By the time of Gaugamela he had founded a number of settlements which probably absorbed most of his wounded men and discharged mercenaries; these took the place of troops guarding the lines of communication, for instance in Cilicia, and constituted an economy in military terms.

The large draft which Alexander probably hoped to have obtained earlier did not arrive until he was at Susa in December 331 B.C. The numbers, given not by Arrian but by Diodorus (17.65.1) and with slight differences by Curtius (5.1.40-42 and 7.1.40) were 500 Macedonian horse, 6,000 Macedonian infantry; from Thrace 600 horse and 3,500 infantry ('*Tralleis*' in Diodorus); and from the Peloponnese 4,000 Greek mercenaries, and 380, or perhaps twice as many, horse. In this case we have an indication in the texts that Antipater sent the Macedonians only; that the Thracians, raised probably by the "General in Thrace," started from Thrace; and that the mercenaries sailed direct from the Peloponnese. They must have had a common rendezvous on the Asiatic coast. The arrival of these reinforcements enabled Alexander to make good his losses (mainly wounded, no doubt) in the Hypaspists and the six phalanx-brigades and also to form a seventh phalanx-brigade (1,500 strong); make good his losses and perhaps increase his "Macedonian" archers; and increase his numbers of Balkan and Greek troops very considerably.

Of his losses we know little, except that deaths in battle were relatively few because the protective armour was very effective except against catapult-bolts. A man was often wounded and fought again, because weapons were not of steel (cf. Livy 31.34.4) and because doctors could cope with sword-cuts and spear-thrusts. Occasionally a death through illness was reported, but we do not hear of any epidemic. Health was evidently good, because Alexander kept his army in camp and not in city billets and because the troops were toughened by their hard training and marching.

Arrian tells us that Alexander added the cavalry which arrived at Susa to the Companion Cavalry, and the infantry "to the other formations" (i.e., other than the cavalry units, *taxeis*), "assigning each group in accordance with national origins," i.e., to units of Lower Macedonia, Elimea, Tymphaea, Lyncus, and Orestis, of which the peoples were called *ethne*, "nations," as in Thucydides (2, 99.2 and 6). At the same time it is doubtful whether Alexander took these 6,000 phalanx-infantry from Antipater's army of 12,000 phalanx-men, not only because Antipater was in as great danger as ever when these troops were requested but also because the officer sent to Macedonia by Alexander seems to have been raising new recruits (C. 7.1.40; cf. A. I.24.2). It makes some sense to suppose that Alexander was now drawing on capable men who had not hitherto been included in the class of "Macedones" proper but were now trained and promoted to that class. This is, of course, conjectural.

When we put these figures together, we can see the order of magnitude of the forces which served under Alexander in the period 334–331 B.C. During the latter part of 331 B.C., he had in Asia some 26,000 men from Macedonia, of whom perhaps 2,400 were not Macedonian citizens; at least 29,000 Greek mercenaries; some 21,000 Balkan troops; and over 10,000 Greek allied troops, including the Thessalian cavalry: a total of about 86,000. Many of these troops served in garrisons, on lines of supply and in new towns founded by Alexander, but they were all under his control. In the Eastern Mediterranean he had begun his campaign in Asia with some 36,000 men in the fleet and had discharged most of them; but in the latter part of 331 B.C. he must have had at least 36,000 men serving with the fleets protecting Egypt, guarding the Hellespont and operating off the Peloponnese (the last under Amphoterus and including 100 ships from Cyprus and Phoenicia). Then in Macedonia itself he had left under Antipater 12,000 Macedonian infantry of the phalanx and 1,500 Companion Cavalry; these were the basis of the army of some 40,000 men, including Greek allies, which served Antipater in the campaign of 331–330 B.C. against Agis of Sparta. In that year, then, Alexander had something like 150,000 men under arms, of whom perhaps a quarter were Macedonian citizens.

The maintenance of his forces must have been a difficult matter from the start. Although he inherited from Philip an efficient army, a strong currency, and productive mines, it seems that there were no substantial reserves. The costs of Alexander's Balkan and Greek campaign may have been covered by the quantities of loot (A. 1.2.1; 1.4.5 and Cleitarchus F I for Thebes), the sale of prisoners and the removal of stock, and he was able to mount and launch his expeditionary force against Persia without losing credit even if he had a current overdraft. If it is true that the army crossed the Hellespont with supplies for only a month, then that was enough, because he won an early victory and his forces lived to a considerable extent off enemy territory from then onwards, whether by gift, requisitioning, purchase, or pillage. Tribute levied from former Persian subjects, contributions paid by Greek cities (especially those liberated in Asia), fines and indemnities imposed on states which were judged unfaithful to the cause—these brought in a steady income to which were added the spoils of war from the Battle of the Granicus onwards. Already in the summer of 334 B.C. he was sufficiently confident of his financial position to forego substantial taxes from Ephesus and Priene; and if financial reasons played a part in his decision to disband the bulk of his fleet, it may have been not that he lacked the funds but that he had a better use for them.

A day's pay for a cavalryman in Alexander's army was probably two drachmae, for a hypaspist one drachma, and for a mercenary soldier two-thirds of a drachma, i.e., four obols. At that time the lowest wage for a workman was two obols a day, and Alexander's men drew basic rations, no doubt gratis. The army's pay at Gaugamela may be estimated as 46,000 drachmae, i.e., some 8 talents of silver per day, and the pay for all troops under arms in all theatres was probably 20 talents a day, or 7,300 talents a year. We may recall for comparison that the output of Philip's mines at Pangaeum alone had been 10,000 talents a year, regarded then as a huge sum.

In order to pay his troops and meet other expenses Alexander had need of a prolific and stable coinage, which, like the gold coinage of Queen Victoria, corresponded in its nominal value to its worth as precious metal.[60] Alexander inherited such a coinage from Philip. Moreover, as Philip had intended to conduct a great campaign in 336 B.C. and in the following years, he had no doubt accumulated a considerable stock of gold "philippeioi" and silver tetradrachms. These seem to have served part of Alexander's needs in 336 B.C. and 335 B.C. In Philip's time the chief mint had been at Pella. It had drawn its minerals mainly from Mt. Pangaeum but also from areas west of the Strymon. The mint at Amphipolis had been of secondary importance. This had corresponded with Philip's interests in the Balkans, Central Europe, and the Aegean, because Pella was at the centre of Macedonia's communications with these areas. But when Alexander crossed to Asia it was Amphipolis which became the chief mint, and the bullion which Alexander obtained in Asia Minor was sent to Amphipolis to be converted into the "philippeioi" which were so useful in recruiting mercenaries.

Alexander acquired large amounts of bullion and coin which had been accumulated by the Persian satraps at administrative centres such as Dascylium and Sardis, and he evidently made use of the gold and electrum ores which were being mined in Asia Minor (as Philip seems to have done, putting Lampsacus, Cyzicus, Phocaea, and Mytilene almost out of operation in these metals). Early in 333 B.C. he had more ready cash in Asia than in Macedonia, since he sent an officer "with money" from Pamphylia to the Peloponnese to recruit mercenaries. But the great change came about after the victory at Issus. Then, in the winter of 333–332 B.C., he obtained a huge amount of Persian bullion and both gold and silver coin in Cilicia and at Damascus (J. 11.10.5 "auri magno pondere"; C. 3.13.16, at Damascus 2,600 talents of coin alone). He began now to make coinage in his own name. The chief mints were first at Tarsus and Myriandrus (renamed Alexandria ad Issum), being close to the source of the metals. Indeed these places had served already as mints for the Persian satraps, and the die-sinkers who had made the last coins of the Persian satraps there went on to produce the first Alexander issues.

Meanwhile in Europe the mints at Pella and Amphipolis began to produce Alexander's own coinages. The standards there had been Attic in gold and Thracian in silver, the latter being appropriate to Philip's interests in the Balkans and (through the Balkans) in Central Europe, but they now became Attic in both metals. Thus Macedonia began to compete with Athens as the issuer of a coinage which was valid throughout the Mediterranean and in Asia in both gold and silver. Possessing large reserves of gold bullion, Alexander was able so to control the rate of conversion into coin that he made ten silver drachmae worth one gold drachma and he maintained the ratio between the precious metals at ten to one. He placed on his gold stater, containing two drachmae, the head of Athena wearing a Corinthian helmet and on the reverse side a winged Victory with a wreath and a *stylis*. The splendid quality of the figures owed much to the contemporary art at Athens. But attempts to derive Alexander's emblems from Athens are most implausible; for since the beginnings of Macedonian coinage in 479 B.C.,[61] no Macedonian king had borrowed any emblem from Athens, and now Alexander was celebrating the victory of Macedonia and not of Athens over Persia. The Athena was in my opinion the Macedonian goddess of war, "Athena Alcidemos," and a lion-gryphon on her helmet has been understood to symbolise Macedonia's enmity with Persia. The wreath and the *stylis* presumably refer to the battle which the winged Victory celebrates. The *stylis* was an instrument for elevating the outlook-post (*aphlaston*) on a ship; it was used here, I suggest, to commemorate the daring of the Companions who took their ship inshore under the nose of Darius when they went to spy out his position (A. 2.7.2).

On his silver tetradrachm, didrachm (issued only in the early years), and drachma, Alexander used the traditional Macedonian emblems (Philip had used them in his first coinage): the head of a young Heracles wearing a lion-skin headdress, and on the reverse Zeus seated on a throne with an eagle and a sceptre. His bronze coin had the same Heracles and the reverse showed Heracles' bow and club. The Zeus was probably Zeus Basileus, the king of gods and men, the sceptre being the emblem of rule and the eagle his messenger—that eagle which had indicated to Alexander that he should defeat the Persian navy on land. Zeus, Athena, and Heracles, although specific to Macedon, were of universal significance to the Greek world, and they were readily identifiable with oriental deities in the minds of Alexander's Asian subjects. In particular the seated Zeus was only a slight modification of the Ba'al portrayed on the Persian coins minted at Tarsus. Alexander's choice of devices was brilliant; for they expressed ideas and aims which were significant for himself, the Macedonians, the Greeks, and the Asian peoples too. Unlike some of his predecessors, he did not place a representation of himself on his coins.

Communications overland from Gaugamela ran through the northern part of the fertile crescent which faces the Syrian desert and then through Cilicia. During the summer campaign he had established his control as far to the north as the Armenian mountains, and his engineers had made a double bridge over the Euphrates at Thapsacus. It is probable that now or soon afterwards he founded some settlements in this northern area, where an Alexandria and a Nicephorium (near Raqqa) are known. In Cilicia too he had bridged the Pyramus and founded settlements. For these districts formed already, and were to form in the future, the channel of traffic between west and east. From Cilicia his communications spread out by land and by sea; and those by sea were protected by flotillas of Macedonian, Greek, Cypriot, and Phoenician ships. Although Alexander did everything possible to improve and secure his line of communications, it still took more than three months for troops to travel from Pella to Susa overland. A courier service could probably cut this time by a month. Thus in terms of communication there was a two-months lag between Antipater and Alexander, and a four-months spell for an answer to a question to be delivered.[62]

In 331 B.C. the slowness of communication between Alexander and Antipater became particularly important, because the situation in the Peloponnese caused much alarm. Sparta, proudly defiant of Philip and Alexander since 338 B.C., had been in open alliance with Persia and had recently been receiving Persian subsidies to support a second front in Greek waters. In summer 331 B.C. Alexander learnt that there was some movement in favour of support for Sparta and Persia in the Peloponnese, and he tried to discourage it by sending a Macedonian fleet to the Peloponnese and reinforcing it with 100 ships from Phoenicia and Cyprus. The fleet's task was to regain lost ground in Crete, cut Sparta's communications overseas and lend help to loyalists in the Peloponnese. This move seemed to be successful. In or around September 331 B.C. a large Macedonian force set off through Thrace for the distant east, and news was reaching Greece by then that Alexander had disappeared into northern Mesopotamia, "almost beyond the limits of the inhabited world" from a Greek point of view (Aeschin. 3.165). By early October Agis III, the young king of Sparta,[63] knew that the forces of Macedon were more widely distributed and more clearly divided than ever before, and he probably had expectations of a rising in Thrace which did occur as soon as the Macedonian force heading for the east was out of reach. Agis then went into action. He attacked and defeated a Macedonian force in the Peloponnese with his own army and with a force of some 10,000 mercenaries, which he had hired with Persian gold. This success brought Elis, Arcadia (except Megalopolis), and Achaea (except Pellene) into open alliance with him. However, the rest of the Greek states, including Athens where Demades was in the ascendancy, remained loyal to the Greek League, their distrust of Sparta being perhaps as strong a factor as their fear of Macedonian power.

Antipater's first concern was to suppress the rising in Thrace and re-open communications with Asia. This he achieved by mustering the full resources of the homeland and by making an agreement with Memnon, Alexander's commander in Thrace, who had evidently instigated the rising (D. 17.62.5) but thought better of it. The news of Antipater's success and of Agis' victory over a Macedonian force reached Alexander at Susa in late December 331 b.c. He sent to Antipater 3,000 talents, a large sum, with which to buy support and mercenaries. (The mints in Europe evidently had no reserves.) What Antipater needed was an army powerful enough to ensure outright victory; for any reverse might cause other states in Greece to defect to the Spartan side. During the winter Agis and his allies seem to have played into Antipater's hands by sitting down to blockade Megalopolis and offering no challenge at all to Macedonia's garrisons and influence in the Isthmus and Central Greece. Antipater took the time which Agis made so conveniently available to him, and it is probable that the 3,000 talents sent by Alexander were in his hands by the end of March 330 b.c.

It was probably in April or May that Antipater came through the Isthmus, apparently unopposed, and raised the siege of Megalopolis. His army, reported to have been 40,000 strong, contained excellent Macedonian troops to the number of at least 1,500 cavalry and 12,000 infantry of the phalanx, large numbers of Balkan troops and contingents from Macedonia's Greek allies. Agis had 2,000 cavalry and 10,000 Greek mercenaries, and, given his alliances, he may have had the 20,000 citizen infantry with which the tradition credits him (Din. 1.34; D.17.62.7). Antipater won the ensuing battle near Megalopolis, in which Agis and 5,300 of his army were killed, and obtained the capitulation of the enemy, Sparta providing hostages. Antipater's own losses were severe, 1,000 or 3,500 being killed, our sources report, and many more wounded, and it is clear that he lacked his king's ability to win by manoeuvre and avoid such losses; indeed, Alexander is reputed to have called it "a battle of rats." Yet the verdict was as clear as it had been at Chaeronea; the pikeman outfought the hoplite.

Antipater referred the treatment of the defeated states to the Council of the Greek League, as the insurgents at least had broken their oaths to the League. The Council in turn passed the matter to Alexander as hegemon. He was apprised of Antipater's victory in August or so, being then probably in Areia, and at about that time the hostages set out from Sparta to make their appeal to him (Aeschin. 3.133). In the end all except the leaders were pardoned by him, and fines were exacted from Elis and Achaea and paid as compensation to the people of Megalopolis.

The inability of Agis to gain adherents outside the Peloponnese doomed the rising to failure. One has to recall that Agis must have known that there were forces of cavalry serving with Alexander from central and southern Thessaly, Malis, Phocis, Locris, Orchomenus, Thespiae, Athens and probably other places, and also that ships and crews from maritime states, including Athens, were at sea with his fleets. Moreover, these states were influenced by the successes against Persia, the material benefits accruing from them, the openings for settlement and investment, and the money brought home by their citizens. It is clear that the Greek states had no substantial grievances under the terms of the Greek League; for a pamphlet *On the Treaty with Alexander* makes only trivial charges against Alexander. The adherents whom Agis did obtain were probably party-leaders who had an eye for power in their own states (e.g., in Elis which had cavalry, i.e., well-to-do men, with Alexander) rather than a zeal for national liberation. Agis himself may have been a political idealist, but he and his fellows seem to have made a faulty assessment of their chances of success. On the other hand, the clemency of Alexander was something no Greek who had seen Thebes destroyed could have counted on in advance. Alexander's mixed methods, of severity and generosity, proved effective during his lifetime.

It seems, then, that Alexander's material resources were not over-strained in 331–330 B.C. As regards money, immense quantities of bullion which the Achaemenid kings had hoarded were there for the taking, and gold would hire any number of mercenaries in Greece and in the Balkans. He had proved too that employment with him was more rewarding and less dangerous than service with the Achaemenids or other employers. His own manpower in Macedonia and the Balkans was able to deal with two risings of some magnitude, and Antipater could have called upon allies in Epirus for help, if the need had arisen. Alexander's main anxiety must have been whether the Macedonians he had with him were becoming exhausted by unending campaigns and distressed by prolonged absence from their homes in Europe. He may already have envisaged the possibility of training Asian subjects so that they would serve the King of Asia.

(C) DEMANDS ON LEADERSHIP AND ADMINISTRATION

The greatest hazard which Alexander faced was that he would be assassinated or killed in action. Because he trusted his friends so implicitly, he had been in serious danger from Alexander the Lyncestian in the opinion of his staff officers, and his Bodyguards and the Royal Pages were constantly on the alert for any conspiracy. In battle he exposed himself recklessly. Perhaps he felt it to be a part of valour (*arete*), perhaps he thought he bore a charmed life; and it was said that the shield of the Trojan Athena was carried by the Royal Hypaspists into battle before him, as a piece of the cross might have been carried before a crusader. To have been so often wounded and yet not incapacitated must have seemed almost miraculous, as in the case of Philip. If he were to be killed, no member of the royal family was fit to take his place. Moreover, so far he had failed to follow the advice of Parmenio to marry and beget an heir. On the occasions when he was dangerously wounded or seriously ill, as at Tarsus, operations came to a standstill and the troops were close to panic; but he seems not to have empowered anyone to act in his place.

Among the leading Macedonians, namely those whom Philip and Alexander had made Friends, Companions, Bodyguards, and Commanders, there was much intermarriage. Influential cliques may have formed and reformed, but there is little to indicate that Alexander was swayed or dominated by any such group. He seems to have assumed that all men in these high grades would be loyal without his making special concessions or currying favour; and in this he relied on the centuries-old tradition of service to the Temenid monarchy as much as on his own personality and open-handedness. He seems to have made his promotions and appointments on the basis of personal merit, and he had an intimate knowledge of his men, because he was constantly in their company in peace, hunting, and war. If he had a fault, it was that he was too trusting where he had given his friendship.

The positions of highest trust were given to those who had proved themselves with Philip, namely Antipater and Parmenio. Otherwise, he provided checks and counter-checks in his administrative service. Thus a garrison-commander was normally independent of the military governor in a satrapy, and a financial officer independent of the civil governor; they were all responsible directly to Alexander, as we have seen in the case of Egypt. Special precautions were taken in the field of finance. Alexander left the Asian communities to collect their own taxes by their traditional methods, and he ordered their senior officials to hand over their dues in money or in kind to Alexander's financial officer—Philoxenus, for instance, in Asia Minor west of the Taurus range, Coeranus in Phoenicia, and Cleomenes in Egypt, each of whom needed only a small staff to keep the records. At a higher level there were regional financial officers who collected, transported, and paid out monies and stores, for example to escort-troops, muleteers, carriers, runners and so on; and they were sometimes empowered to enlist troops, pay them, and conduct them to Alexander.

Such officers were called *hyparchs*, being immediate deputies of Alexander; Menes for instance had Cilicia, Syria, and Phoenicia as his region with a float of 3,000 talents in 331 B.C. (A. 3.16.9–I0). Most important of all were special commissions to take over huge amounts of bullion, these being entrusted for instance to Parmenio and Philoxenus, and the permanent charge of "the money with Alexander," which reached gigantic proportions. This last post was given to Harpalus, a friend and contemporary of Alexander, one of those who had been exiled on his account and then recalled by him. Harpalus played Alexander false, fled into voluntary exile, was recalled, pardoned, and reinstated in 331 B.C. This was to prove one of the rare cases where Alexander's heart misled him.

Ancient democracies, like modern ones, tend to large bureaucracies, especially in ruling others, as Athens did in the fifth century (see Arist. *Ath. Pol.* 24.3). Alexander's policy was the opposite; he let the Asian communities govern themselves and he employed his Macedonian and Greek officials only at the higher levels. In consequence he had no shortage of capable and dependable men to hold senior positions as civil governors, military governors, financial officers, garrison commanders, fleet-commanders, recruiting officers, mint officials and so on; not surprisingly, because he was drawing on those who had been trained within the framework of the Macedonian army. An unsuccessful administrator, such as Arimmas in Syria, seems to have been the exception, and he was dismissed at once. When Alexander appointed Asians as civil governors, it was for reasons of policy, not because he was short of suitable Europeans, and the policy was that of regional self-government, which was being practised in Macedonia, the Balkans, and the Greek states. True, the policy had its defects: Thebes had revolted in 335 B.C., and now Agis had raised some rebels in the Peloponnese, and there had been a recent rising in the Balkans. But in general, the policy had been successful, and it alone enabled Alexander to conserve his military and administrative manpower and concentrate on further conquest.

In Asia risings against a Macedonian satrap had been rare. Admittedly, it was still the honeymoon period, but within it Alexander had done much to win the allegiance of Asians to him as King of Asia. Not the least important factor was the economic prosperity Alexander brought by opening the east to the capitalist system of the west: introducing a full monetary economy, encouraging urban development, protecting maritime commerce, and developing overland communications from the Thermaic Gulf to the Persian Gulf. Men saw the dawn of an economic *koine*, and the benefits of it reached far down into Asian society. The kingship of Asia had begun as a figment of Alexander's imagination in spring 334 B.C. By the end of 331 B.C. it was a reality, extending into the heart of Asia.

No republican, however able, could have succeeded as Alexander had succeeded in his first five years in power, or could have reached the position in which he faced a choice so decisive for the lives of many millions. The coefficient of his achievement was the Macedonian monarchy: that alone made success possible. In 331 B.C. that monarchy was coming under some strain, not through war, to which it was accustomed, but through transplantation. It was true that the Macedonian state functioned where the king himself was, and where a part of the Macedonian people was present in his service; but there must have been many Macedonians who longed to see their king and themselves back in Pella and Aegeae. Alexander took special steps to emphasise that the centre of the state was at his headquarters; for instance, he arranged that "fifty sons of the King's Friends" should be sent "from Macedonia by their fathers to serve as guards of the King's person" (D. I7.65.I; C. 5.1.42), and they arrived soon after the victory at Gaugamela to undergo their training in Asia. Another source of strain was the readiness of Alexander to adopt various *personae*, when his Macedonians would have preferred to have him simply King of Macedon.

(D) THE SOUTHEASTERN SATRAPIES AND THE PURSUIT OF DARIUS

During the winter of 331–330 B.C., Alexander took over the centres of Persian power in the south. Marching in battle-order on Babylon, he was met by deputations of priests, officials, and people, who strewed his way with flowers, showered gifts upon him, and delivered city, citadel, and treasury into his hands. To mark the liberation of Babylon after two centuries of Persian rule, the priests instructed Alexander in the traditional ritual and he made sacrifice accordingly to their chief god, Ba'al; and on his part he ordered the rebuilding of the temples which Xerxes had destroyed, and in particular the temple of Ba'al.

He established a prolific mint at Babylon, which was soon producing silver tetradrachms with the representation of Zeus Basileus or (to his Babylonian subjects) Ba'al. As civil governor or satrap he appointed Mazaeus, the commander of the Persian right wing at Gaugamela, who had surrendered himself and his sons; the command of the troops left at Babylon was given to a Macedonian, and the collection of taxes went to a Macedonian also. At this time he sent another distinguished Persian, Mithrenes, who had joined him at Sardes, to be satrap of Armenia, the region north of Mesopotamian Syria; for that was an area from which attacks might be made on his lines of communication through the northern part of the fertile crescent. What Mithrenes achieved is unknown.

Meanwhile Philoxenus, who had been sent ahead to Susa, reported that the satrap, Abulites, and the people had surrendered the city and treasury. When Alexander reached Susa in twenty days from Babylon, he kept Abulites as satrap of Susiana; but he appointed Macedonians to command the troops in the satrapy, to command the garrison of the citadel, and to guard the treasury. The original bronze statues of Harmodius and Aristogeiton, the tyrannicides, were found among the spoils which Xerxes had brought from Greece and deposited at Susa. With his usual grace Alexander sent them to the Athenian people. The treasury which Alexander took over contained "an incredible amount of specie," including 50,000 talents of silver in ingots. In thanksgiving for his success Alexander made sacrifice in accordance with Macedonian custom and held a festival with athletics events and a torch-race.

With the treasure which had now fallen into his hands Alexander was able to reward his soldiers for their services. He distributed boun-ties which ranged from 600 drachmae for a Macedonian cavalryman to two months' pay for a mercenary (some 50 drachmae), and these gifts were the more timely because Alexander did not permit pillaging and looting. Generous gratuities were paid to men unfit for further service, who were placed in his new towns, in garrisons, or returned home; for instance, 1,000 overage Macedonians garrisoned the citadel of Susa. The war which he expected to fight in the eastern provinces would not be decided by a great pitched battle such as he had fought at Gaugamela; for it became clear that Darius would never muster another great army. Alexander, therefore, reorganised his army in order to fit it for mountain warfare, mobile or guerrilla warfare, and siege-warfare.[64]

The basic unit in the cavalry, apart from the Companion Cavalry, was now made the company of 75 to 100 troopers. Each company was commanded by a Companion cavalryman, chosen by Alexander for his personal courage, and the troopers were allocated to the companies with no discrimination in the matter of race. The chief reason for introducing this system was that Asian horsemen were being brought into the army in large numbers. It is probable that some companies were equipped in the Asian style as mounted javelin-men and archers. The changes in the infantry were designed to encourage initiative, daring, endurance and dedication—qualities which have always been sought in recruiting men for commando units. Alexander held a competition in daring which was judged by a panel, and the first eight men (including Atarrhias and others who had distinguished themselves in the siege of Halicarnassus) were appointed *chiliarchae*, "commanders of a thousand." The 8,000 men who were selected for the eight new units on the grounds of their commando-type qualities came from any unit in the army except the Royal Body-guards and the Hypaspists. When in training and on operations in the Thousands, they obeyed the Chiliarchs; but they evidently retained their affinity with their original units and served in them when that was more appropriate to the conditions. Here too there were changes in training and equipment; for an infantryman of a phalanx-brigade had to use not a pike but a different weapon, and he probably wore different armour for a night operation in wooded, mountainous terrain. Thus Alexander began to develop an army of dual purpose, capable still of fighting in the past style in a set battle, but trained now for mobile warfare in difficult country. It was he who provided the weapons, as Philip had done from the start (D. 16.3.1).

For the advance towards Persepolis, some 600 kilometres southeast of Susa, Alexander took a striking force of 15,000 infantry. His way was blocked by the local satrap Medates, who defended a fortified town in a narrow place. Being informed of a secret route, Alexander sent a turning force of 2,500 Agrianians and mercenaries under Tauron, probably a brother of Harpalus, and himself engaged in an assault on the town, his troops making some siege-equipment from local timber. When Tauron appeared in a position which threatened the town from above, Medates and his best troops withdrew into the citadel and opened negotiations.

Alexander was glad to come to terms with Medates, who was related to Darius and the Queen Mother, Sisigambis. As this success freed the lowland route, Alexander sent on it part of the army and the baggage-train under Parmenio, while he himself led his 8,000 "commando" infantry, together with the Royal Bodyguards and the Hypaspists, against the mountain people called the Uxii. The chieftains of these peoples had demanded from Alexander a payment for passage which they had regularly extracted from the Persian kings, and he had challenged them to meet him at a specified pass. Assuming that they would have taken their troops towards that pass, Alexander made off at night on a different course, raided the undefended villages the next day, and still reached the pass ahead of the Uxian troops. In addition, he had detached en route a part of his force under Craterus who was ordered to seize a strategic point. When the Uxian troops appeared, Alexander attacked them from higher ground and drove them back onto the force under Craterus. The Uxii suffered very heavy losses. According to Arrian (5.19.6), the Uxii stole Alexander's favourite horse, Bucephalus, but in view of Alexander's dire threats, they brought him back.

According to Ptolemy, the terms which were granted to the Uxii were due to the appeal of Sisigambis, whom Alexander had left behind at Susa; they agreed to pay an annual tribute in kind of 100 cavalry horses, 500 draught-animals, and 30,000 head of livestock. In addition the Macedonians had taken much loot. The success of the new commando units was due above all to their astonishing speed in rough country (A. 3.17.4-5) (see Figure 13).

For his next objective, the Persian Gates, a narrow pass ten kilometres long between high mountains in the Zagros range, held by the satrap of Persis, Ariobarzanes, with any army reported variously between 25,000 and 40,000 infantry and 300 to 700 cavalry, Alexander needed his regular army. The troops of the commando units returned to their regiments. While Parmenio took the baggage-train, the Thessalian cavalry, the Greek allies, the mercenaries, and the other "heavy-armed" infantry (probably from each phalanx-brigade) along the lower road which went through Shiraz, Alexander set off for the Persian Gates, taking the Companion Cavalry, the Lancers, the Macedonian infantry (apart from the "heavy-armed"), the Agrianians and the archers along a high mountainous route. Travelling fast to Mullah Susan, he led his army into the pass, which he knew by now was held by the enemy. When he reached the point where Ariobarzanes had built a wall from cliff to cliff, the Macedonians came under heavy fire from catapults, slingers and archers. Withdrawing to Mullah Susan, some five or six kilometres away, he built a fortified camp, ordered Craterus to hold it with two phalanx-brigades, some of the archers, and 500 cavalry, and set off on a circuitous route of which he had been informed by his prisoners. See Figures 40 and 41.

Craterus was ordered to deceive the enemy by keeping the usual number of camp-fires burning, and to be prepared in due course, when he heard Alexander's bugles, to lead his troops into the pass and attack the enemy. Leaving at nightfall with the remainder of the army, he divided it later into two parts: one, consisting of four phalanx-brigades and most of the cavalry, was sent forward into the plain of Ardakan with orders to bridge the river Araxes (Palvar) which lay between the Persian Gates and Persepolis; and the other under his own command, consisting of the Hypaspists, one phalanx-brigade (that of Perdiccas), the Scythian archers, the Agrianians, the Royal Squadron of Companion Cavalry, and a "tetrarchy" of cavalry (perhaps four of the new companies), continued on the circuitous route through difficult and thickly-forested country.

Having rested his troops unseen in the depths of the forest, he advanced again during the night and destroyed or drove off three Persian guardposts between midnight and dawn. His approach still unobserved, he attacked the main Persian force at dawn, and his bugles gave the signal to Craterus who went forward into the assault on the pass. At first Alexander drove the enemy beyond the wall, where he placed 3,000 infantry under Ptolemy, and then Craterus drove them back onto Ptolemy's force. Panic ensued. Ariobarzanes escaped with a mere fragment of his army (he was to be killed later when fighting near Persepolis). Alexander now made full speed for the river, crossed the bridge which his advanced force had constructed, rode through the night, and captured Persepolis and its treasure, before either Ariobarzanes or the Persian garrison could plunder it (apparently the Persians fought one another). The whole operation was one of the most brilliant which Alexander planned and carried out with rapid timing.[65]

When the main army came up, Alexander encamped it outside the city. On the following day he held a council of the commanders of his forces, at which his proposal to destroy the palace of the Achaemenid kings was discussed. Parmenio's views were reported by Arrian, who was drawing no doubt on Ptolemy or/and Aristobulus: namely, that it was a waste of what was now Alexander's property and that the people throughout Asia would not turn to Alexander so readily because they would think that even he had decided not to exercise the rule over Asia but simply to conquer and pass on. His arguments were directed at three of Alexander's known pretensions: that from his landing in the Troad "Asia" had been his possession, that he came to exercise his rule as "King of Asia," and that he was liberating his people, the Asians, from Persian despotism. The alternative policy, "to conquer and pass on," was no doubt one which many of Alexander's commanders would have preferred him to adopt.

Alexander's reply was given in brief by Arrian and by Curtius, to the effect that the palace was the symbol of Achaemenid rule, and that the crimes committed by Darius and Xerxes against the Greek gods and the Greek peoples had to be punished. Thus he drew a distinction between Achaemenid rule and his own rule in Asia, and he reminded his commanders of the declared aim of the Greeks and the Macedonians in their joint war against Persia, to exact vengeance for the crimes committed against them by Persia. To this aim they had subscribed with oaths invoking the Greek gods, and they should honour their commitment to the gods and to their own ancestors by destroying the "regia veterum Persidis regum," the residence of the early kings of Persia.

In January 330 B.C. the Achaemenid palace at Persepolis went up in flames by order of Alexander, Hegemon of the Greek League, King of Macedon and King of Asia. It was symbolic of a vengeance which was intelligible, indeed acceptable, in terms of Greek religion (less so, of course, to the Roman Arrian or to modern Christian writers, but Alexander and his commanders were neither Roman nor Christian); symbolic also of vengeance for Persia's past occupation of Macedonia and now of Macedon's victory over Persia; symbolic finally of the liberation of Asia from Achaemenid rule. Many stories grew up around this spectacular event. Excavation has confirmed that the firing was deliberate and not accidental; for the rooms had been cleared of their contents. It marked too the end of the Greek League's war against Persia. Accordingly, when Alexander reached Ecbatana that summer, he gave full pay and a bounty of 2,000 talents to his Greek troops and had them escorted on their journey home, all except those who chose to continue in his service as mercenaries.

During the three months or so when Alexander's base was at Persepolis he took over Pasargadae, the royal city of Cyrus the Great, the

founder of the Achaemenid empire, and added its treasure to the vast
hoard he had acquired at Persepolis. He was engaged too in the pacification and organisation of the great territories won since the battle of
Gaugamela. As he had done in Babylonia and Susiana, he appointed a
Persian as satrap or civil governor of Persis, and he continued in office
the Persian satrap of Carmania (Kerman), farther to the east.

These were important appointments; for they showed that Alexander's
aim was not to impose Greek or Macedonian governors or even to replace Darius' satraps with anti-Darius Persians (as the Allies imposed
anti-Hitler Germans in 1945) but to let the Persians govern themselves
as the Egyptians and the Babylonians were doing, all within Alexander's
kingship of Asia. It was partly as a gesture of respect for Persian feelings
that he ordered Aristobulus to restore the tomb of Cyrus the Great at
Pasargadae.

In March/April, "at the rising of the Pleiads," when the weather was
still wintry, he conducted a month's campaign with small forces against
the unruly hill-peoples, including the Mardi, who lived in the district
between Persepolis and the Persian Gulf. In April/May he was ready to
take his army northwards. He left only 3,000 Macedonians as a garrison
in the citadel of Persepolis, a remarkably small number when we remember that this was the capital of Persia and that Darius was still at the
head of a loyalist army in Media.

Darius' withdrawal to Media after his defeat at Gaugamela had been
very damaging to his cause. If he had been present to lead and coordinate
the stout-hearted resistance of his satraps Medates and Ariobarzanes,
he might have saved the centre of his realm and kept the bulk of his
treasure under his hand; and from Persis he could equally well have
made the appeal for troops from the northeastern satrapies which he in
fact made from Media. Now, while Alexander was bringing his army on
the 700-kilometre march from Persepolis to Ecbatana and breaking the
resistance of the Paraetacae on the way (here too he put a Persian as
satrap), Darius decided to abandon the defence of Media and began to
withdraw towards the Caspian Sea, a policy which lost him the promised
help of his Scythian and Cadusian allies, whose lands he uncovered to
the advance of Alexander. As his withrawal degenerated into flight,
Alexander made arrangements for the pursuit (see Figure 13).

Three days before reaching Ecbatana (Hamadan), the Persian capital
in Media, Alexander was joined by Bisthanes, a son of the previous Persian king, Artaxerxes Ochus, and so a possible successor, who reported
that Darius had fled with 3,000 cavalry and 6,000 infantry four days before, taking 7,000 talents of specie with him. At Ecbatana Alexander sent
his Greek allies home and ordered Parmenio, who was bringing up the
convoy of treasure, to deposit it on his arrival in the citadel, where it was
to be under the charge of Harpalus. A force of 6,000 Macedonian infan-

try with a few cavalry and light-armed men was detailed to guard the citadel for the time being; and when it was relieved by other troops (we may conjecture), it was to be brought on to Parthyaea by Cleitus the Black, who was then recovering from an illness in Susa. He left orders for Parmenio to march past Cadusia into Hyrcania with the mercenaries, the Thracians, and the remaining cavalry. Alexander himself took the Companion Cavalry, the Lancers and the mercenary cavalry, the rest of the Macedonian phalanx, the Agrianians and the archers on the trail of Darius, who, he suspected, had collected more troops.

In the words of A.P. Wavell "in a sustained pursuit mobility is dependent mainly on the personal will and determination of the Commander-in-chief, which alone can keep alive the impetus of the troops." Alexander drove his force so hard that many fell out and horses died before reaching Rhagae (near Teheran) on the eleventh day. He had come 310 kilometres, or something more, if his route was not direct, in the hope of reaching the Caspian Gates first and heading Darius off. But Darius was still ahead, though losing a number of troops on the way; some went home and others surrendered themselves to Alexander. So Alexander stopped the pursuit one day short of the Caspian Gates, and during the next five days his men rested and his horses grazed in the vicinity of Rhagae. During his stay Alexander appointed an anti-Darius Persian as satrap of Media.

Resuming the advance and passing through the Gates (the defiles of Sialek and Sardar), he paused on the third day in Choarene to send out a foraging party, because the country ahead was desert. During its absence he learnt from a Babylonian notable and a Persian, a son of Mazaeus, that Darius had been arrested by his own cavalry commander and two of his satraps, Bessus and Barsaentes. Alexander set off faster than ever, taking only his Companion Cavalry, the Lancers, and the fittest, least heavily armed infantrymen, with rations for two days. He travelled through the night and next day till noon, when he halted in the great heat. Starting again in the evening and travelling through the night he reached a camp, where he learnt that Bessus, satrap of Bactria, had been acclaimed king by his cavalry, and that the Greek mercenaries, together with Artabazus and his sons, had left Bessus and were following a different route. He forced his weary men and horses on for the next night and day up to noon. He was now where Bessus and Darius had camped the day before.

The natives told Alexander that Bessus was travelling at night, and when he asked if there was a short route which he could take to intercept Bessus' force, they said there was one, but without water. Now that Bessus' cavalry and the Greek infantry were going different ways, Alexander divided his own forces. Selecting the 500 toughest infantry officers and men he mounted them on the surviving horses. They took their infantryman's weapons so that they could fight on horseback or on foot. He ordered the commanders of the Hypaspists and the Agrianians to lead an advance-party lightly equipped on the road taken by Bessus; the rest of the infantry was to follow. Starting towards evening, he and his 500 horsemen rode hard over seventy kilometres of desert, and in the dawn light they came upon the Persians walking without their weapons and in no order beside their slowly moving wagons. Alexander went straight into the attack, it was said with only sixty leading horsemen. Resistance was brief, for the dreaded Alexander had been recognised, but it was long enough for Bessus and the satraps and some 600 cavalry to make off with Darius in a closed wagon. When Alexander was close upon them, two satraps, Satibarzanes and Barsaentes, hurled their spears into Darius and escaped. "Darius died of his wounds soon after, before Alexander could see him" (A. 3.21.10).

If Darius died near Kharian, as seems probable, the Macedonians had covered the 270 kilometres (170 miles) from Choarene in some 108 hours, which may be compared with two Cavalry Divisions in Palestine covering 112 kilometres (70 miles) in 34 hours of pursuit in September 1917. Thus Alexander's picked force almost maintained the speed of Allenby's divisions for more than three times longer. It was an amazing performance. Allenby's loss in horses was considerable; Alexander's must have been very great, and Justin's statement that more than half Alexander's horses died in the heat and the rest were rendered unusable may not be an exaggeration (12.1.2).[66] Since Alexander did not pursue Bessus and the satraps, although their horses too must have been near exhaustion, we may conclude that Alexander's one aim was to capture Darius, at whatever cost to his own men and horses. Now Arrian says that Alexander was told at Choarene what plans Bessus and the satraps had: namely, if he should pursue, they would surrender Darius to him and obtain terms themselves (no doubt using Darius as a bargaining counter), and if he should not, they would set up their own joint authority (no doubt killing Darius, as there would be no question thereafter of bargaining). Some scholars have thought Alexander lucky in that Darius was in fact killed; but if Alexander had wanted that, he would not have pursued. The supreme effort was made, it seems, to take Darius alive.

It will be recalled that Alexander had always treated the family of Darius as royalty, had given a royal funeral in the Persian manner to the wife of Darius, and had himself mourned for her. He had left the Queen Mother and her descendants, including the eight-year-old son of Darius, in royal state at Susa. In the letter which Alexander had sent to Darius from Marathus he had written: "If you come to me, ask and receive your mother, wife and children, and anything else you wish; whatever you persuade me will be yours."

Then in the later negotiations Alexander promised Darius generous treatment, if Darius would come to Alexander, and in the account in Diodorus that generous treatment was to be that Darius would be "king over other rulers." If he had taken Darius alive at Kharian, and if he had carried out his previous intentions, he would have reunited Darius with his family and set him up in the same state. It is probable that within his own overall kingship of Asia, which he had always demanded Darius should recognise, he intended to make Darius king over Persia and whatever territory Alexander chose to go with Persia.

Darius had remarkable beauty and charm; he commanded the affection of his compatriots and the loyalty of his Greek mercenaries; he spoke Greek and had respect for Alexander. If Darius had lived and had agreed to cooperate on such terms with Alexander, the collaboration of Macedonians, Greeks, Persians, and Medes within Alexander's kingdom of Asia might have been effected.

When Alexander found the corpse of Darius, he was deeply moved and laid his own cloak over it. The body was embalmed, sent to Persepolis, and placed in the royal tombs alongside the predecessors of Darius, the obsequies being conducted by his mother, Sisigambis. Thus, Alexander had no intention of proclaiming Darius a usurper, as he had done in his letter of 332 B.C. (A. 2.I4.5). Quite the opposite; he treated Sisigambis as if she were his own mother, and had the children of Darius brought up at court and educated in the Greek language. A brother of Darius, Exathres, was raised to the highest honour in the Macedonian court, that of being Alexander's Friend and Companion.

The death of Darius marked the end of the Persian Empire. Whatever hopes Bessus had of reconstituting it were chimerical. The areas of Persian and Median manpower—Persis, Media, Susiana and Carmania— were firmly in Alexander's control. His base at Ecbatana, the meeting place of the main routes from west to east and south to north, blocked the path of any loyalists from the northeastern satrapies who might seek to invade Media, and the great expanses of desert formed a protection on the east. Darius had strengthened his imperial armies with some 50,000 Greek mercenaries; at the end only 1,500 were with him. Bessus had no access to the Greek mercenary market. Moreover, the speed of Alexander had deprived Bessus of the treasure, some 7,000 talents, which had been taken to Kharian, and Darius had not had the foresight to deposit any part of his hoarded wealth in the northeastern provinces of his empire.

On the other hand, Alexander was now the master of almost unlimited resources in gold and silver bullion. He controlled the amount of coinage which was issued from the bullion as Darius had done (Str. 735), and he made the mint at Babylon the most prolific in Asia, its coins bearing the letter M for "Metropolis." The bullion of the Persian palaces was concentrated at Ecbatana, a central point in the network of main roads, and the guarding of it was entrusted to Alexander's senior general, Parmenio. In order to meet his needs on his campaigns farther east, he took coined money, both Persian (e.g., A. 4.18.7) and his own, in his baggage-train, and he had additional supplies sent forward from Babylon via Ecbatana. Although the cost of transportation was great, Alexander's precautions worked. No consignments of coin or bullion fell into the hands of Asian rebels.

(E) THE NORTHEASTERN SATRAPIES
AND THE THIRD PLOT AGAINST ALEXANDER
(see Figure 15)

To be King of Asia was, in Alexander's mind, to be king over one of the three continents which made up the inhabited world.[67] As Theopompus wrote in his *Philippica*, a work composed mainly during Alexander's reign, "Europe, Asia and Libya are islands around which Ocean flows." Asia was separated from Europe by the Tanaïs (Don) and from Libya by the Nile; but the upper reaches of these rivers and their sources were unknown. The outer edges of the three continents were thought to be desert or steppe, where only nomadic peoples, or none at all, could live; thus northern Asia had its Scythian nomads, and southern Asia great areas of sandy desert. The central feature of Asia was a mountain mass, running from Cilicia in the west to the border of India in the east, and being called from west to east Taurus, Parnassus, Caucasus, and Paropanisus; and to the east of this mountain mass lay India, the last inhabited land, so that anyone crossing the last ridge of Paropanisus would see "the outer sea" (the Ocean), according to Aristotle. Thus Asia east of the Hindu Kush (the ancient Paropanisus) was thought to be a relatively small peninsula running east or southeast into the circumambient Ocean.

Aristotle claimed to know more or less the width of the inhabited world, limited in the north by the cold and in the south by the heat, and also its length from the Pillars of Heracles (the Straits of Gibraltar) to India, beyond which points Ocean intervened, so that the inhabited zone was not continuous round the globe.

> To judge from what is known from journeys by sea and land the length is much greater than the width; indeed the distance from the Pillars of Heracles [at Cadiz] to India exceeds that from Aethiopia [Sudan] to Lake Maeotis [Sea of Azov] and the farthest parts of Scythia in the proportion of more than five to three (*Meteorologica* 362 b, 19–23).

The campaigns of Alexander were in fact journeys of discovery, and the surveyors and the scientists who accompanied him supplied details

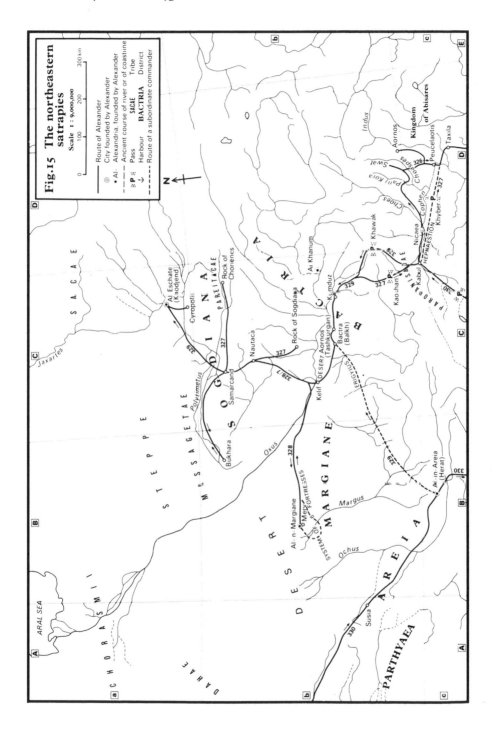

Fig.15 The northeastern satrapies

Scale 1 : 9,000,000

Route of Alexander
City founded by Alexander
• Al- Alexandria, founded by Alexander
Ancient course of river or of coastline
SACAE Tribe
Pass BACTRIA District
Harbour
Route of a subordinate commander

of distance, climate, flora, fauna, and human and animal oecology, which were of the greatest interest to Greek philosophers. For example, the expedition which Alexander sent into Aethiopia brought back measurements of distance which seemed to confirm Aristotle's theory of proportion. Again, when he crossed the width of Asia from Persepolis (which he knew to be near to the Red Sea [Persian Gulf]) to Kharian where he caught up with Darius, it must have seemed clear that the width was decreasing as one went farther east. When Alexander reached the Hyrcanian Sea (our Caspian Sea) soon afterwards, he had no means of determining whether it was an inland sea or a gulf of Ocean. As he had already crossed the mountain mass (at Mt. Elburz) and learnt of nomad Scythians west and east of the Hyrcanian Sea, he had every reason to expect that he was close to the northernmost limits of Asia, or what Aeschines had called "the limits of the inhabited world"; and he will have heard of the belief that "the Ocean flows from India into Hyrcania" (i.e., the Hyrcanian Sea being an arm of Ocean) and that "Lake Maeotis flowed into the Hyrcanian Sea" (C. 6.4.18-19; cf. P. 44. 1–2).

If we look at Figure 16 and consider what territories Alexander expected to find further east, we can better understand the grounds on which he chose to continue his campaigns after the death of Darius. The decision was made public probably at a city later called Hecatompylus (perhaps Shahr-i-Qumis, south of Damghan), where Alexander waited for the rest of his army to join him, and it was made probably because a rumour spread among the Macedonians that they were about to go home, as the Greek allies had done. Alexander persuaded them, apparently without any difficulty, to go forward, conquer the rebels with Bessus and gain possession of "all Asia," the kingdom which he had claimed from the outset.[68] He himself may well have realised that the peoples of the northeastern satrapies would be hardy fighters, since he had seen their cavalry in action at Gaugamela, and he may have thought the extent and nature of the country were less of a difficulty than they proved to be; but even so Alexander was not one to be deterred by any obstacles, real or imagined. The Macedonians went on readily, in devotion to Alexander their king, in fulfilment of their own fighting spirit, and in the hope of the financial gains which Alexander showered upon them from time to time. But both Alexander and his Macedonians were to show the effects of increasing strain during the three years of hard fighting which were to ensue, from July 330 B.C. to summer 327 B.C.

The pursuit of Darius had brought Alexander into the wide corridor between the Parthian desert and the Caspian Sea, through which ran the only route to the northeastern satrapies. This corridor has always been threatened by semi-nomadic tribes from the north; at this time it was the Dahae and beyond them the Massagetae, famous for their for-

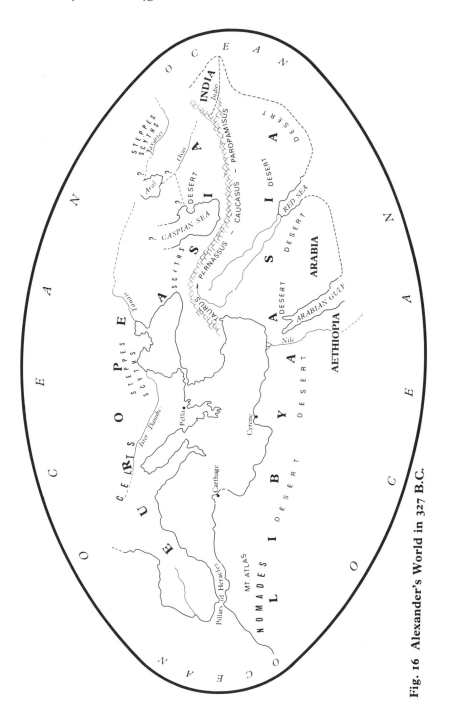

Fig. 16 Alexander's World in 327 B.C.

midable and wide-ranging cavalry. The northeastern satrapies themselves were mainly mountainous, and their inhabitants, being engaged in pastoral life and primitive forms of agriculture, lived in open villages rather than in walled towns. The administrative centres of the local dynasts and the satraps were to be found mainly in natural or fortified citadels.

In areas to the west of the Tigris Alexander had often broken armed resistance by winning set battles and by capturing urban centres, and he had been claiming to liberate civilised peoples from Persian oppression; but now he was faced by open and sporadic warfare against independent, rather primitive peoples upon whom Persian rule had rested lightly. The military methods which he used from now onwards were frequently those he had used against the Uxii: the flying column of commando-type troops, the sacking of villages, and the infliction of heavy casualties on peoples who had no cities to lose. This type of warfare was more exacting for the Macedonians, and unfortunately it not infrequently caused more loss to the enemy than the warfare of set battles and sieges.

Alexander's first objective was complete control of the corridor, on which his operations to the east were to be based, and that meant subjugating the tribes of the Tapurian mountains (Mt. Elburz; 18,934 feet high) and the peoples on the south side of the Caspian Sea.

Arrian has left a much abbreviated but dependable account of this operation, based on Ptolemy and Aristobulus, which I follow here. Dividing his force near Damghan into three parts, Alexander took a flying column of his commando-type troops ("the lightest-equipped part of the force"—A. 3.22.2–3), the Hypaspists, the Agrianians and some archers, and he drove his way through the eastern part of the mountains, defeating the tribesmen en route. The second part—two phalanx-battalions, some archers and some cavalry commanded by Craterus—subjugated the Tapurians of the lowlands, and joined Alexander when he came down to Zadracarta (Sari or Gorgan), the capital of Hyrcania. The third force, commanded by Erigyius, escorted the wagons and the pack-animals of the baggage-train and the accompanying civilians along the Persian road to Zadracarta. Next Alexander led the Hypaspists, two phalanx-battalions, the archers, the Agrianians, half the Companion Cavalry and a squadron of mounted javelin-men against the Mardians of the western part of the Elburz range, primitive and warlike mountaineers who had never submitted to the Persians. Moving fast and partly by night, he took them by surprise, penetrated to their mountain-fastnesses, killing many and taking many prisoners, until the whole tribe capitulated, whereupon he accepted their submission and released his prisoners. Some hostages were probably taken as a guarantee of good conduct in the future, and the Mardians and the Tapurians were both placed under one satrap, Autophradates.

This Autophradates had been Darius' satrap of Tapuria. He and Artabazus, once a friend of Philip, and Artabazus' sons had surrendered to Alexander at Zadracarta. Other Persian notables had done likewise in the Tapurian mountains: Nabarzanes the Chiliarch of Darius, and other leading officers, and Phrataphernes, Darius' satrap of Hyrcania-cum-Parthyaea. Alexander paid special honours to Artabazus and his sons, including them in his entourage, and he made Phrataphernes satrap of Parthyaea, and Amminapes, a Parthyaean, satrap of Hyrcania.

In continuing his policy of appointing Asians as satraps even of strategic areas, Alexander was taking a calculated risk, which his Macedonian officers probably disliked. Darius' Greek mercenaries, 1,500 in number, surrendered unconditionally. Alexander released those who had been engaged before Philip's alliance with the Greek League in 337 B.C. and compelled the rest to serve under the same commander at the same rate of pay in his own forces. Greek envoys who had accompanied Darius gave themselves up. Those from Greek states such as Sinope and Chalcedon which were not members of the Greek League were released; those from member states, such as Athens, and the envoys of Sparta, recently defeated, were kept in custody. Resting his forces at Zadracarta in mid-August 330 B.C., Alexander carried out the traditional Macedonian sacrifices to the gods and held an athletic festival.

The Caspian region was well studied by the Bematistae or surveyors and by the scientists and naturalists with the expedition, such as Aristobulus and Onesicritus. Fragments of their records have survived.[69] The mythical associations of this land so remote to Greek writers were exploited later by Cleitarchus, when he invented a story of the Queen of the Amazons bedding with Alexander for thirteen nights in the hope of getting herself with child by him—a story expressly denied by Aristobulus and by Ptolemy when they came to write their memoirs (P. 46.1).

Cleitarchus, it seems, placed the theft of Bucephalus in the land of the Mardi—another error similarly corrected (A. 5.19.6). He was probably the source, too, of the stories (in D. 17.77.6-7; J. 12.3.10; and C. 6.6.8) that Alexander at this time took over not only Darius' harem of 360 concubines and had them parade for him nightly, but also a host of eunuch prostitutes, headed by Bagoas. Consequently, they said, he fell into Persian vices: "banqueting from an early hour, mad delight in heavy drinking, staying up all night, fun and games, and troops of harlots" (C. 6.2.2). The remarkable energy shown by Alexander on his extensive campaigns during this period and the remoteness of Hyrcania from the seat of any royal harem at Susa are sufficient reasons for rejecting these particular stories.[70]

It was in Hyrcania or Parthyaea that Alexander had to decide on his attitude to Persia and his interpretation of the "Kingship of Asia," because most of the leading Persians had come into his hands and among

them two possible successors to the Persian throne: a grandson of
Artaxerxes Ochus, and a brother of Darius. That Alexander had left the
peoples of Susiana, Persis, and Media to govern themselves in accordance with the existing system may be taken for granted, because Alexander did not impose any Greek or Macedonian framework of local government there or indeed elsewhere; it had been enough for him to appoint a satrap or governor-general as his personal representative, linking the local system to the system of the King of Asia. Where he chose to
appoint Asians—Persians, for instance, in Susiana, Persis, and Media—
he hoped presumably to conciliate local feeling and make use of administrative experience.

Whereas in Egypt and in Babylon he had worshipped the national
gods and behaved as the reigning monarch, there is no evidence that he
ever worshipped Ahura-Mazda, the Persian god, or was acclaimed as
king of Persia by his Persian subjects or by the Persian nobility. It is true
that his power superseded that of Darius, but this is not to say that he
stepped into Darius' constitutional position.

The indications are that Alexander continued to regard himself as
King of Asia, and that all Asians, Persians included, paid their homage
to him in this role. In claiming at Lindus to be "Lord of Asia" he was rival-
ling a claim once made by Cyrus the Great (A. 6.29.8), but he was not
thereby setting himself up as the successor of Cyrus on the Persian
throne. Indeed in invading the land of the Mardians, for instance, and
in his future intentions he meant to carry his conquests beyond the
limits reached by the Persian kings.

As King of Asia he adopted a form of dress which would be acceptable to his Asian subjects: a diadem with two ribbons (that of Philip
probably had one ribbon), sometimes a Macedonian hat (*kausia*), a purple tunic with a white band, a belt and a sword. It should be noted that
he did not adopt the Persian royal insignia, namely the crenelated
crown, the upright tiara (*kitaris*), the long-sleeved robe (*kandys*), and the
trousers (*anaxyrides*), and that to this extent he emphasised the fact that
he was not a Persian monarch, although it suited his critics to imply that
he was none other than the Great King, the model of despotism. The
best summary of his dress in this role is probably that given by Plutarch
(45.2): "He combined fairly well some features of Persian and Median
dress, making his dress less extravagant than the one and more stately
than the other."[71]

The distinguished Persians who entered the service of Alexander
were fine cavalrymen, and they formed now or somewhat later a Royal
Guard with the title "Euacae" (A. 7.6.3; *Epit. Metz* 2). The Asian members of his entourage paid him homage in the Asian manner, of which a
conspicuous feature to a European eye was the bowing and the kissing,
called *proskynesis*. Prominent Asians became court-officials, carrying

rods of office (*rhabdoukhoi*). At first Alexander kept the ceremonial of the King of Macedon in relation to his Macedonians entirely separate from the new ceremonial, but he began soon to display the new ceremonial to his Friends. Thus it became known to his Macedonian and Greek troops. To many of them the distinction between King of Asia and King of Persia was an academic one; what they saw was Alexander going Asian and they resented it.

A pressing problem for Alexander was the maintenance of his army at a number appropriate to his future commitments. Recently he had taken on a mere 1,500 Greek mercenaries, and later in the autumn he received reinforcements, for which he must have sent sometime before his pursuit of Darius began: 500 Greek mercenary cavalry, 130 Thessalian cavalry, 3,000 Illyrians, 2,600 Lydian infantry, and 300 Lydian cavalry. He is likely to have made arrangements by this time for the raising and training of troops from Lycia and Syria; these were to reach him in Sogdiana in the winter of 329–328 B.C.

It is probable that he arranged also for the raising and training of young men in his new towns and in the southeastern satrapies, where they were to be given instruction in Greek language and Macedonian weaponry. As he had already drafted Asian cavalrymen into his army, it is probable that they were to be trained as infantrymen. They were called the Epigoni, "the Successors." Of sheer necessity he was moving towards a multiracial army of both European and Asian stocks; for as we have seen, the Macedonians, although still the élite, had already become only a fraction of the men under arms in his service. And even these men had to recognise the existence of parallel cavalry units, which now shared the prestigious names of the Macedonian cavalry.

Alexander had left a large army at Ecbatana under the command of Parmenio with orders to reduce the Cadusians (east of the Mardians). This Parmenio will have done, since he had 6,000 Macedonians (probably four phalanx-brigades), 200 Companion Cavalry, 5,000 Greek mercenary infantry, 600 cavalry, and other infantry, including some Thracians. Thus Alexander was already confident of his base and his lines of communication when he set off from Zadracarta (Sari or Gurgan) in late August 330 B.C. with an army of which the first-line troops numbered some 20,000 infantry and 3,000 cavalry (P. 47.1). Advancing through Parthyaea into Areia, he received the submission of Satibarzanes, the current satrap, at Susia (probably Tus near Meshhad) and continued him in office. Arrian tells us, evidently from Ptolemy and/or Aristobulus, that Satibarzanes was given Anaxippus, a Companion, and some forty mounted javelin-men in order to head off from the Areians any pillagers—the first indication that Alexander had to take steps to enforce his ban on pillaging.

While he was waiting for the baggage-train to come up, some Persians reported that Bessus had assumed full regalia—the upright tiara and the Persian dress—was calling himself Artaxerxes and saying that he was King of Asia. Thus he not only claimed to be the successor of Darius on the Persian throne, but he also challenged the right of Alexander to call himself King of Asia. Bessus was relying on the support of some Persians who had fled with him to Bactria, of many Bactrians, and of Scythian allies who, he hoped, would join him. Alexander set out for Bactria, and was joined on the way by two groups of cavalry (mercenaries and Thessalian volunteers) who had come up from Media. Then the news reached him that Satibarzanes had killed Anaxippus and his javelin-men and declared himself in support of Bessus.

Turning aside from the main route to Bactra (Wazirabad), Alexander marched about 105 kilometres in two days with part of his army (Companion Cavalry, mounted javelin-men, archers, Agrianians and two phalanx-brigades) to Artacoana (Herat or near it), the capital of Areia, from which Satibarzanes and his supporters fled, amazed at Alexander's speed of movement. While Satibarzanes escaped, Alexander hunted down others responsible for the revolt; some he killed, others he sold into slavery. When the rest of the army came up, he drove south into Zarangaea and reached its capital (by Farah), from which Barsaentes, a Persian leader who had taken part in the arrest of Darius, fled into India. When the Indians arrested him and sent him back to Alexander, he was executed for his crime against Darius. It was characteristic of Alexander that he punished with severity any act of disloyalty, whether to himself or to another.

The Companions may have criticised Alexander for appointing Satibarzanes as satrap. But Alexander proceeded to appoint another Persian as satrap of Areia. He founded a city, Alexandria, in Areia, close to Artacoana, the central point in the communications of Afghanistan; the walls of this Alexandria were five and half kilometres in extent. He was able to settle soldiers there who had served their time or were unfit, because by now he had received the Greek, Illyrian and Lydian troops mentioned previously.

When Alexander was in Zarangaea, there was reported to him a plot which involved the destinies of many leading Macedonian officers: Philotas, Parmenio's son and Alexander's senior cavalry commander, being in charge of the Companion Cavalry; Demetrius, one of Alexander's seven Bodyguards; Amyntas, son of Andromenes, commander of a phalanx-brigade; two of his brothers who in their time also commanded phalanx-brigades; seven officers whose names mean little to us; and Parmenio himself, Alexander's second-in-command. It was naturally a *cause célèbre*, which aroused (and still arouses) widespread speculation and inspired sensational accounts. The briefest, given in Arrian (3.26-27), which is in part an abbreviation of what Ptolemy himself (probably an eyewitness and certainly able to obtain firsthand information) had thought fit to write, is given first, with some comments in brackets.

Ptolemy and Aristobulus said that suspicions of plotting by Philotas had been reported to Alexander in Egypt [almost two years earlier] but they were not believed by him (cf. P. 48.3–49.2). Then, in Zarangaea,

> Ptolemy, son of Lagus, says that Philotas was brought before the Macedones [for trial] and being accused vigorously by Alexander made his defence. The informers came forward and convicted Philotas and those with him on no uncertain evidence and in particular on the evidence that Philotas, having on his own admission been informed of some plot against Alexander, had kept silent despite his twice-daily visits to Alexander's quarters. Philotas and all participants with him in the plot were killed with javelins by the Macedones.

After describing the killing of Parmenio, to which we shall come later, Arrian reported [probably from the accounts of Ptolemy and Aristobulus] the trial and the acquittal of Amyntas, son of Andromenes, and his three brothers "by the Macedones," who also permitted Amyntas to recall one brother who had fled. During the campaign which followed against the Ariaspians, Arrian reported both the arrest of Demetrius by Alexander, who suspected that he had a share in the plot with Philotas, and the replacement of Demetrius among the Bodyguards by Ptolemy, son of Lagus [no doubt Arrian's source here].

Although Ptolemy's opinion is guarded, the words "no uncertain evidence" and "the plot" reveal his belief that Philotas and some others were guilty of conspiring against the king; and in particular that the failure of Philotas to report the information was due to his complicity in the plot and not just a treasonable piece of negligence. It was the verdict of his positive participation which was to arouse suspicion against his father, Parmenio. The facts in Arrian's account are not to be doubted; and where he differs from others in the manner of execution and the number of Amyntas' brothers, his version is to be preferred.

The other accounts are in Diodorus (17.79–80), Plutarch (*Alexander* 48–49), and Curtius (6.7–7.2). As they have many points in common, we can see that they were derived from long, detailed, and sensational accounts. Plutarch and Curtius, for instance, give tête-à-tête conversations and rhetorical speeches which are certainly fictitious. However, the account of Curtius[72] is important in that it helps us to see the procedure which was used. On being informed of a plot Alexander sent guards at once to arrest the named conspirator, Dimnus. He then interviewed Philotas (so too D. 17.79.5–6) and called his Friends together to hear the allegations of the informer, Nicomachus. During the night, with the concurrence and help of the Friends, he had the suspects arrested.

Next morning he made proclamation that "all should assemble under arms" (*omnes armati coirent*, 6.8.23). The "all" were "the Macedones" of Ptolemy (A. 3.26.2; cf. D. 17.79.6 and 80.2). They were some 6,000 soldiers, probably of the Companion Cavalry, the Hypaspists and two phalanx-brigades (such was the flying column Alexander had with him). "In accordance with the ancient method of the Macedones the army used to investigate the grounds of capital charges, . . . and the power of the kings used to have no validity, unless their influence beforehand had had some weight" (C. 6.8.25, the text without any emendation). The only respect in which Curtius is misleading in these words is his description of the Macedones as "the army" (*exercitus*); for they were only an élite part of the armed forces, namely those with the full Macedonian citizenship.[73]

The trial was opened by the bringing in of the corpse of Dimnus, who had committed suicide; next came the informers and those who were under suspicion of having been accomplices of Dimnus. The king acted as state prosecutor. One of the informers, Nicomachus, had been the object of Dimnus' love, and he had been told by Dimnus of a plot to murder Alexander in three days' time. He passed this information to his brother, Cebalinus, who told Philotas and asked Philotas to tell the king. However, Philotas did not do so, either on that day or on the following day, although he talked each day with the king and although Cebalinus reminded him. Realising that the next day was to be the day of assassination, Cebalinus found another intermediary, Metron, gained access to the king and informed him of the plot. Such is the story as given by Curtius. After due investigation "all who had been named by Nicomachus were stoned to death at a given signal in the traditional manner" (6.11.38).

This trial led on to the trial of Amyntas, son of Andromenes, and his two brothers (according to Curtius, whereas Arrian mentions three brothers), who had come under suspicion as close friends of Philotas. They were acquitted by the court's acclamation (7.2.7). At a later date, rather than at the time of the first trial, as Curtius had it (6.11.37-38), Demetrius was held to have been implicated and was executed.

It is clear that the king behaved correctly in accordance with Macedonian procedure; that the verdicts were passed by the assembly, not by the king; and that those killed were guilty by Macedonian standards of justice. Torture was certainly used in the hope of obtaining confessions and names. Diodorus (17.80.2) is probably correct in saying that Philotas was first condemned to death by the assembly and then confessed under torture before his execution (Curtius reports torture during an interval in an extended trial—6.11.10 f).

Modern scholars have no evidence on which to retry the cases of Philotas and the others; and to suppose that Alexander himself instigated the accusers and duped the assembly of 6,000 men into condemning innocent persons is not only to run counter to the texts we have, but also to require in Alexander the supreme folly of arranging to kill Philotas *before* arranging to remove Philotas' father, Parmenio, who commanded a large army, held a huge sum of money (reported as 180,000 talents) and was encamped on his lines of communication at Ecbatana.

That Parmenio was condemned to death by the assembly of the Macedones is reported by Diodorus (17.80.1), who goes on to say that he was tried in absentia and the sentence was made on the supposition that he had formed the plot. Justin (12.5.3) says that he was put to death after trials had been held about him and Philotas (*utroque*). There are no a priori grounds for rejecting this, because neither author is apt to exculpate Alexander. Strabo too (724) says that Alexander sent agents to kill Parmenio as being "an accomplice in the plot" of Philotas. Arrian (3.26.3–4) is less explicit, partly because he was so very concise and partly because he was more interested in the attitude of Alexander. We can be sure that the court did consider the question whether Parmenio, as father of Philotas, was implicated in the plot; but we have not enough clear evidence to decide whether Parmenio was found guilty by the court or not.

Ptolemy and Aristobulus, as well as Arrian, must have been interested in Alexander's attitude of mind; for they knew how devoted he had always been to Parmenio as the first and chief of his Friends. Their views, given in summary by Arrian, were that Parmenio was killed

> perhaps because Alexander did not think it credible that Philotas had made the plot without his father sharing in it; and perhaps because, even if Parmenio had had no share, his survival after the execution of his son was dangerous indeed, since he had so high a reputation with the army—Macedonian and non-Macedonian alike, as well as with Alexander; for he had often been a popular commander of non-Macedonians, in and out of season, by the order of Alexander.

They were right about the danger; for if Parmenio should carry the army of Ecbatana with him, he could split Macedonian power in two and throw the kingdom of Asia into the melting pot.

Alexander sent an officer in Arab disguise and some Arabs on fast dromedaries across the Parthian desert to Ecbatana. They had to get there before any news of the trial, and the officer carried secret orders to the generals in Media. They killed Parmenio, mercifully unaware of Philotas' death, and they quelled the mutinous reaction of his troops by reading them a statement which Alexander had supplied. Back in Zarangaea Alexander founded a new city and called it Prophthasia, "Anticipation." It had been a narrow escape, if the detailed account in

Curtius is correct; but for the persistence of Cebalinus and the prompt-
ness of Metron (A. 6.7.22–24) the assassin would have acted in the
course of the day on which, as it so happened, the trial was held.

If Alexander had been assassinated, his half-brother might well
have succeeded to the throne, but he was not capable of leadership. It
would have been necessary for the Macedones to appoint a supreme
commander who could coordinate the forces in Asia. No one was more
appropriate than Alexander's senior officer in Asia, Parmenio. Able, experienced and popular, he held the key position in Asia and he had
more than once declared a preference for limited territorial conquest,
which would have commended itself to most Macedonians. Moreover,
at the age of seventy he stood above the rivalries of the next generation
of commanders: men such as Craterus, Coenus, Philotas, and Perdiccas. As it was, Alexander lived to advance far into India. But after the
conspiracy he had a diminished sense of security in relation to his leading officers. His judgement of men had proved faulty; and more sinister
was the realisation that Philotas, Demetrius, and others—perhaps even
Parmenio—had been motivated probably not by personal ambition (for
they were at the top already) but by detestation of his policy.[74]

At this time Alexander Lyncestes was put on trial. Accused of treason with his two brothers in 336 B.C., he alone had been acquitted then,
thanks to Alexander's intercession, and since then he had been given
high command by Alexander. In 334-333 B.C. the Friends whom Alexander consulted judged him guilty of treasonous correspondence with
Darius and wanted him to be executed; but Alexander did no more than
arrest him. Now the demand for his trial came in the assembly from
Atarrhias, a tough commander. The prosecutor (Alexander is not mentioned in this connection) made his case, Alexander Lyncestes failed to
muster words in his own defence and he was shot down by the assembly's spears. This too was a man the king had trusted and promoted.

Such methods as the detention of a man for three years or more
without trial, the use of torture during a trial, and the summary execution of a man condemned in absentia (if Diodorus is correct about
Parmenio) are repugnant to those who apply absolute standards of justice and to those who live in a liberal democracy. The historian's task is
less to pass judgement than to understand the conditions of the time
and age. The Macedonians were at war, and the fourth century B.C. was
an age of violence. If historical comparisons are to be made, we shall
learn more from comparison with medieval European monarchical
states than from comparison with twentieth-century democracies,
which use a multitude of methods. It is instructive to recall that the most
civilised state of the fourth century B.C., Athens, required the torture of
slaves who were called to give witness, had a standing panel of 6,000
jurors, and entrusted the verdict in the most important cases to 1,501
jurors. Macedonia was not so very different in 330 B.C. in using as its

constitutional methods 6,000 jurors, its king as state-prosecutor on occasion, and the torture of an accused (probably after conviction); and it is important to note that it followed its constitutional procedure even in time of war on foreign soil. The decision in each trial lay with the Macedonian assembly and not with the king.

Philotas had been sole commander of the Companion Cavalry. Alexander thought it unwise to put anyone in so powerful a position after the conspiracy, and he therefore split the Cavalry into two units, each commanded separately by a "hipparch"—as whom he chose Hephaestion, his closest friend, and Cleitus, who had saved his life at the Granicus river. Disciplinary measures were taken against some troops, perhaps in connection with their reactions to the killing of Parmenio; for a company was formed of "the Disorderlies." Some weeks later, when Amyntas died of an arrow wound, Alexander showed his respect for the acquittal pronounced by the Macedonian assembly by appointing Amyntas' brother, Attalus, brigade-commander then or soon afterwards.

Action was the best cure for dissension. Alexander ordered the army at Ecbatana to join him. If the order went together with the instructions to kill Parmenio, the army will have set off not earlier than the end of October 330 B.C., and having more than 2,000 kilometres to cover it did not catch up with him in Arachosia until late in December. To remove from the centres of Persian manpower an army which we might call "an army of occupation" may have seemed hazardous, even if Alexander did place a garrison at Ecbatana and count on the Epigoni who were being trained in the cities to play their part in maintaining order. The explanation surely is that he judged it imperative to bring his Macedonian units together and reassert his personal authority.

The two months or more between the conspiracy at Farah and the reunion of the army in Arachosia were used by Alexander for extensive operations, about which we have only the most meagre information. First he moved south into the territory of the Ariaspians whom he treated with exceptional generosity, giving them more territory and a financial subsidy and exempting them from tribute. During the sixty days when his headquarters were in Ariaspia[75] he was re-equipping his baggage-train with horses and materials and accumulating supplies for the winter months ahead.

One detachment of Greek mercenary troops, consisting of 600 cavalry and 6,000 infantry, was sent back some 300 kilometres to attack Satibarzanes who had appeared again in Areia; the mission was accomplished successfully, and one of the commanders, Erigyius, distinguished himself by killing Satibarzanes in single combat.[76] Another detachment went south and brought the Drangians and the Gedrosians into submission. Snow was thick on the ground and there was a shortage of supplies when Alexander advanced into Arachosia, passing beyond Kandahar and coming into contact with Indian tribes to the east. Here in midwinter he was joined by the army from Ecbatana and the detachment which had been in Areia.

During these last months of 330 B.C. Alexander laid out the plans and his army built the walls of some new cities: Prophthasia at Farah, Alexandropolis probably at Kandahar, and Alexandria in Arachosia at Kalat-i-Ghilzai. He intended them to become strongpoints on his lines of communication, and he left in Arachosia a garrison of 600 cavalry and 4,000 infantry under a Macedonian satrap, Menon. On the other hand he appointed a Persian to be satrap of the Ariaspians, whose territory lay off the main route. The next stage in the advance from Kalat-i-Ghilzai to Kabul, some 350 kilometres, ran along the flank of the lofty mountains and over the Sher-Dahan pass. Here in January the cold was intense, and wind and snow swept across treeless slopes so that men suffered from frostbite and snow blindness. Their only refuge was in the buried huts of the natives which were revealed by the smoke of their fires; there the Macedonians supplemented their meagre rations, for supplies were running short. Geographers among them reckoned that they were close to the north pole, being on the flank of the Caucasus range beyond which lay the northern part of the Ocean and the eastern part of the Black Sea (D. I7.82.2; C. 7.3.7; cf. 7.4.27).

On the Kabul side of the watershed the climate was relatively kind and the army spent the rest of the winter there, drawing supplies from the basin of Ortospana (by Kabul) and the valley of Charikar. Alexander founded a city there, probably at Begram, and called it Alexandria-in-Caucaso; for it was at the foot of the Hindu-Kush, known then as Paropanisus, which formed a part of the long Caucasus range. The city was at the meeting of three ways: one by which he had come; one leading eastwards to the Indus, of which the Kabul is a tributary; and one over the Hindu-Kush to Bactria, where Bessus had mustered an army. Alexander appointed a Persian to be satrap over the Paropanisades, as the people of the Kabul area were called, and alongside him a Macedonian officer with an armed force. He intended to keep a firm grasp on this gateway to India.

SOURCES

(B) [Dem.] 17; D. 17.48.1-2 and 6; 17.62, 63; 73.5-6; A. 2.13.4-6; 3.6.2-4; 3.16.10; 3.24.4; C. 4.1.38-40; 4.5-9-12 and 19-22; 4.8.12-15; 6.1; J. 12.1.6-11; Aeschin. 3.165; Din. 1.34

(C) A. 3.16.3-22.6; C. 4.16.7-5.13.25; D. 17.64-73; P. 34-38; 42.5-43; Str. 724, 728, 731; Athenaeus. 13.576 d-e

(D) A. 3.23-28.4; D. 17.74-83.2; C. 6.2.12-7.3.23; P. 44-49; J. 12.3.4-5.9; Str. 506-511; see also note 67

VIII

"ULTIMA ASIAE": BACTRIA AND INDIA

(A) BACTRIA

Alexander can have had only the vaguest idea of what lay beyond the massive range of the Hindu-Kush, which rises to 16,872 feet above the sea. To judge from remarks in Curtius (7.3.I9 and 7.7.4), he expected to find there "the deserts of the Scythian region"; for the Scythian race was thought to inhabit a continuous belt from north of the Danube and Black Sea to "the extremity of Asia where Bactra is (*ultima Asiae qua Bactra sunt*), an area generally of "dense forests and vast deserts." And beyond the deserts the circumambient Ocean. No doubt his own curiosity would have impelled Alexander to explore, but on this occasion he had also to deal with the last centre of Persian resistance, organised by Bessus, who had been successfully confined to Bactria by Alexander's systematic conquest of Areia-Zarangaea-Arachosia-Paropanisadae.

The problem for Bessus was that although superior in cavalry he had no trained infantry of Macedonian quality and so could not engage Alexander in pitched battle. He therefore decided to adopt a "scorched earth" policy, such as had been advised by Memnon in 334 B.C.: to withdraw destroying all stores, fodder, and supplies until the pursuers had to stop, close to starvation, and retire in disorder, whereupon his superior cavalry would close in upon them. Such tactics, Bessus knew, had succeeded against Cyrus the Great and Darius I; and if Alexander should advance in the spring when the northern face of the Hindu-Kush was cold and the lowlands were bare, these tactics had an excellent chance of success, particularly since Alexander would be likely to have used up all portable supplies in crossing the mountain. Bessus' cavalry consisted of some Persians who had accompanied Darius, 7,000 Bactrians, and a large number of Scythian Dahae. The risk for Bessus was that his policy would alienate the Bactrians whose lands he proposed to devastate and abandon (see Figure 15).

Alexander made his customary sacrifices in spring 329 B.C. The pass on which he had decided was probably the Khawak Pass, 3545 m high (11,600 ft), some 100 kilometres from Kabul, and he had prepared pack-horses, wagons, and supplies for the long haul over the mountain at a time of the year when there was bound to be much snow on high ground. The combination of the crossing of the Hindu-Kush and the tactics of Bessus brought the army close to disaster. Many horses died on the mountain, grain ran out and men were reduced to eating herbs and any fish they could catch. Then Alexander ordered them to kill the baggage-animals and to eat them raw, there being no wood; and they ate the silphium which grew there, in order to offset the danger of disease from eating only raw meat. "But Alexander advanced all the same," said Arrian (3.8.29), "with difficulty indeed through deep snow and a lack of essential supplies, but still he came on and on." His will and his men's toughness prevailed again. Bessus lost his nerve and withdrew over the Oxus, burning all boats behind him, and the Bactrian cavalry left him and went home. Alexander's army recuperated in the rich country round Drapsaca (probably Kumduz) which his (presumably fastest) men were said to have reached in some sixteen days from Alexandria-in-Caucaso. An amazing achievement, undertaken so early in the year in order to forestall Bessus, who seems not to have contested the army's passage even with light-armed mountaineers, of whom there were plenty in Bactria.

Moving west, he took Bactra (Wazirabad, formerly Balkh) and Aornos (Tashkurgan) at the first assault, and he placed a garrison in the citadel of the latter. These being their chief cities, the Bactrians accepted the rule of Alexander and received as satrap the Persian Artabazus. Alexander founded two cities in which he settled any mercenaries who were willing, 3,000 camp-followers, and 7,000 natives; one, another Alexandria, on the northern side of the mountain, lay "by the pass leading towards Media," i.e., westwards via Herat (keeping the text of D. I7.83.1),[77] and the other perhaps Nicaea, a day's march from Alexandria. The pass towards Media gave him a direct route to Herat (Alexandria-in-Areia) and shortened his lines of communication by two-thirds. He replaced the Persian satrap of Areia with a Cypriote, Stasanor, a distinguished member of the royal house of Soli.

As he was now in excellent horse country and was among tribes famous for their cavalry—the Bactrians alone were credited with 30,000 —Alexander took steps to reorganise his own cavalry. First, he sent home with very generous bounties all his Thessalian cavalry (they had been volunteers) and the oldest of his Macedonians. He then divided his Companion Cavalry into eight hipparchies, each hipparchy into two squadrons (*ilai*) and each squadron into two companies (*lochoi*); eight hipparchies appear in action later (A. 4.22.7; 23.1 and 24.1). As a hipparch held higher rank than an *ilarches*, Alexander was increasing the number of his senior cavalry officers from two to eight after the death of Philotas. This corresponded undoubtedly to an increase in Companion

Cavalry from about 2,000 to about 4,000, if the squadron kept its original strength. A hipparchy thus had some 500 men (see also note 95). The companies within a hipparchy seem to have been variously armed, some being "light" and others "heavy," so that the hipparchy could be effective both in skirmishing and in close fighting and adapt itself to novel tactics, such as those of the Scythians. The additional 2,000 men were probably obtained by drafting the Scouts, for instance, from the old army and by bringing in a number of Persian and Median cavalry. This adulteration of the Companion Cavalry was resented by many Macedonians, even if the number of actual "Companions" within a Companion Cavalry Hipparchy was not thereby increased, at least initially.[78]

Alexander must have realised by now that hard fighting lay ahead. It had become obvious that the area between the Caucasus and the Ocean was no narrow strip, and that it was occupied by tribes which had excellent cavalry forces. When he sent the oldest Macedonians home, he obtained a decision from the rest of the Macedonians that "they would serve for the rest of the war" (C. 7.5.27 *ad reliqua belli navaturos operam pollicebantur*; see note 142 for similar instances).

In midsummer 329 B.C. Alexander marched by night, because of the intense heat, across some 75 kilometres of sandy desert to reach the Oxus (Amu) near Kelif, his men and horses suffering severely from thirst. Bessus was not there to contest the crossing; indeed he was in flight towards Nautaca (Shakhrisyabaz ?) and Samarcand. It took five days to float the army across the huge river, a kilometre wide, on improvised rafts which were buoyed up by tent-covers filled with straw (*Itin. Alex.* 34 describes how the rafts were made). Then a report came from two of Bessus' officers, Dataphernes and Spitamenes, that they had arrested Bessus and would surrender him to "a small force." Alexander sent Ptolemy ahead with three hipparchies of Companion Cavalry, the mounted javelin-men, a Hypaspist chiliarchy, a phalanx-brigade, the Agrianians and half of the archers—not a small force, since he did not trust Dataphernes and Spitamenes. Ptolemy excelled himself. Covering in four days what would normally have taken ten, he took Bessus' officers by surprise. They made off at speed, but they left Bessus behind for Ptolemy to capture alive. On Alexander's orders Bessus was brought naked, in bonds, and wearing a wooden collar, to a place which Alexander and the army were to pass on the march. When Alexander asked Bessus why he had arrested and killed Darius, his king and his kinsman, and when Bessus tried to justify himself, Alexander had him flogged while a herald proclaimed his iniquities.[79]

The end of Bessus was deferred for some months. That winter Alexander accused him before a court evidently of the leading Persians in his entourage (these included Darius' brother and other kinsmen), had his nose and ear-laps cut off (presumably as recommended by the court), and sent him to be tried "at the court of the Medes and the Persians" at Ecbatana, where he was put to death (A. 4.7.3). To Arrian, as to us, the treatment of Bessus was "barbaric." To contemporaries it was in no way unusual, since flogging was a Macedonian and Greek punishment for criminals and mutilation of nose and ears a Persian one. The procedure is of particular interest. In acting as prosecutor before the Persians Alexander appeared as protector of Darius' interests. In referring the matter to the court at Ecbatana he followed his usual practice of making a native people try their own offenders at home, and in so doing he recognised the authority of a native body, which evidently had—and may have had in the past—a regular jurisdiction within a system of autonomous local government. Had there been a Great King of Persia, he would have executed any pretender without trial, for the Great King's word was law. But Alexander was introducing Macedonian forms of procedure into Media and Persia, as Plutarch indicated without reference to this instance (P. 47.3, "He tried to bring the native customs closer to the Macedonian customs").[80]

After capturing Bessus, Alexander made good his losses in horses (*Itin. Alex.* 35) and advanced unopposed via Maracanda (Samarcand), a walled city, the capital of Sogdiana, to what Alexander and his men called the last great river, naming it the Tanaïs rather than the Jaxartes as it was known later. Since leaving the Hindu-Kush he had received the submission of the Bactrians and the Sogdians, and he had left garrisons in a number of Sogdian cities. But the appearance of a peaceful takeover was deceptive. First, some Macedonians in a foraging party were killed by mountaineers. When Alexander led his commando troops against their fastnesses, he was wounded by an arrow which broke a bit off one fibula-bone, and the troops ravaged the whole area and killed more than two-thirds of the tribesmen, estimated in all at 30,000.[81]

The scale of these reprisals may have been responsible for what happened next; for when Alexander convened a meeting of the leading Sogdians, they and some Bactrians rose in revolt and wiped out some of the garrisons in the cities. Alexander's answer to this was *andrapodismos*, the killing of adult males and the enslaving of the rest—a retaliation which Athens had employed against rebel cities. In two days his troops under covering fire from slingers, archers, and catapultists captured by assault and "andrapodised" five cities.

While he was leading a special force along a dry water-course under the wall of a sixth city, he was felled by a stone which struck his neck, and several officers, including his second-in-command, Craterus, were wounded by arrows. But the Macedonians pressed the attack home and captured the city. Of the garrison 8,000 fell in the fighting and 15,000 surrendered; and the walls of the city, Cyropolis (Ura-Tyube) were razed. The seventh and last city was taken by assault, and its population was deported. During these punitive operations the Macedonian troops were allowed to loot and to take personal prisoners.

The next step was a constructive one. Alexander founded Alexandria-on-the-Tanaïs, known also as Alexandria Eschate ("the farthest"), at Khodjend near Leninabad. The soldiers built twelve kilometres of walls and some public buildings in twenty days, and Alexander planted some Macedonians, a number of Greek mercenaries, and thousands of natives, some volunteering, others displaced, for example from Cyropolis, and others whose freedom Alexander purchased from their Macedonian captors.[82] The city was designed to discourage Scythian raiders and deter Sogdian rebels; and in the long term it was the beginning of a new way of life which was to win over the Sodgians and unite them against the Scythians.

Meanwhile an army of Scythians had appeared across the Jaxartes. In the past their mounted archers had defeated Cyrus the Great, Darius I, and other Persian monarchs, and they now taunted the Macedonians. Alexander could not resist the challenge; moreover, he had had experience of Scythian tactics in the plains of the lower Danube. His catapults laid down a covering fire which drove the Scythians from the bank, and his army crossed the river on a huge number of rafts and landing craft, buoyed up on inflated skins. The leading craft carried catapults which were fired from on board, and Alexander went on one of them to direct the disembarkation. He landed the slingers and archers first, and their fire covered the arrival of the infantry and the cavalry. Then his whole force was drawn up in formation without interference from the enemy.

The next thing was to foil the well-known Scythian tactics of withdrawing-and-circling while firing their arrows at their pursuers—tactics encountered by Philip and Alexander in their Danubian campaigns. Alexander used his extended phalanx on the river-bank as a base. From it he sent forward first a hipparchy of mercenary cavalry and four squadrons of lancers, about 1,000 in all, and the Scythians enveloped them in a circling attack with a large circumference. Then he sent forward a mixed force of cavalry and light-armed infantry intermingled, and they broke the circumference at point "X" and stopped the flow of the circling Scythians. Immediately he sent in two attacks, one on either side of point "X"; the first was delivered by the mounted javelin-men and three hipparchies of Companion Cavalry, and the second under Alexander's personal command by the remaining cavalry, each squadron in column formation, which charged into the main concentration of the enemy. The Scythians fled, losing 1,000 killed, and the Macedonians took 1,800 horses; but Alexander drank foul water, suffered violent dysentery, and was carried back dangerously ill. This illness confirmed Aristander's divination, based on the omens of two sacrifices, that to cross the river spelt danger for Alexander.

During these operations on the Tanaïs river a special detachment was on its way to the relief of the Macedonian garrison in the citadel of Samarcand, which was blockaded by Spitamenes and his Sogdian troops. When the detachment arrived, Spitamenes withdrew towards Bukhara and added 600 Scythian cavalry to his Sogdians. The Macedonians pursued incautiously. They numbered 60 Companion Cavalry, 800 mercenary cavalry, and over 2,000 infantry, mainly mercenaries. The Macedonian officers in command of the individual units had been placed by Alexander under the general command of a Lycian, Pharnuches, whose expertise was in the local languages and in diplomacy; and it was evidently the fault of Pharnuches that he brought his troops into action after a forced march, when the cavalry horses were the worse for lack of fodder.

This time the Scythian tactics in the open plain near the desert succeeded brilliantly, and the Macedonians withdrew in disorder to the river Polytimetus (Zeravshan), where they suffered the same fate as the Athenians at the river Assinarus in 413 b.c. They were shot down from a distance. Spitamenes took no prisoners. Only 40 cavalry and 300 infantry escaped. The dead exceeded 2,000 (A. 4.6.2; C. 7.7.39). The different accounts of the survivors were reflected in the narratives of Aristobulus and Ptolemy.[83]

The news of this disaster—the first recorded defeat of Macedonians since 353 b.c.—brought Alexander posthaste to the scene with archers, Agrianians, commando-infantry and half the Companion Cavalry. They covered the 173 miles to Samarcand in three and a half days, that is at the rate of almost 50 miles a day (A. 4.6.4 and C. 7.9.21).[84] Spitamenes fled into the desert. Alexander covered the bones of the dead with a great tumulus and made funerary sacrifices in their honour "in the Macedonian manner." He then made a sweep into the desert on either side of the river Polytimetus. But the enemy were not to be found.

Alexander wintered at Bactra. In 328 b.c. he stamped out revolt in Bactria and Sogdiana by dividing his army into many detachments and capturing numerous fortresses; some rebels he won over by agreement and some he incorporated into his own forces. Little is known of these operations. He had a city founded as Alexandria-in-Margiana in the oasis of Merv, but did not go there himself; its purpose was to prevent the Scythians making use of the oasis. Six hill-sites were chosen for forts, intended as bases for a defence force facing the desert. Spitamenes added 600 Massagetae to his force, won two minor victories, and fled to the desert, where Craterus pursued and defeated him, despite Spitamenes being reinforced by 1,000 more Massagetae. Late in the year, when Spitamenes realised that his strike-and-run raids were rendered impossible by the Macedonian posts, his troops and 3,000 Massagetae made an attack on Coenus in Sogdiana who was in command of 400 Companion Cavalry, the mounted javelin-men, and Bactrian, Sogdian, and other cavalry. Spitamenes was completely defeated. His Sogdian and Bactrian followers mostly surrendered to Coenus, and the Massagetae, frightened by reports of Alexander pursuing in person, cut off Spitamenes' head and sent it to him. The forces of Craterus and Coenus joined Alexander in winter quarters at Nautaca, 328–327 B.C.

Alexander's further plans were revealed particularly by his dealings with the Scythian tribes. When insulted by the Scythians from the far bank of the Jaxartes, he was said to have remarked that "having conquered almost all Asia" he was not going to be mocked by Scythians. But, once victorious, he cultivated friendly relations, sending back prisoners without ransom and replying courteously to the Scythian rulers when they offered alliances to be reinforced by marriages between their daughters and leading Macedonians.

When his newly made friend and ally Pharasmanes, king of Chorasmia on the eastern side of the Caspian Sea, proposed a joint campaign towards the Black Sea, Alexander's reply was reported in the following words. "My concern at present is with India. If I reduce the Indians, I shall indeed possess all Asia, and with Asia mine I shall return to Greece and march from there via the Hellespont and the Propontis into the region of the Black Sea with all my naval and military forces. Your proposal should be reserved for then." This passage in Arrian (4.15.6) was probably the summary of a written reply, recorded in the *King's Journal*. Alexander believed he had reached the limits of northeast Asia and he had only India ahead of him; and a campaign from the Black Sea to the Caspian Sea, he thought, would make his northern frontier complete.

During these two years of intensive fighting, 329 B.C. and 328 B.C., Alexander received only one batch of reinforcements according to our sources, which are probably correct:[85] Greek mercenaries sent by Antipater (600 cavalry, 7,400 infantry), Asiatic troops from Lycia and Syria (1,000 cavalry, 8,000 infantry), and probably Balkan troops as mercenaries (1,000 cavalry, 4,000 infantry), totalling 2,600 cavalry and 19,400 infantry. In addition, he had recruited Bactrians, Sogdians, and other eastern Asians, who were brigaded together "with Amyntas" (A. 4.17.3), and he had incorporated some of them into Macedonian units including the royal guards (C. 7.10.9). It should be noted that no Macedonians were sent by Antipater, doubtless on Alexander's orders. In 329–328 B.C. the king was commanding an army which was increasingly non-Macedonian and Asian. The need for him to impress his personality on the Asians, as well as his love of battle, may explain his personal prowess in those years which earned him wounds and illness but also the love of his men.

He marched on foot interminably like them, helped the laggards, and refused any favours; and at the end of the thirsty march to the Oxus he stood on the roadside, in his cuirass and refusing food and drink, until the whole army had passed him into the camp (C. 7.5.16). If the fact of his unbeaten record created a myth of invincibility, or if his men and his enemies thought he had supernatural powers (C. 7.10.14 and 7.6.6), he did not disillusion them. Such ideas had practical advantages for the King of Asia.[86]

On the other hand Alexander's Asian policy was disliked by most Macedonians. The bitter feelings of some of his officers came out in a quarrel at Samarcand in autumn 328 B.C. The occasion was one of the dinners which Macedonian kings traditionally gave to their Companions, when men drank deep and conversation was uninhibited. Accounts of such dinner parties and especially of drunken brawls by those who have been present are always far from dependable, and in this case we have mainly much later accounts in which elaboration and invention have played their parts. It should be noted that the company was without weapons, but there were some armed guards in the background. Dispute arose, it seems, between the older Companions and the younger ones over the comparative achievements of Philip and Alexander and over some aspects of Alexander's policy in Asia, especially perhaps in the matter of court ceremonial.

The most outspoken and aggressive of the older speakers was Cleitus the Black. He had saved Alexander's life at the Granicus River; now he commanded half the Companion Cavalry and had just been nominated satrap of Bactria and Sogdiana. He and Alexander—both the worse for drink—abused one another so roundly that Alexander tried to strike him but was held back by some of the company, while Cleitus continued to abuse him. During this brawl Alexander shouted out two orders. First, he summoned the Hypaspist Guard, the order being given in the Macedonian dialect which was an indication to the Guard to intervene in "a serious riot" (P. 51.4). Second, he ordered a trumpeter to sound on his trumpet the call for military aid. The trumpeter disobeyed, and Alexander struck him.

Alexander gave these orders because he thought his life was in danger. Fear of a conspiracy can never have been far from his mind, and the combination of drink and anger brought that fear to the surface. When neither order was obeyed, his fear seemed to be confirmed. Meanwhile Ptolemy, son of Lagus, one of the seven Bodyguards, intervened; he hauled Cleitus out of the room, and indeed deposited him outside the citadel (within which the dinner was held). But Cleitus went back. He came in just as Alexander was shouting "Cleitus, Cleitus," and he said "Here am I, Cleitus, Alexander." Alexander struck him with a pike and killed him outright.

We owe this account ultimately to Aristobulus. It was written before Ptolemy wrote his own memoirs, and we can assume that Ptolemy did not express disagreement with it; for Arrian, through whom we have Aristobulus' account, would have noted any discrepancy between Aristobulus and Ptolemy. This then is as close to the truth as we are likely to get. Aristobulus said also that "the fault" (*hamartia*)—not in reference to the drunken brawl but the fault which led to the tragedy— "was with Cleitus alone." He presumably meant that had Cleitus not gone back the tragedy would not have occurred. It is not an attempt to absolve Alexander from the responsibility and the blame for killing Cleitus.

As soon as Alexander struck him down, he saw he was not armed. He realised that Cleitus had not come back to kill him. He knew now what he had done—killed his friend, the brother of his nurse Lanice, the uncle of her sons who had died in his service—and (according to some reports) he tried to kill himself with the pike but was prevented. The majority did not mention any attempt at suicide. All agreed that Alexander lay without food and drink, lamenting and crying out that he was "the murderer of his friends"; that he was then persuaded only with difficulty to eat; and that he made to Dionysus the sacrifice which he had omitted to make on the day of the party. The implication in this sacrifice was probably that Dionysus, having been offended, turned the blessing of wine into tragedy. Alexander made sacrifice to appease him, the Dionysus of *The Bacchae*.[87]

Early in 327 B.C. Alexander undertook two daring enterprises in order to complete the subjugation of the northeastern area. The first was the capture of "the Sogdian Rock," sheer-faced and impregnable, where the women of the rebel leaders were taking refuge. The rock was strongly garrisoned and well supplied, and heavy snowfalls made the task of the Macedonians harder. When Alexander tried negotiation, the tribesmen laughed, saying only winged soldiers could take their rock. Alexander offered huge rewards, ranging from twelve talents to three hundred gold darics, to any who could reach the top of the rock, and three hundred armed men, carrying flags and using ropes and iron tent-pegs as pitons, attempted the ascent during the night. Thirty fell to their death, but at dawn many flags were seen waving on the top of the rock. Alexander's herald announced that Alexander had found winged soldiers, and the enemy, unaware that the number was so small, panicked and surrendered. Among the prisoners were the womenfolk of Oxyartes, a Sogdian leader, and in particular Roxane, a younger daughter of marriageable age, whom men thought "second in beauty only to the wife of Darius among the women in Asia." Alexander fell in love with her. Unlike his Homeric heroes, he did not ravish her as a slave, but he arranged in due course to marry her.[88]

The next target was "the Rock of Chorienes" (Koh-i-Nor), a vast and precipitous rock, defended at the base by a deep encircling ravine. The

Macedonians worked in shifts, day and night without intermission, in bitter weather and deep snow. Felling pines, they made ladders and descended to the bottom of the ravine. There they drove stakes into both sides of the ravine at its narrowest point, and they constructed on the stakes the footings of a bridge. They then made a wicker-work bridge and leveled it up with soil. As these operations were within range of the defenders, screens were used to protect the workers. When the ramp of earth on the bridge rose higher, the Macedonians were able to direct their fire onto the defenders.

At this point Chorienes asked that Oxyartes, who had meanwhile joined Alexander, be sent to advise him. Oxyartes told Chorienes that Alexander was irresistible in war but a man of honour and justice, and Chorienes then surrendered without terms. Alexander gave him custody of the rock and made him governor of the area. His generosity was repaid by Chorienes. The army had carried out this remarkable operation on short rations. Chorienes now issued to the victors, "tent by tent," enough wine, grain, and dried meat to feed them for two months.

The last rebels were in mountainous Pareitacene. Craterus was sent there with a large army, which included 600 Companion Cavalry and four phalanx-brigades, and he won a decisive victory, killing or capturing the rebel leaders. He confirmed his reputation as Alexander's best general. Thus the two years of severe fighting were brought to a successful conclusion. They were not in vain; for Alexander introduced a new way of life into a very large and populous area. The hill-tribes were forced to abandon their raids on the lowlands and adopted a settled life. The marauding Scythians were kept at a distance by a network of fortified places. Peaceful conditions now favoured the growth of agriculture and urbanisation. Where Alexander had found only villages, the Chinese invaders in 125 B.C. found men dwelling in a thousand walled cities—the culmination of a revolution which Alexander had imposed upon the people and promoted by founding eight new cities in Sogdiana and Bactria alone (Str. 517).

When Alexander moved south to Bactra, he took with him large forces of cavalry, which he had recruited from the pacified areas and also from two Scythian peoples, the Massagetae and the Dahae (A. 5.12.2). Craterus, too, brought his forces to Bactra in spring 327 B.C. There Alexander was visited by an old friend of the royal house, Demaratus of Corinth, who rejoiced to see the extent of his conquests. He died of old age soon afterwards, and his ashes were sent on a magnificent four-horse chariot to the Mediterranean coast for shipment to Corinth. A great tumulus, 40 metres high, was built by the army as a memorial to him. Such extravagant honours were in the Asian rather than the European tradition.

At Bactra the third plot to kill Alexander was discovered. Its origin was as follows. A Royal Page, Hermolaus, broke the rules of the hunt in killing a boar which was not his but Alexander's, because it was heading for the king; and for this he was beaten in the presence of the other pages and was deprived of his horse—no doubt standard punishments for pages. To gain revenge Hermolaus persuaded his own lover and four others, all Royal Pages, to join him and kill the king on the night when they alone should be on guard over him. The motives of the others are unknown. When the night came, Alexander returning late from a drinking-party was about to go in when he was intercepted by a Syrian woman "possessed of a divine spirit," who begged him to go back and drink the night out. As the woman had shown second sight previously, Alexander took this to be a sign from the gods. He spent the night with his friends. Next day one of the conspirators told his lover, and he passed the story to his brother who reported it to Ptolemy. Having immediate access to the king as a Royal Bodyguard, Ptolemy reported the matter at once, and Alexander ordered the arrest of those who had been named. This account, evidently from Aristobulus and Ptolemy, except in the one point that Aristobulus alone told of the Syrian woman, is worthy of trust.

The named conspirators admitted their guilt under torture, and they gave the names also of certain others. The Macedonians among them were prosecuted for treason before the assembly of the Macedones. They were found guilty and were stoned to death in accordance with Macedonian procedure. The danger of associating the Royal Pages so closely with the king had been made apparent in 399 B.C., when Archelaus had been killed by a page. But Alexander evidently thought fit to undertake that risk; for as Curtius remarked (8.6.6) the corps of pages was "a training-school for generals and governors," and it had certainly produced a remarkable number of very able men. The way in which Alexander had escaped death may have fostered in him the belief that the gods were protecting his life; but the fact that promising young men should so turn against him must have been a great shock. It was reasonable to suppose that what had set them against him was not so much his personality as his policy.

The pages' conspiracy became famous because it led to the arrest of Callisthenes, the court historian, who had been closely associated with the pages and with Hermolaus in particular as their instructor in philosophy. According to Aristobulus and Ptolemy, those pages who were arrested said that Callisthenes had "incited them to the deed of daring" (A. 4.14.1), but according to others they did not name Callisthenes as a conspirator. Many stories were told of Callisthenes voicing his opposition to Alexander and, if some were true, his words may well have encouraged the pages. Such encouragement was compatible with his not being named as a conspirator at the trial. His arrest and imprisonment were said to have occurred not at Bactra but at Cariatae (Str. 517), presumably on evidence obtained after the trial.

Such an interval of time enables us to understand the citations from two letters of Alexander, which are given by Plutarch (55.6). In the first letter, written to three Macedonian officers who were operating then in Pareitacene, Alexander said that the pages confessed under torture and said no one else was privy to the plot. But in the later letter, addressed to Antipater, he accused Callisthenes of guilt and wrote as follows: "Whereas the pages were stoned by the Macedonians, I shall punish the sophist and those who sent him out and those who harbour in their cities men who plot against me."

What the punishment was is not known for sure. Curtius (8.8.20–21) says that he was tortured to death together with the pages. All other authorities say that he was taken on with the army, being under arrest for seven months, according to Chares, "in order that he might be tried in the *synhedrion* with Aristotle present." This seems most probable. As a Greek, he would be appropriately tried before a court of the Greek League in Greece, where Aristotle, his uncle, could be present. Chares, writing before Aristobulus, said that Callisthenes died of obesity and worms (P. 55.2); Aristobulus said just that he died of disease; and Ptolemy reports that he was tortured and hanged. Chares and Aristobulus, being fellow-Greeks and writing nearer the event, may be preferred to Ptolemy who, as a Macedonian, may not have cared about the exact manner of Callisthenes' end.[89]

Callisthenes was a somewhat enigmatic character. Publishing his history section by section, he propagated the view that Alexander was more than human: he told about the sea bowing down before him in Pamphylia, the priest of Siwah greeting him as son of Zeus, and Alexander himself implying at Gaugamela that he was descended from Zeus (*FGrH* 124 F 14, 31, and 36). Yet in the stories which grew up in the eastern satrapies, it was Callisthenes who urged Philotas to think of the honours paid to tyrannicides, Callisthenes who made stinging remarks at Alexander's expense, and Callisthenes who opposed Alexander over the ceremony of *proskynesis*.

Arrian (4.11) gives a long and clearly fictitious speech by which Callisthenes was said to have killed the idea of asking Macedonians to do obeisance (*proskynesis*) to Alexander. Arrian also recorded the following "story." When a gold loving cup was being passed round, each guest who did obeisance received a kiss from Alexander. When it came to Callisthenes' turn, it happened that Alexander's back was turned; so Callisthenes skipped the obeisance and claimed a kiss. But one of the Companions told Alexander, and Alexander did not kiss Callisthenes. Whereupon Callisthenes exclaimed "I shall go away the poorer for a kiss." Whatever his contemporaries thought of Callisthenes—and Aristotle regarded him as a man of no sense—his end outraged the Peripatetic School of philosophers, and it was they who were to represent Alexander as the worst of tyrants.

As Alexander intended to move his main army over the Hindu Kush, he gave to Amyntas, son of Nicolaus, his satrap of Bactria, a force of 3,500 cavalry and 10,000 infantry, whose task was to maintain law and order in the northeastern area. The unusually large number of cavalry was provided because they could patrol the plains and deal with the chief danger, the Scythian cavalry. The infantrymen were probably Greek mercenaries for the most part, as we shall hear later of Greek mercenaries causing trouble in that area. The army of Amyntas was supported by the settlers—including many Greeks—who became the leading citizens of the new towns.

(B) FROM THE HINDU-KUSH TO THE INDUS
(see Figures 42 and 43)

In preparation for the arduous crossing of the Hindu-Kush Alexander lightened his wagons by burning all superfluous gear; he set the example himself and his men followed it. Late in spring 327 B.C. he took the vanguard over in ten days, perhaps using the Kaoshan Pass (14,300 feet) this time, and made his headquarters at Alexandria-in-Caucaso. There he stayed for six months. Meanwhile horses and oxen dragged the heavy material over the mountain, and merchants and camp followers made their own arrangements for the crossing. Recent levies from "all sorts of tribes" were constantly trained and disciplined; for in those six months he was welding a multiracial force into a single army. Only a few incidents are reported: a Companion executed for abandoning his post as garrison-commander, an officer in charge of Alexandria-in-Caucaso dismissed for incompetence, a Persian rebel executed by Alexander himself, a Companion appointed to the command of Alexandria-in-Caucaso, an Iranian appointed as satrap of Paropanisadae and territory up to the Cophen (Kabul) river, and Alexandria-in-Caucaso enlarged by drafting of more natives and of unfit soldiers. These may serve as indications of much that he must have instructed his subordinates to do in other parts of the kingdom of Asia during those six months.

As usual, Alexander's emissaries had been sent ahead while he was still in Sogdiana, and they had secured the submission of the native rulers in the valleys of the Kabul and its tributaries. These rulers were now his subject-rulers (*hyparchoi*). If they should now disobey or resist, they would be treated as rebels. At first all went well. The rulers obeyed Alexander's summons to a durbar in the autumn; they promised him their twenty-five war elephants (one made a gift of 3,000 horses) and they accompanied the main body on its march via the Khyber Pass to the Indus. The command of this main body was entrusted to Hephaestion and Perdiccas, and the first resistance they encountered was in Peucelao-tis (Charsadda). It took them a month to capture the capital; they executed the native ruler as a rebel and appointed another in his place.

Hephaestion fortified and garrisoned a city, Orobatis, which helped to secure his lines of communication with the base, Alexandria-in-Caucaso. His main tasks were to amass supplies and to bridge the Indus. For this boats up to thirty-oar size were made from local timber in transportable sections, assembled at the river and used as supports of the bridge, whether they were held against the stream by cables in the Persian manner or by anchors in the later Roman manner. Rafts too were used. Hephaestion had the bridge ready before it was needed.

Meanwhile Alexander was engaged on an arduous campaign. Experience in Bactria had taught him that the submission of rulers in mountainous areas was not dependable, and he was determined to secure his northern flank in the area which was to become the Northwest-Frontier of British India. He took with him the Hypaspists, the three Asthetairoi brigades, the Agrianians, the archers, half the Companion Cavalry and the mounted javelin-men; and as he marched up the valley of the Choes (Kunar) to receive the submission of the Aspasians, news reached him that the natives were taking to their strongholds. He moved at top speed. His men routed the first force which stood its ground, and captured the first city in two days of violent assault with scaling ladders and artillery fire; they killed all prisoners in their anger that Alexander had been wounded in the action. The city was razed. The next city surrendered on terms (see Figures 42 and 43).

Leaving Craterus to destroy any nearby city which resisted, Alexander sped on to the capital of the Aspasians, who, taken by surprise, fired their city and fled with heavy losses into the mountains. The next city was fired by its inhabitants. Intent on the next stage, that of pacification, Alexander ordered Craterus to build a fortified city there and people it with native volunteers and unfit soldiers. He himself advanced with three columns against the largest concentration of rebels, defeated them after fierce fighting, and captured 40,000 men and 30,000 oxen. Resistance in Aspasia was at an end. The finest oxen were sent on the long road to Macedonia.

The next people, the Guraeans, offered no resistance. Alexander took men, horses and siege-train "with difficulty" across their rapid river (Panjkora), swollen in midwinter, and his sudden appearance in Assacenian territory caused an enemy concentration of 2,000 cavalry, 30,000 infantry and 30 elephants to disperse. He had now to attack the Assacenians in their cities, where the garrisons were stiffened by Indian mercenaries from beyond the Indus. First came the strongest city,

Massaga, reinforced by 7,000 mercenaries. Here he made a feigned withdrawal until the phalanx turned, charged at the double and routed its pursuers; then came four days of assault with artillery, rams, towers, and gangways, of which one broke under the weight of eager men; finally, on the death of the commander of Massaga, negotiations were opened with his widow, Cleophis, which led to the mercenaries alone coming out and camping near the Macedonians.

According to Arrian, following Ptolemy, the terms of the agreement were that the mercenaries should serve in the Macedonian army, but the mercenaries were in fact planning to escape that night; and when Alexander heard of this, he attacked and slaughtered them. Whether Alexander was in fact justified is unknowable. What is clear is that any commander dealing with mercenaries of any race has only two courses, absorption or elimination. Next day Alexander stormed the city. The whole operation cost him twenty-five dead and many wounded, himself among them.[90]

There was a pleasant break in the fighting when envoys from Nysa claimed that their city was sacred to Dionysus and had been founded by him on his way back from India. Proof of his presence was the ivy, here alone in India; for it was his sacred plant. Alexander and his Macedonians celebrated the presence of Dionysus by making sacrifice and feasting in his honour; and Alexander felt that the Macedonians would not refuse to follow him in their desire to go farther eastwards than Dionysus had done. Alexander granted the Nysaeans their freedom; and he was accompanied by three hundred cavalry and the Nysaean leader's son and grandson on the next campaign.

Ahead of him in the valley of the Choaspes (Swat) lay two fortified cities, Bazira (Bir-kot) and Ora (Udigram). Alexander left a holding force at the first, stormed the second despite its sheer rock walls, and so alarmed the enemy that they abandoned Bazira and occupied Aornos, reputedly impregnable. He now made arrangements for pacification. He appointed a Companion to be satrap of the region west of the Indus, and within the satrapy he fortified Bazira as a Macedonian settlement, converted Ora and Massaga into guardposts, garrisoned Peucelaotis, and won over some small towns near the Indus (see Figures 42 and 43).

As the winter was ending, early in 326 B.C., "the desire" took Alexander to do what Heracles reputedly had failed to do: capture Aornos (Pir-Sar), a flat-topped mountain protected by nature on all sides, which towers some seven thousand feet above the Indus.[91] This desire coincided with a logical purpose, to demonstrate the impossibility of any resistance anywhere succeeding, as he had done at the Sogdian Rock and the Rock of Chorienes. First, a picked forced led by Ptolemy climbed unseen with local guides to a high top, now called Little Una. He fortified it with a palisade and a ditch, and signaled to Alexander to join him. However, the defenders had now occupied the route which Ptolemy had used; so they drove Alexander back and then concentrated their attack on Ptolemy's fortified position. During the night an Indian deserter got through to Ptolemy; he conveyed Alexander's order that Ptolemy was to sally and attack the defenders from above when they attacked the force under Alexander. Next day this tactic succeeded with fierce fighting. Their combined forces now held both the route up and Little Una itself.

The next obstacle was the immense Burimar ravine. Alexander and his men laboured for three days on their side of the ravine, constructing a ramp of rocks and earth and supporting its sides by lines of stakes and trimmed trees. The ramp was built not at the foot of the ravine, as it had been at the Rock of Chorienes, but on a buttress higher up which jutted out and came close to the enemy's side of the ravine. Despite attacks by the Indians the ramp reached a height from which his artillery and his slingers could fire onto the enemy's position.

On the fourth day some Macedonians captured a peak on the enemy's side "with indescribable audacity," and Alexander at once threw a bridge across from his ramp to the captured peak. The defenders opened negotiations. But their intention to disperse under cover of darkness was betrayed to Alexander. He selected men for two climbing parties; they started after nightfall and he reached the top while the others were still pulling one another up. The climbers, seven hundred men of the Bodyguards and Hypaspists, charged at a signal from Alexander and routed the enemy who were already dispersing. Aornos was in his hands. This rock was identified by Sir Aurel Stein. "Alexander's genius and the pluck and endurance of his hardy Macedonians," he wrote, enabled them to overcome the obstacles which Arrian described so vividly and without exaggeration.

After making sacrifice in thanksgiving and appointing an Indian to hold Aornos, Alexander swept through the territory of the Assacenians. Meeting resistance at a narrow place, he himself led the slingers and archers and cleared the way. Where the side of the Buranda river was impassable, his men made a way by constructing a road. Many natives fled across the Indus and joined Abisares, the ruler of central Cashmir, but they had to leave their elephants behind. Indian mahouts in Alexander's service rounded them up, and Alexander took part with them in elephant hunts. His northern flank was now secure. In spring 326 B.C. he joined Hephaestion and gave the united forces a month's rest. While preparations were being made for the invasion of "India," he held a festival of athletic events on foot and on horseback.

(C) THE ATTEMPTED CONQUEST OF "INDIA"

For Alexander, "India" lay east of the Indus and projected eastwards into the Ocean, as Aristotle had taught him. The words of Curtius (8.9.1) reflect this concept: *India tota ferme spectat orientem, minus in latitudinem quam recta regione spatiosa* ("almost all of India looks east, being less extensive in width [i.e., eastwards] than in length [i.e., from north to south]"). When Alexander and his Macedonians crossed the bridge over the Indus, they thought they were entering the last province of Asia. Hitherto Alexander's enquiries had helped him to relate his preconceived ideas to the geographical actuality; but not on this occasion, whether from difficulties of language or from the preponderance of fantasy.

Most accounts of what Alexander actually found in India were full of fantasy, but one was factual, the *Paraplous* ("Voyage") down the Indus, through Ocean and up the Tigris to Babylon, which was written by the commander of the fleet, Nearchus, a Cretan by descent, a Macedonian of Amphipolis by adoption, and an exact contemporary and friend of Alexander. Most fortunately Arrian had the good sense to choose Nearchus as his chief source for the *Indica*, a work appended to the *Alexandri Anabasis* (A. 5.5.1 and 6.28.6). Further, as Arrian included the Indian campaign in the *Anabasis*, we can compare the views of Ptolemy and Aristobulus there with those of Nearchus in the *Indica*, so that we gain a new perspective of Alexander; and we see Arrian's methods in abbreviating and adapting (e.g., compare A. 7.20.9 with *Ind.* 32.8–13). He reduced the fantasia of other accounts to common sense (e.g., compare *Ind.* 30 with Str. 15.2.12) and he added details from later writers, especially Eratosthenes, an academic polymath, and Megasthenes, ambassador to Chandragupta c. 302 B.C. Arrian's aim was not to give a Roman's knowledge of India but to write a historical account of what Alexander and Nearchus found and did (Figure 17).

As he looked across the Indus on a May day in 326 B.C., Alexander knew that the country ahead was very thickly populated and that the Indians were formidable fighters. How large an army did he have? We can work back from a figure of 120,000 men under arms, given by Nearchus at the start of his voyage in November 326 B.C.—a dependable figure because Nearchus and Alexander were concerned with the logistics of supply. It consisted of the original expeditionary force, subsequent recruitments (from Europe), and "all sorts of barbarian peoples equipped in every fashion" (*Ind.* 19.5). The figure but not the context was preserved by Plutarch (66.5) and Curtius (8.5.4). Between crossing the Indus and reaching the Hyphasis Alexander acquired some 10,000 Indian troops; and while returning to the Hydaspes he received nearly 6,000 cavalry and probably 30,000 infantry as reinforcements. He crossed the Indus, then, with some 75,000 men under arms, quite apart from his supply services and the camp followers. Practically all races from the Adriatic to the Indus were represented in his army and his following.[92]

Having sacrificed on both banks of the Indus, Alexander marched to Taxila (Bhir), where he made further sacrifices, held a festival and enjoyed the welcome of Taxiles (the name was a dynastic one). Presents were exchanged, Alexander giving 1,000 talents of coin from his travelling treasury.[93] It was a triumphant moment; for Taxila was where three important routes met in the Indus valley from Bactria, Cashmir, and the Ganges valley. There he received envoys from other rulers, including Abisares of central Cashmir, hitherto hostile. He rewarded Taxiles with further territory, disregarded Abisares on his northern flank, and pressed on eastwards with an accession of 5,000 Indian troops to engage Porus, a ruler who had not sent any envoys. In May 326 B.C. he found Porus on the far side of the Hydaspes, a great river running high with a swift and turbulent current, because the Himalayan snows were melting and the rains had started. The army of Porus on the riverbank could be seen to include more than two hundred elephants, many chariots, and large numbers of cavalry and infantry. Moreover, it was thought that Abisares might join Porus with a comparable army. The river would not become fordable until winter set in, by which time Abisares might be expected to have arrived; on the other hand, if Alexander attempted a direct crossing in face of the elephants, his horses would panic and jump off the rafts (A. 5.10.2). Porus kept his elephants concentrated at his camp but posted detachments under separate commands at various points where the bank presented less difficulty for landing.[94]

Alexander decided to make a surprise crossing by night with a part of his army. He began with various forms of deception. He spread a rumour that he was going to wait until fording was possible; and to support this rumour he openly amassed great quantities of supplies at his camp opposite that of Porus. Then, whenever he went away, he had Attalus impersonate him and mount the guard at the royal tent. Meanwhile he kept moving detachments up and down the bank and launched boats and rafts (brought from the Indus), as if about to cross in daylight, and this caused Porus to move large parts of his army this way and that to oppose any crossing. Moreover, he had his cavalry simulate preparations for crossing at night with much uproar, which at first made Porus move his forces at night. These feints at crossing exhausted Porus' troops. In the end Porus returned to his original dispositions and did not respond any more to such movements.

Craterus now took command of the main camp and openly made preparations as if to cross the river there. Meanwhile Alexander made a personal reconnaissance and chose a place for the secret crossing. He led an assault force, unseen by the enemy, to a thickly wooded bend of the river 27 kilometres upstream; this bend faced a wooded island which blocked the enemy's view. There the Macedonians put together the sections of their boats and timber rafts, the latter being given buoyancy and

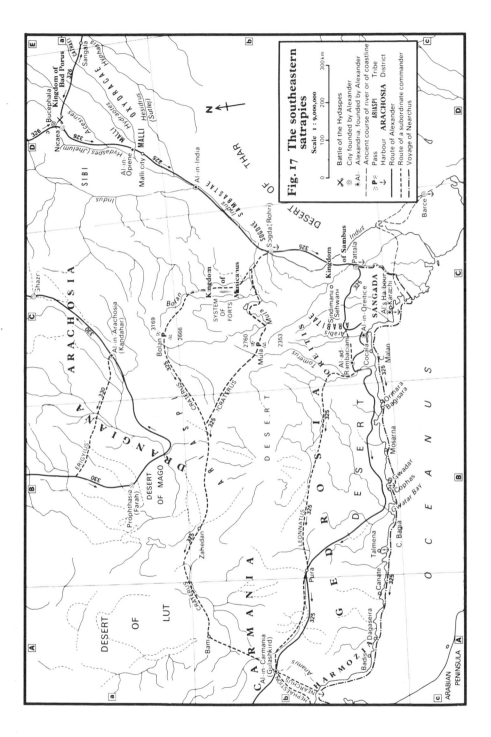

Fig.17 The southeastern satrapies

Scale 1 : 9,000,000

0   100   200   300 km

✕ Battle of the Hydaspes
◎ City founded by Alexander
●Al- Alexandria founded by Alexander
⸺⸺ Ancient course of river or of coastline
⸺ ARIASPI Tribe
⸳P⸳ Pass   ARACHOSIA District
↓ Harbour
⸺⸺⸺ Route of Alexander
⸺ ⸺ ⸺ Route of a subordinate commander
⸺·⸺·⸺ Voyage of Nearchus

balance by large skins filled with chaff and sewn together tightly—corresponding to the empty petrol drums which would have been used today. It was a major task; for the assault force consisted of 5,000 cavalry, requiring for their horses at least 100 large rafts, and 6,000 infantry, whose boats were to tow the rafts across the turbulent river. During the night thunder and heavy rain helped to drown the noise of the preparations. Towards dawn the weather cleared. Meanwhile other detachments had positioned themselves during the night at prearranged points between Alexander and the main camp. A signalling system had been arranged from Alexander to Craterus at the camp—probably by bugle calls.

Alexander's orders for the day of battle were necessarily issued in advance. (They have come down to us, in my opinion, from the *King's Journal*, via Ptolemy and Arrian.) The intermediate detachments were to cross the river *seriatim*, as each saw the Indians to be engaged in battle. Craterus was to "cross at speed" *only* if all the elephants were taken away by Porus to attack Alexander (this did not happen); Craterus was to stay still if Porus were to divide his army and leave some elephants at the main camp; and he was not to cross until either Porus' entire army left the camp or Porus took to flight and the Macedonians were victorious. Of the assault force the cavalry were ordered to disembark first on the further bank. A part of these orders is in direct speech cited by Arrian (5.11.4).

In the half-light before dawn the flotilla set out. Alexander led the way in a thirty-oared boat with a large raft in tow, the two together carrying 500 Hypaspists, and his men were rowing past the island when they were first seen by some Indian scouts, who galloped off to inform Porus. Approaching what they took to be the far bank, the oarsmen manoeuvred the cavalry rafts alongside so that the horses could be taken ashore, and then they returned to pick up the rest of the force. Meanwhile Alexander led the cavalry off, only to find he was on a second island. However, the assault force managed to ford this arm of the river. The men crossed with water to their shoulders and the horses with only their heads above water. (This shows, incidentally, that the cavalry horses were relatively small.) All across, Alexander laid down the order the troops were to adopt in the event of a pitched battle (A. 5.13.4). Then he advanced with the archers and all the cavalry at full speed, the infantry following in formation at normal marching speed. He was four kilometres ahead when he saw an enemy force which he took to be the forward part of Porus' entire army; but it proved to be a separate group sent ahead by Porus, numbering 2,000 cavalry and 120 chariots. Alexander's 5,000 cavalry, charging squadron by squadron, routed the enemy, killing 400 horsemen and capturing all the chariots, which were slowed down by the soggy clay after the night's rain.

When he learnt of his losses, which included his own son, Porus left some elephants and a small force in his camp to face Craterus, who was ostentatiously preparing to cross the river, and led his main body towards Alexander. Warned by the failure of the chariots on soggy clay, he chose a sandy, level area and drew up his forces to await Alexander. His order of battle is shown in Fig. 18. He seems to have assumed that Alexander would attack in an orthodox formation, his infantry phalanx in line and his cavalry on either wing of the phalanx, as at Issus and Gaugamela. For such an attack his order was well designed. The Macedonian infantry, much inferior in number, would be caught and destroyed between the first line of spaced elephants and the second line of infantry, and the Macedonian cavalry could not aid them, because their horses were not trained to face elephants. Porus placed 150 chariots and 2,000 cavalry on each wing; as he expected the enemy line to be much shorter than his own, these forces were in a deep formation, so placed that they could take each wing of Alexander's cavalry forces in the flank. The trap seemed to be well laid. But Porus made the same mistake which Darius had made: he surrendered the initiative to Alexander, and Alexander did not enter the trap.

While Alexander was advancing downstream, he was joined by intermediate groups which crossed the river in accordance with their orders and came up at the double. While they regained their breath and their élan, the Macedonian cavalry circled round the infantry—perhaps by now some 10,000 in number; then behind this moving screen of cavalry the infantry were deployed in the order of Figure 18. The squadrons of cavalry then adopted their formation. The advance opened with Alexander and the bulk of the cavalry riding forward to threaten the extreme left wing of the enemy, and with Coenus and two hipparchies of cavalry (some 1,000 in number) riding in the direction of the enemy right wing, in order to deter Porus from moving the cavalry there to his left wing.[95] The orders of Coenus were that, as soon as the Indian cavalry of the left wing began to ride parallel to the bulk of the Macedonian cavalry, Coenus was to attack them from behind (this involving for him a right-angled change of direction). Meanwhile the infantry advanced slowly. The orders of the infantry commanders were "not to engage until they saw the infantry line and the cavalry of the enemy thrown into confusion by the cavalry under Alexander's own command" (A. 5.16.3).

The length of the Indian line now becomes relevant. According to Arrian (5.15.5) the 200 elephants, posted 100 feet apart, took up some six kilometres (20,000 feet), and the 30,000 infantry would give for that part of the line alone a depth of five men; but according to Polyaenus (4.3.22) the elephants were 50 feet apart, which with Arrian's numbers reduces the line to some three kilometres and raises the depth of infantry to ten there or over the whole line to eight, the normal depth, as Porus must have known, of a Greek or Macedonian line. Evidently Polyaenus has got it right.

The line was further extended by infantry beyond the last elephant at each end, then by chariots and cavalry, but not by very much since the chariots and cavalry were probably in column, their aim being to out-flank the Macedonians as the Macedonians delivered a frontal attack on the Indian centre. At a rough assessment Fig. 18 shows the Indian line at 3,600 metres and Alexander's infantry line at 1,200 metres, the men being eight deep. As we have seen, Alexander's orders were designed to keep the Indian cavalry split with part on either flank and to attack their left wing before their right wing could come across to give support, the distance being some three and a half kilometres.

The first troops to engage the Indians were the mounted archers, 1,000 strong; they destroyed most of the chariots (D. I7.88.1; cf. A. 5.14.3) and threw the 2,000 Indian cavalry into some confusion by their volleys of arrows (A. 5.16.4). Whereas the mounted archers attacked from the front, Alexander now brought his 1,000 Companion Cavalry at speed up to his right of the Indian cavalry, making a show of charging them while in column and still confused, before they could deploy into line and face him. The Indians now concentrated all the mounted forces of the left wing against Alexander. In a series of parallel manoeu-vres Alexander drew the Indian cavalry away from its infantry line.

These parallel manoeuvres were the signal for Coenus. His 1,000 cav-alry, changing direction, appeared suddenly behind the Indian cavalry. Dismayed and disconcerted, the rear files of the Indian cavalry forma-tion tried to turn about and face Coenus' cavalry. In the consequent con-fusion Alexander took the Companion Cavalry into the charge and routed the Indians, who fell back to the protection of the elephants (to which their horses were accustomed). By this time Alexander's right-hand group of cavalry had outflanked and swung to the rear of the enemy line (Polyaenus 4.3.22); and on the enemy side the 2,000 cavalry from the right wing were coming across to give help.

When Alexander's manoeuvres drew the Indian cavalry away from its infantry line, Porus began to move his infantry to his left (he realised that the Macedonian infantry was going to attack the left part of his line), but the timing of the movement was disrupted by the slowness of the elephants. Here too there was a brief period of confusion. Now was the moment for the Macedonian infantry; for "they saw the infantry line and the cavalry of the enemy thrown into confusion by the cavalry un-der Alexander's own command" (A. 5.16.3). Taking the leftwards-mov-ing and confused line of Porus in the flank, the Macedonian infantry at-tacked the elephants in particular and prevented Porus bringing them forward to terrify the Macedonian horses.

At first the elephants made devastating charges, trumpeting, tram-

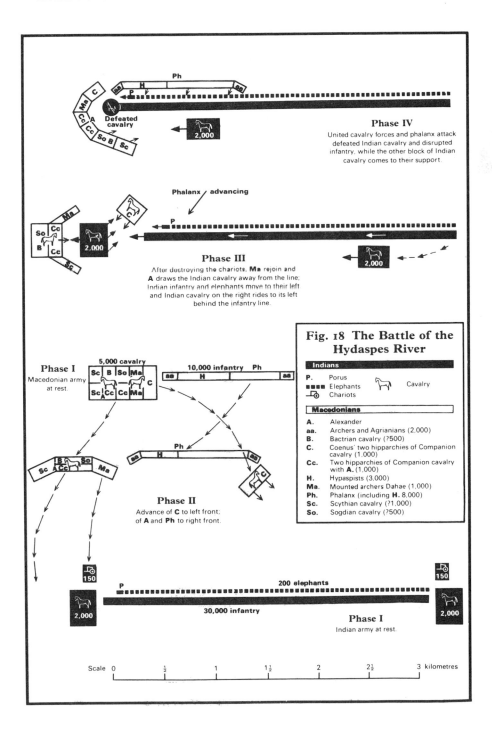

Phase IV

United cavalry forces and phalanx attack defeated Indian cavalry and disrupted infantry, while the other block of Indian cavalry comes to their support.

Phase III

After destroying the chariots, **Ma** rejoin and **A** draws the Indian cavalry away from the line; Indian infantry and elephants move to their left and Indian cavalry on the right rides to its left behind the infantry line.

Phase I

Macedonian army at rest.

Phase II

Advance of **C** to left front; of **A** and **Ph** to right front.

Fig. 18 The Battle of the Hydaspes River

Indians

P.	Porus
∎∎∎∎	Elephants
	Chariots

Cavalry

Macedonians

A.	Alexander
aa.	Archers and Agrianians (2,000)
B.	Bactrian cavalry (?500)
C.	Coenus' two hipparchies of Companion cavalry (1,000)
Cc.	Two hipparchies of Companion cavalry with **A**. (1,000)
H.	Hypaspists (3,000)
Ma.	Mounted archers Dahae (1,000)
Ph.	Phalanx (including **H**. 8,000)
Sc.	Scythian cavalry (?1,000)
So.	Sogdian cavalry (?500)

Phase I

Indian army at rest.

Scale 0   ½   1   1½   2   2½   3 kilometres

pling, seizing, and goring the Macedonian infantrymen, as they had been trained to do, and the Indian cavalry, rallying under their protection and reinforced by the cavalry from the right wing, attacked the Macedonian cavalry, whose mounts were terrified by the trumpeting. The battle hung in the balance. An army less well-trained than the Macedonian would have broken. But the infantrymen, following Alexander's instructions (issued in advance), concentrated the fire of their arrows and javelins on the leading elephants and used their long pikes at close quarters to dismount the mahouts; and the cavalrymen, stronger in physique, armature, and experience, defeated the Indian cavalry and drove them back onto the flank of the elephants. All the left part of the Indian line became a confused mass of elephants, men and horses, enclosed and driven together by Alexander's infantry and cavalry who were attacking in formation from the outer periphery of what was almost a circle.

Wounded and mahoutless elephants went berserk with pain, damaging friends more than foes. Other elephants backed trumpeting onto their own troops, whereupon Alexander ordered his phalangites to lock shields and advance with bristling pike-points, while the cavalry formed three parts of an outer circle round the mêlée. The Indians broke and fled through their own part of the circle, colliding with their own troops, who joined the flight. By this time Craterus had landed at the Indian camp in accordance with his orders; for he had judged the Macedonians victorious. His troops joined in a pursuit which doubled the losses of the Indians.[96]

Porus fought on, despite wounds. Alexander sent Taxiles to offer negotiation, but Porus turned his elephant and attacked Taxiles. Finally an Indian, Meroes, persuaded Porus to dismount and meet Alexander, who asked him what was his wish. Porus replied "Treat me, Alexander, like a king." Alexander was so pleased with the reply that he gave Porus his kingdom and further territory in addition. Later he resolved the quarrel between Taxiles and Porus. This chivalrous conclusion was ensured for Alexander by the magnitude of the Indian's losses: two-thirds of his infantry and cavalry, all the chariots, all leading officers, and all elephants killed or captured. It was Alexander's most bloody and complete victory, and designedly so; for he had reckoned that the greater the slaughter in the pursuit the less need for action there would be in the future (A. 5.I4.2).

The personal bravery and noble bearing of Porus, which won Alexander's admiration, and his exceptional stature and his huge elephant, which delighted later writers, should not conceal from us the fact that his defeat was largely due to his poor generalship. Although swimming across the Hydaspes was not difficult, he seems to have had no agents on the far bank to report enemy movements there; even on his own bank he had no system of signaling; and although he had no idea how many men had crossed at dawn he sent not all his cavalry but only a part, which was inevitably defeated. Deciding on a pitched battle, he divided his forces. In his chosen position he did not rest one wing on the riverbank; in the battle he at first divided his cavalry into two groups, and by anchoring his infantry line to his elephants he sacrificed freedom of manoeuvre. Even so Porus would probably have defeated a lesser general than Alexander; for until that day he had been the greatest power in India.

Because Abisares had not come to the aid of Porus, Alexander had almost twice as many men in the field as Porus. Yet the problem for Alexander was to get enough men into action on Porus' side of the Hydaspes. By the end of the battle all Alexander's army was engaged in the pursuit. The boats and rafts of the assault force no doubt brought the intermediate detachments across. Alexander's planning and logistics were superb. Equally so his speed and daring; for a cautious general might well have waited to bring his entire army to his bridgehead before joining battle with Porus. His tactics resulted in relatively small losses for himself, although higher than at Gaugamela: up to 300 cavalry, including 20 Companion cavalrymen, 80 first-line infantry, and up to 800 other infantry, and very many horses. His intelligence and the Macedonian infantryman's courage overcame a new weapon of war, the elephant.

We owe our understanding of the campaign and the battle to Ptolemy, whose account Arrian used in preference to that of Aristobulus where they differed (5.14.3 – 5.15.2); and Arrian reported that Ptolemy crossed the Hydaspes in Alexander's boat (5.13.1). Ptolemy clearly had access to all of Alexander's orders; for it is these orders which form the framework of the campaign and the battle. In particular the orders to Craterus, cited in direct speech, laid down what he was to do in two contingencies, of which only one eventuated. (We noted the same features in the campaign of Pelium.) The conclusion is the same, that Ptolemy obtained these orders from the *King's Journal* (which he acquired together with the corpse of Alexander). Of course, Arrian has drastically abbreviated Ptolemy's account. It is probable that Polyaenus obtained his remarks from a perusal of Ptolemy's account, but he chose to select different points from those taken by Arrian (e.g., *epikampion, hyperkerasai* as in 4.3.16).

On the other hand the memory of Aristobulus evidently played him false (5.14.3); and other writers gave fictitious but romantic details (5.14.4). Echoes of Aristobulus and others are to be found in the accounts of Diodorus, who has no mention of the river, and of Curtius, who pays much attention to the chariots. Plutarch claims to have drawn his version from *The Letters of Alexander*, which in this case, at least, were not genuine but were constructed probably from an account by Aristobulus (note "the small island" and the 60 chariots in P. 60.3–4 and 8 and in A. 5.14.3).

The victory was commemorated by a silver decadrachm with a symbolic representation of Alexander mounted and wielding a *sarissa* against Porus, who was withdrawing on his elephant, and on the reverse side Alexander, dressed as the King of Asia, holding a thunderbolt.[97] When Alexander designed this coin, he and his Macedonians truly believed that the victory had made him in fact King of Asia. The battle won, Alexander sacrificed to the usual gods and also to Helius, the sun-god, who had granted "the conquest of the world toward his rising" (D. 17.89.3), and summoning an Assembly of the Macedones he told them that Indian power was now overthrown and the riches of India were henceforth theirs for the taking. They had only to advance "to the end of India," where "the farthest East and the Ocean" would be the terminal of their empire (D. 17.89.5; C. 9.1–2; J. 12.7; *Epit. Metz* 63). As after the victory at Gaugamela, the Assembly promised to support the king (C. 9.1.3).

Because "the End of India" was so close, Alexander began plans for his subsequent target, the Ocean, which he proposed to reach by sailing downstream. He had timber floated down the Himalayan foothills and ships built for sea-going, "in order that he might look upon the end of the earth, the sea, when he had overrun all Asia" (C. 9.1.3). He also founded and fortified two cities, one on either bank of the Hydaspes, and named them Nicaea and Bucephala to commemorate his victory and his war-horse, which had died of exhaustion and old age. Generous awards were made to officers and men for distinguished service, and during a month's respite from marching and fighting the army enjoyed festivals of athletic and mounted events. The spirits of the troops were high; their thoughts were of a brief campaign and then the return homewards.

The advance eastwards took Alexander into the foothills of the Himalayas, and he was compelled to cross the tributaries of the Indus high up their courses, because they were swollen with the monsoon rains from July onwards. Taxiles and Porus and their troops accompanied Alexander at first; but he sent them back later, Taxiles probably to organise the sending of supplies and Porus to collect his best troops and also elephants and rejoin him. Alexander usually divided his forces into three groups during this advance: a fast-moving striking force under his own command which supported itself mainly from the countryside, a task force whose duty was to collect and dump supplies for the main army, and the main army under Hephaestion which was bringing up supplies sent from the kingdoms of Porus and Taxiles.

Alexander so directed the task force that it acted at times as a liaison with the main army. The people of southernmost Cashmir, the Glaucae, submitted when the striking force entered their territory; they were added to the kingdom of Porus. Abisares, the ruler of central Cashmir, sent gifts (probably of gold and silver) and forty elephants but refused to come in person despite Alexander's threats. Beyond the Acesines (Chenab) lay the kingdom of "the bad Porus" who was an enemy of "the good Porus" and so now of Alexander. However, Porus did not hold the bank of the raging river which had large, sharp rocks in its bed, and Alexander was able to choose the widest part—fifteen stades (2.7 kilometres) wide, according to Ptolemy—and make the crossing on commandeered boats and on the usual rafts, which the Macedonians built with inflated tent-skins as floats.

Several boats were smashed on rocks in the rapids and "not a few" lives were lost, but the rafts all survived. He left Coenus with his phalanx-brigade to hold the bridgehead and supervise the crossing of the main army and the supply-train. He went on at top speed with his most mobile troops, but the bad Porus fled with his army across the next river, the Hydraotes (Ravi). In order to assume control of Porus' kingdom Alexander detached a force under Hephaestion, which was to reduce all opposition and hand the territory over to the good Porus.

Alexander crossed the Hydraotes without loss and turned not against the bad Porus but against the "self-governing" (republican) tribes. At first they submitted. Opposition started at Sangala (near Lahore), a fortified city on a steep hill, which was held by the Cathaei and their neighbours. The phalanx-men fought their way through the outer defences which consisted of a triple laager of wagons, and Alexander used stockades, night-ambushes and siege-engines against the beleaguered city.

Then the Macedonians themselves stormed the defences. They killed 17,000 and captured 70,000 at a loss to themselves of 100 killed and over 1,200 wounded, and Alexander went in pursuit of any other tribes which refused to submit and fled. On his return he razed Sangala and gave its land to the "self-governing" tribes which had submitted.[98] During these operations Porus had helped Alexander with 5,000 Indians and a posse of elephants; he was now sent back to occupy the leading cities with garrisons. Northeast India thus secured, Alexander advanced to the Hyphasis (Beas) which flows into the easternmost tributary of the Indus. According to the arguments which he had expressed after the victory at the Hydaspes he should now be close to "the end of India."

For some time now, Alexander must have been coming to the realisation from reports which he was receiving (e.g., A. 5.25.1) that this was not so. Now the rank and file of the army realised it too and rumours circulated of a mighty river called Ganges and of huge armies and gigantic elephants—rumours which local Indians said were true. Faced with this new situation, Alexander's soldiers showed by their behaviour that they would go no further, and Coenus as spokesman for officers and men alike, in a meeting of the leading officers which Alexander summoned, spelt out the reasons for turning back (though not in the words reported by our sources).

Alexander was determined to go on, no doubt in the belief that beyond the Ganges he would soon reach the Ocean; he made his determination clear and dismissed the meeting. Next day he reconvened the meeting. This time he said any who wished could leave their king and go home, but he would go on, since he would have those who would follow their king of their own will. These words were spoken in an angry manner, and the hint was taken that the Asians would willingly go on with Alexander as King of Asia. Alexander then shut himself up in his tent for three days. He knew that his words would reach the Macedonians, and he thought they might change their minds. But no, there was silence throughout the camp. On the fourth day Alexander made sacrifice, which was customary before crossing a river. The omens proved unfavourable. Calling to him his leading Companions and closest Friends, he declared to the army that he had taken the decision to turn back. The announcement was greeted with shouts of joy and tears of relief.

The clash of wills may be considered in two ways. Militarily the Macedonians alone were involved in the standstill. There is little doubt that the Asian troops, and not least the Indians of the native rulers, were prepared to follow Alexander; and Porus seems to have considered that they were capable under Alexander's command of conquering the Indians of the Ganges valley (D. 17.43.2–3). Yet the Macedonians, even if less than a sixth of the army, were indispensable as the spearhead in battle and the lynch-pin of control and communications. To go on without them was military nonsense, whatever Alexander chose to hint.

The constitutional issue was simple and decisive. The King of Macedon could not proceed as such without the approval of the Assembly of the Macedones. After his victories at Gaugamela and at the Hydaspes river he had obtained that approval and acted on it (P. 30.1 and C. 9.1–3); if now the Assembly were to say no, he was bound to accept it and turn back. Given these considerations, Alexander handled the clash with skill, at least if we follow Arrian, our best source, and not Diodorus and Curtius. Alexander kept it to the military level. He convened not a meeting of the Assembly but a meeting of the leading officers, among whom were non-Macedonians. Such groups gave advice only. The decision rested with the Commander. When the standstill continued, he called a meeting of Macedonian leading officers only. He conveyed through them his military decision to turn back. He had avoided the constitutional issue, except insofar as the sacrifice was made and the omens were respected by him as king of Macedon. He emerged unscathed in this role, and even as commander of the army he earned his soldiers' gratitude.

The conduct of the soldiers was equally striking. They conveyed their attitude by their silence, and there were no acts of indiscipline. When Coenus spoke, he bared his head before the king in the customary manner. Respect was shown by king and subjects alike. Neither side bore malice; and Alexander gave Coenus a magnificent funeral when he died of disease at the Hydaspes.

In fact, the Macedones won, both as soldiers and as an unconvened Assembly, and any military historian will acclaim their good sense, even granted the belief that it was only twelve days' march to the Ganges and that the Ocean lay not far beyond it. Already the lines of communication were immensely long, the dilution of Macedonian forces very great, and the size of the subjugated populations enormous without adding that of further India. Yet Alexander wanted desperately to go on. Why? We must consider the answer in the last chapter.

The cure for disappointment was action. As rumours of gigantic elephants had dismayed his troops, so he set them to work on building gigantic defences, equipment, and fittings which would make the eastern Indians hesitate to attack him. To mark the limit of the army's advance towards the east, twelve gigantic altars of stone were dedicated to deities chosen by Alexander: Athena Pronoia (meaning Foresight) and Delphic Apollo, familiar to Greeks and Macedonians alike; Heracles, ancestor of the royal house; Zeus of Olympus and the Cabiri of Samothrace particular to the Macedonians; Ammon, personal god to Alexander; the "Indian Helius" (the Sun); and other gods whose names have not come down to us. At these altars thanksgiving was made "to the gods who had brought him so far victorious." The twelve altars were also intended to be "memorials of his own labours," comparable to the twelve labours of Heracles, and they were set up at the eastern end of Alexander's world, even as the Pillars of Heracles had been set up by Heracles at the western limit, the Straits of Gibraltar. Nothing could have demonstrated more strikingly that Alexander had accepted the decision of the army for all time, even though he expected that most of his life lay ahead of him. He had just reached the age of thirty.

The clash at the Hyphasis should not be misunderstood. Since Alexander gave no order, no order was disobeyed. In this sense there was no mutiny. The army did not put forward any demand, such as to go home, and Alexander agreed only not to go farther east. Army and Alexander alike knew that the next move was not to retreat as they had come but to conquer south India.

SOURCES

(A) A. 3.28.5-4.22.3; D. 17.83.3-9; P. 50-55; C. 7.4-8.8; J. 12.5.10-7.3; Str. 517 *Epit. Metz* I-38

(B) A. 4.22.4-30.9; 5.1.1-3.4; D. 17.84-86.3; P. 56-59; C. 8.9.1-12.3; J. 12.7.4-12; Str. 697f.; Polyaenus 4.3.10 and 20; *Epit. Metz* 39-49

(C) A. 5.3.5-29.2; D. 17.86.4-95.2; P. 60-62; C. 8.12.4-9.3.19; J. 12.8.1-17; Polyaenus 4.3.9, 21, 22; Str. 686, 698, 700 f.; *Epit. Metz* 49-69

IX

THE CONQUEST OF SOUTHERN "ASIA"

When Alexander first entered the Indus valley, he thought that the river was the upper Nile (just as he had supposed the Jaxartes to be the upper Tanaïs), and that it flowed through a great desert before reaching upper Egypt. He was led to this belief by current theories about great rivers and by his observation of similar flora and fauna, e.g., crocodiles, in the Indus and Nile valleys. His theory was a measure of his ignorance of the southern part of his world. When means of communicating with the Indians were established, he learnt that the Indus flowed into the sea but very far from where he was (in fact some 800 miles as the crow flew).

It was not only the size of India which amazed him; it was also the huge and warlike population. Egypt and Mesopotamia were almost as populous, but they had welcomed Alexander without a sign of resistance. Here for the first time a very large settled population was prepared to oppose him, both west and east of the river. On the figures which Arrian gives the thirty-seven cities and the comparable number of large villages of the Guraeans had at least half a million inhabitants, and the losses of the Cathaeans implied a similar population. When the territory of Porus was extended to the Hyphasis by Alexander, his realm was said to include more than two thousand cities. The India south of Nicaea and Bucephala might be even larger and more difficult to conquer.

His first need was to safeguard his base. Philippus, son of Machatas, controlled as satrap the line of communications towards Bactria, territory west of the Indus in the Kabul valley, and an enclave east of the river. Otherwise Alexander put his trust in native rulers (as did the British many years later). Taxiles and Porus had served him well in war, ship-building, and supply, and he had managed to reconcile them to one another and link them by dynastic marriages. When Abisares submitted and sent thirty elephants as a proof of his sincerity, he was confirmed in his kingdom by Alexander, and his neighbour, Arsaces, was made dependent on him. To have devised and imposed any other form of government in north India would have imposed impossible demands on Macedonian manpower, and Alexander's policy was justified by the results. The native rulers paid a tribute which he assessed, and they pro-

217

vided troops and goods, and they supported the cities which Alexander had founded and fortified within their territories. These arrangements, covering Cashmir, most of the Punjab and northern Pakistan, were completed before he launched the invasion of south India (see Figure 17).

Preparations had been started some months earlier. Now on the way back from the Hyphasis to the Hydaspes he met a convoy of reinforcements: nearly 6,000 cavalry from Greece and Thrace, 7,000 Greek mercenary infantry raised by his treasurer in Asia (Harpalus), and 23,000 Greek infantry collected from his Greek allies in Europe, Asia, and Africa. The prospects of making a fortune in the service of Alexander were such that he had no longer any need to take troops from Macedonia. Together with the men came two and a half tons of medical supplies and 25,000 "panoplies" (sets of armour), engraved with gold and silver, which Alexander distributed forthwith. Now, if not earlier, the Hypaspists were given the silver-faced shields which earned them the nickname *Argyraspides*, "Silvershields" (C. 8.5.4; cf. 8.8.16; 9.3.21; D. 17.95.4); and they and the rest of the front-line infantry were equipped with the new panoplies. As the Asian troops had their native armour, we may infer that Alexander had at least 25,000 Macedonian, Greek, Agrianian and similar infantrymen before he received the accession of some 30,000 Greek infantry. It is at this time that Nearchus put the number of men under arms at 120,000.

We may distribute the total as follows:

Front-line infantry:	Macedonian and Balkan	15,000
	Greek from the Greek world	40,000
Second-line infantry:	Balkan and Asian	35,000
	Indian (brought by Taxiles, Porus and Philippus (*Ind.* 19.5)	15,000
Cavalry: (total in P. 66.5)	Macedonian, Iranian, and Indian	7,000
	Newly arrived from Greece and Thrace	6,000

It was a total which Alexander took steps to reduce. He settled veteran mercenaries in his cities (e.g., A. 5.29.3) and strengthened the garrisons on his lines of communication and at fortified points in India. Even so his army was in the region of 100,000 men under arms for the invasion of south India. The medical supplies remind us of Alexander's care for his men, and we learn at this time of free issues of corn to the soldiers' women and children, some of whom had been born on campaign nine years before.[99]

For the conquest of south India Alexander had an original plan: to use the great river both as a supply line and as a base of operations. His fleet of 1,800 vessels (so Ptolemy in A. 6.2.4) had been built in advance by shipwrights from the Mediterranean and by local craftsmen. They ranged from thirty-oar warships to cargo-vessels, rafts, and local river craft, being equipped to carry troops, horses, heavy equipment, and supplies. They needed helmsmen and oarsmen to control their downstream passage, and these were drafted from other duties—Greeks of the islands, Hellespont and Ionia, Phoenicians, Cyprians, Carians, and Egyptians. Commanders of warships were Macedonian, Greek, Cyprian, and in one case Persian, and the admiral-in-charge was Nearchus whom we have already met. Information about the hazards of rivers—the Hydaspes entering the Acesines, and the Acesines the Indus—was presumably obtained from local boatmen, and the presence of rapids must have been known in advance.

As the fleet perforce travelled faster than any army, Alexander planned to use it as a platform for launching a special assault under his own command, if attack was needed. The rest of the army was to operate in three groups: one including the 200 elephants on the left bank under Hephaestion, another on the right bank under Craterus, and the third as a rearguard and reserve under Philippus. The movements had to be timed, the supplies organised, and the routes defined all in advance, since Alexander intended the groups to rejoin him at prearranged points, sometimes three days' drift downstream, sometimes more. It was an unprecedented operation, requiring excellent foresight.

When his own force began to embark at dawn on a November morning in 326 B.C. (Hypaspists, archers, Agrianians, and the Royal Cavalry squadron being 8,000 men and 300 horses), Alexander sacrificed to the river-god Hydaspes and his usual deities, not omitting Athena Foresight. Then as he embarked, he poured libations to the Acesines and the Indus as well as to the Hydaspes, to Heracles and Ammon, and to his other deities. At the bugle call the vessels rowed out at prearranged intervals, and the riverbanks rang with the boatsongs and coxes' cries, as the whole flotilla passed downstream to the amazement of the native Indians. Hephaestion had already started at elephant pace; Craterus set out at the same time as Alexander; and Philippus waited three days before advancing. They all rejoined him five days after he had sailed. From there they proceeded in the same way.

At first the tribes submitted.[100] But considerably before approaching the confluence of the Hydaspes and the Acesines, Alexander learnt that the two largest and most warlike tribes, the Mallians and the Oxydracans, were placing their families in fortified cities and preparing to meet him in battle in the area between the two rivers. They were not under native rulers, but were "republican" like the Cathaei, and each as formidable as the Cathaei.

Anxious to avoid a pitched battle such as he had fought at the Hydaspes, Alexander moved fast. His laden fleet shot the rapids at the confluence with only slight loss due to the collision of two warships. Sending the fleet ahead to the frontier of Mallian territory, he led his own force northeastwards against the Sibi, who submitted, and the Agalasseis, whose resistance was broken when he stormed their chief cities. His flank thus secured, he returned to the fleet, where the other groups awaited him. From there he launched a concerted operation of which the object was to prevent the Mallians and the Oxydracans from joining forces and to take the Mallians by surprise. Its success depended upon precise timing and the speed of Alexander's own group.

Craterus was given command of Philippus' Asian troops, one phalanx-brigade, the mounted archers and the elephants, which were transported to the right bank of the river. Nearchus then set off with the fleet, keeping three days ahead of Craterus' force, which had to isolate and reduce the tribes west of the right bank. Nearchus was to halt at the junction of the Acesines and the Hydraotes, and Craterus was to join him there and await Alexander. Meanwhile, Hephaestion took a force down the left bank of the Acesines; in due course he would reach the same rendezvous. Five days after Hephaestion had set out, Alexander started on a surprise strike deep into Mallian territory east of the Acesines. Ptolemy with a separate force was to start three days later, follow Alexander's route and join him ultimately. This five-pronged movement was designed to split enemy forces along the river-line, to shatter the Mallians in such a way that refugees would fall into the hands of Ptolemy and Hephaestion, and to cut off and discourage the Oxydracae from coming to the help of the Mallians (A. 6.11.3 fin.).

Much depended on the secrecy of Alexander's strike. Starting from the Acesines, probably at night, he camped next day at a pool (probably Āyak), fed and watered men and horses, and made a forced march, carrying water, across a desert (Sandarbār) with half the Companion Cavalry, the mounted archers, the Hypaspists, one phalanx-brigade and the Agrianians (approximately 7,500 men). The cavalry covered 72 kilometres (45 miles) in some 18 hours; they arrived at dawn outside the first Mallian city, ahead of any report (A. 6.6.2). Alexander killed those in the fields and ringed the city with his cavalry. When his infantry came up, the cavalry and light-armed men were sent on under Perdiccas to surround the next city. In their absence the infantry broke their way into the first city, stormed the citadel and put everyone to the sword. Alexander was in the thick of the action throughout.

Perdiccas found his city deserted but galloped on and massacred many fugitives. After a rest and a meal Alexander marched all night to reach the Hydraotes at dawn, when he caught and destroyed the rearguard of a Mallian army which was probably about to join the Oxydracae. Following the rest of the Mallians across the river, he killed or captured many, but the main body reached a stronghold. Leaving Peithon with a detachment to take the stronghold (which he did), Alexander recrossed the Hydraotes and attacked a city of Brahmans which was sheltering

Mallian troops. In a desperate assault Alexander was first to mount the citadel wall. As the enemy fought to the death, only a few were taken alive.

This breath-taking strike had broken any attempt at coordinated resistance and inflicted over 10,000 casualties, apart from noncombatants killed or enslaved. Alexander changed now to a less rapid pace. While some cavalry and light-armed troops destroyed any refugees in the woods, the main body approached city after city, to find them deserted, and then located an army of some 50,000 men on the far side of the Hydraotes. Arriving first with his cavalry, Alexander led them alone into the river, whereupon the Mallians retreated in good order. When the infantry came up in formation, the Mallians fled and were hotly pursued by the cavalry; but most of them escaped into a fortified city. Alexander began the assault next day, dividing his men into two groups. The group which he led broke into the city first and attacked the strongly-held citadel. The other group under Perdiccas came later into the city and brought no ladders, thinking the siege to be over. Under the impression that Perdiccas' men were malingering, Alexander seized a ladder, set it against the citadel wall and went up it, huddling under his shield. Peucestas, bearing the sacred shield from Troy, followed close and after him Leonnatus, a Bodyguard. Another ladder was set up alongside, and Abreas, a man distinguished for courage, was first to go up it. Both ladders rested on a stretch of wall between two towers, and on the inside a high mound came close to the top of the wall.

Alone though he was, Alexander pushed the defenders off the top of the narrow wall by using his shield and sword. He was joined on the wall by Peucestas, Leonnatus, and Abreas. Then both ladders broke under the weight of those who were climbing up in support of their king. The four men were a standing target for missiles from the two towers and the mound. Alexander jumped down inside, landed on his feet and defended himself with shield, sword, and stones against attackers and even killed the enemy commander. The others jumped down and fought beside him. Abreas was struck dead by an arrow fired at short range. Alexander was hit by another arrow which went through his cuirass, pierced his chest above a nipple and entered a lung. He fought on for a moment and then collapsed into his shield. Peucestas crouched over him, holding the sacred shield against the hail of arrows, and Leonnatus guarded his other side. Both were wounded before the Macedonians reached them and drove off the attackers.

There being no intact ladders available, some Macedonians outside had made pitons from the broken ladders, driven them into the mud-bricks and climbed the wall; others had made human ladders; and others had smashed their way through the gates by brute force. Once inside they raised the battle-cry and killed man, woman, and child in the belief that Alexander had been wounded to the death. He was carried away semi-conscious on his shield.

To extract the arrow the wound was widened, probably by Perdiccas with his sword-point. The consequent gush of blood was great, although after Alexander had fainted from the pain, the bleeding stopped. A rumour that he was dead reached the camp, where men were overcome with grief and despair. They refused to believe that he was alive even when he was brought downriver on a barge. Then he was seen to be raising his arm in the royal greeting (perhaps as shown on a coin of Philip, his father). They shouted for joy, lifting their arms to heaven in gratitude and pointing towards him. Carried ashore on a stretcher, he nonetheless insisted on riding his horse to his tent, and when he dismounted, the soldiers wreathed him "with such flowers as India then was producing."

We owe our account to Arrian's use of Ptolemy and Aristobulus. Others embellished the story (e.g., D. 17.99.1–4). Cleitarchus substituted Ptolemy for Leonnatus in an attempt to flatter his royal patron (for Ptolemy was then ruler of Egypt), but Ptolemy to his credit denied it when he wrote his personal record after the publication of Cleitarchus' romances.

The huge losses inflicted on the Mallians by Alexander, Hephaestion and Ptolemy had the desired effect. The report of the irresistible Macedonian troops and their king who "was descended from the gods" moved ahead of them. The Oxydracans submitted at once, and all other peoples in the region except the Abastanes, whom Perdiccas subjugated during Alexander's convalescence. All forces came together at the confluence of the Acesines and the Indus. There Alexander set the southern limit of Philippus' satrapy. The peoples within his satrapy recognised Alexander as their king, paid the stipulated tribute, and provided military contingents, supplies and services on demand or voluntarily. Thus the Mallians and Oxydracans together were required to send 2,500 cavalry, and the Oxydracans voluntarily sent 500 manned war-chariots. Alexander released the thousand hostages whom the Oxydracans had been required to provide. Other tribes built warships and cargo-vessels for him. Alexander put under Philippus all the Thracians and drafts of troops from other units in the army, in order that he should be able to maintain order; and he commanded him to build a new city and dockyards at the confluence of the two rivers (at Sukkh?). It was called Alexandria-in-Opiene (St. Byz. s.v. *Alexandreiai*).

Resuming his advance with the same strategic plan, Alexander received the submission of the tribes—the Sambastai, for instance, who were even more powerful than the Oxydracans—and sometimes was given "heroic honours" as their king. Stopping at the capital of the Sogdae, he founded and fortified a new city—another Alexandria—and built dockyards. There he learnt that Musicanus, reputedly richer than Porus, was intending to resist. Taking an assault force on board and setting off at once, he made the fleet race under oar downstream and was at the heart of Musicanus' realm before anyone even knew about his departure. Caught unprepared, Musicanus surrendered all his elephants and asked for a pardon. This Alexander granted, but arranged for Craterus to fortify and garrison the capital city (near Rohri) as a centre of control. He appointed Oxyartes and Peithon, probably as satrap and military commander, respectively, to administer the region from the confluence of the Acesines and the Indus down to the sea. The various tribes, the native rulers, and their deputy rulers were thenceforth under the orders of Oxyartes and Peithon. He appointed another native ruler who had made submission, Sambus, to be satrap of "the mountain Indians" to the west, through whose territory there was access to Arachosia by the Mullah and Bolan passes. No contact had yet been made with the ruler of the Delta.

At this point Alexander was taken unawares by a resistance movement. It was planned by the Brahmans, some of whom he had encountered in the Mallian campaign. Their leaders were priests and philosophers, and their followers were fine soldiers; all were fired by a fanatical spirit, and they were exceedingly numerous. These leaders organised revolts not only of the Brahmans but also of the subjects of a deputy ruler called Oxycanus (or Porticanus), Sambus, and Musicanus; but they failed completely to coordinate their efforts and to combine their huge forces.

Alexander was too quick for them. The riverborne assault force drove Oxycanus into a fortified city, which Alexander took by storm on the third day. The standard punishment for rebels was exacted: Oxycanus was executed, the prisoners were sold in the slave market, the possessions of the city became the loot of the soldiers, and the fortifications were razed to the ground. Only the elephants were kept by Alexander. All other cities capitulated. Turning to the realm of Sambus, Alexander received the surrender of the capital city, Sindimana (Sehwan), but severe fighting was needed to master the other cities, since this was the chief country of the fanatical Brahmans. In one siege the Macedonians tunneled under the wall and emerged inside the city to the surprise and discomfiture of the enemy. The losses of the Brahmans in this campaign were reported as 80,000 by Cleitarchus, who was given to exaggeration, but they were certainly as great as those which had been suffered by the Mallians.

The defenders of the last city, Harmatelia (Bahmanabad ?), were drawn into making a sortie by the feigned retreat of 500 Agrianians and were then so heavily defeated by the main force that those who were left to hold the city surrendered. (For the story of the snake poison and

Alexander's dream told in this context, see Note 2). Alexander pardoned them. Sambus survived only by fleeing eastwards with thirty elephants. The attack on Musicanus was delivered by two army groups, Peithon capturing the central area and Musicanus himself, and Alexander reducing the outer provinces. Where the rebels resisted to the end, any survivors were sold into slavery and their cities were looted and destroyed. Where they capitulated, they were spared, but the citadels were fortified and occupied by Alexander's troops.

Alexander ordered the public hanging of Musicanus and the Brahman instigators in the recovered territory; in the same way he had provided for the execution of Bessus in his homeland. The suppression of so widespread and so formidable a rebellion in such a short time is the more remarkable when we recall that the great majority of his forces were not Macedonian but Greek, Balkan, and Asian.

Warned by the fate of the rebellion, Soeris, the native ruler of the Delta, came to Alexander's camp on the Indus and put himself, his possessions, and his territory in his hands. He was reinstated and instructed to prepare for the arrival and provisioning of the army in his territory. Alexander was now preparing for the next phase of operations, the creation and consolidation of a southern frontier. In June 325 B.C., he detached Craterus with three phalanx-brigades, some archers, all his elephants, and those Macedonians who were no longer fit for military service and were to be repatriated; no doubt Craterus was also given Asian cavalry, whether Iranian and/or Indian. His task was to march to southern Arachosia, Zarangaea, and Carmania—areas into which forays had been made in 330 B.C., to deal with any problems in these areas and to await the arrival of Alexander in Carmania. Alexander himself moved southwards from Rohri. Hephaestion led one force down the left bank.

Peithon with the mounted javelin-men, the Agrianians and some Asian troops was ferried over to the other bank. The task of Peithon was to reorganise those parts of Musicanus' dependent territories in which citadels had been fortified and garrisons planted; he was to concentrate the scattered populations into new urban centres, deal with any signs of further insurrection, and meet Alexander at Pattala. The assault force under Alexander's command set off downstream, and on learning that Soeris was in flight raced ahead with all speed of oar to his capital at the apex of the Delta, Pattala (Hyderabad ?). His light-armed troops were in time to catch up with most of Pattala's fleeing population, who were persuaded in general to return. Alexander promised to them what he had promised to the hillmen after the battle of the Granicus: they would be free to till their fields and occupy their city under the same conditions as in the past. Alexander set his army to work at Pattala, excavating a harbour and constructing dockyards, and when Hephaestion arrived his troops began the fortification of the citadel.

For the last stage to the sea Alexander took his warships and fastest vessels down the right-hand branch of the river and had Leonnatus march alongside with 1,000 cavalry and 8,000 infantry on the left bank. As the Indians fled, Alexander had at first no pilots, and a sudden and violent storm coming up from the sea battered and wrecked the ships; but with repairs and the help of captured Indians the crews found shelter in a side channel. There to their surprise (for they were accustomed only to the almost tideless Mediterranean) an ebb tide left them high and dry, and then the flow augmented by the storm caught some craft off keel and smashed them. Going ahead with the best sailors, Alexander came to an island, proceeded 37 kilometres further and saw the sea for the first time in six years, and in the sea an offshore island (Abou Shah ?). At both islands Alexander made sacrifices of thanksgiving to those deities and with those rituals which, he said, Ammon had revealed and enjoined; and then sailing into the open sea he sacrificed to Poseidon, slaughtering bulls and casting a gold chalice and gold bowls into the waters. He prayed that Poseidon would give safe passage to "the expedition by sea."

It was now July 325 B.C. and the adverse trade winds were blowing from the southwest. On his return to Pattala Alexander arranged for the fortification of the harbour there, explored the eastern arm of the Indus, and finding a brackish lake before the mouth, decided to build another harbour and dockyards there; for its situation closely resembled that of Pella harbour with an intake of fresh water and an outflow into the sea. From there he sailed out to sea. The two outlets of the Indus were found to be 330 kilometres apart. Each certainly had a silt bar, and the continuous trade winds made the surf dangerous. Alexander chose the western outlet as the more navigable for "the expedition by sea."[101]

Leaving his ships on the coast there he disembarked some cavalry, explored the coast westwards for a distance of three days' march, and arranged for wells to be dug up to that point and further west along the coast. On his return to the ships he went upriver to Pattala. Later he supervised the construction of the harbour-works and the dockyards at the lake and posted a garrison at the place, which he named Barce. Meanwhile four months' supply of grain was being collected for the army, and other preparations were in hand for the expedition by sea along the coast. A part of the fleet was to stay at Pattala, and no doubt other ships at Barce. Finally, he founded some cities in the delta area (C. 9.10.3). His arrangements for south India were completed by the end of August 325 B.C.

The conquest of "India" south of the station on the Hydaspes took seven months (P. 66.1), from December to July. Although patchily described in our sources, it was probably Alexander's most brilliant military achievement. Undeterred by vast numbers, warlike reputations, innumerable fortified cities, war-elephants and war-chariots, and having none of the advantages conferred on Europeans by the invention of gunpowder but using virtually the same weapons as his opponents, Alexander executed a masterly plan which hinged upon the use of the river-line and the coordination of multiple forces. The Macedonian units were at the peak of their experience, led by officers and men often of Philip's training, who excelled themselves in speed of movement, resourcefulness on land and water, and in the storming of city after city in never more than three days. It was natural enough that Arrian (and ultimately the *King's Journal*) should concentrate on their amazing achievements. But at the same time we can see that the conquest was due to a multiracial army of some 100,000 men responding to the magnetic personality of their commander and to the use of non-Macedonian cavalry in gaining possession and maintaining control of the great plains, which were ideal for cavalry action.

Alexander's methods with the Indians were a mixture of harshness and clemency (the point is made in Polyaenus 4.3.30). Merciless towards the Mallians as the first to resist and towards the Brahmans as the fulcrum of revolt, he pardoned the Oxydracans and won their cooperation. His aim was to overcome all resistance, impose peace on often quarreling tribes and rulers, and gain the support of the peasantry. No doubt he encouraged any belief in his divine powers and his divine descent which arose among the Indians; but it is striking that he never offered sacrifice to Indian deities, as he had to Egyptian and Babylonian deities, perhaps because he found Indian religious ideas radically different from his own. When his trust in native rulers proved mistaken, he replaced them with a system of self-governing cities; otherwise, he made no change in the local systems of administration (see A. 7.20.1). His representatives, the satraps, operated at the viceroy level. They exercised military and police control from a number of garrison-points, securely fortified, and they dealt directly with the heads of the civil communities.

Alexander acquired a vast amount of treasure (e.g., A. 6.16.4), which he spent in part on the equipping of the harbours and dockyards, which were to stimulate water-borne trade and revolutionise commercial exchange, and on the construction and adornment of his new cities, each of which he founded with 10,000 citizens at the outset and planned to be "famous in the world" (D. 17.102.4; A. 6.15.2). His concern for economic development was shown by the creation of native urban centres and the digging of wells to make the desert productive (A. 6.18.1).

Having renounced the advance to the East, he found the Indus valley to have natural defences towards the east and the rivers to be natural routes of communication. In particular he established garrison-points at the head of the delta and by the eastern outlet, beyond which lay the desert; his system of defence in India resembled that in Egypt. His communications with the West were maintained throughout the Indian campaign. Reinforcements, supplies, visitors, envoys, despatches, prisoners, and no doubt traders, artists, and adventurers reached him without hindrance; and to some extent it was a two-way traffic, since Alexander was directing the administration of the central and western satrapies. Little of this interested our sources. We hear of Oxyartes, father of Roxane, reporting in person to Alexander, and of Tiryaspes being tried by Alexander and demoted for embezzlement as satrap of Paropanisadae; and of Greeks in the new cities in Bactria fighting one another, recruiting natives and finally revolting against the satrap. If these were the worst troubles of the King of Asia, they were trivial in significance. The consolidation of his control over so great an area was attested by the fate of the last Persian organiser of resistance, Barsaentes, who had raised troops and elephants in India. He was arrested by loyalist Indians and executed on Alexander's order as an accomplice of Bessus in betraying Darius.

(B) THE CONQUEST OF THE SOUTHERN DISTRICTS BETWEEN INDIA AND MESOPOTAMIA

In June 325 B.C. Alexander sent Craterus to establish and extend control of the southern hinterland, and then to wait for him in Carmania; he himself evidently intended to reach Carmania by a more southerly route. Then in July, on sailing out from the Indus Delta, he decided to send an expedition by sea, which would form a third column of conquest. But this expedition was designed also to solve the question as to whether this southern sea was an inner, self-contained sea or a part of the great sea, "Ocean," which encircled the whole of the inhabited land mass.

Alexander was certainly familiar with Herodotus' story of the Greek captain over one hundred and fifty years earlier having sailed from the Indus to "the Arabian Gulf" (our Red Sea) in thirty months; but the story can hardly have seemed credible since the period of time was absurd and a passage by sea was not known to contemporary Indians. He was guided rather by his own sense of geographical probability. Aristotle had talked of "the other sea, Ocean," being visible to the east of India;[102] that might still be true if one went farther east, but it seemed more likely to be true if one turned south.

For Alexander had seen in the southern sea abnormally big fish and even whales, and on either side of the delta there was desert land, which according to Greek theorists was typical of the Ocean's shores. To send an expedition by sea was the only way to ascertain the truth; starting in a westerly direction, either it would eventually be driven southwards and eastwards round an inner sea, or it would continue westwards and reach the "Red Sea" (our Persian Gulf). If a sea passage could be discovered, the benefit of linking India and Mesopotamia for commerce and control would be enormous. So Alexander sacrificed to Poseidon, Oceanus, and other gods (*Ind.* 18.11; D. 17.104.1) and asked them to favour the sea expedition. It was an act of faith in Greek geographical theory and in the goodwill of the gods; but it was fraught with danger.

Some hazards were known to Alexander from his own experience. He had seen that the summer winds, blowing strongly onshore, and the strong tides caused continuous lines of steep surf. With such weather a fleet had to stay at sea unless it could find a river mouth with a good entry; and if there was a shelving, sandy beach, it was only the light ships (*kerkouroi*) which had a chance of landing through the surf. Accordingly Alexander instructed Nearchus, his chosen admiral, to wait until late October when the trade winds would give place to favourable light winds (A. 6.21.2). What alarmed Alexander, according to Nearchus, was "the length of the voyage and the chance of total disaster if the expedition met with a desert coast or one without anchorage or one with inadequate supplies." He was thinking not of merchant ships under sail, which could carry a heavy cargo of supplies for a small crew, but of ships under oar with a large crew and very little storage space—thirty-oared longboats (*triakontoroi*) and light boats under oar (*kerkouroi*).[103]

They could use a favourable wind, but they were not, like cargo vessels at sea, dependent on the wind; thus they could row in a calm which left a cargo vessel standing. "The length of the voyage" was dangerous because only a limited amount of water and food could be carried in such ships and conditions at sea in open boats in hot weather were very exacting. "A desert coast" would offer neither water nor food; Alexander had seen such coasts on either side of the Indus, and he had arranged to dig wells in advance so that the fleet could get water there. "A coast without anchorage" would keep the fleet at sea in any adverse weather; this in turn might lead to starvation, or an onshore gale which would wreck the ships. "A coast with inadequate supplies" emphasises the fact that oared vessels soon ran short of water and food and therefore needed to draw them from a well-inhabited coast or from prepared dumps and wells. Nearchus felt he could succeed only if "the sea in those parts was navigable, and if the task was not beyond human capacity" (see Figure 19).

In order to offset these dangers for the fleet Alexander intended to start some two months ahead of the fleet, and keep near the coast with at least part of his forces and find harbours, dig wells, dump supplies, arrange native markets, look for anchorages and make whatever provision was possible under the circumstances (A. 6.23.1, for instance). He must have devised some means of indicating to the fleet that such facilities were available, when he had already gone far ahead. In addition to oarsmen and naval hands the ships carried enough troops to overcome any minor resistance and force a landing; they were well armed and had siege-catapults. The men were fired with Alexander's enthusiasm and interest, and they trusted in his "extraordinary good fortune."

The army which was to prepare the way for the fleet had a dangerous task also. Even if Alexander did not know the full extent of the difficulties in Gedrosia (and Nearchus believed he did not), he expected some stretches of desert from what he had seen west of the Indus delta. He prepared for this hazard as far as possible by accumulating four months' supplies of food for men and beasts; these were to be transported on wagons. When all was ready, Alexander's army set off from Pattala in late August 325 B.C., so that he could benefit from the monsoon rains (Str. 721) and have a good lead in order to stay ahead of the fleet. He expected to meet Nearchus not en route but at the mouth of the Tigris or the Euphrates (A. 6.19.5; D. 17.104.3; C. 9.10.3).

As the overtures which had been made in advance were rejected by the first two peoples, the Arabitae and the Oreitae, Alexander achieved a surprise by crossing a desert during the night and appearing on the edge of the fertile valley of the Purali at dawn. His cavalry, riding ahead, killed those who resisted and took many prisoners. When the main body under Hephaestion joined him, he advanced to the Oreitae's largest village, Rambacia, where he decided to found an urban centre for Oreitans and Arachosians. While Hephaestion was putting this in train, three raiding forces pillaged Oreitan territory, and then Alexander advanced against a concentration of Oreitans and Gedrosians at a defile (Kumbh Pass) which gave access to Gedrosian territory. At his approach the Oreitan leaders capitulated. They were told to summon their people and send them home on the assurance of Alexander that they would suffer no harm.

Apollophanes was appointed satrap of Oreitis, and Leonnatus was left behind as military commander for the time being with all the Agrianians, some archers, some cavalry, and a force of Greek mercenaries, both infantry and cavalry. Leonnatus was to complete the urban centre and enforce law and order among the Oreitae; he had also to arrange provisions for the fleet on its arrival. In fact Leonnatus carried out both commissions brilliantly and was crowned with a golden crown by Alexander later; for he defeated the Oreitans and their neighbours in a major battle, inflicting 6,000 casualties, and he gave ten days' supplies to Nearchus and replaced some of Nearchus' men with his own. Before Alexander left he founded an Alexandria on the coast near the mouth of the Phur, at a place where there was a sheltered harbour.

In October—the month during which Nearchus had been told to

start—Alexander entered Gedrosia. He intended to conquer the Gedrosians whose leaders had not yet submitted and to make provision for the fleet. Sixty days were to pass before he reached the capital of Gedrosia, Pura. At first there was still water available from the monsoon rains, as Alexander had been led to expect (Str. 721), and some wild life and trees; indeed the Phoenician traders with the army loaded their carts with myrrh-gum and spikenard, which commanded a good price in the west. The primitive aborigines who lived on the coastal strip had little to offer, and the army lived largely on the supplies which were being transported on the wagons. Then they had difficulty in finding water.

Alexander kept some cavalry on the coast to mark anchorages and find means of getting water for the fleet, but he took the main body to inland watering-points and finally to a place inland where grain and other foodstuffs were available. Alexander intended these for the fleet; so he loaded them on wagons, sealed the wagons with his royal seal and sent them on their way to the coast. But the escort of troops broke the seal and distributed the food to "those who were most distressed by starvation" (A. 6.23.4), not soldiers, to whom rations would have been issued, but camp-followers. Alexander pardoned this act of indiscipline when he learnt of their need; but when more grain was captured by his raiding force, he sent it down to the coast to be held for the fleet. Later, he made a dump of meal for the fleet. As they advanced, the forwarding of supplies from Oreitis declined (Str. 722); convoys were rarer and each convoy brought less. Groups of Gedrosians were sent inland to obtain grain, dates, and sheep; these were bought by the soldiers and the traders.

At this point Alexander had to make a decisive choice. If he took the inland route for the next stage, his army would reach the Gedrosian capital without difficulty—as that of Leonnatus did a month or two later—and he must have had information about the route itself from the Gedrosians. But the fleet would then be abandoned to its own devices; and from what he had seen of the coast so far and may have learned of the coast he was approaching, the chances of the fleet failing completely without his help must have seemed high. If he took the coastal or near-coastal route, about which local information was probably discouraging but vague, his army would be in some danger; but he would be near enough to "provide the bare necessities for the fleet" (A. 6.24.3). What should he do? It was an agonising choice. He decided to take the coastal route in order to provide for the fleet, as Nearchus later reported. Even when he reached Pura by that route, he was still to fear that the fleet might be a total loss (*Ind.* 34.1 and 35.2); but at least he knew he had done all in his power to help Nearchus.

The army which set off on the coastal route consisted of the Hypaspists, three phalanx-brigades, some archers, the Royal Cavalry Guard, some cavalry hipparchies, and the mounted archers—perhaps 12,000 men if the units were at full strength and in any case a predominantly Macedonian force.[104] The wagons of the baggage-train, carrying the supplies, the sick and the weak (including some of the soldier's women and children), and the wagons of the traders reduced the pace of the army, because detours were necessary in order to avoid steep inclines. Soon they came into a hilly wilderness of soft sand and excessive heat (see Figure 44). There men and animals sank knee-deep and grew exhausted. Moreover, the wide distances between water-points extended the all-night marches into the roasting day.

As morale declined, the men began to kill the draught-animals and eat them, as they had done in the pursuit of Bessus, and they destroyed the wagons and used the wood for cooking. Soon there was no transport for the sick and weak. Most of those who fell behind "died in the sand like men who have fallen overboard at sea." One night when they encamped in a wadi, a cloudburst in the hills caused a sudden flood, which swept away most of the remaining draught-animals, the wagons, and the royal gear, and drowned many women and children.

Still Alexander led them on, walking himself at the head of the column. When all were panting with thirst, his Guards brought him some water in a helmet. He thanked them and poured it out upon the sand; water was to be for all or none, and certainly not for the king alone. When the guides lost their way after a sandstorm, he rode ahead with a few cavalrymen, reached the sea and discovered himself some clear, fresh water in the shingle.

Thereafter for a week the army marched by the shore, relieved from thirst and living on short rations, until the guides took them inland. There they reached food and water in plenty. When they came to the Gedrosian capital, they rested and recouped their energies. From there they covered some 300 kilometres to reach the heart of Carmania, where they met Craterus and his army. Large numbers of draught-animals and camels were brought there from Zarangaea and Areia to make good the losses in the Gedrosian desert; for the satraps of these two provinces had anticipated such losses as soon as they had heard that Alexander was taking the coastal route.

The reunion of the two armies was a ground for rejoicing and revelry, which was magnified by sensational writers into a Bacchic procession with Alexander impersonating Dionysus! Arrian regarded that as nonsense (6.28.1; D. 17.106.1 transferred the procession to the emergence from the desert, i.e., to Gedrosia; C. 9.10.24 f. and P. 67 kept it in Carmania). Alexander was still suffering from his greatest anxiety. It was December and still there was no news of Nearchus. Had all the sufferings of men, women, and children, and beasts in the desert been in vain?

Nearchus started earlier in October than had been intended, because the neighbouring Indians were hostile and threatened his base (Str. 721). The wind being still unfavourable, he was unable at first to clear the mouth of the Indus. He succeeded only by digging a channel a kilometre in length, which was a laborious and time-consuming operation with pick, shovel, and basket. During the first stage of the voyage, as far as the mouth of the Arabis river, he was able to use the wells and the dumps of stores which Alexander had prepared; but even so he lost precious time, since violent southerly winds held the fleet stormbound at Bibacta for thirty-three days. During this delay they ate deep into their stores and had only brackish water to drink. Between the Arabis river and Cocala high surf kept the thirty-oared ships constantly at sea. Even so Nearchus followed the Mediterranean custom of hugging the coast, and because he was too close inshore a sudden squall destroyed two of these ships and also a lighter vessel. At Cocala the crews were able to land and rest. Nearchus replaced exhausted or discontented personnel and took on ten days' supplies of food which had been prepared by Leonnatus on Alexander's orders. At a point between Cocala and the last place in Oreitis they drove off 600 natives who resisted their landing; and they spent five days there repairing their ships, which had now covered some 500 kilometres (Figure 19).

The next stretch of coast, occupied sparsely by aborigines whom Nearchus called "Fish-eaters," extended for 1,370 kilometres (Str. 720). The passage proved almost as difficult for the fleet as the march had been for Alexander. Supplies ran out three times. Nearchus kept the crews on board in case they should desert. That they survived must have been due in part to the dumps and the indications of water, etc., left by Alexander (although Arrian did not mention them in the *Indica*); and thereafter they lived thanks only to whatever the aborigines gave them or were forced to surrender—a little grain, a few sheep, goats and camels, fish and fish-meal, dates and palm-buds. They owed much to a Gedrosian interpreter and a Gedrosian pilot, under whose guidance they rowed and sailed night and day, whereas hitherto they had usually travelled by day only. They reached safety only when they turned northwards off the entry to the Persian Gulf and set their course for Carmania.

On reaching Harmozia in Carmania Nearchus built a fortified camp, beached his ships for repair, and set off with Archias and five others to find Alexander. It was now January. News of their coming reached Alexander ahead of them. When he saw them so ragged, long-haired, and emaciated, he assumed they were the sole survivors. He took Nearchus aside and wept. Then he said, "That you and Archias here have come back to us safe will mitigate this utter disaster for me; but how were the ships and the men lost?" Nearchus assured him all was

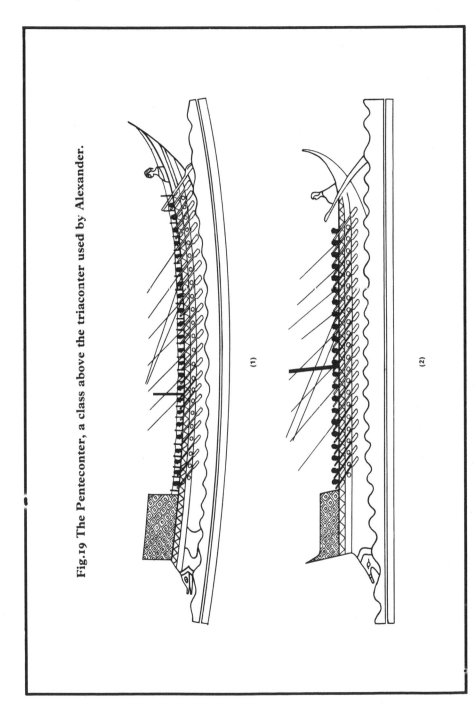

Fig.19 The Penteconter, a class above the triaconter used by Alexander.

(1)

(2)

well. "Thereupon Alexander wept the more, because the survival of the expedition seemed to him too good to be true."

The accounts we have given of Alexander's march through the Gedrosian desert and of the voyage of the fleet are derived through Arrian mainly from two participants, Ptolemy (cf. D. I7.104.6) and Nearchus.[105] They certainly did not minimise the dangers and the sufferings with a view to exculpating Alexander. They appreciated the fact that the two expeditions were inter-related. Other writers did not have that perspective. Some believed that Alexander chose the desert route *only* to put himself in rivalry with a mythical Babylonian queen, Semiramis, and the founder of the Persian Empire, Cyrus the Great, who were each said to have lost almost an entire army there. Others magnified Alexander's losses for sensational purposes. Thus Plutarch (66.4–5) reported that "not even a quarter of his armed force returned from India" and that it had numbered there 120,000 infantry and 15,000 cavalry—leaving the reader to infer losses in the desert of over 100,000![106] In fact it is doubtful if the army itself suffered serious loss; for Aristobulus recorded that Alexander made sacrifice in Carmania "on behalf of the army for its salvation in Gedrosia" and held a festival of arts and athletics. It was chiefly the baggage-animals and the non-combatants that died, according to Arrian's account; and the latter looked not to the army but to the traders for their provisions.

The voyage of the fleet as described by Nearchus and retold by Arrian owed its success to the skill and courage of Nearchus. But that was not the whole story. Alexander's provision of wells, dumps, and information must have played a very important part. Much credit was also due to the chief navigator Onesicritus, who made good use of offshore islands. The size of the fleet on this voyage is not stated by Arrian. We may conjecture that the crews of Greek, Egyptian, and Asian oarsmen numbered a few thousand and that the marines hardly exceeded a thousand; for if he had had many more marines, he would not have fortified his camps as he did even in thinly populated areas.[107] The larger vessels were like a British navy "whaleboat," but bigger, being thirty-oared instead of twelve-oared. Being designed primarily for rowing, they were undecked and had room for only a few marines and a limited amount of supplies, perhaps just enough for ten days (*Ind.* 23.7). Water for five days (*Ind.* 40.11) may have been about as much as they could carry, and water was essential for survival in open boats under a scorching sun.

Only a fool would deny that the success of the fleet was due in part to good luck or divine aid. Alexander, believing the latter, sacrificed to Zeus the saviour; Heracles; Apollo, averter of evil; Poseidon and the gods of the sea; held a festival of arts and athletics and led a procession in honour of the gods. During it the army decorated Nearchus with flowers and ribbons.[108] The risks which Alexander took both in the desert and at sea were incalculable. That was in the nature of exploration. The effect was the establishment of sea-communication between two great centres of civilisation. Further, Alexander's faith in Greek geographical theory was confirmed. The sea between India and the Persian Gulf was indeed "the great sea, Ocean," and it was to be presumed that the southern parts of Arabia, Aethiopia, Libya, and of the land of the nomads beyond Mt. Atlas were also washed by the Great Sea. In his pleasure at the success of Nearchus, Alexander dreamed of circumnavigating what we call Africa and arriving at the mouth of "our sea," as the Mediterranean was then called (A. 7.1.2 and P. 68.1).

(c) THE DEVELOPMENT OF THE PERSIAN GULF AND THE CONTROL OF THE CENTRAL PROVINCES

Nearchus was entrusted at his own request with the exploration of the eastern coast of the Persian Gulf. Many parts were found to be uninhabited and barren, but the problem of supplying the fleet was eased by the foresight of Alexander, who had a large supply dump made at the mouth of the river Sitaces. There Nearchus stayed for three weeks to repair his ships and take on food and water. Strong tides, sandbanks offshore, shallow lagoons, hidden reefs, and steep surf caused dangers and difficulties, but Onesicriticus was helped in his navigation by the Persian governor of the island Organa and by local pilots. At the head of the Gulf Nearchus sailed first to the mouth of the Euphrates, his objective, but he then turned back to the mouth of the Pasitigris and proceeded upstream. There he met Alexander and his army in February 324 B.C. at a place near Susa where a bridge using rafts as pontoons had been built for the crossing of the army. Sacrifices were offered and games were held by Alexander in thanksgiving that his fleet and his men had completed the voyage in safety. In the presence of the assembled forces Alexander crowned with golden crowns for their distinguished services Peucestas, Leonnatus, the other six Bodyguards, Nearchus, and Onesicritus. It was a fitting climax to the fleet's adventures (see Figure 13).

Alexander had commanded Nearchus to examine the coasts during his voyage; explore anchorages, islands of any size, and bays; record any peoples, their customs, and their cities; and note where water was available and where the land was barren or productive. All this information was included in the form of a *Paraplous*, which like the Portulan or Mariner's Guide in medieval times made long-distance voyaging possible, and the way was now clear for maritime trade between Mesopotamia and India. On being informed locally that the Arabian coast was almost as long as that from the Euphrates to the Indus but that it had anchorages and sites suitable for cities which, if founded, would become prosperous, Alexander pressed on with the exploration of that coast and with the investigation of the possibility that one could sail round Arabia into the Gulf of Egypt (our Red Sea). During the next twelve months he sent three separate groups of explorers, each in a thirty-oared ship. The last, who got farthest, returned after reaching Cape Macetia (the Macedonian name for the Oman peninsula on the western side of the entry to the Persian Gulf), and reported that the peninsula of Arabia was almost as large as that of India and much of its coastline was desert. Meanwhile another party sailed down the Gulf of Egypt; they reached Yemen near its mouth and learnt of Aden in the outer sea.

In order to develop and protect the Persian Gulf as the base of maritime trade with India and Arabia and (if Arabia should prove circumnavigable) with Egypt, Alexander created a great fleet of ships on the Euphrates.[109] The nucleus was formed by Nearchus' fleet. Next ships were built in Mesopotamia with cypress, the only suitable local timber, by shipwrights brought from the Eastern Mediterranean; and copper, hemp, and sails were sent by the kings of Cyprus. Ships ranging from quinqueremes (in which a sweep or long oar was rowed by five men) to triremes (in which a crew of 180 men rowed individual oars in three banks) were transported in sections from the Phoenician coast via Syria to Thapsacus on the upper Euphrates, reassembled and floated down. Other ships were built at Thapsacus with timber brought from the Lebanon. Crews and divers for the fleet were attracted from Phoenicia and elsewhere in the Eastern Mediterranean by the offer of high wages in the service of the king. Slave rowers, too, were purchased, probably from Greek owners. The fleet was to be based at Babylon. The Euphrates was an important waterway. Ships could be rowed or towed upstream as far as Thapsacus (Str. 766), and there was easy passage down to the Persian Gulf. A huge basin for a thousand ships was to be excavated at Babylon and dockyards built; and work on these was started with the king's money.

As the ships came into service, Alexander instituted competitions for oarsmen and for helmsmen and races for quadriremes and for triremes, and he kept the fleet constantly under training. The Pasitigris was also opened up to direct traffic; for Alexander removed a system of weirs which the Persians had built as a hindrance to any sea-borne invaders. Alexander intended to be the master of the southern seas.

The prosperity of Mesopotamia depended largely on irrigation from the Euphrates. Alexander explored the whole system of rivers and canals, and discovered a deposit of boulder clay near the junction of the Euphrates and the Pallacopas canal. He arranged to build a dam with this impermeable clay at the junction and to control by sluices the diversion of water; in this way he superseded the Persian system which had employed 10,000 Assyrians for three months each year with less effect (A. 7.21 and Str. 740-1).

On the western side of the Euphrates delta he chose a suitable site for a city, such as he had founded on the western side of the Nile delta; he had it fortified, and settled it with Greek mercenaries—some volunteers, others discharged from active service—and with natives. He planned also to found colonies on the coasts and the islands of the Persian Gulf and to people them with settlers of maritime experience, especially from Phoenicia and Syria, some of whom were to be attracted by financial subsidies and others to be bought out of slavery and rehabilitated (A. 7.19.5). He foresaw a time when these colonies would be prosperous as the cities of Phoenicia and Cyprus were then.

Since the Gulf and Mesopotamia were clearly to be the centre of administration and economic prosperity in the kingdom of Asia, the relatively narrow waist of land between the Gulf and the Caspian Sea gained a new significance. With his view of the world's surface it seemed to him possible that the Caspian Sea might be part of the outer sea, the Ocean, and that there might be a seaway eastward from the Caspian to India and westward from the Caspian to Lake Maeotis (the Sea of Azov), the last link in the latter case being the Tanaïs (Don). Alexander therefore sent a Macedonian officer to supervise the felling of suitable timber in the Hyrcanian forests and the building of a fleet of warships on the Caspian coast. Some of the fleet was ready in 323 B.C., and he planned then a voyage of exploration to ascertain whether the Caspian was an inner sea or a bay of Ocean. In either case he expected the south coast of that sea to become the terminal of northern sea routes. Thus the main trade routes within the kingdom of Asia from north to south and from east to west were certain to cross within the area which we now call Iran-Iraq.

For a year after the meeting of Nearchus and Alexander in Carmania the operations of the armed forces by land and sea were in this vital area. Early in 324 B.C. Alexander marched inland with a fast-moving force of Companion Cavalry, archers and commando-infantry and headed for Pasargadae and Persepolis in Persis, where there had been signs of revolt. The main army, the elephants and the baggage-train were placed under the command of Hephaestion and sent by the coastal route through fertile country in Persis and Susiana. Alexander rejoined Hephaestion near Susa, and it was there that Nearchus with his fleet reported in February 324 B.C. Alexander's keen interest—his so-called *pothos*—led him next to explore the river system and deltas of lower Mesopotamia; these have changed radically since his time. He embarked the Hypaspists, the Royal Guard and a few Companion Cavalry on the fleet. The main army under Hephaestion moved first towards the Persian coast and then up the Tigris, where it met Alexander. The whole force proceeded up the Tigris valley, the river being navigable, to Opis at the end of the summer. In the autumn his army followed the trade-route used by caravans through Celones and Bagistane and the breed-ing-ground of the famous Nysaean horses to Ecbatana (Hamadan) in Media, where Alexander made sacrifices and held a festival of arts and athletics. He was probably celebrating the consolidation of his authority in these rich areas.

After the death of Hephaestion at Ecbatana (see below), Alexander entrusted the command of the main army to Perdiccas and sent him back to Babylon. He himself conducted a campaign in rugged Luristan against the Cossaei, a mountain people like the Uxii, who had remained independent of Persian rule and refused to submit to the Macedoni-ans.[110] They lived by raiding the lowlands and taking their toll of the trade along the caravan route, and they used the guerrilla tactic of dis-persing into their mountain fastnesses and villages, when they were at-tacked in force, and of emerging later to resume their raids. Alexander's reply to this tactic was to attack with an equally mobile army of cavalry and commando-infantry in severe winter conditions, when the enemy could be tracked down and isolated.

He gained possession of a strategic defile by a ruse which delighted Polyaenus (4.3.3I); for he lulled the Cossaeans into a false confidence by spreading the rumour that he was going to Babylon to celebrate the funeral of Hephaestion, made a night march with his cavalry and found the defile unguarded. Sweeping through the mountains and winning all engagements, the Macedonians killed many and captured a great many more until the Cossaeans despaired and capitulated at the end of forty days. Alexander returned the prisoners and their lands to the Cossaeans on the conditions that they accepted his rule and that they lived in cities which he founded. His purpose, as expressed by Nearchus (*Ind.* 40.8), was that "they should cease to be nomads, become tillers and workers of the soil and have possessions which would discourage them from raid-ing and pillaging." This policy of founding native urban centres was one which he had used in the realm of Musicanus. It is possible that he founded similar centres among the Uxii and the Mardi.

In the spring of 323 B.C. Alexander joined Perdiccas at Babylon. There he found some of his new fleet ready, became keenly interested in exploring the Caspian Sea, and went ahead with his plans for develop-ing the Persian Gulf and colonising its shores and islands. He returned to Babylon in April or May in order to make his final dispositions before undertaking a summer campaign. Babylon was evidently to be the capital of his administrative system in central Asia and his base for fu-ture operations.

The maintenance of order in central Asia must have been one of his chief concerns during this period. His long absence farther east, the rumour of his death among the Malli, and then the rumour of disaster in the Gedrosian desert had encouraged some of his administrators and commanders to abuse their authority and contemplate revolt. Craterus, for example, brought before Alexander Ordanes and others whom he had arrested for conspiracy, and they were put on trial and executed. Cleander, Sitalces, and Agathon, who had held commands in the battle of Gaugamela and had shown loyalty to Alexander in the execution of Parmenio, were summoned from Media, where they were in command of the occupying force. When charges were laid against these officers by some of their troops and by the natives, Alexander heard their cases and condemned them to death. Punishments were not confined to selected commanders: of the 5,000 infantry and 1,000 cavalry whom they had brought with them from Media no less than 600 were executed for having committed crimes in accordance with their orders. The punishment of such offences was, as Arrian remarked (6.27.5), a major factor in reconciling the people of Asia to Alexander's rule, for it showed that he would not permit anyone in his service, Macedonian or Asian, to maltreat his subjects.

The satrap of Susiana, Abulites, was imprisoned for maladministration, and his son, Oxyartes, being judged guilty evidently of some crime, was executed by Alexander in person, using his *sarissa*. Baryaxes, a Mede, who proclaimed himself King of the Medes and Persians, and Orxines, a Persian, who usurped the position of satrap of Persis, were tried and executed. Alexander used the capital sentence as a deterrent to all other satraps, governors and commanders. Incompetence, too, led to dismissal or imprisonment: for example, Apollophanes, satrap of Oreitis, who had probably failed, like Abulites, to send supplies urgently at the time of the march through the Gedrosian desert. It was easy for detractors to exaggerate the number of abuses and defections (e.g., P. 68.3); but what is remarkable is not the number, given the extent and the newness of the conquests, but the measures taken by Alexander at once. The Roman Republic did not attain that standard even in a hundred and fifty years.

The troops which endangered law and order were mainly Greek and Thracian. For instance, the Greek mercenaries settled in Bactria by Alexander fell out among themselves, enrolled natives in their internecine strife, and then, some 3,000 of them, in fear of being punished by Alexander, tried to make their way back to Greece. The troops who were punished with Cleander, Sitalces, and Agathon were presumably Greek mercenaries and Thracians; for Greeks and Thracians had been under their command at Gaugamela. The Philippus whom Alexander left as satrap in India was plotted against and killed by "the mercenaries." There too Alexander had left Thracians; and in this case it was the Macedonians serving as Bodyguards of Philippus who executed the troublemakers and maintained control until Alexander appointed a successor, probably Eudamus, "a commander of Thracian troops." Whenever a satrap planned revolt, he was apt to hire mercenaries; this at least is implied by Alexander's order to his satraps and commanders that "they should dismiss their mercenaries at once" (D. I7.I06.3).

Alexander placed an increasing reliance on Asian troops for the support of his Macedonian striking force and for the maintenance of order in Asia. In February 324 B.C. he was joined at Susa by 30,000 young men principally from his new cities but also from other parts of Asia, who had been trained as infantry in accordance with his orders of 330 B.C. in Greek language, Macedonian weapons, and Macedonian battle tactics. They were called "the new generation" ("Epigoni"). Their Macedonian training was one of the things which alarmed the Macedonian soldiers at Opis and when "the barbarian army" was baptised with the honoured Macedonian infantry names of *pezhetairoi* and *asthetairoi* and *argyraspides* it was thought that Alexander really did intend to replace the Macedonian units with these barbarian units. In fact Macedonians and barbarians seem to have served concurrently in parallel units (like the English Buffs and the Palestine Buffs in 1941).

Another innovation was introduced on Alexander's orders by Peucestas, who had been made satrap of Persis; for he brought to Babylon in May 324 B.C. some 20,000 archers and javelin-men from Persis, Cossaea, and Tapuria. With these Alexander formed a mixed infantry army, each file of sixteen men having a Macedonian commander, three Macedonians on high rates of pay, and twelve Asians. The Macedonians alone were equipped in Macedonian style; the others kept their native fashion. For this mixed army some 6,700 Macedonians were needed. We may conjecture that the parallel army of 30,000 Asian Epigoni and the mixed army of some 26,700 men were intended for different duties: the former to support the Macedonian striking force and the latter to keep order in Asia. In each case there were cavalry units as well; but they had already served Alexander for several years.

At the same time Alexander reduced the Macedonian striking force by sending home some 10,000 men in the late summer of 324 B.C. A draft of as many young Macedonians was to be sent to him in due course, but not in time to take part in the campaign which he planned for summer 323 B.C. The reinforcements which did reach him in time were drafts from Lydia and Caria and cavalry under Menidas (the last being perhaps Greek mercenaries); they helped to fill the gap left by the homeward-bound Macedonians. In any case we can see that the Asians were by far the greater part of the two armies and of the navy in 324–323 B.C.

When Alexander fell ill at the end of May 323 B.C., he had arranged for the main field-army to march first from Babylon and for the élite force under his own command to sail downstream from Babylon on a later day. His anxieties during his illness centered on "the voyage", which Nearchus was evidently to command. There is no doubt that the fleet of ships larger than thirty-oared vessels was to attempt the circumnavigation of Arabia. The army was to conquer the last of the southern provinces of Asia, Arabia (Str. 741 = Aristobulus F 55; Str. 785; A. 7.20.1), and his improvement of the flood-control system had been designed to make the invasion of Arabia less difficult (Str. 741). When the conquest was accomplished, he expected to meet Antipater and the 10,000 young Macedonians, probably in Palestine (C. 10.1.17), or perhaps in Egypt, in the spring or summer of 322 B.C. But on 10 June, 323 B.C., Alexander died at the age of thirty-two years and eight months from an incurable illness, which probably was the form of malaria known as *malaria tropica*. We shall describe his last days in the next chapter.

SOURCES

(A) A. 5.29.3-6; *Ind.* 18-19; D. 17.95.3-104; P. 63-66.2; Plut. *Mor.* 327 b, 341 c, 344 d; C. 9.3.20-9.10.3; J. 12.9.1-12.10.7; Str. 692, 701. *Epit. Metz* 70-78

(B) A. 6.21-28.5; *Ind.* 20-36.3; D. 17.105-106; P. 66.3-68.1; C. 9.10.4-10.1.15; J. 12.10.7; Str. 720-723

(C) A. 6.28.6-7.23; *Ind.* 36.4.43; P. 68-73.1; D. 17.107-116; J. 12.10.8-13.6; Str. 730

X

THE LAST YEAR
AND THE ACHIEVEMENTS OF ALEXANDER

(A) AS KING OF THE MACEDONES

Whatever Alexander may have become in Asia, he was from first to last, and above all king to his Macedones. The relationship was personal; it existed wherever and whenever he and they were together, and it was thus not confined within the limits of any "national territorial state." In other words, the Macedonian state—*to koinon ton Makedonon*—[111] consisting of king and Macedones, was in action only when and where the king and the Macedones happened to be: for example, at Aegeae in 336 B.C., at the Hyphasis river in 326 B.C. and at Babylon in 323 B.C. The king deputed his authority where he was not present in person. Thus he gave to Antipater powers of command in Macedonia and Greece (A. 1.11.3). Within Macedonia we may assume that Antipater raised taxes, conscripted troops, and administered justice in the name of the king, but the order and the money for the despatch of a fleet by Antipater to the Hellespont in 333 B.C. came from the king. Antipater's powers in Greece were exercised by him as a deputy of the Hegemon of the Greek League. He also had a deputed authority over "Illyrians, Agrianians, Triballians, and (the northern parts of) Epirus."[112] In these capacities he was called Alexander's "general in Europe" in a loose sense, just as Alexander the Lyncestian or Memnon had the title of "general in Thrace." But Antipater was not "regent" in the sense that he was operating the machinery of the Macedonian state in Macedonia in the absence of the king. Rather the Macedonian state travelled with the king.

When a clash of wills developed between the king and the Macedones at the Hyphasis river, one principle of the monarchy was well expressed in the following words attributed by Arrian to Coenus. "You, O King, do not wish to command the Macedones by decree; you say yourself that you will lead them when you have persuaded them, and that you will not enforce your will if you are persuaded by them." As we have seen Alexander persuaded them after Gaugamela in Parthyene

(C. 6.4.1), and probably after the defeat of Porus (C. 9.1.3). When the Macedones stood still at the Hyphasis river, he tried to persuade them by threatening to go on alone; but in the end he was persuaded by their attitude and by unfavourable omens (we must remember that Aristander did not belie the omens at the Tanaïs, A. 4.4.2–3); so he turned back. The principle of persuasion is still the mark of a libertarian or democratic government.

In 324 B.C. a new crisis arose at Opis, where the forces which had been serving under Alexander, Craterus, Hephaestion, and Nearchus were assembled together. The events which led to the crisis had their beginnings in 325 B.C., when Alexander put under the command of Craterus those Macedones who were unfit and whom he therefore intended to send home to Macedonia. Early in 324 B.C. at Susa he made some provision for these and other Macedones who had lived with Asian women and had had children by them: he recognised the associations as legitimate and himself gave to each pair a wedding present. The number proved to be some 10,000. No modern state has shown so humane an attitude in the matter of its soldiers' sexual liaisons, whether in Europe or in Asia. Next, he tackled the problem of the debts which these and other Macedones might owe, not to the army but to civilians such as Phoenician and other traders. A modern state, of course, does not consider itself responsible for soldiers' debts.

Alexander thought otherwise. He announced that he would pay all soldiers' debts and asked the soldiers to record their debts. However, only a few did so; for the majority thought that he might want the record for some ulterior purpose. When he realised why they were holding back, he announced a further principle of the monarchy (so Arrian 7.5.2): "The King must speak nothing but the truth to his subjects, and none of them must suppose that he speaks anything but the truth." The principle is correct, whether one is applying it to a monarch or the president of a republic; for a lying head breaks the confidence of the body.

To demonstrate that his only motive was, as he had indicated, to pay off the soldiers' debts to civilians, he had his accountants pay the debts without recording the name of the soldier debtor, to a total amount, it was said, of 20,000 talents. "So the soldiers did believe that Alexander told the truth." Moreover, the way was now clear for a number of Macedones to leave Asia under conditions which Alexander judged to be honourable in relation to themselves and the Asians.

At Opis Alexander called a meeting of the Macedones and announced the intentions which he had no doubt had in mind for a year and more. "I release from service and send to their homes those who are unfit for war through age or injury; I shall give freely to those who remain[113] such sums as will make them the object of greater envy to those at home and will inspire the other Macedones to undertake willingly the same dangers and labours."

It might have been supposed that the first part of this announcement would be welcomed, because the desire of the men to go home had been made clear at the Hyphasis river and elsewhere, and that Alexander's difficulty would be in persuading the others to stay with him. The actuality was quite different. Those due to be released felt insulted by being described as unfit for war; they associated his supposed contempt for them with his preference for Asians, as shown by his wearing Asian dress, forming Asian units with Macedonian names, and importing Asians into the Companion Cavalry; and they expressed their anger in a general uproar from which two slogans emerged: "Discharge *all* Macedonians from service," and "Go campaigning yourself with your father at your side" (meaning not Philip but Ammon). Thereupon Alexander and his commanding officers jumped down from the platform and, as Alexander pointed out with his hand the most conspicuous leaders of the general riot, the guards arrested them on his orders and led them off to be executed. In the ensuing silence he returned to the platform and addressed the troops.

The first part of the address, as reported by Arrian, probably has points from the original speech; for being concerned with Philip it had little topical interest for writers of the Roman Empire. But the second part, both in Arrian and in Curtius, was a victim of rhetorical elaboration. The general tenour of Alexander's speech was certainly that he discharged the Macedonians one and all, as that was what they wanted, and that they should tell those at home that they had deserted their king. Then he jumped down alone, entered the royal tent and stayed there for two days, refusing admission even to his bodyguards. On the third day he summoned the leading Asians, gave them command of the newly named units (Asian *pezhetairoi, asthetairoi*, etc.), called them after the Persian fashion his "kindred," and authorised them and them alone to kiss him.

The Macedonians, officers and soldiers alike, had been waiting and watching. They had hoped, no doubt, that as at the Hyphasis river he would be persuaded to go back with them to Macedonia. Now it was clear that he would stay, alone if need be. Were the Macedones deserting their king, or was the king deserting the Macedones? In either case the Macedonian state was splitting apart. However, what settled the dispute was not reasoning but emotion. When the Macedonians saw the names of their units being conferred on the Asians,

> they no longer mastered their feelings but rushing to the King's quarters threw their weapons down as tokens of supplication to their King, stood outside shouting to be admitted, and promised to hand over the instigators of the trouble and the starters of the uproar. They would not leave his door day or night, unless some pity for them was shown by Alexander.

When this was reported to Alexander, he came out at once. Seeing them so humble and hearing cries and sobs from most of them, he too shed tears. Then he came forward as if to say something, but they kept beseeching him, and Callisthenes, a leading Companion cavalryman, . . . said as follows: "O King, what hurts the Macedonians is that it is Persians you have made your kindred, and it is Persians who are called 'kinsmen of Alexander' and Persians who kiss you. No Macedonian yet has tasted that privilege." Then indeed Alexander interrupted, saying, "But all of you I regard as my kinsmen and from now on I shall call you so." At these words Callisthenes came up and kissed him, as did anyone else who wished. So then they picked up their weapons and returned shouting and singing the song of victory to their camp. And Alexander sacrificed to his customary gods in gratitude for the outcome.

Thus Alexander imposed his will on the army. First, the unfit and the other Macedonians were to go home. But Alexander now gave them the choice of going or staying, and some 10,000 opted for home. They were to be paid up to the day of their arrival in Macedonia, and each man received from him a gratuity of one talent. Those who had Asian wives and children were advised to leave them in Asia, where Alexander promised to maintain and educate them at his own expense, bringing them up in Macedonian ways and training the boys to become Macedonian soldiers, until such time as they grew into manhood; they would then be brought to Macedonia and handed over to their fathers. They would be conducted home by Craterus, his most honoured general, and if Craterus should become too ill, by Polyperchon. When they were ready, Alexander embraced them all; he and they were in tears, as he dismissed them from his presence.

Second, he kept with him those Macedonians who wanted to stay on the terms he had outlined. They were probably less than 10,000, and 6,700 of these were needed for the mixed army which he was creating. Third, he made the Macedonians accept his position as King of Asia, in that they took the Persian title of "kinsmen" and they adopted the Persian practice of kissing the king. It was in celebration of this acceptance that he held the banquet for Macedonians, Persians, and other Asians which we shall describe later.

The love which bound Alexander and his Macedonians together was shown in other ways. He was particularly loyal to those boyhood friends who were exiled by Philip—Harpalus, Nearchus, Ptolemy, Erigyius and his brother Laomedon; and his strong affections for other Macedonian officers are mentioned—Alexander the Lyncestian, Peucestas, Craterus, Coenus, and above all in Alexander's last years, Hephaestion. Whether these loyalties and affections had their origins in homosexual practices (such as were sometimes attested among the pages) is anyone's guess. It should, however, be noted that the ancient Alexander-historians did not make any statements or suggestions to that effect in these cases; that has been left to some of the modern historians.[114] The closeness of these friendships are equally likely to have been due to the sharing of common aims and common dangers for the ten years during which they were away from their Macedonian womenfolk. When a friend died, Alexander was able to pay him a tribute of royal proportions: mourning throughout the entire army for Alexander the Molossian in 330 B.C., a giant tumulus forty metres high (three times the height of the Vergina "Great Tumulus") for Demaratus, and a magnificent funeral for the brigade-commander, Coenus.

Hephaestion died in 324 B.C. after a brief illness. Alexander lay fasting for three days, proclaimed mourning throughout Asia and made provision for a funeral more lavish then that of Coenus. Hephaestion's tomb was covered by a tumulus (P. 72.5). At the time of his death Hephaestion held the highest single command, that of the Companion Cavalry; had been repeatedly second in command to Alexander on campaigns; and ranked second to Alexander in the hierarchy of the Asian court, holding the title of Chiliarch, which had been held under Darius by Nabarzanes. Thus Alexander honoured Hephaestion both as the closest of his friends and the most distinguished of his Field Marshals. He planned a memorial more striking than that for Demaratus (it was to be built in the form of a ziggurat at Babylon), and a festival of arts and athletics to surpass all others. Hephaestion's name was to be attached to his last command for ever, and a likeness of Hephaestion was to be carried into battle with the Companion Cavalry. His fellow-officers dedicated themselves and their weapons to his memory, and they had gold-and-ivory images of him made for his tomb, like those found in miniature at Vergina and Naoussa in Macedonia. And during the campaign against the Cossaei, Alexander killed young Cossaeans as human sacrifices to the dead Hephaestion.

These tributes and memorials seem absurdly extravagant in comparison to what we say and do in church and state for a deceased Field Marshal in this enlightened century. But we have to remember that Alexander was much closer emotionally to his ancestor Achilles than to us, and that he wished to immortalise his love for Hephaestion as signally as Achilles had done for Patroclus. The recent discovery at Vergina has provided antecedents or analogies for lavish funerary offerings, human sacrifice, gold-and-ivory images and a "Great Tumulus" in Macedonia itself. The fellow-officers of Hephaestion may have acted spontaneously, for Macedonian commanders and veterans had a sense of achievement and a sense of their self-importance which it is difficult for us to recapture. And when Alexander himself died, they had a coffin and a funerary carriage made which were of unparalleled extravagance (D. I8.26–28).[115]

Alexander enquired of the oracle of Zeus Ammon at Siwah whether Hephaestion should be honoured as a god or as a hero. He had in mind the divine honours paid to his grandfather Amyntas and his father Philip in Macedonia, or to Lysander and Timoleon in Greece. But the oracle replied that the honours should be those of a hero, and it is known that cults in honour of Hephaestion as a hero were established in Greece and in Asia before the time of Alexander's death. Here too there were precedents. Many mythical and historical commanders and states-men were worshipped as heroes after death in the Greek states.

During his own illness Alexander's first concern was for the state. He made sacrifice daily, even on the day during which he lost the power of speech. Two nights and two days of unremitting high fever followed, and it was clear that he was sinking. Then the soldiers pressed into his tent, longing to see him while he yet lived.

> "As the army filed past him, he was unable to speak, but it is said that even so he welcomed each of them, raising his head with difficulty and greeting them with his eyes. *The King's Journal* reports that Peithon, Attalus, Demophon, Peucestas, Cleomenes, Menidas, and Seleucus, keeping an all-night vigil in the shrine of Sarapis, asked the god whether it would be better for Alexander to be brought into the shrine, to make sup-plication and to be healed by the god. But the god indicated that he should not be brought into the shrine; the better thing for him would be to stay where he was. This was reported by the Companions, and shortly afterwards Alexander died, as this was surely the better thing."[116]

The thoughts of the dying king were for his Macedonians, the rank and file, with whom he had shared twelve years of dangers and labours not from the remoteness of a throne but as a man among men, marching and fighting, thirsting and sleepless, carousing and triumphant. He loved them and they loved him as their king and as a man, and they could not bear to let him die without their greeting him. That they ad-mired him beyond all others goes without saying; for they were profes-sional soldiers and they knew that no one matched him in personal bravery and in power of command. In their eyes, since they had been trained from boyhood for war, he was the ideal king of a warrior state. And the glory which he had brought to Macedonian arms was a justifi-cation of his life and theirs. Because they had such faith in their royal house, which "they were conditioned by custom to honour and venerate" (C. 10.7.15), the Macedonian rank and file at Babylon insisted that the successor to Alexander should be Philip Arrhidaeus, son of Philip, half-brother of Alexander, and his associate hitherto in state sacrifices and ceremonies.

Had Alexander lived and returned to Macedonia, he would no doubt have brought all the Macedonians under his spell. But his absence during eleven years meant that he had little personal influence with the Macedonian army in Europe; it was 13,500 men strong in 334 B.C. and must have been considerably stronger in 323 B.C., since he proposed to draft 10,000 men from it. That army may well have been critical of Alexander. It had received little help from him, except in finance, during the hard-fought war against Agis, and it faced the prospect of other risings in Greece and in Thrace. The triumphs in Asia were counterbalanced at home by the list of casualties through battle, privation, and disease.

His policy in the east had been carried out in the face of strong opposition. Parmenio had advised against proceeding beyond Asia Minor; Philotas and Cleitus had shown bitter opposition to Alexander's adoption of Asian ceremonial; and in the mutiny at Opis this opposition was shared by the Macedonian rank and file. In quelling the mutiny Alexander seemed to indicate that to be king of Asia meant more to him than to be king of Macedonia. Moreover, Alexander had failed in one of the primary duties of a reigning king, to beget sons early, as Parmenio had advised him to do. That failure was to be a contributing factor in the war between the generals which began so soon after his death; for had there been a son ten years old in 323 B.C. he might have constituted a centre of loyalty.

The judgement of the Macedonians on their king was expressed by the granting or withholding of divine honours. Amyntas and Philip were worshipped as gods, perhaps during their lives and certainly after death, not only at Pydna and Amphipolis but also at Aegeae, as it seems from the excavations at Vergina; and such worship must have been accorded by the Macedonian assembly. In his later years Alexander wished to be granted divine honours. It appears from Curtius (I0.5.11) that he made a request of the Macedonians and that it was rejected.[117] After his death the Macedonians at Babylon did not vote him divine honours. On the other hand they voted a huge sum for a life-sized gold coffin and a splendid funeral car "worthy of the glory of Alexander," on which the corpse was to be transported to Aegeae for burial in the cemetery of the Macedonian kings. He was certainly a great king but not the greatest in the opinion of contemporary Macedonians.

We have the advantage of hindsight. We can see that it was Alexander's leadership and training which made the Macedonians incomparable in war and in administration and enabled them as rulers of the so-called Hellenistic kingdoms to control the greater part of the civilised world for a century or more. In a reign of thirteen years he brought to Macedonia and Macedonians the immense wealth which maintained their strength for generations. All this was and is an unparalleled achievement. Moreover, as king of Macedonia he did not drain his country unduly in his lifetime, since Antipater had enough men to defeat the Greeks in 331 B.C. and 322 B.C. Yet the system he was creating— quite apart from any further conquests he had in mind in 323 B.C.—was certain to put an immense strain on present and future Macedonians. They were spread dangerously thin at the time of his death, and the prolonged absence of so many Macedonians abroad was bound to cause a drop in the birth-rate in Macedonia itself. Of course Alexander expected his Macedonians to undertake almost superhuman dangers and labours, and it was their response to his challenge that made them great. But the dangers and labours were being demanded for the sake of a policy which was not Macedonian in a nationalistic sense, which the Macedonians did not wholly understand, and which they never fully implemented. Philip's singlemindedness made him the greatest king of Macedonia. Alexander's wider vision made him at the same time something more and something less than the greatest king of Macedonia.

(B) AS HEGEMON OF THE GREEKS, AND HIMSELF AS A GREEK

As hegemon in the war against Persia, Alexander overthrew the power of Persia and sent the troops of his Greek allies home from Ecbatana in 330 B.C. All Greeks in Asia had then been liberated from Persian rule, and the East was opened to Greek enterprise for employment, settlement, and trade to a degree unparalleled in the past. Hundreds of thousands of Greeks emigrated from the mainland, the islands, and the Asiatic coast, as they have so often done when profitable occupation elsewhere has become available. Alexander's service to Greece far surpassed that even of Timoleon, who had liberated the Greeks of the west from Carthaginian rule and attracted great numbers of settlers to Sicily from the mainland.[118] The improvement of conditions in Greece through emigration of surplus populations and through growth of trade in the eastern Mediterranean helped to remove the two main causes of revolution in the Greek states and inter-state war on the mainland. But social and economic relief was not enough by itself to ensure stability and peace; for the Greek states lived as much for politics as for bread.

The political situation of the Greek cities in Asia was clear from the outset. In claiming Asia as his and in describing himself as "Lord of Asia" he did not except the Greeks in Asia; they were to be and became as much his subjects as anyone else in Asia.[119] This was not surprising; for liberation from Persia had always entailed not liberation from the liberator but absorption into the liberator's system of power, as Sparta and Athens had shown in the last fifty years (quite apart from modern parallels). Alexander ordered the replacement of the existing tyrannies and oligarchies by democracies in all cities in Asia, and he laid down the terms of the relationship between himself and each city in accordance with its services or disservices in the war against Persia.

In general his rule was much lighter than that of previous rulers; payments to him were less than they had been to Persia, and opportunities for employment and trade were immensely greater. The most favoured cities were described as "free and autonomous," in that they were relieved from payment, exempt from conscription, not subject to the satrap, and they issued silver and bronze coinage; but they were still subject to the overall authority of Alexander as king of Asia. The cults and the compliments with which they honoured Alexander were probably genuine expressions of their gratitude.

The political status of the offshore islands varied.[120] Some were admitted to the Greek League, Tenedos, for instance, having an agreement "with Alexander and the Greeks" (A. 2.2.3). Others were associated with Alexander alone; Mytilene in Lesbos, for instance, had a treaty of alliance "with Alexander" (A. 2.1.4) and was rewarded for good service by Alexander who granted it some of a neighbour's territory (C. 4.8.13). During the war at sea some pro-Persian Greeks were captured. Those from cities associated only with Alexander were handed over by him to them for judgement, Methymna in Lesbos being mentioned specifically, but those from Chios were held in Egypt, probably so that when the winter was over they could be sent by sea to Greece for trial by the Greek League. It seems then that Lesbos was associated only with Alexander, and that Chios was a member of the Greek League in winter 332–331 B.C. Samos, being a possession of Athens, was certainly a member of the League, but Rhodes, the island of greatest strategic importance, surrendered itself to Alexander and was held by him alone, its defectors being imprisoned by Alexander's deputy, Philoxenus, at Sardis.

Alexander's relations with the Greek League had two aspects: he was hegemon or commander of the league for life, and as head of the Macedonian state he was in alliance with the league certainly until 330 B.C. and probably until his death. In addition he had separate pacts with individual states such as Athens, and he held the special position of president (*archon*) of the Thessalian League. So long as these states or leagues honoured their contractual obligations they were treated as free and sovereign states. Thus they issued their own coinage; even Corinth where a Macedonian garrison held the citadel by agreement with the Greek League, coined profusely. Did Alexander as hegemon act beyond his legal powers and infringe the freedom of the Greek states? Late in 336 B.C. he approved a change of constitution from oligarchy to democracy at Ambracia, which was a member of the Greek League, and, as far as we know, this act of approval was not criticised. Between then and probably early 331 B.C. he arranged or imposed changes of constitution in Messenia, where he restored exiles; and at Pellene in Achaea, where a democracy was succeeded by what a hostile critic called a tyranny.

That critic was the unidentified writer of a speech *On the Treaty with Alexander* which has come down to us among the speeches of Demosthenes. He claimed that Alexander acted *ultra vires* in Messenia and at Pellene, because the member-states of the Greek League had undertaken not to intervene in one another's constitutional affairs (Tod 177, 14 f.). This argument, however, is unconvincing; for the hegemon certainly had some overriding powers (e.g., in imposing a garrison, which was expressly forbidden as between members), and during the war of the Greek League against Persia the hegemon was exercising his "full powers" to ensure that a member-state remained loyal to the cause. Thus, if these two cases in Messenia and Pellene were the worst the unidentified writer could find, we may conclude that he acted only as he was entitled to do.[121]

What shocks a modern commentator is Alexander's destruction of Thebes in 335 B.C., probably only four years before the composition of the speech. Why did the writer not even mention it? The fact that the formal decision to destroy the city was taken by the Council of the Greek League would not have deterred this writer, because he paid no heed to the formal powers of the hegemon. It may be that the fate of Thebes was as acceptable in 331 B.C. to many Athenians as it was to Thebes' rivals in Boeotia and Central Greece. That of course does not excuse Alexander in our eyes. He was certainly calculating and cold-blooded in his use of severe methods throughout his career, whether in Greece, Sogdiana, or India, and as we have previously argued, his severity with Thebes put an end to the possibility of full cooperation between the Greek states and Macedonia.

The Council of the Greek League can have laid down only very general guidelines for the hegemon in the war against Persia, such as that traitors were to be arrested for trial by the Council and that escaping traitors "were to be banished from the territory of all states sharing in the common peace" (Tod 192, 12–14). In most respects Alexander had a free hand. He used his powers to conscript warships, impose garrisons, or replace a pro-Persian government, as at Chios; and he showed remarkable generosity to his Greek allied troops when he added to their wages gratuities totalling 2,000 talents. He referred certain matters to the Council for decision—the treatment of Thebes, the arrangements with Tenedos, and the trial of Chiot renegades. He was generous in his release of Greek prisoners and Greek envoys, and he did not treat captured works of Greek art as his own spoil, but sent them to the original owners. When Antipater defeated Sparta and the rebel states, and the

Council referred the decision about them to Alexander, he acted with clemency. His aims were clearly reconciliation and cooperation with the Greek states, but within the framework of the Greek League, which required the member states to keep the peace, act constitutionally "according to the laws," and in general maintain the status quo.

When all his forces were assembled at Susa, early in 324 B.C., Alexander announced to them that all exiles from the Greek states of the mainland and the islands would be recalled and reinstated, except those under a curse and exiles from Thebes.[122] This was the best way of spreading the news through Asia. There had not been time since the return from Carmania for Alexander to have consulted the Council of the Greek League in advance, and the occasion of the announcement was inappropriate for any ruling given by that Council. Further at the end of July 324 B.C., a personal agent of Alexander, Nicanor of Stageiros, who was in no way connected with the Council of the Greek League, made the same announcement to the company assembled at Olympia for the Olympic Games, a company which included more than 20,000 Greek exiles. This was the best way of informing exiles in Greek lands. It was not an order (*diatage*) but an announcement (*diagramma*); to say no to it was not an act of disobedience or rebellion but the start of a discussion. States which decided to conform with the announcement, e.g., Tegea (Tod 202), referred to it as such. States which objected sent envoys to argue the case with Alexander at Babylon in 323 B.C. (D. I7.113.3), not to the Council of the League. There is no doubt, then, that Alexander chose not to work through the Greek League or act as hegemon of it, probably because the recall of all exiles was not within the competence of an organisation concerned with the maintenance of "the common peace." Rather, he acted as the ally of the Greek states; but an ally of overwhelming strength, whether or not Nicanor issued the threat (reported in D. 18.8.4) that Antipater had orders to compel any unwilling state to recall its exiles.

Alexander's action was not of immediate advantage to himself. Most of those exiled in 336–323 B.C. had been enemies of Macedonia and were likely to remain so. He knew that he would arouse the bitter hostility of Athens and the Aetolian League; for Athens, having seized Samos in 365 B.C., would have to remove her citizen-settlers from Samos and restore the island to the Samians, and Aetolia, having seized Oeniadae, would have to evacuate it and restore it to the Acarnanians. His aim was rather to remove a general cause of instability and suffering in the Greek world, and indeed beyond it, by reducing the large floating population of embittered émigrés and unscrupulous mercenaries to which Isocrates had drawn Philip's attention (*Philippus* 96), a population which was momentarily increased by the dismissal of the mercenaries recruited in Alexander's absence by his satraps. That he took a personal interest in the proper rehabilitation of the exiles is clear from the case of Tegea (Tod 202). Had he lived and reached the eastern Mediterranean in spring 322 B.C., there is no doubt he would have restored all exiles, even using force if necessary against Athens and Aetolia.

Alexander made the same direct approach to the Greek states in seeking honours for Hephaestion and himself. When Hephaestion died in October 324 B.C., Alexander asked the oracle of Zeus Ammon at Siwah whether Hephaestion should be worshipped as a god; he received the response that Hephaestion should be honoured as a hero. On Alexander expressing his wish many Greek states, Athens included (Hyperides, *Epitaphios* 21), established a cult in honour of Hephaestion as a hero early in 323 B.C. There were precedents for such conduct. The case of Alexander was more complicated. The League of Ionian cities and many of the Greek cities in Asia individually, as well as Thasos and Rhodes, granted "divine honours" on their own initiative to Alexander in 334–333 B.C. as their liberator and benefactor and established a cult in his name with a shrine, games and sacrifices. There were a few precedents, Lysander, for instance, having been so honoured as the liberator of Samos from Athenian rule.

To grant "divine honours" to a living man was not to regard him as a god on earth but to recognise his services as comparable to those which a god might render to a community; it was the highest form of compliment. It had no political application, as Tarn and others have suggested; for Greek cities in Asia continued to negotiate with Alexander purely as a temporal power. With this immediate background Alexander announced in the winter of 324–323 B.C. that he wished to be granted "divine honours" by the Greek states of the mainland, and our sources contain echoes of discussions on this subject in Athens and Sparta. In general his wish was implemented: Athens, for instance, dedicated a temple, an altar, and a cult-image to Alexander (Hyperides, *Epitaphios* 21). In spring 323 B.C. envoys from the Greek states came to Alexander in Babylon. "They wore crowns in approaching Alexander and they crowned him with golden crowns, having come indeed on a sacred mission to pay divine honour" (A. 7.23.2).

Philip and Alexander were alike in seeking that open and public recognition which was to them a part of "glory." The scenes at Aegeae in 336 B.C. and at Babylon in 323 B.C. when Philip and Alexander respectively were crowned with gold crown after gold crown by individual Greek city-states had been planned in advance and were carefully stage-managed, and neither the kings nor the states regarded the performance as spontaneous. We must remember too that Philip and Alexander were Greeks, descended from Heracles; they wished to be recognised by the Greeks as benefactors of the Greeks, even as Heracles had been. In asking for divine honours Alexander must have known he was exposing himself to ridicule from such men as Hyperides and Demosthenes;[123] but his personal longing for recognition was evidently overwhelming and he sought to obtain it in time for his own victorious return to the Greek world, prospectively in 322 B.C. In voting to grant divine honours the citizens of any Greek state may have been divided. Some realised the great benefits and opportunities which Alexander's conquests had brought to them. The majority, no doubt, resented the power of Alexander and the shackling of their foreign policy. For all of them the grant of divine honours was only another step along the road of flattery.

In other matters too the behaviour of the Greek states during the last year of Alexander's life was correct. For instance, Alexander's dishonest treasurer, Harpalus, reached Greece in June or so of 324 B.C. with the huge sum of 5,000 talents, 6,000 mercenaries, and 30 ships and tried to raise Athens in revolt. The Assembly refused. No other state offered him sanctuary, and he was killed by one of his company during a foray in Crete. One effect of Harpalus' dealings with Athens was the condemnation and exile of Demosthenes, Demades, and others for accepting bribes from Harpalus. Alexander did not demand repayment of money deposited by Harpalus at Athens nor any further punishment of Demosthenes and the others. His attitude was one of moderation and conciliation.

It is difficult to find fault with the conduct of Alexander as hegemon of the Greek League. He conducted its war against Persia brilliantly, made few demands on the member states, suppressed rebellions by Thebes and by Agis' allies, and referred the final decisions in these cases to the Council of the League. He respected the formalities of his position; he was conciliatory, especially to Athens, and unfailingly courteous to the envoys of the member states. Where he may have feared opposition, in the restoration of exiles and the request for divine honours, he did not put the Council of the League to the test but dealt directly with individual states. Even the offers of Harpalus did not shake the loyalty of the League members, and there is no doubt that Alexander would have held the League together if he had lived longer.

The question as to whether his policy of maintaining the Greek League was justified raises larger issues. Its cooperation at first and its non-intervention later were essential factors in his defeat of Persia and his opening of the east to Greek enterprise; if he had begun by disbanding the League and leaving the individual states to pursue their own policies, he could never have succeeded. The destruction of Thebes was calculated to discourage the support of Persia by other states; if she had been spared, she would probably have joined Agis and might well have disrupted the Greek League.

As a Greek Alexander was attempting to change the age-old course of city-state politics from imperialistic particularism and internecine warfare to a federal system and an expansion outwards in terms of influence, settlement, and trade. He thought that the change was beneficial and that the attempt was succeeding in 323 B.C., and that was why he sought and obtained recognition from the Greeks. The opposite view was arguable then, and it is arguable today, that for all its faults an untrammeled nationalism develops higher qualities than a controlled federalism even with a benevolent controller. So Demosthenes believed, and the Athenians expressed their faith in his belief when they upheld his policy in the law court in 330 B.C. But there were other Greeks, less favourably placed than the Athenians, who may have welcomed the escape from the growing anarchy and indecisiveness of the decades which preceded the formation of the Greek League.

(C) AS A COMMANDER

Alexander was below average in height; he was well-built and strong, a fast sprinter, and an excellent horseman from boyhood. He was in love with hunting and combat and as quick to kill a man as an animal; in this he was a true Macedonian. By training and temperament he was passionately eager to win glory in war; his favourite book was the *Iliad*, and his favourite character Achilles. His joy in action is shown most vividly in the painting of the Battle of Issus. He courted every danger—fighting at the head of every formation, leading any wild venture, and scaling first the parapet of a besieged city. When he was nearly killed by the Malli and his friends advised him not to run such risks he was indignant; for, as Arrian observed, "His impetuosity in battle and his passion for glory impelled him to such conduct." Moreover, it added a special dimension to his power of leadership; for he was the first to do whatever he asked his men to do, and his survival of danger after danger created the myth that he personally was invincible in war. Indeed he may have come to believe it himself. Youth too was on his side; for he did not pass the peak of his physical powers, and his self-confidence in combat was unabated.

As constitutionally elected king, Alexander had sole right of command and an inherited authority. From the age of twenty onwards he appointed his deputies without let or hindrance, issued all orders, and controlled all payments, promotions, and discharges. His authority as a commander was almost absolute, his discipline unquestioned, and his position unchallenged. As religious head of the state, he interceded for his men and was seen daily to sacrifice on their behalf.

Unique in his descent from Zeus and Heracles, he was acclaimed "son of Zeus" by the oracle at Didyma, the Sibyl at Erythrae, and the oracle of Ammon (the last at least in the opinion of his men), and he fostered the idea of divine protection by having the sacred shield of Athena carried into battle by his senior Bodyguard (it saved his life against the Malli; A. 6.10.2). Before engaging at Gaugamela Alexander prayed in front of the army, raising his right hand towards the gods and saying, "If I am really descended from Zeus, protect and strengthen the Greeks." That prayer, apparently, was answered. In the eyes of most men—and most men then had faith in gods, oracles, and omens—Alexander was favoured by the supernatural powers. To those who were sceptical he had extraordinarily good luck.

The brilliance of Alexander's mind is seen most clearly in his major battles. As Thucydides said of Themistocles, he was "the ablest judge of situations which developed immediately and admitted of least consideration, and the best anticipator of future and even remote developments." For example, he saw at once the advantages and disadvantages of Darius' position on the Pinarus river and he anticipated the effects of his own detailed dispositions and orders to a nicety. "He surpassed all others in the faculty of intuitively meeting an emergency," whether in besieging Tyre or facing Scythian tactics or storming an impregnable fortress. He excelled in speed and precision of thought, the calculation of risks, and the expectation of an enemy's reactions. Having himself engaged in every kind of action and having grappled with practical problems from a young age, he had a sure sense of the possible and extraordinary versatility in invention. Unlike many famous commanders, his mind was so flexible that at the time of his death he was creating an entirely new type of army.

A most remarkable quality of Alexander's was the concern for his men. No conqueror had so few casualties in battle, and the reason was that Alexander avoided "the battle of rats" by using his brains not just to win, but to win most economically. He made this his priority because he loved his Macedonians. He grew up among them and fought alongside them, both as a youth admiring his seniors and as a mature man competing with his companions. He honoured and rewarded courage and devotion to duty in them, paying a unique tribute to the first casualties by having bronze statues made by the leading sculptor, and he felt deeply with them in their sufferings and privations. He aroused in them an amazing response. He not only admired courage and devotion to duty in his own men but in his enemies, whom he treated with honour. In return he won the respect and loyalty of Asians of many races whom he had just defeated in battle.

No doubt he had a magnetic quality which attracted most of the men and women who knew him, from Porus and Sisigambis downwards. But the myth or romance of the irresistible conqueror preceded him. Sometimes his enemies fled at his approach, because they thought him more than man, and his control of his Asian troops was such that he was prepared to go ahead with them alone, if the need should arise. Some commanders may have rivalled him in the handling of his own race. None have had such a capacity for leading a multiracial army.

(D) AS A STATESMAN IN EUROPE AND ASIA

We have already touched upon his statesmanship in enhancing the prestige of the Macedonian monarchy and advancing the power of the Macedonian state. He reduced the harshness of customary law, (for instance, he no longer required the execution of the male relatives of a convicted traitor), and he was concerned for the welfare and the birth rate of Macedonia. He provided tax reliefs for the dependants of casualties, brought up war orphans at his own expense, and sought to avoid conflicts between the European and Asian families of his Macedonians by maintaining the latter in Asia. He increased the number of young Macedonians when he legitimised the soldiers' children by Asian women, and he sent the 10,000 veterans home in the expectation of their begetting more children in Macedonia.

His choice of Antipater as his general in Europe was wise. A man of sixty in 336 B.C., of proven loyalty and wide experience, Antipater handled the rising in Thrace and the war with Agis successfully, maintained regular communications with the king and sent men and materials at his request. By 323 B.C. Antipater was aged seventy-four, and the strains of dealing with the strong-willed Queen Mother, Olympias, and with the temperamental Greek states must have been cumulative. Alexander might well have retired him. Instead he paid him the compliment of asking him to bring out the 10,000 Macedonians to Asia. He appointed as general in Europe a man twenty-five years younger and of equal experience, Craterus. In making this change Alexander did and said nothing to diminish the stature of Antipater (A. 7.12.7).[124]

In Macedonia and in the Balkan Empire Alexander was consolidating what Philip had constructed in twenty-three years of intense activity. After the whirlwind campaign of 335 B.C. peace brought prosperity and Macedonia became the economic centre of southeastern Europe. Much wealth came from the east in subventions from Alexander, the earnings of Macedonians, Illyrians and Thracians, and the purchase of arms and materials. The fusion of Upper Macedonia with the original kingdom became complete, and Greco-Macedonian culture spread through the cities which had been founded, especially in Thrace. Alexander attended to land-reclamation near Philippi and improved the breeding of stock by sending cattle, for instance, from India. Illyrians and Thracians served in large numbers with Alexander, and the Thracians held a favoured position in the satrapy of Philip in India.

The importance of Macedonia in international commerce is seen in the history of its coinage. Whereas Philip had used the Attic standard in gold and the Thracian standard in silver, Alexander adopted for both metals the Attic standard which prevailed in the Eastern Mediterranean. The mint at Pella provided gold and silver coin for the South and the West, and Damastium in northwesternmost Macedonia coined silver until 325 B.C. for the West, an area enlarged by the campaigns of Alexander the Molossian in South Italy. Amphipolis became the most prolific mint in Alexander's domains and struck a prodigious amount of coinage—in silver tetradrachms alone some thirteen million coins, it has been estimated, were issued in eighteen years—and nearby Philippi served as a subsidiary mint in gold and silver until c. 328 B.C. These mints provided coin for Thrace and for Asia north of the Taurus range and to some extent for Asia south of that range. In addition to the Alexander coins these mints produced the coins of Philip in gold and silver for the Balkans and the West and in gold for Asia during the period 336–328 B.C. approximately. It is possible that Alexander was beginning to reduce the number of mints and to issue only his own and not Philip's types in the years after 328 B.C. When we recall that the Greek states were coining as hitherto and that Alexander added greatly to money circulating in Greece by establishing a prolific mint at Sicyon in the Peloponnese in 330 B.C., we may realise the stupendous increase in coined money, expenditure, and employment which Alexander brought about in Europe alone, quite apart from the economic revolution in Asia.

While Philip invented and inaugurated the Greek League, it was Alexander who demonstrated its efficacy as a *modus operandi* for the Macedonians and the Greeks and used their joint forces to overthrow the Persian Empire. By opening Asia to Greek enterprise and culture Alexander relieved many of the social and economic pressures which had been causing distress and anarchy in the Greek states.[124a] At the same time he was personally concerned with affairs in Greece, as we see from the large number of embassies which came to him in Asia rather than to his deputy, Antipater, in Macedonia. Only a few details are known: plans for draining Lake Copais in Boeotia, advice to the federal assemblies of Achaea, Arcadia, and Boeotia, and the minting of much coin at Sicyon in 330–329 B.C. It was Alexander's success in driving the double team of Macedonia and the Greek League which inspired Demetrius to revive the Greek League in 303 B.C.

Alexander's originality is seen most clearly in Asia. He set himself an unparalleled task when he decided in advance not to make the Macedonians and the Greeks the masters of the conquered peoples but to create a self-sustaining Kingdom of Asia. Within his kingdom he intended the settled peoples to conduct their internal affairs in accordance with their own laws and customs, whether in a Greek city or a native village, in a Lydian or a Carian state, in a Cyprian or a Phoenician kingdom, in Egypt, Babylonia, or Persis, in an Indian principality or republic. As his power extended, he did not introduce European administrators at a level which would inhibit native self-rule (as so-called colonial powers have so often done); instead he continued native administrators in office and raised the best of them to the highest level in civil affairs by appointing them as his immediate deputies in the post of satrap (e.g., Mazaeus at Babylon) or nomarch (e.g., Doloaspis in Egypt).

Parallel to these senior civil servants and, like them, answerable directly to Alexander were the senior financial officers, some dealing with a large region (e.g., Harpalus and Philoxenus) and others dealing with a satrapy (e.g., Cleomenes with Egypt), and the senior military officers commanding an army group (e.g., Parmenio), a satrapal force (e.g., Amyntas in Bactria) or garrison troops (e.g., Pantaleon at Memphis); these officers were from Europe, being Macedonian, Greek, and Thracian. A few native rulers combined civil, financial, and military powers, and one of them, Taxiles, was appointed together with Eudamus, a Greek, to administer Philip's satrapy. At the time of Alexander's death there were some twenty-five satrapies in Asia and they were administered by several hundred senior officials of European and Asian blood.

In creating this (by our standards) very small administrative service Alexander drew on experienced Asians, mainly Persians since they had exercised power under Darius, and on European amateurs who were without the special training a modern government would provide. The administrators, being few, had great authority within their own sphere, and opportunities for corruption were as frequent as they were to be under the Roman Republic or in many parts of the modern world. Alexander provided from the start the safeguards which Rome devised under the Empire: the separation of civil, financial, and military functions into different hands, and the appeal of the individual subject to the head of government. When we consider the area involved and the recentness of the conquest, the number of condemnations for corruption and misgovernment of which the sources tell us is remarkably small.[125]

What is important is the effectiveness of Alexander's system: native civilians and armed forces alike lodged complaints with Alexander, the accused were tried legally and openly, and those found guilty were executed forthwith, in order "to deter the other satraps, governors, and civil officers" and to make it known that the rulers were not permitted to wrong the ruled in Alexander's kingdom. In the opinion of Arrian, who lived at the zenith of the Roman Empire and had a standard of comparison, it was this system which "more than anything else kept to an orderly way of life the innumerable, widely diffused peoples who had been subjugated in war or had of their own will joined him" (6.27.5). In the same way rebels, sometimes in the form of native pretenders, were put on trial; and, if found guilty, they were executed, often in the manner native to the particular area (A. 6.30.2). Where the rights of his subjects were at stake, he showed no mercy or favouritism for any Macedonian, Greek, Thracian, Persian, Median, or Indian.

One exception may be suggested. In connection with the honouring of Hephaestion Arrian reports (7.23.8) that a letter from Alexander to Cleomenes in Egypt included a sentence pardoning Cleomenes for any past offences and for any future offences, if Cleomenes made two shrines for Hephaestion. Any letter alleged to be from Alexander has to be scrutinised with a critical eye. The content is suspect in itself in this case, and the fact that Ptolemy later executed Cleomenes for his crimes is relevant. Where Alexander erred, Ptolemy acted justly; that may have been the impression a forger wished to convey.[126]

What Alexander sought in his senior administrators was summed up in the word "excellence" (*arete*). He assessed it by performance in his own army and in that of his enemy; for he approved courage and loyalty, wherever he found it. But a particular kind of excellence was needed where conquerors had to accept the conquered as their equals in administering the kingdom of Asia. The Macedonians justifiably regarded themselves as a military élite, superior to Greeks and barbarians, and closer to their king than any foreigner; and the Greeks despised all Asians as barbarians, fitted by nature only to be slaves. Yet here was Alexander according equal status, regardless of race, not only to all his administrators but also to all who served in his army! Resentment at this was the chief factor in the mutiny of the Macedonians at Opis. On that occasion Alexander enforced his will. He celebrated the concept of equal status in an official banquet, at which the Macedonians sat by their king, with whom they were now reconciled; next were the Persians; and after them persons of "the other races." All the guests were men who ranked first in reputation or in some other form of excellence (*arete*).

The guests were of many races. Those who were neither Macedonian nor Persian were invited not as spectators but as participants in a ceremony of fellowship and celebration, now that the integration of the various races into the army had been accepted by the Macedonians. The seating arrangements and the fact that Greek diviners and Persian Magi carried out the religious ritual gave priority of importance to the Macedonians and the Persians, which accorded with the status of the Macedonian veterans and the Persian "Apple-bearers" and "Epigoni" in the armed forces. "All 9,000 guests poured the one libation and sang the song of victory." And they all heard Alexander pray for many blessings and above all for concord between Macedonians and Persians and for the sharing in the rule (of the kingdom) between Macedonians and Persians. In this ceremony we see Alexander's welcoming of excellent men from various races and his according of special honour to Macedonians and Persians.[127]

Some months before the banquet at Opis Alexander had set the seal of his approval on the intermarriage of Macedonians and Asians in a striking manner. Whereas his marriage to Roxane in 327 B.C. had been an affair of the heart, for reasons of policy he and more than eight of his Companions married women of the Persian, Median, and Bactrian nobility in a mass wedding at Susa,[128] and he gave dowries to all the brides. He took Darius' eldest daughter and Artaxerxes Ochus' youngest daughter; Hephaestion married another daughter of Darius, Craterus had a niece of Darius; and so on; and the wedding was conducted in the Persian manner with the bridegroom kissing the bride. It was a gesture of the greatest goodwill towards the leading families of Asia, and it was the intention of Alexander that the children of these marriages should share in the administration of the kingdom. At Susa too he converted the unions of some 10,000 Macedonian soldiers and Asian women into official marriages, and he gave them all wedding gifts. The women of very many races must have been represented.

When Alexander encountered nomadic or marauding peoples, he forced them, often by drastic methods of warfare, to accept his rule and to adopt a settled way of life. Many of his new cities were founded among these peoples so that "they should cease to be nomads," and he encouraged the concentration of native villages to form new urban centres. For he intended to promote peace, prosperity, and culture within these parts of his kingdom too, and the cities and centres were means to that end. Strongly fortified and well manned, they were bastions of peace, and the young men in them were trained by Macedonian and Greek veterans to join Alexander's new army and maintain his peace. They were sited to become markets for agricultural produce and interregional exchange, and their citizens, especially in the new cities by the deltas of the Nile, the Euphrates, and the Indus, learnt the capitalistic form of economy, which had brought such prosperity to the Greek states in the fifth and fourth centuries.

The cultural model for the new cities was the Macedonian town, itself very strongly imbued with Greek ideas and practices. The ruling element from the outset was formed by Macedonian and Greek veterans; and the Asians, although free to practise their own religion and traditions, were encouraged to learn Greek and adopt some forms of Greco-Macedonian life. According to Plutarch (*Mor.* 328e) Alexander founded 70 new cities, which started their life with 10,000 adult male citizens as the norm, and he must have envisaged a fusion of European and Asian cultures developing within and spreading out from these arteries into the body of the kingdom.

Ceremony plays an important part in monarchy. Alexander invented his own ceremonial as King of Asia. He himself wore the Macedonian type of diadem but with two ribands, and an Asian style of dress, specifically not the "Median" or Persian royal style[129] but such as is shown on the Hydaspes medallion; and his travelling "tent" or reception-marquee, supported by thirty-foot columns sheathed in gold and silver and studded with precious stones, was large enough to hold a hundred couches for a state banquet. When granting an audience to Asians Alexander was attended by eunuchs and guarded by "Apple-bearers," the Persian equivalent of the English "Beef-eaters"; those who were admitted bowed with a gesture of homage or prostrated themselves (as in Aeschylus *Persae* 152), and the mark of royal favour was permission to kiss the king and to be given by him the title "Kinsman." Such pomp and ceremony, extravagant in Macedonian eyes, were designed to appeal to the oriental mind, but they were also symbolic of Alexander's own reaction to oriental splendour as shown by his immense gifts, the giant tumulus to commemorate Demaratus, the quenching of the sacred flames throughout Asia in mourning for Hephaestion, and plans for a funerary ziggurat for Hephaestion and a funerary memorial for his father Philip to rival the greatest pyramid in Egypt.

In theory Alexander might have practised one form of ceremonial for the Macedonians and another for the Asians. In fact he wanted the leaders of both to participate in the Asian kingdom and so in the ceremonial which he had invented. This was understood and accepted by his closest friends, Hephaestion and Peucestas. Indeed as satrap of Persis, Peucestas learnt Persian, wore the "Median" style of dress, and adopted native ways, to the delight of Alexander and the Persians and the distress of many leading Macedonians. For most Macedonians opposed Alexander openly and bitterly. With extraordinary strength of will he insisted, despite the fact that his insistence alienated Philotas, Cleitus, and Callisthenes and provoked the mutiny at Opis. Yet he gained his objective, at least in outward form, when he let repentant Macedonians at Opis kiss him and granted them the title of kinsman. So much did it matter to him that European and Asian should be treated with equal esteem and receive the same honours in his kingdom of Asia.

The effects of a statesman's ideas, especially if he dies at the age of thirty-two, are rarely assessable within his lifetime. Yet before Alexander died his ideas bore fruit in the integration of Asians and Macedonians in cavalry and infantry units; the training of Asians in Macedonian weaponry; the association of Asians and Macedonians in each file of the army; the settling of Macedonians, Greeks, and Asians in the new cities; the spread of Greek as a common language in the army and in the new cities; the development of Babylon as the "metropolis" or capital of the kingdom of Asia; the honouring of interracial marriage; and the raising of Eurasian children to a privileged status.

Peace reigned in this kingdom of Asia, and its people now had little to fear from their neighbours. Urbanisation, trade, water-borne commerce, agriculture, flood-control, land-reclamation, and irrigation were developing fast, and exchange was stimulated by the liberation of hoarded treasure. The gold and silver coinage of Alexander, uniform in types and weights, was universally accepted because it was of real, bullion value. In the eastern satrapies especially the gold darics and silver shekels of the Persian treasuries continued to circulate, and in the western satrapies local currencies were provided by the Greek, Cyprian, and Phoenician cities.

The chief mint of Alexander's coinage in Asia was at Babylon; its output was second only to that of the mint at Amphipolis, and it was closely followed by the mint at Tarsus. During the 320s B.C. many subsidiary mints of Alexander coins came into operation; for example at Lampsacus, Sardis, Miletus, and Sidea in western Asia Minor, at Aradus and Sidon in Phoenicia, at Citium in Cyprus, at Alexandria in Egypt, and at Ecbatana in Media. Already in the 320s B.C. Asia enjoyed an unprecedented prosperity, of which the huge amount of Alexander coinage is an index, and that prosperity was to last despite the wars which followed his death. The skill with which Alexander changed the economy of Asia into that system of commercial exchange which the Greeks had invented and we call capitalism, and at that within so few years, is one of the most striking signs of his genius.

The Asian response to Alexander is seen in the "Alexander Romance," which began to grow within his lifetime. Its background was the welcome accorded by the ordinary people of Egypt and Babylon to their liberator, and its testimony is that they and other native peoples adopted Alexander as their own king. Thus, in an Armenian version

> Nectanebos, the last king of Egypt, went to Pella and set up as a soothsayer. When Olympias was in labour, he delivered her, saying, "Give birth now, O Queen, and the one you bear is a world conqueror." Thereupon Olympias cried out louder than a bull and gave birth to a boy child, and as the boy fell to the earth, there was an earthquake and thundering and frequent lightnings so that nearly the whole world trembled.

For the boy was the seed of Ammon, implanted in Olympias by this same Nectanebos. The founding of Alexandria on the native soil of Egypt by the conqueror—an action which modern nationalists would detest—was celebrated in the romance by the soothsayers declaring "This city . . . shall feed the entire world and men born in it shall be everywhere; for they shall travel like birds throughout the world." So it remained until the regime of President Nasser. Even in Persis, where national resistance might have been strongest, the Romance makes Alexander carry the dead Darius, give him a state funeral, and issue an edict to all the people of Persis, which includes these words:

> You are each to observe the religions and customs, the laws and conventions, the feast days and festivities which you observed in the days of Darius. Let each stay Persian in his way of life, and let him live within his city. I make no claim to your possessions; each shall administer his own property, except for gold and silver. . . . For I wish to make the land one of widespread prosperity and employ the Persian roads as peaceful and quiet channels of commerce.

The native peoples understood and accepted the purposes of Alexander as their king.

Alexander was even brought into the usually exclusive fold of Judaism. In his history of the Jews, published in A.D. 93/94, Josephus wrote that Alexander prostrated himself before the High Priest, who had come in his ceremonial robes to meet the conqueror before the gates of Jerusalem. When Parmenio asked Alexander why he had done so, Alexander replied:

> It was not before him that I prostrated myself but the God of whom he has the honour to be the high priest; for in my sleep at Dium in Macedonia I saw him in this dress, and he urged me, as I was thinking to myself how shall I become master of Asia, "Do not hesitate, but cross over in confidence; for I myself shall lead your army and give you the empire of the Persians" (*AJ* 11.329).

The fulfilment of Alexander's plans was impaired by his early death and by the strife between the generals which ensued. Yet even so, within the span of thirteen years, he changed the face of the world more decisively and with more longlasting effects than any other statesman has ever done. He first introduced into Asia the Greco-Macedonian city within the framework of a monarchical or autocratic state, and this form of city was to be the centre of ancient and medieval civilisation in the southern Balkans, the Aegean, and the Near East. For the city provided that continuity of Greek language, literature, and culture which enriched the Roman world, fostered Christianity, and affected Western Europe so profoundly. The outlook and the achievements of Alexander created an ideal image, an apotheosis of kingship which was to inspire the Hellenistic kings, some Roman emperors, and the Byzantine rulers. And his creation of a state which rose above nationalism and brought liberators and liberated, victors and defeated into collaboration and parity of esteem puts most of the expedients of the modern world to shame.

(E) AS A PERSONALITY

Ancient and modern writers have studied various aspects of Alexander's personality. His sexual life, for instance, has been the subject of wild speculation. Some have supposed that his closeness to his mother and his continence in the presence of Darius' mother, wife, and daughters were signs of sexual impotence; others just the opposite, that he travelled with a harem which provided him with a different girl each night of the year; and others that he had homosexual affairs with herds of eunuchs, Hephaestion, Hector, and a Persian boy. The truth is not attainable nor of much importance; for in the Macedonian court homosexual and heterosexual attachments were equally reputable, and the sexual life of Philip, for instance, seems to have had no effect on his achievements in war and politics. Disappointingly for sensationalist writers Alexander's relations with women seem to have been normal enough for a Macedonian king: three or four wives at the age of thirty-two and two or perhaps three sons—Heracles by Barsine, widow of the Rhodian Memnon and daughter of the Persian Artabazus (P. 21.7–9 and Plut. *Eum.* 1 fin.; C. 10.6.11–13; J. 13.2.7; Suidas s.v. Antipatros); by the Bactrian Roxane a boy who died in infancy (*Epit. Metz* 70) and a boy born after Alexander's death, who became Alexander IV.

Alexander's relations with his parents have been interpreted in differing ways. Some have held him guilty of patricide, planned in advance with the connivance of his mother; others have pictured him publicly disowning his "so-called father," Philip; and others have made him praise the services of Philip to his country and plan to raise a gigantic memorial over Philip's tomb. If we consider these matters from the viewpoint not of the twentieth century but of the fourth century B.C., we should note that patricide, being the most heinous crime in Greek religion, was hardly conceivable in a man of strong religious faith; that to believe one was the son of a god was not to disown one's human father (whether Amphitryon or Joseph); and that praise of Philip was natural in every Macedonian and not least in the successor to his throne. Indeed if the first unplundered tomb at Vergina is that of Philip, as I believe, its unparalleled splendour is a measure of Alexander's affection for and admiration of his father. He was always loving and loyal to his mother, Olympias. Her tears meant more to him than any triumph, and in taking her side he endangered his own chances of the succession to the throne. When he went to Asia, he made her guardian of the kingship and his representative in the performance of state religion and ceremonial in Macedonia,[129a] and he sent to her, partly in that capacity, his regular despatches and a part of the spoils of war. As son and king, he seems to have had full control over her.

In the course of the narrative we have described many facets of Alexander's personality: his deep affections, his strong emotions, his reckless courage, his brilliance and quickness of mind, his intellectual curiosity, his love of glory, his competitive spirit, his acceptance of every challenge, his generosity and his compassion; and on the other hand his overweening ambition, his remorseless will, his passionate indulgence in unrestrained emotion, his inexorable persistence, and his readiness to kill in combat, in passion, and in cold blood and to have rebellious communities destroyed. In brief, he had many of the qualities of the noble savage.

What is left to consider is the mainspring of his personality, his religious sense. The background is essential. Members of the Macedonian royal house worshipped the Olympian gods of orthodox Greek religion in the orthodox way; participated in the ecstatic religions of Orpheus, Dionysus, and the Cabiri (in Samothrace); consulted oracles, apparently with credulity, for instance of Zeus Ammon at Aphytis in Chalcidice, Apollo at Delphi, and Trophonius at Lebadea in Boeotia; and believed in omens and their interpreters. Further, they had at Aegeae and Pella their particular worship of Heracles Patroüs as their heroic ancestor and semidivine exemplar; for Heracles himself was a "son of god," even of Zeus.

To emulate, even to surpass his father Philip, or the conquering prototype, Cyrus the Great; to rival the journeys and achievements of Heracles and Dionysus; and in his turn to win "divine honours" was probably Alexander's youthful ambition. Europe had been the scene of Philip's triumphs, and Italy was to be invaded by the Molossian Alexander; so Asia was the continent for Alexander. But would the gods give it to him? As he landed in the Troad Alexander gave expression to his faith: "From the gods I accept Asia, won by the spear." He reaffirmed this after his victory at Gaugamela, when he dedicated spoils as "Lord of Asia" in thanksgiving to Athena of Lindus and wrote to Darius, "the gods give Asia to me." And in the end he was to see himself, and others —even the remote Libyans—were to see him as "King of all Asia" (A. 7.15.4; *Ind.* 35.8).

But in 334 B.C., he must have asked himself whether he was indeed a "son of god," capable of such heroic achievement. The answers came unambiguously from oracles and priests in whose words he had belief: in 332 B.C. the priests of Egypt greeted him as "Son of Ra"; the priest of Ammon at Siwah probably led him and certainly led others to think he was "Son of Ammon," and then the shrines of Didyma and Erythrae declared him to be a "Son of Zeus." It was tempting to put such faith to the test, and his prayer at Gaugamela did so. The victory there reassured him that he was indeed "descended from Zeus."

Many signs and wonders—some self-evident, others interpreted by seers—showed that the gods were on his side. There is no doubt that he and his men believed in them implicitly. We must remember that Alexander's preferred readings were the *Iliad*, the plays of the three great tragedians, and dithyrambic poetry, in all of which the gods revealed their purposes to men in a variety of ways—signs and wonders being among them. Of those which happened to Alexander Arrian, drawing on Ptolemy and Aristobulus, mentions the following: the swallow at Halicarnassus, the knot at Gordium untied by the future "ruler of Asia," the thunder and lightning there, the dream before the attack on Tyre, the bird of prey at Gaza, the grain marking the bounds of Alexandria, the rain and the crows on the way to Siwah, the soaring eagle at Gaugamela, the adverse omen at the Jaxartes, the Syrian clairvoyant in Bactria, the springs of oil and water by the Oxus, and the oracle of Belus (Ba'al) before the entry into Babylon (A. 7.16.5–17.6). Even when death was overshadowing him Alexander might have said, like old Oedipus, "in all the signs the gods themselves have given me, they never played me false."

The gods were the authors also of all success in the opinion of Alexander (Plut. *Mor.* 343B), and to them he gave the credit and the thanks. He was constantly engaged in religious acts; he sacrificed every morning of his adult life, on any evening of carousal with his Companions, on starting any enterprise, crossing any river, entering battle, celebrating victory, and expressing gratitude. He was more self-effacing in his devoutness than his father. For example, whereas Philip had portrayed himself on his coins taking the salute, probably at a victory parade, and advertising his successes at the Olympic games, Alexander showed gods only on his regular coin issues. In the famous sculptures of Alexander by Lysippus he was represented with a melting and liquid softness of the eyes "looking up towards the heavens," and this was interpreted at the time as looking up towards Zeus, from whom his inspiration came. In his early years, for instance on landing in Asia, he paid special honour to Athena Alcidemus (the Macedonian war-goddess who protected Philip and Alexander according to Pliny *NH* 35.114), [129b] Zeus the King ("of gods and men") and Heracles, ancestor of the royal house; and throughout his reign he showed them, and them alone, on his gold and silver coins. It is only on the Porus medallion that the figure of Alexander appeared: diminutive in a symbolic combat. On the reverse his face is not thrown into relief. For later portraits see Figures 20 and 36.

After the pilgrimage to Siwah he put Zeus Ammon, or Ammon of the Libyans (in contrast to Ammon at Aphytis), or just Ammon on the same level as Athena, Zeus, and Heracles in his regard; for instance, on meeting Nearchus he called to witness "Zeus of the Greeks" and "Ammon of the Libyans" (*Ind.* 35.8). The thunderbolt which is carried by Alexander on the Porus medallion was probably the weapon of Zeus Ammon, with which he had armed Alexander to win the Kingdom of

Asia. In the paintings by Apelles, Alexander was portrayed wielding the thunderbolt, probably as King of Asia. It was the oracle of Zeus Ammon, not an oracle in Greece, that Alexander consulted about the honouring of Hephaestion, and at the mouth of the Indus, for instance, he made two sets of sacrifices with the rituals and to the gods prescribed by the oracle of Ammon.

He sacrificed occasionally to other non-Greek deities, such as Tyrian Melkart (identified with Heracles), Apis and Isis in Egypt, and Belus (Ba'al) in Babylon, whose temple he intended to rebuild. And his readiness to turn to Greek and non-Greek gods alike for help is shown by his consulting not only Greek seers but also those of Egypt, Persia (the Magi), and Babylon (the Chaldaeans). It was no doubt because of his faith in these divine powers that during his last illness Sarapis was consulted; that his corpse was embalmed by Egyptians and Chaldaeans; and that the ram's head, the emblem of Ammon, was added to the head of Alexander on the coins of Lysimachus. It is evident that Alexander did not think in terms of his national gods defeating those of other races, as the Greeks and the Hebrews for instance had done; rather he was ready to accord respect and worship to the gods of other peoples and to find in some of those gods an excellence equal to that of the Macedonian and Greek gods.

That Alexander should grow up with a sense of mission was certainly to be expected. For he was descended from Zeus and Heracles, he was born to be king, he had the career of Philip as an exemplar, and he was advised by Isocrates, Aristotle, and others to be a benefactor of Macedonians and Greeks alike. His sense of mission was inevitably steeped in religious associations, because from an early age he had been associated with the king, his father, in conducting religious ceremonies, and he was imbued with many ideas of orthodox religion and of ecstatic mysteries. Thus two observations by Plutarch (*Mor.* 342 A and F) have the ring of truth. "This desire (to bring all men into an orderly system under a single leadership and to accustom them to one way of life) was implanted in Alexander from childhood and grew up with him"; and on crossing the Hellespont to the Troad Alexander's first asset was "his reverence towards the gods." Already by then he planned to found a Kingdom of Asia, in which he would rule over the peoples, as Odysseus had done, "like a kindly father" (*Odyssey* 5.11). He promoted the fulfilment of that plan "by founding Greek cities among savage peoples and by teaching the principles of law and peace to lawless, ignorant tribes." When he had completed the conquest of "Asia" through the favour of the gods and especially that of Zeus Ammon, he went on to establish for all men in his kingdom "concord and peace and partnership with one another" (*Mor.* 329 F).

This was a practical development, springing from a religious concept and not from a philosophical theory (though it led later to the philosophical theory of the Cynics, who substituted for Asia the whole inhabited world and talked of the brotherhood of all men), and it came to fruition in the banquet at Opis, when he prayed in the presence of men of various races for "concord and partnership in the ruling" of his kingdom "between Macedonians and Persians."

What distinguishes Alexander from all other conquerors is this divine mission. He had grown up with it, and he had to a great extent fulfilled it, before he gave expression to it at the banquet at Opis in such words as those reported by Plutarch (*Mor.* 329 C). "Alexander considered," wrote Plutarch, "that he had come from the gods to be a general governor and reconciler of the world. Using force of arms when he did not bring men together by the light of reason, he harnessed all resources to one and the same end, mixing the lives, manners, marriages and customs of men, as it were in a loving-cup." This is his true claim to be called "Alexander the Great": that he did not crush or dismember his enemies, as the conquering Romans crushed Carthage and Molossia and dismembered Macedonia into four parts; nor exploit, enslave or destroy the native peoples, as "the white man" has so often done in America, Africa, and Australasia; but that he created, albeit for only a few years, a supra-national community capable of living internally at peace and of developing the concord and partnership which are so sadly lacking in the modern world.

Figure 20. A copy in glass paste of a late fourth
century B.C. gem showing the head of Alexander.
Augustan period. *Source: Antikenmuseum, Berlin,
Germany.*

Figure 21. The plain of Poloskë, viewed from Wolf's Pass, looking westwards. The water on the right, now the Ventrok Channel, is where the Eordaïcus ran. The hill beyond it was the fortified citadel of Pelium. *Source: A. Harding.*

Figure 22. The eastern exit of Wolf's Pass, Lake Little Prespa and the ridge of Mt. Peristeri, beyond which lies Florina. *Source: A. Harding.*

Figure 23. The plain of Adrasteia and the ridge on which the Greek mercenaries stood. Viewed from the right bank of Kocabaş (Granicus) River. *Source: N.G.L. Hammond.*

Figure 24. The Kocabaş (Granicus) River just below the Cinar Köprü bridge. Note trees, shrubs, and the meandering course of the river in June. *Source: N.G.L. Hammond.*

Figure 25. The bed of the Payas (Pinarus) River near Mt. Amanus. Note the scattered boulders and the silhouette of the sickle-shaped hill. *Source: N.G.L. Hammond.*

Figure 26. The Payas (Pinarus) River entering the steep-sided channel. Viewed from the left bank just below the first bridge. *Source: N.G.L. Hammond.*

Figure 27. The second bridge of the Payas (Pinarus) River with level ground and shelving banks beyond. Viewed from the right bank. *Source: N.G.L. Hammond.*

Figure 28. The "dead ground" and the sickle-shaped promontory of high ground. Viewed from the south side of the Payas (Pinarus) River. *Source: N.G.L. Hammond.*

Figure 29. Ivory head of Philip from the tomb of Philip II at Vergina (Aegeae). The right eye is blind. Height 2 cm. *Source: Spyros Tsavdaroglou.*

Figure 30. Ivory head of Olympias from the tomb of Philip II at Vergina (Aegeae). Height 2 cm. *Source: Spyros Tsavdaroglou.*

Figure 31. Ivory head of Alexander from the tomb of Philip II at Vergina (Aegeae). Height 2 cm. *Source: Spyros Tsavdaroglou.*

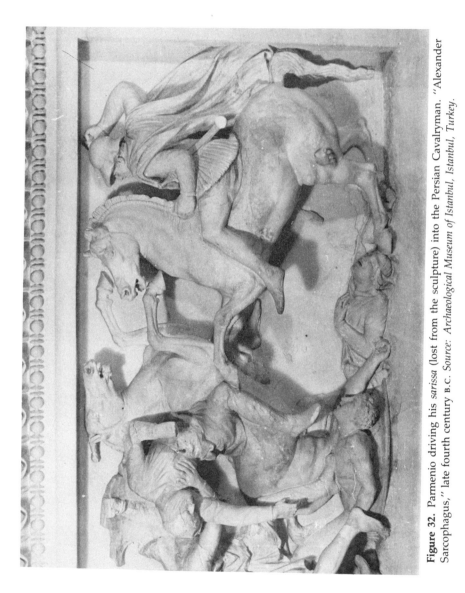

Figure 32. Parmenio driving his *sarissa* (lost from the sculpture) into the Persian Cavalryman. "Alexander Sarcophagus," late fourth century B.C. *Source: Archaeological Museum of Istanbul, Istanbul, Turkey.*

Figure 33: Alexander (bareheaded) and Darius (in chariot) at the Battle of Issus in a first century A.D. Roman mosaic from Pompeii. *Source: National Museum, Naples, Italy: "Fotografie della Soprintendenza alle Antichità della Provinze di Napoli e Caserta-Napoli."*

(a) Gold stater, 8.58 g(rammes). *Obv(erse)*. Head of Athena wearing triple-crested Corinthian helmet; on bowl, coiled snake. *Rev(erse)*. Nike holding wreath and stylus; trident-head; inscribed 'of Alexander'. Minted at Amphipolis, probably from gold taken after Issus (J.11.10.5). Celebrates victory of Issus: Athena probably Alcidemos, Macedonian goddess of war; Nike with wreath of victory; trident of Poseidon, whom Alexander invoked on preceding night (*P.Oxy.*1798. p. 129); and stylus commemorating naval exploit of Alexander's Companions (see p. 94 and p. 157).

(b) Silver tetradrachm, 16.72 g. *Obv*. Young head of Heracles. *Rev*. Zeus seated legs together on throne with back, holding sceptre and eagle; helmet crest, M, monogram; issue marks below throne. Inscribed "of king Alexander." Minted at Amphipolis. Heracles as ancestor of Temenid house. Zeus Basileus with sceptre of rule and eagle-messenger, which guided Alexander's strategy with Persian navy; helmet crest may recall crest shorn from Alexander's helmet at Granicus. Royal title suggests later than (a). Seated Zeus resembles seated Baal on Persian coins of Tarsus (see p. 157).

(c) Silver tetradrachm, 16.52 g. *Rev*. As (b), but with facing head of Helios (sun-god) with bursting rays, as on caskets in the Vergina tomb. Alexander sacrificed to Helios after victory at the Hydaspes (D.17.89.3 and C.9.1.1), as god of the Orient; also suggestive of Indian worship of Mithra.

(d) Silver tetradrachm, 17.18 g. *Rev*. As (b), but with Macedonian shield of distinctive design, token of armed defence (perhaps of Kingdom of Asia). From a hoard at Demanhur in Egypt.

(e) and (f) Rare silver decadrachms, 42.20 g. and 39.62 g. *Obv*. Alexander on horseback, wearing head-dress as on *Reverse*, with *sarissa*, attacking rider on elephant; mahout turning to throw javelin and holding two javelins. Greek letter *ksi* (Ξ) above. *Rev*. Nike about to crown Alexander with wreath of victory; he holds a thunderbolt forward, rests on a spear, wears sword in scabbard, skirted cuirass, cloak, close-fitting helmet with crest between two very high plumes (as at Granicus, Plut. *Alex*. 16.7) and with the ends of two ribbons of the diadem, worn under the helmet. The coins commemorate victory after battle, as Alexander is in full battle-dress of Macedonian style; but the two ribbons show him as King of Asia, and the thunderbolt (cf. Plut. *Alex*. 44.3) as vicegerent of Zeus. The salient feature of the battle, Alexander with lance against a large elephant with large rider, may represent either the clash of cavalry and elephants (A.5.17.3 init.) when Alexander led the Companion Cavalry or the moment before Porus fainted and Alexander lost his horse (C.8.14.33-4) in the battle of Hydaspes. No other battle is likely. Same *ksi* (Ξ) and same monogram with poorly executed elephant on silver tetradrachm in *Arch. Rep.* 20 (1973-4) 68 fig. 9, which may commemorate an elephant hunt in India (A.4.30.8).

Figure 34. Description of the coins in Figure 35.

(a) Obv.   (a) Rev.

(b) Obv.   (b) Rev.

(c) Rev.   (d) Rev.

(e) Obv.   (e) Rev.

(f) Obv.   (f) Rev.

Figure 35. Gold and silver coins of Alexander. *Source: Ashmolean Museum, Oxford, England (a-d); British Museum, London, England (e,f).*

Figure 36. Head of Alexander, a marble copy of a late fourth century B.C. original. c. 100 A.D. *Source: Dr. E. Schwarzenberg.*

Figure 37. Satellite photograph of Southwestern Macedonia and its southern neighbours. The northernmost lakes are the Prespas, the southern that of Ioannina. See Fig. 5 on same scale. *Source: Department of Interior, EROS Data Center, Sioux Falls, South Dakota.*

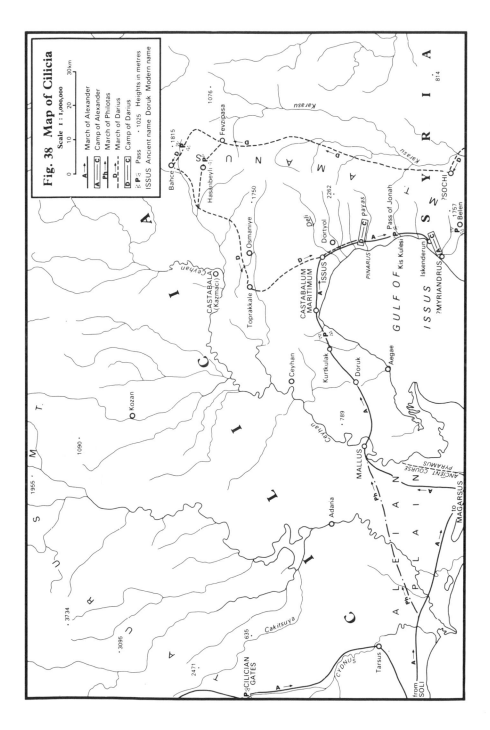

Fig. 38 Map of Cilicia

Figure 39. Satellite photograph of Cilicia. *Source: U.S. Department of Interior, EROS Data Center, Sioux Falls, South Dakota.*

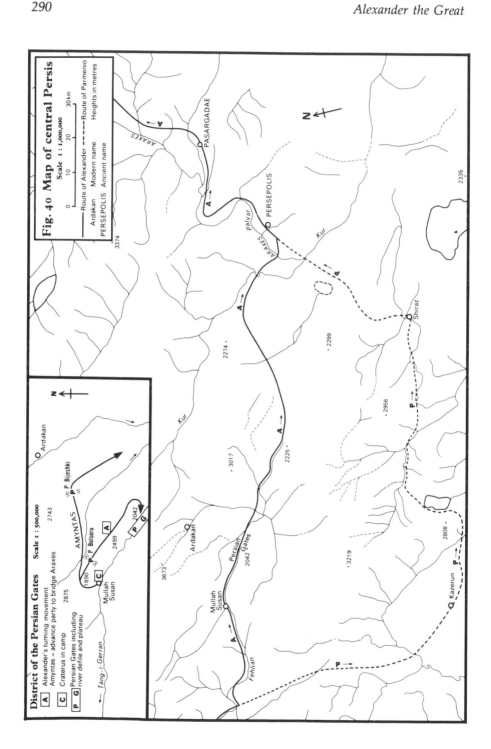

Fig. 40 Map of central Persis

Figure 41. Satellite photograph of Central Persis. *Source: U.S. Department of Interior, EROS Data Center, Sioux Falls, South Dakota.*

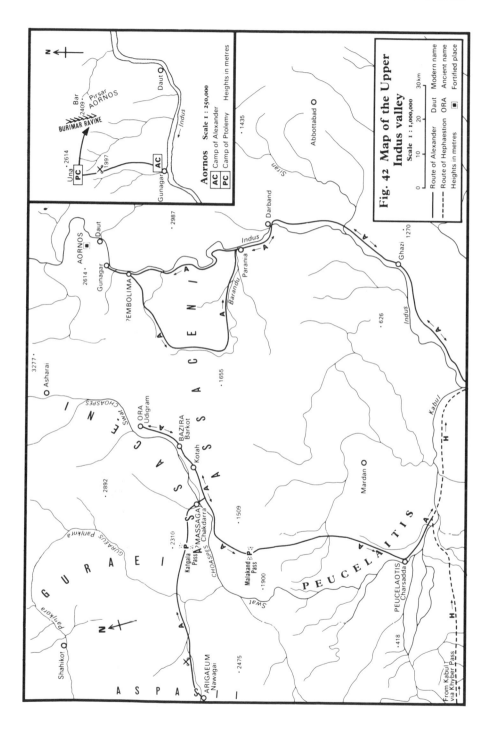

Fig. 42 Map of the Upper Indus valley

Figure 43. Satellite photograph of the Upper Indus valley. *Source: U.S. Department of Interior, EROS Data Center, Sioux Falls, South Dakota.*

Figure 44. Satellite photograph of the Makran coast and the Gedrosian desert. *Source: U.S. Department of Interior, EROS Data Center, Sioux Falls, South Dakota.*

APPENDIX I

THE *KING'S JOURNAL* ON THE LAST DAYS OF ALEXANDER

Before quoting from the *Journal*, Arrian states that Alexander was banqueting with "the Friends," that is, at an official banquet, and was drinking far into the night. (This statement was derived from the accounts of Ptolemy and Aristobulus in accordance with Arrian's practice.) Arrian then goes on to add a report (from other sources) in the accusative and infinitive, that it was a time of general festivity for the whole army, and that when Alexander wanted to leave the party, he was invited to join in a carousal in honour of a god (a *komos* or feast, probably in honour of Heracles); the invitation was given by Medius, his most trusted Companion at the time. Arrian then continues:

> And the *King's Journal* is as follows. He made the carousal and he was drinking at Medius' place. Then he got up, bathed and slept, and once again dined at Medius' place and again drank far into the night, and on breaking off from the drinking he bathed. After bathing he ate a snack and slept there, because he already had a fever. However, as was his custom every day, he made sacrifice, being carried on a stretcher to the ceremony, and after completing it he lay down in the men's room until nightfall. During this time he was issuing orders to the commanding officers about the march and the voyage—the march to begin in three days' time, and the voyage, led by himself, in five days' time. From the men's room he was carried on the stretcher down to the river (the Euphrates), and embarking on a boat he sailed across the river to the garden, and there bathed again and rested. Next day he bathed again and made the customary sacrifice; and going to his room lay down, conversing with Medius; and ordered the commanding officers to meet him at dawn. After doing that he had a light dinner, was carried to his room again and was now in continual fever all night long.
>
> But next day he bathed, and after bathing he sacrificed. And he issued orders to Nearchus and the other commanding of-

295

ficers about the conduct of the voyage in three days' time. On the next day he bathed again, made the appointed sacrifice, and on completing the service he had continual fever from then on. However, even so, he summoned the commanding officers and gave them orders for setting sail, so that all should be ready for him. That evening he bathed, and after bathing he was now in a bad way. Next day he was carried across to the house by the swimming-pool, made the appointed sacrifice, and although grievously ill summoned the most important of the commanding officers and again issued orders for the voyage. On the following day he just managed to have himself carried to the sacred area and make sacrifice, and nonetheless was issuing orders still about the voyage to the commanding officers. Next day he was indeed in a bad state; yet he made the appointed sacrifice. He ordered the generals to wait in the courtyard and the commanders of the brigades and the battalions to wait in front of the gates, and he was carried through (them) into the palace, grievously ill though he already was. As the commanding officers came in, he knew them but no longer spoke at all but remained speechless. In the night he had a bad fever and in the day, and next night and next day.

So it is written in the *King's Journal*, and next that the soldiers longed to see him, some in the hope of seeing him still alive, and others because of a report that he was already dead but his death was being concealed, they supposed by the Bodyguards —at least I think so. And I think that most of them felt grief and longing for their king and so pressed in to see Alexander. As the army filed past him, he was unable to speak, they say, but even so he welcomed each of them, raising his head with difficulty and greeting them with his eyes. The *King's Journal* reports that Peithon, Attalus, Demophon, Peucestas, Cleomenes, Menidas, and Seleucus, keeping an all-night vigil in the shrine of Sarapis, asked the god whether it would be better for Alexander to be brought into the shrine, to make supplication and to be healed by the god. But the god indicated that he should not be brought into the shrine; the better thing for him would be to stay where he was. This was reported by the Companions, and shortly afterwards Alexander died, as this was surely the better thing. What Aristobulus and Ptolemy have written is not far from that.

That the above is only part of the original is clear from a freer citation of the same *Journal* by Plutarch (P. 76), who omitted many of Arrian's points and added some. Each author felt free to select what he wanted and use his own words, but there are enough details and words in common to establish that they were drawing on the same account.

APPENDIX II

ALEXANDER: A DRINKER OR A DRUNKARD?

Alexander was not a lonely but a sociable man, and sociability in Macedonia was inseparable from drinking. Banqueting with the Companions or the Friends, drinking in honour of a god and drinking in a private party were the traditional activities of a king. "By God," said some charmed Athenian envoys, "Philip is the greatest man to drink with." A king could not be less, and we may be sure that Alexander could and did drink with the best of his officers, as in the party which ended with the death of Cleitus. Moreover, the Macedonians drank harder liquor than most southern Greeks; for they did not put water in their wine, as the Greeks usually did, and the Paeonians, for instance, had some form of beer or gin. We hear too of drinking contests, as in Bavaria, when sometimes the winner died of the effects.

In the hot plain of Babylon, where the water lacked the purity of Macedonian springs (see C. 10.10.10–11), we may be sure that what Alexander drank daily was not water but wine, and that the night was the time for a party in June and the day or part of it was for sleeping. Whatever a rabid teetotaller may think, this form of drinking was not incompatible with brilliant leadership, as a Philip and a Churchill (another late riser) have shown. When the fever came on, Alexander, we may assume, quenched his raging thirst with wine; indeed, Aristobulus said, according to Plutarch (P. 75.6) "in the madness of his fever and in his thirst he drank wine excessively, and thereupon became delirious and died."[130] As we see from the account in the *King's Journal*, Alexander was not in a hospital or even under the supervision of doctors; rather, he was the king, and he managed his affairs to the end.

Those who hated Alexander transferred this last desperate act from the end to the beginning of his illness. "He was earnestly invited" writes Diodorus," to go to one of the Friends, Medius the Thessalian, for a carousal (*komos*), and there after filling himself up with much unmixed wine he ended with a huge 'Heracles' beaker of the stuff and drank it off. Suddenly, as if struck by a powerful blow, he uttered a loud cry, groaned and groaned, and was led off by the hand by his Friends and was put to bed" etc. (D. I7.117.1-2; so too *Itin. Alex.* 53 and J. I2.13.8 in more sensational style). This was indeed the drunkard's doom! A different story but with the same moral was produced by Ephippus of Olynthus, a contemporary of Alexander (*FGrH* I26 F 3); and yet another variant by one Nicobule (*FGrH* I27 F 1). Some of the ingredients passed into the *Romance of Alexander*.

The dispute between those who thought of Alexander as a drinker (e.g., Aristobulus, his close friend, who said that Alexander's long drinking sessions arose not for the sake of the wine, since Alexander did not drink much wine, but out of friendliness for his companions, A. 7.29.4) and those who pictured him as a drunkard has continued through the ages. It was summarised more than four hundred years after the event by Plutarch in *Moralia* 623 e; he put forward on the one side an argument of the Aristobulan type and on the other an appeal to the *King's Journal* to show that Alexander was a drunkard, since there it was stated very often "today he slept after the drinking," and sometimes "also the next day." If the *King's Journal* was forged, as some have held, it is worth noting *en passant* that it was forged by those who wished to represent Alexander as a drunkard.

We have in this connection two citations from the *Journal*, one for the month Dios which starts with a party *chez* Eumaeus, and the other, which we have already cited, for the month Daisios starting with a party *chez* Medius. The one covers the period from the 5th to the 3rd of the following month; the other only twelve days up to the 28th of the month. The one has Alexander dining with Eumaeus, Perdiccas, and Bagoas; the other only with Medius. To any objective reader they are extracts from different parts of the *Journal*. Yet not so the emenders of the text: they change Dios to Daisios and Eumaeus to Medius! Such emendations, without any palaeographic justification and devised for a preconceived purpose, are to be rejected out of hand. Yet scholar after scholar has treated the two citations as variant versions of the same event, the last illness of Alexander[131] (e.g., Hamilton P 210 and Lane Fox 465).

The citation for the month Dios (Ael. *VH* 3.23 = *FGrH* 117 F 2a) is not verbatim but gives the sequence and some phrases from the *King's Journal* (it is inference only that it comes from the *Journal*). On the 5th Alexander drank, it says, at the house of Eumaeus, and on the 6th he slept after the drinking, got up and dealt with the commanding officers about the morrow's march, saying it would be early. On the 7th he banqueted at Perdiccas', drank again and slept on the 8th. On the 15th he drank and did as usual after the drinking. On the 24th he dined with Bagoas, whose house was nearly twenty kilometres away from the palace. On the 3rd he slept. Now this passage was evidently chosen to show that Alexander was a drunkard who gave up many days to toping.

But what does it amount to, if we look at it in a detached way? Within a month he attended three dinners at which he drank with his friends; on one other occasion he drank, we are not told with whom. Hardly an excessive programme for royalty![132] As the parties were night-parties he can hardly be blamed for sleeping a part of the next day, or even after a couple of such parties for a couple of days (as in Athen. 434b). As that is the best evidence his detractors could produce, whether from a genuine or a forged document, we may conclude for sure that Alexander was a drinker and not a drunkard.

On the matter of forgery is it likely that a forger, aiming to prove Alexander a drunkard, would have produced such a feeble case as the two citations from the *King's Journal* provide?[133] Further, if Arrian compared his copy of the *King's Journal* with the accounts of Ptolemy and Aristobulus and concluded that their accounts were not far from the facts of the *Journal* (A. 7.26.3), is it possible that their accounts, probably as eyewitnesses, coincided by chance with a forged *Journal*? The answer to both questions is surely no.

APPENDIX III

LAST PLANS: GENUINE OR FORGED?

The information about Alexander's last plans comes mainly from Diodorus (18.4.1–6). Since most of what Diodorus has to say about Macedonian affairs in this book comes from Hieronymus of Cardia, a follower of Eumenes and a dependable writer, there is a strong presumption that this piece of information comes from Hieronymus and was believed by him to be true. It is of two kinds. First, part of the plans were implicit in "written orders" which Alexander had given to Craterus, who was to take over from Antipater the post of "General of Europe," or as we might say, Governor-General both of the Balkan area west of the Nestus line, and of the Greek peninsula. These orders, of which there was certainly a copy at Babylon, were reviewed after Alexander's death by his successors, and they decided not to implement them. Diodorus tells us nothing of the orders' content, but he connects the orders with the "memoranda" of the king which Perdiccas, as senior general, took over. It is evident, then, that the written orders were related in some aspects at least to the major plans which were found in the memoranda; and Craterus, we may infer, was to embark on the European side of those plans for the reason that Alexander would not be in Europe himself to conduct the operations. No scholar, I think, has suggested that these written orders were forged by Craterus. Second, Diodorus writes about the contents of the "memoranda" in two stages. First, he dwells on the unprecedented expenditure which Alexander's "many and great enterprises and in particular the completion of Hephaestion's memorial" would involve—this with reference to Craterus' written orders, which means that some of the enterprises were there. Second, Diodorus lists "the largest and most memorable items in the memoranda." It is this list which some scholars regard as a forgery.[134]

Before we turn to the list, it is advisable to summarise what we know of Alexander's intentions from the narrative of events before his unforeseen death. The plans for the memorial to Hephaestion were certainly on paper and under way; it was to be in the form of a gigantic ziggurat, and in connection with it the Friends and the commanding officers had prepared "gold and ivory likenesses" of Hephaestion—a Macedonian practice now made familiar to us through the discovery of such likenesses in miniature in tombs at Vergina and Naoussa.[135] The order of expenditure was estimated in our sources to be 10,000 to 12,000 talents, and the ziggurat would have been one of the artistic wonders of the world, had it been completed (D. I7.115).

Alexander intended also to build shrines for Hephaestion elsewhere, to rebuild the temple of Ba'al at Babylon, and to build temples in Greece to the cost of 10,000 talents (Plut. *Mor.* 343d). He planned to settle in Persis all the Greeks who had served with Darius and with the satraps of Darius, these totalling some 50,000 (Paus. 1.25.5 and 8.52.5; the number recurs in C. 5.11.5),[136] and he intended to plant other settlements for military purposes in Media (Polybius I0.27.3). For this programme he would have needed immigrants from Europe.

Embassies which came to Alexander did so often in response to his requests for free passage or alliance, and the fact that embassies came to Babylon from Libya and from the Bruttians, Lucanians, and Etruscans (A. 7.15.4) may well indicate that he intended to go in that direction.[137] In any case, if he had not fallen ill, the army would have set off on June 6th and the fleet would have started downriver from Babylon on June 8th for the conquest of Arabia. Then in the following year[138] he intended to meet Antipater and the draft of Macedonian troops on the coast of the Mediterranean. During the advance of his army and his fleet he hoped to choose sites on the coasts and islands of the Persian Gulf for new cities and to plant in them settlers who were experienced in maritime trade; for he expected that area to become as prosperous as Phoenicia itself (A. 7.19.4–5).

Of "the largest and memorable items in the memoranda," those which Craterus presumably had orders to carry out were the building of temples, costing 1,500 talents each, at Delos, Delphi, and Dodona; and in Macedonia at Dium, Cyrrus (for Cyrnus in the manuscript), and Amphipolis (the total 9,000 talents was close to Plutarch's 10,000 for the same purpose); and the construction of "a tomb for his father Philip which should be like the greatest of the pyramids in Egypt." (The temples were both a form of thanksgiving by Alexander and a symbol, like Pericles' buildings on the Acropolis, of triumph over Persia; they were entirely in keeping with Alexander's ideas. As Alexander had conducted the burial of Philip in 336 b.c., this "tomb" was a memorial, similar in its conception to the huge tumulus, some 40 metres high, which he had built in honour of Demaratus of Corinth; and there is little doubt that the "Great Tumulus" at Aegeae [Vergina] was built for this purpose but several years after the death of Alexander.)[139] The orders of Craterus may well have provided for the construction of ships and the recruiting in Greece of naval personnel and maritime settlers; for Miccalus of Clazomenae was raising men in Syria and Phoenicia for this purpose (A. 7.19.5).

For Asia the memoranda included the building of a temple to rival all others in honour of Athena at Troy. [It was to her that he had dedicated his armour on setting foot in Asia, and it was her sacred shield which had saved his life against the Malli. Now that the kingdom of Asia had indeed been given to him, he intended to pay his tribute to Athena of Troy and make her city great (Str. 593). The temple was to be a counterpart to the great temple to Ba'al which he planned to erect in the "metropolis" of that kingdom, Babylon.] Then Asia was to make its contribution to the next campaign, the Mediterranean campaign, by building in Phoenicia, Syria, Cilicia, and Cyprus a fleet of a thousand warships of classes larger than the trireme. Next, "cities were to be founded and persons transplanted from Asia to Europe and vice versa, in order that he might bring into general concord and family relationship the greatest continents by means of intermarriage and bonds of affection." (One area for such a development was the coast and islands of the Persian Gulf, to which we may assume Alexander hoped to attract Greeks, whether freemen or purchased slaves, as well as Phoenicians, if necessary by financial subsidy (as in A. 7.19.5); but Asians going to Europe must have depended on the making of preparations by Craterus and the General in Thrace.)

The last items which Diodorus included in his selection were some preparations for the Mediterranean campaign. The newly built fleet of a thousand warships larger than triremes was to operate against the Carthaginians, the peoples of the African, Spanish, and following coasts up to Sicily. A road was to be built along the African coast as far as the Pillars of Heracles (the Straits of Gibraltar). Harbours and docks for so large an expedition were to be built in advance at appropriate places. (With such arrangements the fleet and army could advance together, as they had done from Amphipolis to Miletus and again from Tyre to Egypt, and there was abundant information from Greek and Phoenician sailors. No formidable land power existed on the African coast. The new fleet was to be additional to the fleets which Alexander already had in the East Mediterranean; for it must have seemed possible that the Athenians, threatened with the loss of Samos, might side with the fleets of Carthage, Etruria, and Sicily, or with some of them. Alexander had no intention of being outnumbered, because he had limitless funds, timber, and shipwrights; so too Xerxes had sailed with more than a thousand warships in 480 B.C. Larger ships than triremes were now the fashion,[140] and they had proved themselves in the West in the first half of the century.)

All these plans of the memoranda are fully in the spirit of Alexander.

They are consistent with his pursuit of glory by conquest and with his rivalry with Heracles, who, it was believed, had set up his pillars at the mouth of the Mediterranean and had sailed to the islands of the West, the Hesperides. Nor were they chimerical. He had abandoned or at least postponed his earlier dream of sailing to the south of the purely hypothetical coasts of "Aethiopia, Libya, and the Nomads beyond Mt. Atlas and so of reaching Gadeira (Cadiz) at the mouth of our sea." The plans of the memoranda were entirely practical, dealing with known coasts and predictable enemies; for the Greeks of the coasts of Libya, Sicily, Italy, France, and Spain had a wealth of experience in peace and war, and most recently Alexander the Molossian and the Greeks of South Italy had fought with and against the many warlike peoples of Italy.[141]

Just as the "written orders" were rejected by the successors to Alexander's executive powers, so the plans of the memoranda (not just the selection we know) were brought by Perdiccas to the Assembly of the Macedonians at Babylon and were rejected by them as being "immoderate and difficult to achieve" (D. 18.4.3 and 6).[142] The Macedones were right. Without the unifying power and the master hand of Alexander the fulfilment of the plans was wellnigh impossible.

It seems, then, definite that there were genuine "written orders" to Craterus and genuine "memoranda" of Alexander. The former were executive orders for implementing plans contained in the latter. On Alexander's death Craterus was in Cilicia; the written orders were known at Babylon because there was surely a copy of them in the archive there (the *gazophylakion*), and they were cancelled by "the successors," i.e., a council of the leading officers and Philip Arrhidaeus (D. 18.4.1). The plans, then, had been formulated some weeks, even months, before Alexander's death; they had no doubt been discussed by him with his leading officers, and in any case they were known to Eumenes and others who were concerned with the drafting of the plans and the recording of the orders issued in relation to them. In fact too many people knew what was in the memoranda for anyone after that, even Perdiccas, to put a bogus set of plans before the Assembly of the Macedonians (D. 18.4.3) and expect not to be challenged as a liar. Thus the genuine memoranda and the plans contained in them were made public to all Macedonians and became known to the army and navy in general at Babylon; from then on these plans passed into the historical tradition of all Alexander-historians of that generation, since they were a matter of common knowledge and of common interest.

Those, then, who believe that what we have in Diodorus is a forgery have to answer the question: by whom, how, and when did the forged memoranda displace the genuine memoranda from the fully established tradition? No one has suggested a plausible name; or how anyone managed to silence the accounts of many previous writers and impose a new set of plans. But Tarn has proposed a "when," in the form of "after 181 B.C." By then there must have been in the library at Alexandria alone many works by Hellenistic historians, Hieronymus of Cardia among them, who had set down or referred to the genuine last plans of Alexander. How were these expunged? And for what purpose at that date did anyone wish to forge new plans for Alexander? It seems to make no sense at all. Rather, the plans which Diodorus chose to select from the "memoranda" are genuine.[143]

APPENDIX IV

TWO MISCONCEPTIONS

Whereas there is the strongest evidence that Alexander claimed Asia as his and called himself "Lord of Asia" and "King of Asia," he has been regarded by many scholars as the successor to the Persian throne[144] and the ruler of the Persian empire. There is, however, no good evidence for their view. It is true that some Greeks who resented his Asian policy portrayed him and no doubt thought of him as "the Great King," the personification of the tyrannical despot, demanding obeisance and suppressing liberty (so Callisthenes in A. 4.11.6–9 by implication when Alexander was asking for *proskynesis*); but that was rather a form of vituperation than a definition of his actual status.

Stories, too, were told of Alexander as if he were the successor to the Persian throne: Demaratus of Corinth, for instance, remarking that any Greek who had not seen Alexander "sitting on the throne of Darius" had missed a great joy in life (P. 37.7 and 56 and before the death of Darius, D. 17.66.3); Alexander compelling the Macedonian Companions to wear Persian dress and Alexander himself as the heir to Darius' signet ring and Darius' harem of women and numerous eunuch-prostitutes, headed by Bagoas the Beloved of Darius (C. 6.6); and the Persians mourning the dead Alexander as "their nation's justest king" (C. 10.5.17, *ut gentis suae iustissimum regem*).

But Alexander never wore the robes of the Persian king nor the distinctive upright tiara (*kitaris*). He did not occupy a palace in Persia nor rule there as a Persian monarch. In his administrative system Persia was like any other satrapy, and the execution of Bessus as a traitor to Darius was carried out "in the assembly of the Medes and Persians," the body responsible for internal administration. Alexander's claim from start to finish, even in the eyes of the Libyans (A. 7.15.4), was that he was King of Asia, a territory which included not only Darius' empire (A. 2.14.9) but also much more. Cyrus the Great, and other Persian kings with less justification, had made that claim in the past (A. 6.29.8); consequently, Alexander sought to rival and surpass Cyrus, not as King of Persia but as King of Asia.[145]

Another misconception is that Alexander aspired to the rule of the whole inhabited earth, the *oikoumenē*. The idea found expression in some ancient authors. In the exchanges between Alexander and Darius before the confrontation of the armies at Gaugamela, Alexander is made to play on a Persian claim to universal rule by saying that, just as the universe could not maintain its equilibrium and order if there were two suns, so the inhabited earth could not be free from war and confusion if it was subject to two kings; thus the decision at Gaugamela was for "sole and universal rule" (D. 17.54.5–6). In the fictitious questions and answers at the oracle of Siwah, Alexander asked the great question and received the response that he would be "Lord of all" (P. 27.6), and "Ruler of all the world" (C. 4.7.26 *terrarum omnium rectorem*).[146] In the fictitious speech of Alexander at the river Hyphasis the rhetorical climax is reached that "the frontiers of the empire here will become the frontiers of the earth as God has made them" (A. 5.26.3). And this concept was the centrepiece of the *Alexander Romance*. It has been adopted as historical by some modern writers.

Thus C.A. Robinson attributed to Alexander the "extraordinary idea" of "world conquest," and F. Schachermeyr saw in the "memoranda" the indication that Alexander was aiming at "a universal conquest of the inhabited earth."[147] But there is no solid evidence for this view. Rather, Alexander turned back at the Hyphasis river and marked his agreement to go no further by erecting twelve altars. In his opinion the inhabited earth consisted of three continents: Europe extending from the Pillars of Heracles to the Tanaïs, Asia extending from the Tanaïs to an unknown distance eastwards and back to the Nile, and Libya extending from the Nile to the Pillars of Heracles (A. 3.30.9 and 4.7.5).

At the time of his death he had yet to conquer Arabia and to explore the northwestern part of Asia between the Caspian Sea and the Sea of Azov, and his plans were subsequently to campaign along the African seaboard and along the north coast of the Mediterranean as far as Sicily. In as far as the "memoranda" reveal his distant plans, he hoped to create a kingdom in the west, comprising the coastlands of the Mediterranean and dependent largely on sea power, which would balance the kingdom of Asia and give to Macedonia the central position in his structure of power. It was the strategic and imperial plan of a man aged thirty-two , who had already shown in practical terms that he had a remarkable understanding of what was practicable.

NOTES TO THE TEXT

1. The fullest analysis of the sources in English is by Tarn II 1–133, but some of his views have not carried conviction (e.g., his supposed "mercenaries' source," and his late dating of Cleitarchus). Pearson's is the best overall study, and Brown, Brunt, Goukowsky, and Hamilton, *P* are very useful and give references to recent literature. The *King's Journal* is at the centre of controversy. A.E. Samuel, 'Alexander's Royal Journals', *Historia* 14 (1965) 1 ff., showing that such journals were kept at Babylon, has provided a possible source from which Philip adopted the practice of keeping a journal (for the Persian Artabazus spent many years at Philip's court). The supposition of Samuel and others that a forged version of Alexander's *Journal* was in circulation only indicates that a genuine one existed. The passage describing Alexander's last days as cited from his *Journal* have been held by many scholars (e.g., Pearson) to have come from a forged version. This is discussed in Appendix I. We conclude there that Arrian has given us the true account, either from the genuine version of the *Journal*, or from Ptolemy's citation of it. The importance attached to the *Journal* and the nature of its contents are shown in Plutarch, *Eumenes* 2: when a fire destroys some papers on which Eumenes was working, Alexander orders "his satraps and generals" to make good the loss by providing "copies which Eumenes was to take over." Citations from the *Journal* are so rare because ancient writers hardly ever quoted primary evidence; their emphasis was on artistic writing, not footnotes. It so happened that Alexander's death was described with art in the *Journal*; see Appendix I.

2. Another example of blatant flattery attaches to the story of Alexander's dream of an antidote, so saving Ptolemy from the deadly effect of snake poison on an Indian barb which had wounded him (C. 9.8.20-27; D. 17.103.7-8). As Goukowsky 142 notes, the episode is an invention of Cleitarchus to show that divine favour, sending the dream, saved Ptolemy.

3. An excellent study of Arrian, which I had the good fortune to read, will shortly be published by the University of North Carolina Press from the pen of P.A. Stadter. Attempts to find serious errors in Arrian, *Anabasis*, for instance by A.B. Bosworth in *CQ* 26 (9176) 117 ff., are not convincing (see my comments in *CQ* 28 [1978] 136 ff., Hammond, *A* and Hammond, *G*). Errors of omission and obscurity do occur, because Arrian was making a drastic abbreviation of his sources' much longer accounts and also he was capable of carelessness at times.

4. On this subject see *Mac.* I 3–211; for Macedonian institutions see *Mac.* II, especially 150 ff. and 647 ff.; for Philip II see *Mac.* 11 203 ff., Ellis, and Cawkwell. On trials for treason by the Macedonian assembly see also N.G.L. Hammond, '"Philip's Tomb" in Historical Context', *GRBS* 19 (1978) 340 ff.; *contra* R. Lock, 'The Macedonian Assembly', *CPh* 72 (1977) 91 ff., who seems to assume that any conceivable explanation of the presence of the Macedones at such a trial is more likely to be true than that of the sources, even if they derive from Ptolemy, a contemporary. See also Hammond, *A.*

5. For Illyrian tribes see N.G.L. Hammond, 'The Kingdoms of Illyria *circa* 400–167 B.C.', *BSA* 61 (1966) 239 ff.; A. Stipčević, *The Illyrians* (Noyes Press, NJ 1977); F. Papazoglou, *The Central Balkan Tribes in Pre-Roman Times* (Amsterdam, 1978). For Thracian tribes J. Wiesner, *Die Thraker* (Stuttgart, 1963) and G. Mihailov in *The Cambridge Ancient History*, new ed., III.2.ch.33*b* (forthcoming). For the Greeks, T.T.B. Ryder, *Koine Eirene* (Oxford, 1965); and for the Greek League, G.T. Griffith in *Mac.* II 623 ff.

6. See J.K. Anderson, *Ancient Greek Horsemanship* (Berkeley, 1961), especially 129 and 151 f., which show that even the best cavalry could not put their horses at the spear or pike points of an unbroken infantry formation.

7. For *pezhetairoi, asthetairoi,* and *asthippoi* see A.B. Bosworth in *CQ* 23 (1973) 245 ff., G.T. Griffith in *Mac.* II 405 ff. and N.G.L. Hammond in *CQ* 28 (1978) 128 ff. For Lancers see R.D. Milns in *JHS* 86 (1966) 167.

8. See Parke, *M* and G.T. Griffith, *The Mercenaries of the Hellenistic World* (Cambridge, 1935). For the army in general, see Tarn II 135 ff., G.T. Griffith in *Mac.* II 405 ff., and Milns in *EH* 87 ff.

9. For equipment see Snodgrass; for *sarissa*, see M.M. Markle in *AJA* 81 (1977) 323; for siegecraft, see Marsden, *A.*

10. For supply see Wavell 8, "The most important [mental quality in a general] is . . . common sense, knowledge of what is and what is not possible. It must be based on a really sound knowledge of the 'mechanism of war', i.e., topography, movement and supply." See also Engels' interesting study, which became available after this text was written. We differ in a point which is vital to his calculations. To him food was transported mainly by pack-animals (the technical terms in Greek being *skeuophora* and *achthophora*), a method which in his opinion restricts the orbit of effective supply to some 60 miles, since the animal soon eats as much as it carries. To me the sources show clearly that food was usually transported by draught-animals (*hypozygia* and *zeuge*) drawing wagons, as we see even in the Gedrosian desert (so too Cyrus had 400 wagons of flour and wine for his 13,000 or so Greeks, Xen. *Anab.* 1.12.18); and that pack-animals, such as camels and mules, were employed mainly in the deserts or mountains, or as additional to wheeled transport (e.g., D. 17.71.2; 17.105.7; A. 3.23.2; and P. 37.4). Wagons had to be manhandled in adverse conditions (A. 6.25.2; cf. Xen. *Anab.* 1.5.8). The use of wheeled transport greatly enlarges the orbit of supply, especially when relays of horses and mules are obtainable locally. The relative inefficiency of pack-animals was familiar to me in 1943.

10a. See further Hammond, *A.*

11. For various views see E. Badian in *Phoenix* 17 (1963) 244 ff., J.R. Ellis in *JHS* 91 (1971) 15 ff., Kraft, and N.G.L. Hammond in *GRBS* 19 (1978) 339 ff.

12. The reports so far are preliminary; the last article in the preceding note is concerned with the identification of the tomb.

13. See *StGH* 534 ff. and *Mac.* II 596 ff. for Chaeronea, and *HG²* 505 and 509 f. for Pelopidas and Epaminondas.

14. Wilcken 67 ff. and N.G.L. Hammond in *JHS* 94 (1974) 66 ff.

15. Emending *Philippous polin* to *Philippoupolin* in A. 1.1.5 and comparing Str. 7 fr 36; see *Mac.* I 193 and 199. See also Hammond, *A.*

16. For *pothos* see Ehrenberg 52 ff., reproduced in Griffith 73 ff.; and Kraft 81 ff.

17. For this campaign see N.G.L. Hammond in *JHS* 94 (1974) 66 ff. with Plates x-xi showing the scene of the battle of Pelium.

18. For a discussion of Alexander's route see N.G.L. Hammond in a volume of studies on Alexander to be published by the Society for Macedonian Studies, Thessaloniki.

19. D. I7.8.2–I7.I3.6 and P. 11.6–12 come directly or indirectly from a Greek account, probably that of Cleitarchus, whereas D. I7.14–15 seems to come from a different source representing Alexander as agent of "the Greeks," i.e., the Greek League. It is significant that Cleitarchus fr. 1 applied the figure of 440 talents not as in D. I7.14.4, and that Duris gave the number of Athenian leaders as in D. I7.15.1. Polyaenus 4.3.12, wrongly bringing Antipater to Thebes, smacks of Cleitarchus.

20. As Thebes had a field army of 7,000 hoplites, some 12,000 men defended the walled city (cf. Hegesias F 15). The surprising capture was due to Perdiccas' initiative and Alexander's tactics. Perdiccas was certainly commended for his courage (he was severely wounded) and he was later made a Bodyguard. To suppose that Ptolemy fabricated the whole incident in order to blacken Perdiccas as a rival and in order to shift the blame for the destruction of Thebes from Alexander to Perdiccas is to misread Arrian, our only source for Ptolemy's views, and to underestimate Ptolemy's intelligence. Thebes' fate depended not on how it was captured, but on what the Greek League and Alexander as hegemon decided. For the supposition see R.M. Errington in *CQ* 19 (1969) 263 f. and Brunt 35.

21. For the widow Timoclea the version of Aristobulus F 2 is to be preferred.

22. The League Council met probably twice: first deciding to rebuild Orchomenus and Plataea, to garrison the Cadmea and to destroy Thebes—those attending this meeting being mainly from areas which had joined Alexander in the siege (D. I7.14.1; J. 11.3–4; A. 1.9.9), so that Alexander could have probably obtained a different decision if he had waited for a fully attended meeting; the second, to plan the war against Persia, a meeting not reported in our sources.

23. For the festival at Aegeae see *Mac.* II 150; *contra* F. Geyer, *Hist. Zeitschr.* Beiheft I9.I00 and A.B. Bosworth in *CQ* 1976. 120.

24. See R.A. Tomlinson in *AMac.* I 310 and 313 ff.

25. See *Mac.* I 16 ff. for population figures. The warlike peoples of the Macedonian kingdom, of whatever ethnic origin, were certainly organised to resist the raids of neighbouring peoples and in this way to support the field army, which excelled in mobility. So too in Roman times the Roman troops were supported by a militia of *epaktoi stratiotai* (ibid. 185).

26. See Brunt lxix-lxxi; the number of archers and Agrianians in D. 17.17.4 is probably corrupt (cf. A. I.6.6); for Macedonian infantry *Itin. Alex.* 7 gives 10,000.

27. The account of the Battle of the Granicus river which follows is based on a longer study of the evidence and a refutation of other interpretations, especially those of Fuller, Green, and Lane Fox. This longer study is Hammond, *G.*

28. The share which the Greeks played in Asia Minor is usually disregarded, e.g., by Lane Fox, who says of Granicus (123), "a battle in which Greeks had only featured prominently on the enemy side"; and to suppose that Alexander kept part of the Greek fleet to "serve as hostages" is to overlook the fact that he could not control those Greek ships when at sea, and that he would entrust his siege-train to those ships (D. 17.22.5) ready and able, once at sea, to defect to the enemy.

29. Marsden, *A* 101. Figures in our sources about the highest walls and towers in this period are consistent; towers such as those of Aegosthena, Dodona, and Perge, built on rock and of massive proportions, were certainly capable of being carried to such a height. A siege-tower needed to be only slightly higher than the enemy's wall.

30. For other examples of payment to or by "Macedones," i.e., the Macedonian state, see D. 16.71.2, *Mélanges G. Daux* 24, and Hammond, *A.* The routes taken by Alexander in Lycia and Pamphylia are not known for certain; the problems are well expounded by F. Stark in *JHS* 78 (1958) 102.

31. See *HG*² 454 f.; Agesilaus' difficulty over supply in *Oxyrhynchus Historian* 17.2, and his raiding for food in 6.4, 7.1, 16.1 and 5.

32. For the connections of Macedonia and the Phrygians see *Mac* I 407–14 and E.A. Fredricksmeyer, 'Alexander, Midas and the Oracle at Gordium', *CP* 56 (1961) 160 ff.

33. This march may be compared with the one by cavalry only of 70 kilometres (44 miles) in some 16 hours in the final pursuit of Darius, and another against the Malli, by cavalry with infantry close behind, in some 18 hours. As the Macedonians had been breeding horses for speed and endurance for generations (e.g., Philip bringing in Scythian stock from the Lower Danube), the best comparison is with cavalry mounts of early in this century. W.R. Brown, *The Horse of the Desert* (New York, 1929) 178 ff. records a mounted horse which covered 90 miles in 7 hours and 52 minutes and 400 miles in four consecutive days; another travelled 61.8 miles in 8 hours 7 minutes; and three others made a continuous ride of 154 miles in 30 hours and 40 minutes or so each. Two cavalry divisions in Palestine in 1917 covered some 70 miles in 34 hours, and this is comparable to Alexander's force against the Malli covering some 94 kilometres (59 miles) in 30

hours. See N.G.L. Hammond in *CQ* 28 (1978) 137 ff. Mr. Paul Mellon kindly drew my attention to W.R. Brown's book.

34. The Pyramus river flowed then nearer to Tarsus than it does today; see *RE* 24 (1963) col. 3.

35. C. 3.7.8, who has been giving the marches day by day, presumably from a detailed record, is preferable to A. 2.6.1–2, who has telescoped four days of marching into two without mentioning Castabalum and Issus. Curtius puts the consultation at Issus. For the marches and the problems of the battle of Issus see especially C.L. Murison in *Historia* 21 (1972) 399 ff.

36. The synchronisation of events is given clearly in the sources (C. 3.8.13; P. 20.4; in A. 2.7.1 Darius' two days from the Amanian Gates to the Pinarus corresponds with Alexander's one day to Myriandrus and one day of rest there in A. 2.6.2).

37. I identified the Pinarus with the Payas in *HG*¹ (1959) 609. Some of those who identify it with the Deli Cayi, for example Walbank 372–73 and Fuller 154, consider Callisthenes' figure to be wrong. That the Jonah Pass was on the coast is clear from Xen. *Anab.* 1.4.4, since the walls of the fortresses at either end of the "Gates" reached the sea and Cyrus intended to turn the position by landing troops from ships. See F. Vollbrecht ed. (Leipzig, 1870) ad loc. "die am Meere gelegenen Pässe." Engels' pass "a mile high" (p. 132) is a fantasy. The Jonah Pass was where the Kersus river entered the sea at that time, perhaps by Kis Kulesi. The modern road has a gradual ascent to a higher level than that of the ancient pass.

38. As Walbank 366 and most scholars have held.

39. See *Mac.* I 135. When I made my survey and wrote the description, I had not read Hossbach's report of November 1913 in H. Delbrück, *History of the Art of War* (transl. by Renfroe, London, 1975), 206 f. We have to compare my (1) with his (4) and (5). His (4) begins with the ford just above the uppermost bridge, correctly 3½ kilometres from the present mouth of the Payas, and he notes the "unusually stony river bed" there. Upstream from there his (5) proceeds 1½ kilometres into the rift, which quickly becomes impassable. Next, my (2) coincides with his (3) with its conglomerate rock channel. Lastly, my (3) corresponds with his (1) and (2), where considerable changes have occurred through the removal of material for road and railway construction; but this last part has changed more radically since antiquity. Although Hossbach did not note the "dead ground," he mentioned in his (4) the "flattened-off river bank" on the north side and the steep path down (from my ridge or swell) into the river on the south side.

40. See *HG*² 666. The words *enthen kai enthen* in A. 2.8.6 mean "here and there" and are different from *hekaterothen*, "on either side" as in A. 3.11.7.

41. Callisthenes in Plb. 12.20.8, keeping the MS *poiei*.

42. A. 2.8.3–4 seems to have lost a sentence giving Craterus a brigade of the phalanx.

43. A. 2.10.4 may exaggerate, because there was time for the Macedonian centre to get into difficulties.

44. This reference seems not to have been suggested; numismatists have looked for associations with Athens, but these would be historically out of place at Issus where Athens played no part.

45. This letter is cited in *oratio recta* by Arrian at 2.14.4-9, evidently from Ptolemy's account, Ptolemy drawing on Alexander's papers in his possession. What Arrian gives is certainly true in substance to the meaning of the original letter, but it is probably not verbatim, since ancient historians very rarely gave the original words. The summary of Darius' letter which Arrian gives in 2.14.2–3 is a further degree in paraphrase from the original. See L. Pearson in *Historia* 3 (1955) 448 and G.T. Griffith in *PCPS* 1968. 33.

46. See Marsden, *A* 102.

47. For Gaza the narrative of A. 2.25.4-27.7 is preferable to that of C. 4.6.7-30, which was drawn evidently from Hegesias F 5, a rhetorical, inventive and hostile writer. Hegesias gives Alexander two wounds instead of one, makes him fight again at once after the flow of blood from his major wound is staunched and then collapse, lead the final assault with his wound still open, get hit by a rock, lose his temper and devise for the enemy commander alive a form of punishment which Achilles devised for Hector dead, being dragged behind a chariot. Alexander knew that Homer condemned Achilles for these "shameful deeds," and he had no wish to be regarded as guilty of an even more shameful deed. Lane Fox 193 thinks otherwise.

48. For relations with Greek cities in Asia see Ehrenberg and also E. Badian in *Ancient Societies and Institutions* (Oxford, 1966) 37.

49. For instance, the Arab at Gaza in *FGrH* 142 F 5 and Alexander in C. 4.6. 20–25.

50. Josephus *AJ* 11.317 seems to be historical, unlike 329–39; see Appendix C in Loeb edition, vol. VI.

51. The settlements and the satrapy-divisions are disputed for Syria. See *RE* XI (1921) 1050 *Koile Syria*, Strabo 752, and H. Seyrig, *Antiqu. Syrien.* no. 87.

52. On Alexandria see Fraser. As the analogies he makes are with Greek colonies, he takes a different view from that in the text about the size of Alexander's foundation-city and about the reason for the two grades of citizen. A map of the site is given on p. 8, and he shows the importance of Osor-hapi at Memphis on p. 253.

53. See Parke, *Z* 1947. The connection between the Libyan Zeus Ammon and the Hellenic Zeus of Dodona was very ancient (Hdt. 2.54–55). The origin of the worship of Ammon at Aphytis in Chalcidice is not known; the head of Zeus Ammon figured on coins there from 424 B.C. Alexander was familiar with Dodona and Aphytis.

54. Unlike Marsden, *G*, who had Alexander slow-march his army at some six miles a day for some two months from Thapsacus to the Tigris; this is incom-

patible with Alexander's methods (20 miles a day is more his pace), his system of supply and his temperament; and the emendation of C. 4.9.14 from four to fourteen which Engels accepts (p. 69) is arbitrary. They are driven to these interpretations by supposing that the calculation of the distance from Thapsacus to the Tigris which comes probably from Eratosthenes (Str. 91) was possible only if Alexander had marched that way. The two seem to me totally unconnected.

55. Fuller 176 disposed of Tarn's belief that the base camp was raided; Arrian made it clear that it was the advanced camp and that it contained some "barbarian captives." The episode was inflated by Cleitarchus or another writer into heroic proportions with the Queen Mother refusing to be liberated (as if Persian officers would not have taken her willy-nilly), Alexander scoring a verbal hit against Parmenio, and both sides sending further troops back to the camp. The idea that the Persian cavalry returned through the same gap and clashed head-on with Alexander is a recent one (D. 17.59.8 made them flee to Mazaeus; C. 4.15.22 said they could not re-form their ranks). Alexander had a bilingual officer (a Persian-speaking Greek) in charge of the "barbarian prisoners" (A. 3.6.6). One imagines that the family of Darius was left at the base camp in greater safety; the other prisoners were surely not brought from across the Euphrates. Those in the advanced camp were probably captured during the campaign in the north and the advance down the Tigris valley (A. 3.8.2). Alexander may have split the prisoners as well as the guards between his two camps.

56. Other views of the battle will be found for instance in *JHS* 67 (1947) 77, where G.T. Griffith had Alexander after his break-through turn right with the Companion Cavalry to help the Lancers, while Marsden, *G* thought Alexander aimed to encircle the whole of the enemy's right centre. The idea that Parmenio's call for help arrived when Alexander was already in full pursuit has arisen mainly from a misunderstanding of A. 3.14.4 where *taute* resumes the preceding sentence and of A. 3.15.1 where *tou diokein* is absolute and *eti*, as is usual, goes with the following word (as translated in my text, not as in Brunt 270). Much has been made of the clouds of blinding dust which appear in C. 4.15.32–33. However, they are as fictional as the adventures of the returning Alexander in C. 4.16.20–25; for as we know from Xen. *Anab.* 3.5.1–15 and as we can see from the photographs in Fuller 168–69, the plain was not a dusty desert but pasture and ploughland, famous for its villages and cattle. Fuller 178 n. 2 was influenced by his experience in India; but Arrian, Ptolemy, and Aristobulus, knowing this region, had nothing to say of dust. A.M. Devine in *Phoenix* 29 (1975) 374 ff. brought out Alexander's skill in feeding the cavalry battle to his right, and forming his own force into a wedge for the decisive blow. Polyaenus 4.3.17 is excellent on the aim and the effect of Alexander's advance to his right front.

57. The passage in P. 33.12 has been wrongly attributed to Callisthenes by some writers. The subject of *aitiontai* there is not stated; it is a loose amalgam by Plutarch, whose aim is to point up Alexander's energy by mentioning Parmenio's age and slowness. Callisthenes is cited for the "*onkos*" of Alexander, a word meaning pretentiousness and implying Callisthenes' disgust at Alexander's oriental pomp and *proskynesis*. See the good remarks by Brunt 512 f.

58. King of Asia: I emphasised this in *HG²* 621 but failed to realise it was a claim greater than and in practice excluding being heir to Darius.

59. See Brunt. lxii and 526 with R.D. Milns, 'Alexander's Seventh Phalanx Battalion', *GRBS* 7 (1966) 159 ff., and in *EH* 117. Tarn's suggestion that Antipater sent an annual draft of Macedonians to Alexander has nothing in the sources to commend it.

60. Coinage: A.R. Bellinger, *Essays on the Coinage of Alexander the Great* (New York, 1963); G. Kleiner, *Alexanders Reichmünzen* (Berlin, 1949); C. Seltman, *Greek Coins* (London, 1933) 203ff.; M. Price, *Coins of the Macedonians* (London, 1974) 23-26; G.R. Edwards and M. Thompson 'Gold coins of Philip, and Alexander from Corinth', *AJA* 74 (1970) 343 f.

61. See *Mac.* II 104 ff.

62. Herodotus 5.50 and 5.53 gave 14,040 stades from Ephesus on the coast to Susa; thus the army which reached Alexander at Susa in December 331 B.C. had left Pella probably in September.

63. Agis' War: Brunt xlv and 480 with E. Badian, 'Agis III', *Hermes* 95 (1967) 170 ff.; G.L. Cawkwell, 'The Crowning of Demosthenes', *CQ* 63 (1969) 163 ff.; and E.N. Borza, 'The End of Agis' Revolt', *CPh* 66 (1971) 230 ff.

64. Army reorganisation: A. 3.16.11; C. 5.2.1–6; D. 17.65.2–4. For the 8,000 see A. 3.17.2.

65. Persian Gates operation: A. 3.18.1–10; C. 5.3.17 to 5.5.5; D. 17.68; Polyaenus 4.3.27; and P. 38.1–2. Arrian's account is a summary evidently of one by Ptolemy who mentioned his own part, while Diodorus, Curtius, and Plutarch drew in part at least on Cleitarchus. Polyaenus may have got his narrative from Aristobulus, since he gave to the officers of Alexander's forces different places from those in Arrian's account. Arrian seems to have omitted Polyperchon's phalanx-brigade by error.

66. See Brunt 494 ff.; N.G.L. Hammond in *CQ* 28 (1978) 136 ff.; A.P. Wavell, *The Palestine Campaign*[3] (1931) 210; see n. 33 above.

67. For geographical ideas, see Theopompus *FGrH* 115 F 75 C 2; Arist., *Meteor.* 350 a 18, 362 b 19 (Loeb ed. Lee with pp. 102–105); C. 6.4.19; and *HG*[2] 627 f.

68. Alexander at Hecatompylus: D. 17.74.3; C. 6.2.15; P. 47.1; and J. 12.3.2–5.

69. D. 17.75.3–7 with references given by P. Goukowsky 226–228.

70. Athenaeus, citing as his authorities Dinon, father of Cleitarchus, and Dicaearchus, described Persian harem practice, and since he did not mention Alexander in this connection it is clear that Athenaeus believed Alexander to have abandoned the harem; not so Green 185 f. and Lane Fox 277. Curtius throws in "herds of eunuchs, practised in (homosexual) prostitution" for Alexander's benefit, as well as the 365 girls of the harem (6.6.8).

71. See P. 45.1–2; 47.3; D. 17.77.4–5 and the references given by Goukowsky ad loc.

72. Curtius' account is overlaid with phrases and incidents which were introduced to please contemporary Roman readers. He has Alexander invite Philotas to dinner first, even as Tiberius had C. Asinius Gallus to dinner while his fate

was being sealed (Dio. C. 58.3.2–3). The trial before "the army" and the long silence of Alexander (C. 6.9.2) are reminiscent of the army and Scipio Africanus at Sucro (Livy 28.26.I5). Then he makes Alexander speak in Greek but confront Philotas with the problem of speaking in Greek or in the Macedonian dialect, even as Tiberius required a centurion to speak in Latin after he himself had spoken in Greek (Dio. C. 57.15.3-4; cf. Suet. *Tib.* 71). And the defence by Amyntas is on the lines used by M. Terentius (Dio. C. 58.I9.3–4 and Tac. *Ann.* 6.8.2–11). Scenes of torture were introduced into his account as being so much to Roman taste. Even in the wording of the parts played by the army and the king in the trials for treason there is a reminiscence of the "potestas" and the "auctoritas" of Augustus in the *Res Gestae*. Some of these points were brought to my notice by A.M. Devine, whose article on Curtius will be published in a forthcoming number of *Phoenix*.

73. The procedure in a trial for treason is discussed, together with the passage from Curtius 6.8.25, by N.G.L. Hammond in *GRBS* 19 (1978) 340 ff. See also Hammond, *A.*

74. In giving the background to the conspiracy of Philotas against Alexander in 330 B.C. Plutarch produced a story of reports being made in 332 B.C. on Philotas by his mistress, Antigone, formerly a slave-girl of Macedonian origin at the Persian court; as the story is decked out with secret comings and goings, tête-à-tête conversations and the leading on of Philotas by Antigone, it is palpably fictitious (P. 48–49). The climax of the story is that Alexander did *not* act at all in 332 B.C. The story is clearly a blow-up of the report in Egypt which Ptolemy and Aristobulus mentioned (A. 3.26.1), where the climax is the same. In telling the story Plutarch had Alexander encourage the girl to lead Philotas on, and Plutarch used the phrase "Philotas did not know he was the object of a plot"; and so he spoke freely to her. This phrase has been used by E. Badian, 'The Death of Parmenio', *TransAPA* 91 (1960) 324 ff., to mount a charge against Alexander that he organised a conspiracy *against* Philotas in 330 B.C. This charge is not to be found in any ancient author, and the passage in P. 48.1 is of no worth as evidence for 332 B.C. or for 330 B.C. Tarn 2. 271–272 omitted to mention Diodorus, Justin, and Strabo in his analysis of Parmenio's death.

75. Brunt 499 has an excellent note on Alexander's movements at this time. He denies the stay in Ariaspia which Curtius 7.3.3 mentioned, but some such delay is needed somewhere, in order to allow the army from Ecbatana to reach him in Arachosia (C. 7.3.4). While he was in Ariaspia, he organised the affairs of the "Benefactors" (*Euergetae*), so-called from their loyalty to Cyrus I, and he was said by Curtius to have given them "much money," probably in payment for horses and supplies. The timing which I am suggesting in my text involves the rejection of Strabo 724 fin. or the assumption that his phrase "the setting of the Pleiades" referred not to the passage through Paropanisadae but to Alexander's first arrival among the Euergetae.

76. In A. 3.28.2-4 the account of Erigyius' mission seems to be attached to his return in the sequence of Arrian's incidents (probably following the original sequence in the *King's Journal*); his placing of it is preferable to that of D. 17.83.4–6 and C. 7.4.32, who located in Bactria the news of Erigyius' success.

77. For the emendation of D. 17.83.1 see Goukowsky ad loc. with references.

78. For hipparchies see G.T. Griffith, 'A Note on the Hipparchies of Alexander', *JHS* 83 (1963) 68 ff. and Brunt lxxiii ff. I put the reform before A. 3.29.7 and 4.4.7, since I do not believe that Ptolemy, Arrian's source, a cavalryman, could have used the word in a non-technical sense if the change had either been made or came soon after. See also Hammond, *A*.

79. For the capture of Bessus, Ptolemy is preferable to Aristobulus, whose version may be due to abbreviation as much as faulty memory (he kept Ptolemy in the story). The elaborate stories about Bessus in C. 7.4.1–19, 7.5.19–26, and 7.5.36–43 seem fictional and due to Cleitarchus (so too D. 17.83.7–9; for cutting up Bessus into gobbets see a similar piece in Livy 8.24.14–15, again perhaps deriving from Cleitarchus).

80. Bessus was not prosecuted as a pretender to the throne of Persia, because Alexander had put that throne in abeyance and Persia was now a republic.

81. Reprisals: C. 7.6.1–7 has the wounded Alexander receive the surrender of the mountaineers, but the probability is that the troops acted on their own when he was incapacitated, as in A. 4.23.5.

82. For captives planted in new cities by Philip see J. 8.6.1.

83. Disaster at Bukhara: Aristobulus and Ptolemy gave different accounts (A. 4.5.2–4.6.2); the former was critical of individual officers and their motives, whereas Ptolemy (aware of Aristobulus' account) concerned himself mainly with tactics and seems more trustworthy; C. 7.7.30-39 has the flavour of Cleitarchus with individual *aristeiai*, the great horse, and Alexander's astute trickery.

84. Also *Epit. Metz* 13. C. Neumann, 'A Note on Alexander's March-rates', *Historia* 20 (1971) cites convincing parallels.

85. A. 4.7.2 and C. 7.10.12 (reading Melamnidas for *maenidas*).

86. In the narrative I have not included the destruction of the Branchidae as in C. 7.5.28 f. and Str. 714-715, since it is generally regarded as unhistorical.

87. Cleitus: A. 4.8.1–4.9.8 gave his own personal account and added his comments in a way which shows that he had abandoned his usual method of giving what was agreed by Ptolemy and Aristobulus. P. 50–52, drawing on a number of sources, produced a hotch-potch which included such improbabilities as verbatim conversations. C. 8.1.19–8.2.12 blew up his account with rhetorical exaggerations, verbatim lamentations, and even a Macedonian decree of a most unlikely kind, and J. 12.6.1–17 is of little worth. Berve 206 ff. gives full references; he saw that Alexander suspected he was the victim of a conspiracy (208).

88. For the Sogdian Rock see A. 4.18.4–4.19.4 and, with more detail (partly fictional) C. 7.11, whose description of Alexander having the leaders flogged and crucified is not historical; for had they been so treated, it is incredible that Oxyartes would have come over to Alexander and that Chorienes (below) would have surrendered so readily.

89. The letters of Alexander to various Macedonian generals to which Plutarch refers (P. 55) show that *at the time* the pages said no one else was privy to the

plot and that *at a later date* Callisthenes was accused by Alexander. These letters were probably authentic, but it cannot be proved. For the trial of Callisthenes before a Greek League court see also the words of the letter to Antipater.

90. For the mercenaries see A. 4.27.2–4; D. 17.84; P. 59.6–7; Polyaenus 4.3.20 and *Epit. Metz* 43 f. (C. 8.10.22-36 describes the siege but makes no reference to the mercenaries.) Tarn 1.89 thought the massacre may have been due to a mistake; but Ptolemy (evidently Arrian's source for the campaign; cf. 4.24.8 and 25.4) made no such excuse. The addition, that Alexander had a son by Cleophis (C. 8.10.35–36; J. 12.7.10), is surely a romantic invention in the manner of Cleitarchus. The Macedonian losses are probably from Ptolemy and ultimately from the *King's Journal;* they are remarkably small, if Arrian and Curtius are correct in saying that the city was defended by "over 30,000" and "38,000" infantry respectively (A. 4.25.5; C. 8.10.23). For the site see Stein 44. For details of the siege see *Epit. Metz* 39–41.

91. Stein 128 f. and Fuller 250, both with illustrations. Aornos is the Greek version of the local Sanscrit name which meant "strongpoint."

92. Brunt 530 f. with the *a priori* assumption that the proportion of Asians in the army "must be vastly too high." By what criterion? Nearchus, the source of *Ind.* 19.5, was giving fact, not theory when he mentioned *pantoia ethnea barbarika*. As reinforcements C. 9.3.21 gives 5,000 cavalry "from Thrace" and "7,000 infantry from Harpalus," and D. 17.95.4 gives nearly 6,000 cavalry and over 30,000 infantry being "allies and mercenaries from Greece" and two and a half tons of medical supplies. The only point which Curtius and Diodorus have in common is 2,500 "panoplies" (sets of armour). The infantry from Harpalus may be included in Diodorus' infantry from Greece, as Harpalus controlled the funds for hiring mercenaries, and the two forces of cavalry may well be the same. If so, the figures indicate a total reinforcement of nearly 6,000 cavalry and some 30,000 infantry.

93. P. 59.5 and C. 8.12.15–17. Alexander was conforming with the custom of the Indian rulers, as in A. 6.14.1 and 6.15.6; see also *Epit. Metz* 32, 52, and 68 for enormous gifts to Alexander.

94. The location of Porus' camp is uncertain (see a good discussion by Hamilton, *P* 163 f.), and my acceptance of Stein's placing of Alexander's crossing at Jalalpur is only tentative (Stein in *Geog. Journal* 80 [1932] 31 ff.). See also *Epit. Metz* 59.

95. Arrian says there were five hipparchies in all. Craterus, a regular infantry brigade-commander (Berve 114), had "his own hipparchy" as commander at the camp (5.11.3), and Alexander crossed the river with four hipparchies, the crack one being named by "the Royal Guard" which it contained (5.12.2 and 5.13.4 *kai tōn allōn hipparkhiōn*). In the main battle Alexander led "the Royal Guard" hipparchy and Coenus led "his own hipparchy" (5.16.3–4). Coenus, like Craterus, was a regular brigade-commander, and the brigade of his name was in action on this occasion (5.12.2); so it is clear that Coenus led this hipparchy only for the action itself. It was not "the hipparchy of Coenus" in the continuing sense of "the brigade of Coenus." As Craterus had one hipparchy at

the camp, Alexander divided the four hipparchies in the battle into two for himself and two for Coenus. Alexander engaged, then, with 1,000 mounted archers (5.16.4), Bactrian, Sogdian, and Scythian cavalry (5.12.2) who in comparison with the number of the mounted archers can hardly be less than 2,000, and his two hipparchies. As he had in all some 5,000 cavalry (5.14.1), the hipparchy numbered some 500 men. The four hipparchies made up 2,000 Companion Cavalry, of whom we find 1,700 sailing down the Hydraotes (6.14.4). Tarn 2.192, followed by Brunt and Griffith in *JHS* 83 (1963) 41 and 71, nn. 13 and 16, thinks Arrian failed to mention a hipparchy of Coenus at 5.12.2; if so, the army had both an infantry and a cavalry unit named after Coenus! See further Hammond, *A.*

96. The movements of the cavalry on both sides are in some doubt. See a good discussion by J.R. Hamilton, 'The Cavalry Battle at the Hydaspes', *JHS* 76 (1956) 26 ff., although it seems very unlikely that Coenus' cavalry rode *behind* the enemy line from right to left, as Hamilton supposed. Rather Coenus was sent towards the enemy right (5.16.2–3, since we have the enemy left in 2) and had to keep the Indian cavalry of the enemy left in sight; then on seeing them engaging he was to attack their rear. This last point is spelt out in C. 8.14.15, since once Coenus sees Alexander engaged he is to move his forces right and attack the confused enemy (*ipse dextrum move et turbatis signa infer*), where I suggest that *dextrum* is a corruption of *dextrorsum*. As I understand the battle, Arrian is describing the cavalry manoeuvres on the left wing *only* at 5.16.4–5.17.1, and his *pantothen* refers to all parts of the left wing. The Indian cavalry on the right wing, when it saw the change of direction by Coenus, must have realised his purpose and hastened to the aid of the left wing; but this is not stated by Arrian, and we infer it only from Arrian's statement that 3,000 Indian cavalrymen were killed. Hamilton cites the earlier literature on the battle in his article.

97. See a study of this medallion in *JDAI* 77 (1962) 227 ff. and P. Goukowsky in *BCH* 96 (1972) 447 f.

98. For Sangala see A. 5.22–25, D. 17.19.2–4, C. 9.1.14–18, and Polyaenus 4.3.30; the operations against Pittacus in Polyaenus 4.3.21 seem to have taken place in this region.

99. For the reinforcements see n. 92 above. I have argued in *CQ* 28 (1978) 135 that the Argyraspides received their name in Alexander's lifetime and this is the time which fits the ancient evidence. The distribution is only approximate. The total of cavalry is taken from P. 66.5; the figure may be correct, although Plutarch's 135,000 is an error since he exceeds Nearchus' total by 15,000. Tarn's trick of converting 120,000 men under arms into 120,000 "souls" including women and children despite the evidence commands no respect (*CAH* 6.401); for it is most unlikely that camp-followers were ever counted, since they were not on the ration strength but followed at their own risk.

100. The placing of the various tribes is uncertain, and the problems are summarised by O. Stein in *RE* 18² (1942) 2024 f. The narrative in the text is based on the following considerations: (a) Str. 701 puts the Sibi (D. 17.96.1), the Malli, and the Oxydracae "in order," i.e., from north to south below the Hydaspes. (b) If the Sibi are among the tribes which Alexander raided in order to prevent

them from helping the Mallians (A. 6.5.4), the Sibi lay north of the Mallians. (c) The pool of water and the desert extending at least to the river Hydraotes (A. 6.6.2) have been identifed with Āyak and Sandarbār; they were both in Mallian territory. (d) The Oxydracae, then, lay east and south of the Mallian territory; as they were not invaded in force and as their cities lay close to those of the Mallians (D. 17.98.2), they lay south and east of the Hydraotes. (e) As the courses of the rivers have changed greatly, even the points of confluence in antiquity cannot be determined.

101. The delta has changed greatly since antiquity. When Alexander sailed down to the sea the second time, it was "to learn which outlet was more navigable" (A. 6.20.2); and subsequently (at A. 6.20.4) "he learnt that the outlet on this side of the Indus was more navigable" (mistranslated by Robson in the Loeb edition; compare *epi tade* in A. 3.25.8 and 4.28.6, meaning in effect "on the writer's side"). It was from this outlet, the western one, that Nearchus sailed; and his description of it is naturally very different from the description of the eastern outlet by Arrian (compare *Ind.* 21.2–6 and A. 6.20.3–4). The words *epi tade* have generally been misunderstood since, e.g., Tarn in *CAH* 6.414. He wrote of a "bore" moving upriver, but the danger was the steep surf at the mouth; my personal experience in 1941 is that the crew can get a naval whaleboat out by manhandling and then rowing, but it would not be possible with a heavier vessel such as a thirty-oared boat (triaconter). Lane Fox 386 writes of "triremes," mistakenly; the use of "trierarch" for the naval officers was purely honorary. See further Hammond, *A.*

102. Visible from the top of "Caucasus," the mighty range to which the Hindu Kush belongs (Arist. *Meteor.* 1.13.15).

103. Alexander's river-fleet is described in A. 6.1.1, 6.2.4, 6.3.2 and *Ind.* 19.7. It consisted of the following. (1) "Long ships," i.e., warships (*nēes*) of three kinds in descending order of size (*triakontoroi, hemioliai* and *kerkouroi*), all built primarily for oarsmen. (2) Transporters, called "round ships" (*strongyla ploia*), a general term for cargo-vessels (e.g., A. I.11.6). (3) Horse-carriers (rafts with low sides, e.g., A. 6.3.4). (4) Troop-carriers and corn-carriers (nature unknown). (5) Local and improvised river-craft. On the river they were all under oar (e.g., A. 6.3.3, 6.4.5 and 6.5.1–3), but the cargo-vessels had only a few oars for steering and got out of control in the rapids. Once Alexander knew the conditions at the mouth of the Indus and out at sea, he took only the first two kinds of warships, no doubt as the most seaworthy (compare A. 6.18.3 and 6.20.3). For Nearchus' expedition warships alone were used (his vessels are always described as *nēes*, and named ones are *triakontoroi* and *kerkouroi*), mainly under oar (e.g., *Ind.* 22.4) and occasionally with some sail (*Ind.* 24.1), and they loaded supplies of corn onto these warships (*Ind.* 23.7). The only *ploia* mentioned were those of natives on the coast.

104. Units with Alexander during the first stage of the march from the Indus valley are mentioned in A. 6.21.3 and 6.22.1. Of them the Agrianians, some archers and cavalry, and Greek mercenaries, both infantrymen and cavalrymen, were left with Leonnatus—a large force as it inflicted 6,000 casualties on an army of 8,400 Oreitans and an unknown number of their neighbours (A.

7.5.5; *Ind.* 23.5; C. 9.10.19), but a smaller force than that which Alexander took into the desert (A. 6.33.2 fin.)—let us say about 8,000 soldiers. As I shall suggest below, the personnel of the fleet was probably nearer 5,000 than 10,000. Craterus had taken the main body on a northern route with three phalanx brigades, some archers, a large number (later 10,000 in A. 7.12.1) of Macedonians due for repatriation, and the elephants. These alone are mentioned, but we have to add large cavalry forces, including such cavalry of northeast Iran and Afghanistan as Alexander wished to take to Mesopotamia, the siege-train, the ancillary services, Greek mercenaries, and Asian light-armed infantry. We may estimate the men under arms with Craterus at 24,000, with Leonnatus at 8,000, with Alexander at 12,000 and with Nearchus at 6,000, totalling 50,000.

105. Arrian's use of the sources is best seen at A. 6.24, where he records the general consensus of many authors and notes that Nearchus was alone in saying that Alexander did *not* realise the difficulty of the coastal march, and that Alexander was motivated not only by rivalry with Semiramis and Cyrus but also by his desire to provide the necessaries from nearby (i.e., from the coastal route) for the fleet (A. 6.24.3, a passage mistranslated by Loeb R and Engels 112). Arrian quotes from Nearchus in indirect speech, i.e., until *stratian* in 6.24.5. He then resumes his narrative, which was drawn in accordance with his general stated practice from Ptolemy and Aristobulus, except when he introduced a "saying" or "story" from elsewhere (e.g., 6.26.1–5). This was not understood at all by H. Strasburger, 'Alexanders Zug durch die gedrosische Wüste', *Hermes* 80 (1952) (followed by Lane Fox 539), who disregarded the change from indirect to direct speech and attributed almost all Arrian's account to Nearchus (476 ff.). Our other main source of information, Strabo, drew on Nearchus at 686 for Alexander's rivalry with Semiramis and Cyrus and at 721–722 for the start of the fleet before the winds were favourable; otherwise he used different authors (e.g., as saying that Alexander *did* know the difficulty of the coastal route) and one in particular who gave distances both differing from those in Arrian and fantastic in themselves (e.g., marches of 600 stades = 110 kilometres). In my opinion Strasburger 478 ff. erred in attributing much of Strabo's narrative to Nearchus.

106. Strasburger, op. cit. 486 f., accepting Plutarch's "a quarter" and making his own assessment of Alexander's force, produced a loss of some 50,000 soldiers; Lane Fox 398 made an open guess of 25,000 lost out of "40,000 people."

107. Alexander had 80 triaconters at the start on the Hydaspes (A. 6.2.4) and it is doubtful if he had need of more than 100 at any point; if we allow 20 hands and marines to each for Nearchus' expedition and suppose that he had 100 triaconters, their personnel totalled 5,000. The *kerkouroi* had a much smaller complement, say 20 men each, and let us allow 50 such vessels. The total then would be some 6,000 men. This is, of course, a very rough estimate, based on only a few figures. Tarn in *CAH* 6.414 thought of 100–150 vessels and 3,000–5,000 men.

108. For a different view of the voyage and march to Carmania see Engels 110 f., whose assumptions run counter to the evidence in Arrian. He holds that the fleet was to leave soon after the army (*contra* A. 6.21.1–3), that Alexander did

not know the behaviour of the trade winds (*contra* A. loc. cit. to his p. 114), that the fleet's function was to carry and land supplies for the army (*contra* A. 6.23.4–6 and 24.3, the latter interpreted correctly on p. 141 n. 91 but wrongly on p. 113, since the recipient in the dative is the fleet), that the delay of the fleet was due to *unexpected* winds (*contra* A. 6.21.1–3; according to Strabo 721 fin. Nearchus would have waited longer but for pressure from the Indians). He constructs his own figures for the size of the naval force: 114 warships, some 400 merchantmen (see n. 103 above for the absence of *ploia*) and 20,000 men. These figures are reached partly by computing the quantity of stores they had to carry to feed the army on land (this being in his view the fleet's function), an army which he estimates at 150,000 personnel, 18,000 mounts and 3,648 baggage animals, since he accepts P. 66.4–5 (but see note 104 above). If the fleet was such as Engels supposes, its speed would have depended upon the speed of the merchantmen *under sail*; yet we hear only once of a wind being favourable. It is clear from Alexander's preparations for the voyage round Arabia that the fleet was to be one of warships, not merchantmen (A. 7.19.3–4). E. Badian, 'Nearchus the Cretan', *Yale Classical Studies* 24 (1975) 163, "cannot easily accept *another* round of games," that is one for the fleet's survival after one for the army's survival; he is evidently less fond of games than Alexander was, but then it must be remembered that in Alexander's day games were a form of thanksgiving to the gods. Badian also doubts the story of the first meeting of Alexander and Nearchus; but Nearchus was writing for contemporaries, who knew where and when they did meet, whereas Diodorus 17.106.4 and anyone since then have been free from that limitation.

109. For naval preparations see A. 7.7.1–7, 7.19.3–6, 7.21.1–7, and 7.23.5; and C. 10.1.19 (the building of 700 septiremes, very large warships).

110. For this campaign A. 7.15.1–3; *Ind.* 40.8; D. 17.111.4–6; P. 72.4; Str. 744; and Polyaenus 4.3.31.

111. The phrase occurs in the speech of Alexander at Opis (A. 7.9.5). The expression was commonplace in fourth century Greece before and in the time of Alexander; it occurs c. 370 B.C. in the case of the Molossian state (see *Epirus* 531), which had many analogies with the Macedonian state and was generally at a more primitive stage of evolution.

112. His authority ran "up to the Ceraunian mountains," i.e., to the southern shore of the Bay of Valona and included Parauaea and Chaonia (*FGrH* 156 [Arrian] F I section 7), which thus lay outside the Molossian kingdom's sphere; see *Epirus* 558 f. and *BCH* 90 (1966) 156 ff., which shows that part at least of northern Epirus was not under the Molossian Cleopatra c. 330 B.C., even if the restorations proposed in the inscription are wrong. The extent of Antipater's authority lets us see that "Thrace" as a separate command began to the east of the Triballi, the Agrianes, and the Macedonians, i.e., of the Nestus river. See Figure 2. In foreigners' eyes Alexander was sometimes represented by the Queen Mother, Olympias, rather than by Antipater (see *SEG* IX 2 of 330 B.C.). For her position see Hammond, *A.*

113. I retain the manuscript reading *menousin* at A. 7.8.1, because it was the gifts to those staying that would encourage the men of the new draft from

Macedonia, and because Curtius (10.2.8-9) mentions those who were to stay. The number of those staying was probably less than 10,000 Macedonians proper (C. 10.2.19); with the addition of Balkan troops who often fought alongside them the numbers were probably 13,000 infantry and 2,000 cavalry (C. 10.2.8). Milns in *EH* 112 mistranslates C. 10.2.8; the ablative absolute is anterior to the selection of those who were to stay.

114. The homosexual activities which interested the ancient writers were those between a man and a boy. We have already (note 70 above) mentioned as incredible the "herds of eunuchs" Alexander was said by Curtius to have taken over from Darius for his own use, together with the 365 harem girls. The other story with a generalising moral is just the opposite; for according to P. 22.1 Alexander reprimanded two Macedonian officers on separate occasions for offering him beautiful slave-boys. Perhaps this is less improbable, but that is not to say much. The famous case appears first in a fragment of Dicaearchus, a contemporary of Alexander, who wrote that Alexander was so overcome by the eunuch, Bagoas, that he kissed the boy before a theatre-full of people and on their applauding, kissed him again (Athen. *Deipn.* 603 a-b). In itself the story is of no significance, since to kiss an actor even twice was no more a homosexual act than it would be in acting circles today. (Alexander loved actors like Thessalus, not in a sexual sense.) This story was retold by Plutarch (67.7) from Dicaearchus, whether directly or indirectly (here I disagree with E. Badian, 'The Eunuch Bagoas', *CQ* 8 [1958] 151, n. 3, 153, and 156, who postulated a different source) in order to show not that Alexander was a homosexual but that he was a drunkard (for he makes him drunk); and he adds the point that Bagoas had won a victory in a song-and-dance competition and sat down beside the king. So the whole story may be true; but it gives no real insight into Alexander's sexual life. For that we turn to Curtius again. This Bagoas was a Persian boy, "a eunuch of singular beauty, in the very flower of boyhood, who had been the beloved of Darius and was later to become the beloved of Alexander." At their meeting Alexander was so moved by Bagoas' appeals that he "pardoned" Nabarzanes who had already been promised his safety by Alexander (C. 6.5.22; this high-ranking Persian had joined Bessus in placing Darius under arrest, but had had no part in killing him and had left Bessus in order to come over to Alexander— so A. 3.21.1 and 3.21.10). To suppose that in so important a matter Alexander was influenced only by love at first sight for the boy seems highly improbable. But more is to come. Having prostituted himself with Alexander, Bagoas engineered the execution of Orxines by Alexander. He did so because Orxines had failed to give him a present, and he managed it by saying Orxines had robbed the tomb of Cyrus the Great. What with a pardon for Nabarzanes and an execution for the "innocent" Orxines, Alexander did indeed "at the caprice of a catamite give kingdoms to some and take life from others" (C. 10.1.42, trans. J.C. Rolfe). All this has a sexual and rhetorical colour calculated to suit the taste of Romans who knew their Nero! Its relevance to Alexander is questionable. Arrian's account both of the robbing of Cyrus' tomb being unsolved and of Orxines' execution being due to charges laid by Persians is far more likely to be historical (A. 6.29.5–6.30.2).

115. Hephaestion's funeral was variously described and judged (A. 7.14.2; D.

17.110.8 and 114–15; J. 12.12.12 and P. 72). The plans for the memorial in the form of a ziggurat (a Babylonian monument) were not implemented (*pace* D. loc. cit.); we hear only of Alexander's orders and intentions in the short time before his own death (P.72.5 and 8; A. 7.14.8 and 10). The cult of Hephaestion at Athens is attested by the contemporary writer, Hyperides, in his *Epitaphios* 21; see C. Habicht, 28 f., 236 f., and 272.

116. The illness is described in the *King's Journal* in P. 76 and A. 7.24.4–7.25.6. For the dependability of Arrian's account see note 1 above. The symptoms were those of *malaria tropica* (so Goukowsky 276), colloquially known as "blackwater fever" with terrible thirst and periods of coma (a man in my group died of this fever within a week in Macedonia in 1943, when the medical advice was merely not to move him). Hephaestion, too, had had a high fever and died quickly, probably of the same disease. The worship in Babylon of the Egyptian god, Osor-hapi, or, in Greek form, Sarapis, the patron of the god of healing, should not surprise us; for when Alexander left Egypt he was followed throughout by Egyptian seers and by Egyptian people, who may well have made a shrine of Sarapis in the great city. See Hamilton, *P.* 212 f. On the allegation of alcoholism see Appendix 2. After his death through an undiagnosed and swift illness, rumours that he had been poisoned spread quickly (D. 17.117.6 – 17.118.2; C. 10.10.14–19; and J. 12.13.10); they were dismissed by Arrian and Plutarch on sensible grounds, and are incompatible with the symptoms as they are described, but commend themselves to A.B. Bosworth in *CQ* 21 (1971) 112 f., since he regards the description in the *King's Journal* as a forgery. Curtius reported, although with disbelief, that Alexander's body was not corrupted or discoloured when the Egyptians and Chaldaeans came to embalm it (10.10.12). In the deep coma of *malaria tropica*, death may have occurred considerably later than was thought at the time.

117. Worship of Amyntas and Philip in N.G.L. Hammond, *GRBS* 19 (1978) 333. Antipater was opposed to granting him divine honours after his death (Suidas s.v.).

118. For Timoleon, who defeated Carthage and liberated the Greeks in Sicily from the rule of tyrants in 337 B.C. see *HG*² 557; we know of 50,000 male settlers, and there may have been more.

119. See Ehrenberg, better than E. Badian in *Ancient Studies and Institutions, Studies presented to Victor Ehrenberg* (Oxford, 1966) 37 f.; Badian, assuming Arrian to be incorrect where he disagrees with Badian's view, holds that the Greek cities in Asia were admitted to the Greek League. It should be recalled that Athens in 477 B.C. did not admit those cities to the Greek League of that period. For example, Priene was much favoured but still subject to Alexander's decree (*GHI* 184 and 185). Both Priene and Ilium (Troy) had cults of Alexander, as did the Ionian League (Str. 593 and 644).

120. See *GHI* 192 (Chios) and *GHI* 191, 35, 57, and 127 f. (Eresus in Lesbos).

121. See G.L. Cawkwell, 'A Note on Ps.-Demosthenes 17.20', in *Phoenix* 15 (1961) 74 f.

122. In recalling exiles Alexander acted within the terms of the Greek League

charter according to E. Bikerman, 'La lettre d'Alexandre aux bannis grecs', *REA* 42 (1940) 25 ff., otherwise E. Badian, 'Harpalus', *JHS* 81 (1961) 29 f. I do not support the latter's view that Alexander wanted to place in the Greek cities his worst enemies, the unemployed mercenaries.

123. Hyperides, *Epitaphios* 8; Demosthenes, according to Deinarchus, *in Dem.* 94 and Hyperides, *in Dem.* 31, remarked, "Let him be son of Zeus, or, if he prefers it, son of Poseidon, for all I care."

124. Arrian's judgement is better than that of other writers in this matter (7.12.4 as compared, e.g., with Plut. *Mor.* 180 E); if Alexander had feared Antipater, he would not have given him command of 10,000 Macedonians.

124a. See *HG²* 525 ff.

125. For instance, Tiryaspes in 326 B.C., Astaspes in 325 B.C., a group of four military officers, Abulites and his son, and (Auto)phradates all in 324 B.C. E. Badian in *JHS* 81 (1961) 17 deduces more from these few cases than the evidence justifies.

126. For other cases where an anecdote seems designed to favour Ptolemy, see note 2, and p. 127.

127. The two Royal Guards, one of Macedonians and the other of Persians, were given the posts of honour by the king in the funerary car (D. 18.27.1), no doubt in accordance with the known wishes of Alexander.

128. These are described in A. 7.4.4-8; Chares F. 4 = Athen. 538b-539a; Ael. *VH* 8.7; D. 17.107.6; C. 10.3.11–12; Plut. *Mor.* 329 E–F and 338 D; and J. 12.10.10.

129. The Macedonian diadem probably had one riband; for dress see especially P. 45.2 and *Mor.* 330 A.

129a. See Hammond, *A.*

129b. The head of this Athena was represented on the iron helmet in Philip's tomb at Vergina; see M. Andronikos in *AAA* 10 (1977) 47.

130. This passage refers directly to Alexander's death "on the thirtieth of Daisios," not to the banquet of Medius, as A.B. Bosworth asserted in 'The Death of Alexander the Great', *CQ* 21 (1971) 115; indeed, Aristobulus did mean what he said, that the immediate cause of death was the excessive drink of wine. Doctors, then, as doctors today, probably knew they could do nothing to check *malaria tropica*.

131. Hamilton, *P* 210 "the version given by Aelian" and Lane Fox 465. As the month Dios fell in October-November and as the reference to the house of Bagoas, a Lycian high in Alexander's favour, suggests that Alexander was at Babylon, the party was held either in 324 B.C. before the campaign against the Cossaei or in 331 B.C.

132. Nor a justification for such phrases as "a drinking marathon unique in history" (Bosworth, op. cit. 122), "a continuous record of carousing," and "Alexander's final month of debauchery" (Lane Fox 467).

133. If the forger's motive was not to portray Alexander as a drunkard (although

he produced that effect on Plutarch, Athenaeus, Aelian, and several moderns), what was it? The details of the fever and the taking of Alexander hither and thither seem to have no ulterior significance at all. Bosworth op. cit. argued that the forgery must have been perpetrated within the eighteen months which followed the death of Alexander. As Alexander's papers, including the genuine *King's Journal*, were in Babylon during that period, and as Eumenes, the compiler of the *Journal*, was high in Perdiccas' favour, there is every reason to suppose that the genuine description of Alexander's death was well known; moreover, the leading Macedonians and no doubt others knew the nature and the details of the king's illness and death from being with him or hearing day-by-day reports. How then did the forger convince these persons that his forged version was more true than what they had seen, heard, and perhaps read or, in the case of Eumenes, written in the genuine *King's Journal*?

134. Notably Tarn. 2.378 ff. and F. Hampl, 'Alexanders des Grossen Hypomnemata und letzte Pläne', in *Studies presented to D.M. Robinson* 2 (Washington, 1953) 816 ff. = Griffith 308 ff. Opposed by E. Badian in *HSCP* 72 (1967) 183 ff.

135. See N.G.L. Hammond in *GRBS* 19 (1978) 336 f.

136. See *HG²* 667 for numbers of Greek mercenaries in Persian service. Alexander may have planned to move some discontented Greek mercenaries from Bactria and Sogdiana to Persis. As they often had Asian wives and Eurasian children, they were useful providers of soldiers in the next generation, like his own Macedonians.

137. Arrian reported but did not vouch for embassies from Carthage and Aethiopia, and from Celts, Iberians and Romans (7.15.4). That there had been communication between Alexander and the Romans was attested by Strabo 232.

138. F. Schachermeyr, 'Die letzten Pläne Alexanders des Grossen', *JOAI* 41 (1954) 137 = Griffith 341, thought that the Mediterranean campaign could not have been planned to start before spring 320 B.C. But the conquest of Arabia may not have been thought by Alexander to need more than a six-months campaign, especially if he meant to strike overland from Kuwait to the Gulf of Aqaba and up the Dead Sea rift into Syria (C. 10.1.17, implying a projected arrival in Syria). His plan was to let the Arabs maintain their traditional forms of self-rule (A. 7.20.1).

139. See N.G.L. Hammond in *GRBS* 19 (1978) 333 f. This memorial offended Tarn, Hampl op. cit. 825 and even Schachermeyr op. cit. 129, but they failed to note the analogy of the gigantic tumulus for Demaratus and the Great Tumulus at Vergina. They also disliked the words, "his father Philip," because they thought Alexander had disowned his father publicly. Schachermeyr, believing the plan to be genuine, supposed that Perdiccas had inserted the expression to please the Macedonians, but that still does not explain why Alexander devised a special honour for a man whom, in Schachermeyr's view, he had disowned.

140. Mnesigeiton in Pliny *NH* 7.208 attributed to Alexander the first building of septiremes; this is likely to have been in 324–323 B.C. in the Mediterranean, and Curtius probably refers to them in a corrupt passage (I0.1.19).

141. The distinction between (1) dreams of circumnavigation of Africa, (2) the campaign to conquer Arabia, and (3) the Mediterranean campaign was not kept clear by Hampl op. cit. 826 and Schachermeyr op. cit. 137 f. Nor by Curtius at I0.1.17–19. He used a single phrase "once all the coastal region of the Orient was subjugated" for the conquest of Arabia, but he described the preparations for conquest in some detail (19). On the other hand, he gave the plan for the Mediterranean campaign in full (17–18), but he did not describe the preparations at all. He placed all this soon after Nearchus' arrival, whereas A. 7.1.2 and P. 68.1 mentioned at that time the dream of circumnavigation, and Arrian also the possible subjugation of Carthage.

142. Army and fleet were poised ready to go, and Perdiccas had to gain the consent of the Macedonians to whatever he wished them to do. Similarly Alexander had sought their agreement after Gaugamela (P. 34.1), at Hecatompylus after Darius' death (D. 17.74.3; C.6.2.20–21 and 6.4.1), in Bactria (C. 7.5.27), and after the victory at the Hydaspes (C. 9.1.1–3).

143. This was the conclusion of Schachermeyr op. cit. 344 = Griffith 140 but on different grounds. For instance, his argument that Alexander meant to transplant slaves from Asia to Europe and vice versa is unacceptable, since it would not have led to intermarriage and general concord (D. 18.4.4, where the contrast between *poleon* and *somaton* is between cities and persons).

144. E.g., P.A. Brunt, 'Persian Accounts of Alexander's Campaigns', *CQ* 12 (1962) 147, saying that Alexander posed as Darius' legitimate heir and citing A. 3.22, 3.23.7, 3.25.8, 3.30.4-5, 4.7.3, etc.; but to punish treachery is not to claim the succession to the throne. Tarn in *CAH* 6.384 presents Alexander as "the new Great King."

145. Tarn's dogmatic statement in *CAH* 6.402, "to the end of his [Alexander's] life, 'Asia' meant to him, as to everyone, the empire of Darius I," is typical of Tarn, but not of Alexander's generation, who thought of Asia as including many areas untouched by Darius I, e.g., the area east of the Tanaïs and the Black Sea, that east of the Upper Nile, Arabia, and the land of the Scythians.

146. The conceit of universal rule was typical of Rome from Livy's time onwards: "it is the will of Heaven that my Rome shall be the capital of the world" (1.16.7 *caelestes ita velle ut mea Roma caput orbis terrarum sit*).

147. Respectively in *The American Historical Review* 42 (1957) 344 = Griffith 72 and op. cit. 119; Schachermeyr holds to the view of "einer universalen Weltgestaltung" in *EH* 66 and 79.

NOTES TO THE FIGURES

Figure 1. Boundaries of cantons and national frontiers are based on *Mac.* and N.G.L. Hammond in *CQ* 30 (1980) passage 1.

Figure 2. It is assumed that there were two islands called Peuce in the Danube, one upstream where the Triballian king took refuge, the other in the Delta. For Alexander's return to Troy after the battle of the Granicus see Str. 593.

Figure 3. For a full account see N.G.L. Hammond in *JHS* 94 (1974) 66 f. The Greek form of Pelium is "Pēlĕŏn" in Procop. *Aed.*4.4.3.

Figure 4. Based on the ancient tactical handbooks. Three men at the point, Aelian, *Tact.* 47.3; pikes in closest order, Asclepiodotus 5.1; wedge formation (*embolon*) in Aelian, *Tact.* 47.5, Asclepiodotus 11.5 and Arrian, *Tact.* 29.5. The phalanx here is in close but not the closest order.

Figure 5. See a full account by N.G.L. Hammond in a forthcoming book on Alexander from the Society of Macedonian Studies.

Figure 6. For the advance to the Granicus river and the Asian Gates see C. Foss in *Anc.Mac.* II 495 f. and his Map 1.

Figures 7 and 8. A full account by N.G.L. Hammond in *JHS* 100 (1980), forthcoming.

Figure 9. Based on Marsden, *A,* and W. Soedel and F. Foley in *Scientific American* 240.3.120 f. The composite bow of wood, horn and sinew was strung and stretched on a slider, which was forced back into the case and triggered mechanically (the dotted lines in [1] show the back position). The heavy bow of Zopyrus who flourished c. 350 B.C. discharged two six-foot arrows or stone balls, and the light (for mountain warfare) a four-foot arrow, with great velocity and a range of 300 m. The torsion catapult, developed by Alexander's engineers, had two powerful sinew springs under tension which were housed in vertical frames, one each side of the case; to these the slider and trigger were attached, and the arms moved only a short distance when the slider was forced back. This catapult discharged stone balls heavy enough to smash masonry. The housing of the sinew springs is shown in a front view in (3). Both the bow and the catapult were used at Tyre (Diod.17.42.7). They were mounted, like guns, on a stand, carriage or deck, as suited the occasion.

Figure 10. For two distinct places, Castabala and Castabalum Maritimum, see the evidence cited in Pauly-Wissowa, *Realencyclopadie* s.v. The Pass of Jonah is described by X.*An*.I.4.4; the distance from it to Myriandrus, as given by Xenophon and confirmed by *Stadiasmus Magni Maris*, puts Myriandrus near Büyükdere. The grazing for more than 10,000 horses was in the coastal plain round Iskenderun, and the camp probably extended north of Iskenderun itself (Alexander intended to go on to the Belen Pass).

Figure 11. The map is a magnification of the 1:200,000 map of Turkey, German version Staff, Adana sheet, 1943.

Figure 12. For Siwah direct to Memphis see P.M. Fraser in *Opuscula Atheniensia* 1967, 23 f.

Figure 13. Thapsacus is placed by W.J. Farrell in *JHS* 81 (1961) 153 f. at the rail-way-bridge over the Euphrates by Jerablus. The route for invading Hyrcania is revealed by Curt.6.4.2-3, especially his "campestri itinere"; *contra* A.F. von Stahl in *Geogr. Journal* 64 (1924) 312 f.

Figure 14. The plan of the battle is schematic because the exact position of the battlefield is not known.

Figures 14, 15 and 17 are based on Pergamon Press World Atlas. The courses of the Indus and its tributaries in antiquity are uncertain. H.T. Lambrick, *Sind, a general introduction* (Hyderabad, 1964) has been used for the delta in antiquity. Details of Gedrosia are based on F.J. Goldsmid in *Journal of the Royal Geographical Society* 33 (1863) 181 f.

Figure 19. Both ships are drawn from vase-paintings of the period 550–500 B.C. The number of oars, twenty-three on one side, shows that the ships are pente-conters ("fifty-oarers"). In order to show the oars the painter has put the oar-handle at head-level which is impossible for an oarsman; the oars were rowed through the port-holes which are visible in (1) and also for but not shown in (2). Undecked with a single bank of oarsman, the pentecounter (perhaps 125 feet long and 13 feet beam) and its smaller sister, the triaconter ("thirty-oarer," per-haps 75 feet long), were basically the same in Alexander's time. Compare graffiti at Delos of the first century B.C. in L. Casson, *Ships and Seamanship in the Ancient World* (New Jersey, 1971) figs. 109-110. Note the ram, steering-sweep and rigging for the (imagined) sail on one mast, which could be lowered.

Figure 20. A cast of glass-paste, taken in the Augustan period (23 B.C.–A.D. 14), from a gem of the late fourth century B.C., which portrays Alexander with his strong brows, alert expression and naturally wavy hair.

Figure 21. The plain of Poloskë with the Ventrok Channel on the right, just where the Eordaicus ran, and beside it the fortified hill of Pelium. Viewed from Wolf's Pass, looking westwards.

Figure 22. The eastern exit of Wolf's Pass, Lake Little Prespa and the ridge of Mt. Peristeri, beyond which lies Florina. Other photographs of the Pass in *JHS* 94 (1974) pl. X and *Iliria* 4 (1976) 197.

Figure 23. The plain of Adrasteia and the ridge on which the Greek mercenaries stood. Viewed from the right bank of the Kocabaş (Granicus) a little below Dimetoka.

Figure 24. The Kocabaş just below Cinar Köprü bridge. Note trees and shrubs, tyre marks on the hard clay bed and the meandering course of the river in June.

Figure 25. The bed of the Payas (Pinarus) near Mt. Amanus, looking south from the right bank, a little above the first (highest) bridge. Note the scattered boulders in the bed and the silhouette of the sickle-shaped hill.

Figure 26. The Payas entering the steep-sided channel. Viewed from the left bank just below the first bridge, looking westwards.

Figure 27. The second bridge of the Payas with level ground and shelving banks beyond. Viewed from the right bank, looking westwards.

Figure 28. The "dead ground" and the sickle-shaped promontory of high ground. Viewed from the ridge on the south side of the river by the first bridge, looking south.

Figures 29-31. Ivory heads, 2 cm high, from the tomb of Philip II at Vergina (Aegeae). Identified by M. Andronikos in *National Geographic* 154 (1978) 1.75, and supported by N.G.L. Hammond in *GRBS* 19 (1978) 4.336 f. Alexander, aged probably eighteen, still has some "puppy" fat and already the typical set of the neck and head and the upturned eyes.

Figure 32. From the marble "Alexander Sarcophagus" of Sidon, now in the Istanbul Museum, so-called because it portrays Alexander and others in battle—here probably Parmenio wearing the Macedonian cavalry hat (as in Figure 33) at the Battle of the Granicus River. Late fourth century B.C.

Figure 33. Roman mosaic, 5.12 m x 2.71 m, of the first century A.D. at Pompeii, reproducing a late fourth century B.C. painting with Alexander and Darius as the central figures at the Battle of Issus, where the right wing of the infantry phalanx was rolling up the Persian centre and Alexander, at the head of the Companion Cavalry, was closing in on Darius. Here Darius has faced about for flight. Alexander, wielding a very long *sarissa* in his right hand, comes in from the left of Darius' original position (before he faced about), and the pikes of the Hypaspists are seen as they approach along the left front of Darius' original position. The Macedonians are recognisable by their head-gear: a cavalryman in the Macedonian hat with an eight-foot spear in his right hand behind Alexander's head, and infantrymen in crested helmets by Darius' outstretched arm and beyond his driver's left arm. There is no doubt about the length of the Hypaspists' pikes, carried aloft by the rear ranks as the phalanx moves forward (see Figure 4). That the original was painted probably in Alexander's lifetime is indicated by the portrait with naturally wavy hair, the eye distended in the thrill of battle, and by the inclusion of the dead tree which was featured in the painting of the royal hunt above the entry to Philip's tomb at Vergina. The cuirass with shoulder pieces and gold heads with rings and the sword-pommel resemble closely those in Philip's tomb. The armour worn by Alexander at Gaugamela is described in Plut. *Alex.* 32.8-11; it is not the same as in the mosaic.

Figure 36. Marble copy, c. A.D. 100, of a late fourth century B.C. head of Alexander with naturally wavy hair. The best extant portrait, it is in Vienna in the possession of Dr. E. Schwarzenberg, who kindly permitted its reproduction. See his account of it in *EH* 230 fig. 1 and text.

Figures 37-44. The satellite pictures and the corresponding maps, both at 1: 1,000,000, provide a vivid impression of the terrain. The maps are based on the U.S. Army 1:1,000,000 series, GSGS 2555. The Persian Gates of Figures 40-41 are in territory surveyed only from the air; the inset was made from such a survey, *Tactical Pilotage Chart* H-6 BG, 1: 500,000, and from the sketch-map in *Geographical Journal* 92 (1938) facing p. 384 by Sir A. Stein.

Figure 42. The route of Alexander is far from certain; see Hamilton, *P* fig. 2 on p. 168. Here identifications are taken from Stein. The inset map is based on Stein's map at the end of his book and on U.S. Army Map Service, NI 43-5, which is superior. See excellent photographs of Pirsar in Fuller 250.

Figure 44. This satellite picture of the Makran coast and the Gedrosian desert shows what Goldsmid described as "a confused and intricate mass of hills and hillocks . . . pure sandstone bare of vegetation and intersected by torrents," i.e., torrent-beds (*JRGS* 33.199). The coast is obscured by a sandstorm, such as caused Alexander's guides to lose the way. The range parallel and nearest to the coast is the Taloi range, 1,275 m high in the east and 925 m high in the west; the range to the north of it reaches 1,454 m. Forced to turn inland east of Barabu and to enter the area between the ranges, the expedition underwent its worst sufferings. "The killers were burning heat, absence of water and deep sand, especially on the high ridges, into which draught animals and people sank as if into mud or a snowdrift" (Arr.6.24.4). Alexander found the way to the coast probably near Pasni.

End Paper. In Alexander's absence Antipater had responsibility for the Greek League, Macedonia, North Epirus (here shown as Chaones), Illyrii, Triballi and Agrianes. The Ep(irote) All(iance) was independent. The "General of Thrace" was in charge of the Pontic tribes also. The districts India I and India II were set beside the kingdoms of Porus, Taxiles etc. Lists of satrapies after Alexander's death are to be found in Diod. 18.3 and parallel passages.

CHRONOLOGICAL TABLE
OF DATES ADOPTED IN THE TEXT

336 B.C.	June	Accession of A; Parmenio advances in Asia Minor.
	Autumn	A gains support of Amphictyonic Council; A appointed *hegemon* of Greek forces v Persia.
335 B.C.	Spring to Sept.	A campaigns in the Balkans. Memnon counter-attacks in Asia.
	Oct.	Fall of Thebes; arrangements for war v Persia concluded with the Greek League Council.
	Nov./Dec.	Festivals at Dium and Aegeae.
334 B.C.	May	A lands in Asia.
	May/June	Battle of the Granicus river.
	Summer	Capture of Miletus and isolation of Persians at Halicarnassus.
334/3 B.C.	Winter	A conquers Caria, Lycia, Pamphylia and Phrygia
333 B.C.	March–June	Naval offensive by Memnon; he dies in June.
	April–July	A is based on Gordium and campaigns in adjacent areas.
	July–Sept.	Pharnabazus conducts his naval offensive.
	Aug.	A enters Cilicia; ill until late in Sept.
	Oct.	Parmenio sent ahead to "Syrian Gates"; A campaigns in Rough Cilicia.
	Nov.	Battle of Issus

332 B.C.	Jan.–July	Siege of Tyre; disintegration of the Persian fleet.
	Sept./Nov.	Siege of Gaza; Macedonia supreme at sea.
	Dec.	A enters Egypt.
331 B.C.	Jan.	A founds Alexandria.
	Feb.	A visits Siwah.
	Spring	Festival at Memphis.
	Early summer	A in Phoenicia and Syria. Reinforcements leave Macedonia in July.
	Late July	A sets out for Thapsacus.
	Aug.–Sept.	A campaigns in northern Iraq.
	Sept. 20–21	Eclipse of the moon.
	Oct. 1	Battle of Gaugamela in Oct. Agis raises a coalition in Greece.
	Dec.	A at Susa learns of Antipater's settlement of Thrace and of Agis laying siege to Megalopolis.
330 B.C.	Jan.–March	A at Persepolis.
	March/April	A campaigns v Mardi.
	April/May	Antipater defeats Agis.
	May	A leaves Persepolis
	Summer	Campaigns in Tapuria, Hyrcania, Parthyaea and Areia. Pursuit and death of Darius in July.
	Oct.	Plot of Philotas.
	Nov.	A in Ariaspia.
	Late Dec.	Armies unite in Arachosia.
329 B.C.	Jan.	A advances to Kabul; he winters there.
	Spring	A crosses the Hindu Kush
	Summer	A reorganises his cavalry. Crosses Oxus. Captures Bessus. Advances to Jaxartes.
	Autumn	Rising of Sogdians and Bactrians.

329/8 B.C.	Winter	A at Bactra
328 B.C.	Spring/Summer	Campaigns in Sogdia and Bactria.
	Autumn	Death of Cleitus at Samarcand.
328/7 B.C.	Winter	A at Nautaca. In late winter A captures the Sogdian Rock and the Rock of Chorienes
327 B.C.	Spring	Forces unite at Bactra. Plot of the Pages.
	Spring/Summer	Army crosses the Hindu Kush.
	Summer–Autumn	A at Alexandria-in-Caucaso.
327/6 B.C.	Winter	Hephaestion advances to the Indus. A Campaigns in Swat, and late in the winter captures Aornos.
326 B.C.	Spring	Forces unite at the Indus.
	May	Battle of the Hydaspes.
	Summer	A advances to and returns from the Hyphasis.
	Nov.	The fleet starts down the Hydaspes.
326/5 B.C.	Winter	A campaigns against the Malli; is wounded in an assault on a Mallian city.
325 B.C.	Feb.	Forces unite at the confluence of the Acesines and the Indus.
	Spring	The Brahman rebellion.
	June	Craterus starts for Carmania.
	July	Other forces unite at Pattala.
	Late Aug.	A starts for Carmania.
	Oct.	Nearchus starts on his voyage.
	Oct.	A enters Gedrosia.
	Dec.	A meets Craterus in Carmania.
324 B.C.	Jan.	A meets Nearchus in Carmania; A advances into Persis.
	Feb.	A's army and Nearchus' fleet meet on the Pasitigris.

324 B.C.	July/Aug.	Recall of exiles announced at Olympic Games.
	Late summer	Mutiny at Opis. Veterans set off with Craterus for Cilicia and Macedonia.
	Autumn	A at Ecbatana; Hephaestion dies there. Perdiccas takes main army to Babylon.
324/3 B.C.	Winter	A campaigns v Cossaei.
323 B.C.	April/May	A joins Perdiccas at Babylon.
	May	Final preparations for summer campaign against the Arabs.
	End of May	A falls ill.
	June 10th	A dies.

ABBREVIATIONS

AJA	*American Journal of Archaeology*, 1897–
AMac. I	*Ancient Macedonia* I (Institute of Balkan Studies, Thessaloniki, 1970)
AMac. II	*Ancient Macedonia* II (Institute of Balkan Studies, Thessaloniki, 1977)
BCH	*Bulletin de Correspondance Hellénique*, 1877–
Berve	H. Berve, *Das Alexanderreich auf prosopographischer Grundlage* (Munich, 1926)
Brunt	P.A. Brunt, *Arrian* I in the Loeb edition (London, 1976)
BSA	*Annual of the British School at Athens*, 1895–
Burn	A.R. Burn, *Alexander the Great and the Hellenistic World* (New York, 1962)
Cawkwell	G.L. Cawkwell, *Philip of Macedon* (London, 1978)
CPh	*Classical Philology*, 1906–
CQ	*The Classical Quarterly*, 1907–
EH	Fondation Hardt, *Entretiens* XXII: *Alexandre le Grand, image et realité* (Geneva, 1975)
Ehrenberg	V. Ehrenberg, *Alexander and the Greeks* (Oxford, 1938)
Ellis	J.R. Ellis, *Philip II and Macedonian Imperialism* (London, 1976)
Engels	D.W. Engels, *Alexander the Great and the Logistics of the Macedonian Army* (Berkeley, 1978)
Epirus	N.G.L. Hammond, *Epirus* (Oxford, 1967)
Epit. Metz	*Epitoma rerum gestarum Alexandri et liber de morte eius*, ed. P.H. Thomas (Leipzig, 1966)
FGrH	F. Jacoby, *Die Fragmente der griechischen Historiker* (Berlin, 1923–30; Leiden 1940–58)
Fraser	P.M. Fraser, *Ptolemaic Alexandria* I (Oxford, 1972)
Fuller	J.F.C. Fuller, *The Generalship of Alexander the Great* (London, 1958)
Goukowsky	P. Goukowsky, *Diodore de Sicile XVII* (Budé ed., Paris, 1976)
GRBS	*Greek, Roman and Byzantine Studies*, 1958–
Green	P.M. Green, *Alexander the Great* (London, 1970)
Griffith	G.T. Griffith, ed., *Alexander the Great: the Main Problems* (Cambridge, 1966)

Habicht	C. Habicht, *Gottmenschentum und griechische Städte* (Munich, 1970)
Hamilton, *A*	J.R. Hamilton, *Alexander the Great* (London, 1973)
Hamilton, *P*	J.R. Hamilton, *Plutarch, Alexander: a Commentary* (Oxford, 1969)
Hammond, *A*	N.G.L. Hammond 'Some Passages in Arrian Concerning Alexander' *CQ* 30 (1980) (forthcoming)
Hammond, *G*	N.G.L. Hammond 'The Campaign and the Battle of the Granicus River' *JHS* 100 (1980) (forthcoming)
*HG*²	N.G.L. Hammond, *A History of Greece*² (Oxford, 1967)
HSCP	*Harvard Studies in Classical Philology*, 1890–
Itin. Alex.	*Itinerarium Alexandri*, ed. Volkmann
IG	*Inscriptiones Graecae*, 1873–
JHS	*The Journal of Hellenic Studies*, 1880–
JOAI	*Jahreshefte des österreichischen archäologischen Instituts in Wien*, 1898–
Kraft	K. Kraft, *Der 'Rationale' Alexander* (Kallmünzen, 1972)
Kromayer	J. Kromayer and C. Veith, *Antike Schlachtfelder* (Berlin, 1903)
Lane Fox	R. Lane Fox, *Alexander the Great* (Omega Books, 1975)
Mac. I	N.G.L. Hammond, *A History of Macedonia* I (Oxford, 1972)
Mac. II	N.G.L. Hammond and G.T. Griffith, *A History of Macedonia* II (Oxford, 1978)
Marsden, *A*	E.W. Marsden, *Greek and Roman Artillery* (Oxford, 1969)
Marsden, *G*	E.W. Marsden, *The Campaign of Gaugamela* (Liverpool, 1964)
Milns	R.D. Milns, *Alexander the Great* (London, 1968)
Parke, *M*	H.W. Parke, *Greek Mercenary Soldiers* (Oxford, 1933)
Parke, *Z*	H.W. Parke, *The Oracles of Zeus* (Oxford, 1967)
Pearson	L. Pearson, *The Lost Histories of Alexander the Great* (New York, 1960)
PCPS	*Proceedings of the Cambridge Philological Society*, 1882–
POxy	*Oxyrhynchus Papyri*, ed. B.P. Grenfell and A.S. Hunt, 1898–
RE	A. Pauly, G. Wissowa, and W. Kroll, *Realencyclopädie d. klassischen Altertumswissenschaft*, 1893–

REA	*Revue des études anciennes*, 1899–
REG	*Revue des études grecques*, 1888–
SEG	*Supplementum epigraphicum Graecum*, 1923–
Snodgrass	A.M. Snodgrass, *Arms and Armour of the Greeks* (London, 1967)
Stein	Aurel Stein, *On Alexander's Track to the Indus* (London, 1929)
StGH	N.G.L. Hammond, *Studies in Greek History* (Oxford, 1973)
Tarn	W.W. Tarn, *Alexander the Great* I and II (Cambridge, 1948)
Tod	M.N. Tod, *Greek Historical Inscriptions* II (Oxford, 1948)
TransAPA	*Transactions of the American Philological Association*, 1870–
Walbank	F.W. Walbank, *A Historical Commentary on Polybius* II (Oxford, 1967)
Wavell	A.F. Wavell, *Generals and Generalship* (London, 1941)
Wilcken	U. Wilcken, *Alexander the Great*, trans. by G.C. Richards and ed. by E.N. Borza (New York, 1967)

ABBREVIATIONS OF ANCIENT AUTHORS AND BOOKS

A.	Arrian, *Anabasis Alexandri*
Ael. *VH*	Aelianus, *Varia Historia*
Aeschin.	Aeschines
Arist.	Aristotle
Ath. Pol.	*Athenaion Politeia*
Meteor.	*Meteorologica*
Arr.	Arrian
Tact.	*Tactica*
Ascl.	Asclepiodotus
Athen., *Deipn.*	Athenaeus, *Deipnosophistai*
C.	Quintus Curtius, *Historiae Alexandri*
D.	Diodorus Siculus, *Bibliotheke Historike*
Din.	Dinarchus
Dio C.	Dio Cassius
Frontinus, *Strat.*	Frontinus, *Strategematica*
Hdt.	Herodotus
Ind.	Arrian, *Indike*
Isoc. *Epis.*	Isocrates, *Epistulae*
J.	Justin, *Historiae Philippicae*
Josephus *AJ*	Josephus, *Antiquitates Judaicae*
P.	Plutarch, *Alexander*
Paus.	Pausanias
Pliny, *NH*	Pliny (the Elder), *Naturalis Historia*
Plut.	Plutarch
Eum.	*Eumenes*
Mor.	*Moralia*
Polyb.	Polybius
Str.	Strabo
Suet. *Tib.*	Suetonius, *Tiberius*
Tac. *Ann.*	Tacitus, *Annales*
Xen.	Xenophon
HG	*Historia Graeca*
Anab.	*Anabasis*

REFERENCES

Translations

For *A.* and *Ind.* the Loeb edition vol. I by P.A. Brunt, vol. II by E.I. Robson.

For *C.* the Loeb edition by J.C. Rolfe.

For *D.* the Loeb edition vol. VIII by C.B. Welles.

For *J.* the Bohn Library edition by J.S. Watson.

For *P.* the Loeb edition vol. VII by B. Perrin.

For *FGrH* concerning Alexander the translation by C.A. Robinson, *The History of Alexander the Great* I (Providence, 1953).

Bibliography, E. Badian, 'Alexander the Great, 1948–67' in *Classical World* 65 (1971) 37 ff. and 77 ff., and J. Seibert, *Alexander der Grosse* (Erträge der Forschung 10, Darmstadt, 1972) with Goukowsky's additions in *REG* 87 (1974) 425 ff. Lists of select works are given by Engels, Green, Hamilton, Lane Fox and Milns. The books listed here under the List of Abbreviations and the articles cited in the Notes of this book will set the reader on the way.

References to the ancient sources are given at the end of each chapter. Further references will be found in the Notes.

Representation of Alexander *in art* see M. Bieber, *Alexander the Great in Greek and Roman Art* (Chicago, 1964) and comments by E. Schwarzenberg in *EH* 223 ff. Handsome illustrations are provided in vol. IV of *The History of the Greek Race*, published in 1973 by Ekdotike Athenon, and in T. Saranti, *O megas Alexandros* (Athens, 1970) and in M. Renault, *The Nature of Alexander* (London, 1975). A spirited account with a grasp of practical problems had been published in demotic Greek by G.A. Christides (Ioannina, 1978).

Coins of Alexander are well illustrated in *Sylloge Nummorum Graecorum* vol. V; Ashmolean Museum, Oxford, Pt. III: Macedonia (London, 1976) Plates 46-65.

Illustrations of places are given in vol. IV of *The History of the Greek Race*. The following are mentioned in the geographical order of Alexander's campaigns: Pella p. 13, Sardis 57, Halicarnassus 64-65, Gordium 73, Cilician Gates 75, Tyre 92, Euphrates by Raqqa 114, Susa 127, Persepolis 130, Pasargadae 135, Caspian Gates 138, Elburz Mts. 142, Caspian Sea 143, Alexandria-in-Areia = Herat 144, Alexandria-in-Arachosia = Kandahar 147, Hindu Kush passes 148, 151 (Khawak) and 156, Aornos in Bactria = Tashkurgan 153, Salang pass leading to the Oxus valley 157, Bactra-Zariaspa = Balkh 159, Cophen valley 171, Choaspes valley 172-3, Swat valley 174, Khyber pass 176, and Taxila 181.

339

The index includes names and topics in the text and notes as well as references to the Figures. A. stands for Alexander, D. for Darius III.

Eagle: 80, 138, 157, 267
Earth: 45, 132
Ecbatana (Hamadan): Figure 13 Ca;
    167f, 171f, 179, 183, 185f, 190, 238,
    249, 263, 315, 334
Ece Gol: Figures 6 Ba, 7
Echedorus R.: 1 Ba; 12
Eclipse, of moon: 132, 135, 332
Edessa: Figure 1 Ba; 123
Edessa, re-named Aegeae: 8
Edoni: Figure 1 Ca; 122, 128f
Egypt: Figures 12, End Dc; Lower: 122,
    129, 266, 268; Upper: 122, 128f; as a
    whole: 1, 116, 118f, 123; A.'s ar-
    rangements in: 129; 150f, 153f, 155,
    178, 181, 217, 219, 226, 234; Gulf of:
    236; 241, 250, 259, 262, 302; seers of:
    323
Eidomene: Figures 1 Ba, 2 Ba
Ekaterini: Figure 1 Ba; 8
Elaeus: Figure 6 Aa
Elburz Mts· 174, 176
Electrum: 156
Elephantine (Aswan): Figure 12 Ac; 128
Elephants: 140, 142, 199f, 202, 204, 206f,
    212; as gifts: 213, 217, 219, 223f, 226f,
    237, 320
Elimeotis: Figure 1 Aa; 18, 27, 58, 115,
    154
Elis: 58, 63, 152, 159
Emathia, of Lower Macedonia: Figure 1
    Ba; 8, 10
Emathia, of middle Axius: 18
Embolima: Figure 42
Engineers: 1, 3, 67, 82, 116f, 132, 158
Eordaea: Figures 1 Aa, 5 Ba; 3
Eordaea, western: Figures 1 Aa, 5 Ba;
    18, 58
Eordaïcus R.: Figures 1 Aa, 3; 18, 49, 58,
    328
Epaminondas: 31, 45, 142, 151, 309
Ephemerides, see *King's Journal*
Ephesus: Figure 2 Cb; 65f, 78f, 155, 314
Ephippus: 298
Epigoni: 179, 185, 240, 260
Epirote Alliance: Figure End Bc; 330
Epirus: Figures 1 Aa, 5 Ab; 16, 35, 123,
    160, 242, 321, 330
Eratosthenes: 203, 313
Eresus: 65, 323
Erigon R. (Cerna Reka): Figure 1 Aa; 49
Erigyius: 37, 176, 185, 245, 315
Erikli: 96
Er Rastan: 119
Erythrae; 128, 255, 266
Eskişehir: 82, 87
Etruscans: 301
Euacae: 178

Euergetae: 315
Eulaeus R.: Figure 13 Cb
Eumaeus: 298
Eumenes: 1, 300,303, 307, 325
Euphrates R.: Figures 13 Aa-Cb; 106,
    119f, 130f, 151, 158, 229, 235f, 237,
    295, 328
Euripides: 21
Europe: Figure 16; 13; Central: 156f,
    172; General in: 242, 300; 264, 266;
    emigrants from: 301; 306
Europos: Figure 1 Ba; 18
Eurybotas: 61
Eurydice, see Cleopatra, ward of Attalus
Eurymedon R.: Figure 2 Db; 85
Exathres: 171
Exiles, restoration of: 252f, 323f, 334

Farah: 180, 185f
Feasting: 16, 34, 194, 201; at Opis: 245,
    260f; 267, 269, 295, 297f
Fehlian R.: Figure 40
Fertile Crescent: 118, 158, 163
Festivals: 14, 25, 38, 63, 93, 117, 123,
    129, 164, 177, 202, 204, 212, 234, 238;
    commemorating Hephaestion: 246;
    321
Field-defences: 53, 58-62; at Issus: 100,
    105; 201
Financial officers: 79, 129, 161f, 250, 259
Fish-eaters, aborigines: 232
Fleet: 29f, 33f, 47, 66f, 79, 310; A.'s
    disbanded: 89, 155; re-assembled: 89;
    in Egypt: 129, 155, 158; Macedonian:
    158; commanders of: 162; on Hydaspes:
    218f; 228-234; size of: 234; on
    Euphrates: 234; 242; on Caspian: 237;
    at Susa: 237; for Mediterranean: 302
Flood-banks: 12, 29, 72
Flood-control: 241, 263
Florina: 49, 328
Foot-Companions, see *pezhetairoi*
Forts: 192
Fragmentum Sabbaiticum, on Issus: 110
Friends: 15f, 25, 27, 38f, 54, 63; council
    of: 87f, 92; 161, 163, 171, 179, 181, 183f,
    214, 295, 297
Funerary carriage of A.: 246f, 248, 324

Gabiene: Figure 13 Db
Gadara: Figure 12 Cb; 119
Gadeira: 303
Gaius: 4
Ganges R.: 204, 213f, 215
Garrisons, in Greece: 22, 44, 57f, 250;
    Persian: 79, 81, 86, 116f, 119, 166;
    A.'s in Chios and Rhodes: 129; in
    Egypt: 129, 153; 155, 159, 164, 168,
    186, 190, 192, 200, 213, 226, 251; troops

sarissophoroi, see Lancers
Saryekshan: Figure 13 Aa; 132
Satibarzanes: 170, 179f, 185
Scardus Mt (Šar Planina): Figure 1 Aa; 10
Scientists with A.: 3, 172, 177
Scombrus Mt (Vitosha): 49
Scouts *(prodromoi)*: 28, 31, 67, 189
Scythia and Scythians: 16, 20, 30f, 41, 139f, 143f; archers with A.: 166; allies of D.: 168; 172, 174, 180, 187, 189; tactics of: 191f, 256; 192f, 199, 310, 318, 326
Sea-level, changes in: 125
Seaway: 29
Sehwan: Figure 17 Cb; 223
Seleucia (Silifke): Figure 10 Ab
Seleucia Pieria: Figure 10 Bb
Seleucus: 106, 247, 296
Self-government: 18, 124, 162, 168, 178, 190; in India: 226; in Arabia: 325
Selge (Sirk): 85
Semiramis: 234, 320
Septiremes: 321, 325
Serfs: 19
Sestus: Figures 2 Ca, 6 Aa; 62, 66, 68
Shahikot: Figure 42
Shahr-i-Qumis: 174
Shahrud: Figure 13 Da
Shakhrisyabaz: 189
Sher-Dahan: 186
Shipka Pass: Figure 2 Ca; 46, 144
Shipwrights: 34, 218, 222, 236, 302
Shiraz: Figures 13 Dc, 40; 166
Shpilë Mt: Figure 3
Sibi: Figure 17 Da; 220, 318
Sicily: 302, 306, 323
Sicyon: 258
Side: Figure 2 Db; 85
Sidea: 263
Sidon: Figure 12 Cb; 111, 115f, 263, 329
Siege-craft: 1, 33f; Greek: 81; Persian: 81; Phoenician: 81
Siege-train, Macedonian: 28, 49, 52, 60, 66f; at Halicarnassus: 80f; 94; at Tyre: 114f; at Gaza: 116f; 164f, 200f, 213, 229, 320
Sillyum (Asar Köyü): Figure 2 Db; 85
Silphium: 188
Silver: 15, 156f, 163f, 171, 213, 258, 263f, 267
Silver-Shields, see *argyraspides*
Simmias: 142, 145f
Sinai: 123
Sindimana (Sehwan): Figure 17 Cb; 223
Sinope: 177
Siphnos: Figure 2 Bb; 92, 111
Sisigambis: 165, 170, 256; see Darius, family of

Sisines: 87
Sitaces R.: Figure 13 Inset; 235
Sitalces, Odrysian king: 13; member of Odrysian house: 239
Siwah: Figure 12 Ac; 40, 123; visit of A. to: 125f, 128, 198, 247, 253, 266f, 306, 327, 332
Slaves: 10, 20, 34, 60, 62, 78f, 115, 117; at Alexandria: 124; 180, 190, 195, 223f; rowers: 236; redeemed: 237; 260, 302, 326
Slingers: 47, 49, 102; Persian: 166; 190f, 202
Sochi (Kirikhan): Figures 10 Cb, 38; 93f
Socrates: 74, 76, 118
Soeris: 224
Sofia: 30, 49
Sogda (Rohri): Figure 17 Cb
Sogdae: Figure 17 Cb; 222
Sogdiana: Figures 15 Cb, End Lc; 179, 190, 192; cavalry with A.: 193f, 196, 199, 318; 251, 325, 332f
Sogdian Rock: Figure 15 Cb; 195, 201, 316, 333
Soli (Viransehir), in Cilicia: Figures 2 Db, 10 Bb; 93, 114, 129
Soli, in Cyprus: 188
somatophylax, King's Bodyguard: 3, 27, 38f, 40, 52, 118, 130, 160, 164, 180f, 194, 202, 221; all crowned: 235; 244, 256, 296; of Philippus: 239
Spain: 302
Sparta: Figure 2 Bb; 21f, 45, 62, 77f, 79, 89, 92, 110f, 117, 129f, 155, 158f, 177, 251; as liberator in Asia: 249f; 253
Spercheus R.: 58
Spitamenes: 189, 192f
Spithridates: 74
Stageiros: 252
Stasanor: 188
stasis, party-strife: 78
Stateira: 170, 195; see Darius, family of
Stein, Sir Aurel: 202
Steppes: 47, 56, 172
Štip: 49
Strabo, sources of for Gedrosia: 320
Strumitsa: Figure 1 Ba; 7
Strymon R.: Figures 1 Ba, 2 Ba; 19f, 26, 30, 46, 66
stylis: 110, 157
Sucro: 315
Sudan: 128, 172
Suez, Gulf of: 129
Sukkh: 222
Sun: 45, 128, 132, 212, 215
Supply: 28, 34, 50, 53, 58, 66f, 80f, 86f, 92f, 94, 107, 114, 118, 130f, 132, 134f, 155, 185f, 187f, 195, 200, 203, 212f, 217, 219, 227-232; 234f, 239, 308, 310